www.wadsworth.com

www.wadsworth.com is the World Wide Web site for Wadsworth and is your direct source to dozens of online resources.

At *www.wadsworth.com* you can find out about supplements, demonstration software, and student resources. You can also send email to many of our authors and preview new publications and exciting new technologies.

www.wadsworth.com
Changing the way the world learns®

Why Nations
Go to War

Why Nations Go to War

Ninth Edition

John G. Stoessinger

University of San Diego

Australia · Canada · Mexico · Singapore · Spain
United Kingdom · United States

THOMSON

™

WADSWORTH

Publisher: *Clark Baxter*
Executive Editor: *David Tatom*
Assistant Editor: *Rebecca Green*
Editorial Assistant: *Reena Thomas*
Technology Project Manager:
   Michelle Vardeman
Marketing Manager: *Janise Fry*
Marketing Assistant: *Mary Ho*
Advertising Project Manager:
   Kelley McAllister
Project Manager, Editorial Production:
   Ray Crawford

Print/Media Buyer: *Rebecca Cross*
Permissions Editor: *Sommy Ko*
Production Service: *Dennis Troutman,
   Stratford Publishing Services*
Cover Designer: *Sue Hart*
Cover Image: *Getty Images /
   Scott Nelson*
Compositor: *Stratford Publishing
   Services*
Printer: *Transcontinental / Louiseville*

For more information about our products,
contact us at:

**Thomson Learning
Academic Resource Center
1-800-423-0563**

For permission to use material from this text,
contact us by:

Phone: 1-800-730-2214
Fax: 1-800-730-2215
Web: http://www.thomsonrights.com

Library of Congress Control Number:
2004100654

Casebound ISBN 0-534-63148-7
Paperbound ISBN 0-534-63147-9

**Wadsworth/Thomson Learning
10 Davis Drive
Belmont, CA 94002-3098
USA**

Asia
Thomson Learning
5 Shenton Way #01-01
UIC Building
Singapore 068808

Australia/New Zealand
Thomson Learning
102 Dodds Street
Southbank, Victoria 3006
Australia

Canada
Nelson
1120 Birchmount Road
Toronto, Ontario M1K 5G4
Canada

Europe/Middle East/Africa
Thomson Learning
High Holborn House
50/51 Bedford Row
London WC1R 4LR
United Kingdom

Latin America
Thomson Learning
Seneca, 53
Colonia Polanco
11560 Mexico D.F.
Mexico

Spain/Portugal
Paraninfo
Calle/Magallanes, 25
28015 Madrid, Spain

Acknowledgments

Acknowledgments and copyrights appear at the back of the book on page 348,
which constitutes an extension of the copyright page.

For my son
Richard
and his generation

Preface

The twenty-first century brought with it two new kinds of war. The horrendous events of September 11, 2001, precipitated an invasion of Afghanistan that toppled the Taliban regime but failed to find the elusive perpetrator of the 9/11 disaster, Osama bin Laden. Instead, the United States, under the Bush administration, decided to bring the battle to the terrorists wherever they could be found regardless of national boundaries. In addition, in March 2003, the United States embarked on a highly controversial preemptive war against Iraq in order to depose Saddam Hussein. These events are analyzed in Chapter 9 of this edition.

Seldom has the world changed so much in so little time as it has since the new millennium began. These changes are reflected in the chapters on Korea, India and Pakistan, the Balkans, and the Middle East.

The analytical framework that has held the book together over the years has served the present edition well. Overall, the book remains essentially a product of reflection. I have benefited greatly, however, from the excellent and dedicated research work of my teaching assistant at the University of San Diego, Alexander Salita. He has my gratitude and appreciation. So does Janis Lasser for a number of creative suggestions. Finally, my students at the University of San Diego have been most helpful, sharing many comments that showed extraordinary intellectual and emotional maturity. No teacher could be more fortunate.

I continue to hope that this book might make a modest contribution to the understanding of humanity's most horrible self-imposed affliction.

John G. Stoessinger

Contents

Preface   ix
List of Maps   xiii
About the Author   xv
Introduction   xvii

1 The Iron Dice: World War I   1

The Kaiser's Fateful Pledge   *3*
The Austrian Ultimatum to Serbia   *5*
The Closing Trap   *8*
The Iron Dice   *14*
Conclusion   *20*
Selected Bibliography   *24*

2 Barbarossa: Hitler's Attack on Russia   27

Hitler and Russia   *28*
Stalin and Germany   *38*
Conclusion   *49*
Selected Bibliography   *54*

3 The Temptations of Victory: Korea   57

President Truman's Decision   *58*
General MacArthur's Gamble   *70*
Conclusion   *78*
Afterthoughts: Fifty Years Later   *80*
Selected Bibliography   *85*

4 A Greek Tragedy in Five Acts: Vietnam   87

Act One: Truman—Asia Was Not Europe   *88*
Act Two: Eisenhower—The Lesson of France Ignored   *91*
Act Three: Kennedy—The Military   *96*
Act Four: Johnson—The Catastrophe   *101*
Act Five: Nixon—Full Circle   *109*
Conclusion   *113*
Selected Bibliography   *116*

5 From Sarajevo to Kosovo:
The War over the Remains of Yugoslavia   119

The Dismemberment of Yugoslavia Begins   *122*
The War in Bosnia   *125*
The Tide Turns against the Serbs   *131*
The Dayton Peace Accords   *133*
The UN War Crimes Tribunal   *135*
Kosovo: The War against Europe's Last Dictator   *138*
Conclusion: A New Dawn of Peace with Justice?   *151*
Selected Bibliography   *154*

6 Four Battles over God: India and Pakistan
in 1947, 1965, 1971, and 1998   157

Colonialism, Partition, and War   *158*
The Kashmir War of 1965   *166*
The Bloody Dawn of Bangladesh   *169*
Nuclear Viagra   *178*
Conclusion   *182*
Selected Bibliography   *184*

7 The Fifty Years' War in the Holy Land:
Israel and the Arabs   187

The Palestine War of 1948   *188*
The Sinai Campaign and the Suez Crisis of 1956   *198*
The Six-Day War of 1967   *204*
The October War of 1973   *212*
The Lebanese Tragedy   *222*
The Palestinian Uprising   *225*

The Peace Process: Between Fear and Hope   *228*
The Second Palestinian Uprising and the Road Map   *231*
Conclusion   *237*
Selected Bibliography   *241*

8 Saddam Hussein's Wars against Iran and Kuwait   245

The Iran-Iraq War: The Price of Martyrdom   *246*
Saddam's Aggression against Kuwait   *251*
Selected Bibliography   *270*

9 New Wars for a New Century: America and the World of Islam   273

George W. Bush: From Pragmatist to Crusader   *276*
War Drums   *281*
The "War after the War": Dilemmas of Occupation   *286*
The Capture of Saddam and Beyond   *301*
Selected Bibliography   *307*

10 Why Nations Go to War   309

The Determinants of War   *311*
Heart of Darkness   *324*
Learning from History   *327*
Selected Bibliography   *337*

Epilogue   341
Index   349

Maps

MAP   1   Europe in 1914   xxii

MAP   2   Europe in 1945   26

MAP   3   Operation Barbarossa and the Eastern Front,
            1941–1942   40

MAP   4   The Korean War, 1950–1953   56

MAP   5   Vietnam, 1954–1975   86

MAP   6   Yugoslavia and the Breakaway Republics, 1991   118

MAP   7   Crisis in Kosovo   143

MAP   8   The Indian Subcontinent   156

MAP   9   Israel and Its Neighbors   186

MAP   10   Israeli Conquests, 1967   210

MAP   11   Iraq and the Persian Gulf Region   244

MAP   12   The Gulf War, February 1991   263

MAP   13   Iraq, Afghanistan, and Neighboring Countries   272

MAP   14   Iraq: Ethnic-Religious Groups   287

About the Author

John G. Stoessinger (Ph.D., Harvard) is Distinguished Professor of Global Diplomacy at the University of San Diego in San Diego, California. He has taught at Harvard, MIT, Columbia, Princeton, the City University of New York, and Trinity University in San Antonio, Texas. In 1969 he led the International Seminar on International Relations at Harvard University, and in 1970 he received honorary doctor of law degrees from Grinnell College, Iowa, and from the American College of Switzerland.

Stoessinger is the author of ten leading books on international relations, including *The Might of Nations: World Politics in Our Time,* which was awarded the Bancroft Prize by Columbia University in 1963 and is now in its tenth edition. He is also the author of *The Refugee and the World Community; Financing the United Nations System; Power and Order; The United Nations and the Superpowers; Nations at Dawn: China, Russia, and America;* and *Henry Kissinger: The Anguish of Power.* Dr. Stoessinger also served as chief book review editor of *Foreign Affairs* for five years and as acting director of the Political Affairs Division at the United Nations from 1967 to 1974. He is a member of the Council of Foreign Relations.

In 2002, Dr. Stoessinger was selected for inclusion in Marquis's *Who's Who in America* and, in 2003, *Who's Who in the World.*

Introduction

This book attempts to take a new look at the age-old scourge of war. Ever since I was a student, I have found most explanations of war somehow wanting. I read that wars were caused by nationalism, militarism, alliance systems, economic factors, or some other "fundamental" cause that I could not connect directly to the actual outbreak of a given war. Often I was told that war was an ineradicable part of human nature. Having lived through most of the major wars of the twentieth century, I wondered if this could be true. I yearned for a deeper understanding, in the hope that insight might bring healing. The conventional wisdom left me totally dissatisfied, both intellectually and emotionally. It somehow always missed the human essence of the problem. Forces over which people apparently had no control were frequently enthroned as "fundamental" causes. Yet it was *people* who actually *precipitated* wars. This personality dimension was seldom given its due weight in traditional books on war. The outline for this book grew out of my need to know the human truth behind the mechanistic forces.

In this edition, I decided to embark on ten case studies of the major international wars fought in this century: the two world wars, Korea, Vietnam, the Balkans, India and Pakistan, the Arabs and Israel, Saddam Hussein's attack on Iran and on Kuwait, Osama bin Laden and the war on terrorism, and the American-led invasion of Iraq. What interested me most in each case was the "moment of truth" when leaders crossed the threshold into war. I decided to blow up that fateful moment, to capture it in flight, as it were, in all its awesome, tragic meaning. In the process, I sought answers to the questions that have always haunted me: At what moment did the decision to go to war become irreversible? Who bore the responsibility and why? Could the disaster have been averted? Did the ten cases, different though they were, reveal some common truths about war in our time?

My first unforgettable exposure to World War I was Erich Maria Remarque's classic, *All Quiet on the Western Front,* a book dedicated to the memory of a generation that "had been destroyed by war even though it may have escaped its guns." Yet many old people to whom I spoke about the war remembered its outbreak as a time of glory and rejoicing. Distance had romanticized their memories, muted the anguish, and subdued the horror of what followed. I have attempted to recapture the atmosphere of those few weeks in July 1914 that changed the world forever, and I have tried to portray the leading personalities who contributed to the disaster.

I remember well the charismatic nature of Hitler's grip on the German nation. Most of my boyhood years were spent fleeing from the Nazi terror. I have always been haunted by the personality of Hitler and driven by a need to understand his demon. That is why I chose to examine Nazi Germany's attack on the Soviet Union—an assault that witnessed Hitler at the zenith of his power but also bore the seed of his ultimate destruction. Why did he launch this suicidal assault? Why did Stalin, who trusted no one, place his trust in Hitler? And what explains the fact that so many German soldiers followed Hitler to their doom in the Soviet Union like obedient schoolchildren?

When the Korean War broke out, I remember that I applauded President Harry Truman for repelling the armed aggression from the north. But when General Douglas MacArthur's forces crossed the thirty-eighth parallel into North Korea, I began to worry about China. And when, indeed, the general drove on toward the Chinese border, I shuddered with anxiety that China might intervene militarily. My fear was justified. I have attempted in this case study to recapture each decision separately and to place responsibility where it belongs.

In no war did personalities play a greater role than in Vietnam. I believe that, in the course of a single generation, five American presidents based their policies in Indochina not on Asian realities but on their own fears and, ultimately, on their hopes. Each president made a concrete policy decision that escalated the war and left it in worse shape than before. It is for this reason that this case, like a Greek tragedy, has five "acts," each a virtually new step in a gradually escalating conflict that became the "Thirty Years' War" of our century.

The story of the dismemberment of Yugoslavia is the story of one man's destructive hubris: Slobodan Milosevic, who now faces trial on charges of genocide.

Some of the most dreadful wars of the twentieth century were fought on the Indian subcontinent. The human suffering that accompanied them was on a scale so vast as to defy imagination. I have attempted to convey the personalities of the Hindu and the Moslem leaders, for whom religious war was just as real in our secular era as it was at the time of the Crusades a thousand years ago.

A Fifty Years' War was fought between Arab and Jew. Six times over three generations these two peoples have turned on each other with a terrible ferocity. Both Arab and Jewish leaders have seen their cause as just and firmly based on the will of God, morality, and reason. And in the name of two appeals to justice, they have done things to one another that neither side will easily forget. I have attempted to capture the human truth of this great tragedy, in which right does not clash with wrong, but with another right. I have also chosen to examine Saddam Hussein's attack on Iran in 1980 and his invasion of Kuwait ten years later.

Finally, I have included the two wars that have ushered in the new century: the worldwide war against terrorism precipitated by the shattering events of September 11, 2001, and the preemptive war against Iraq in 2003, in which President George W. Bush applied a doctrine that opened a new chapter in American history.

As I studied these cases and surveyed the entire spectacle of war in our time, a number of themes emerged that I had never noted before. I have presented these new ideas in the concluding chapter. A pattern emerges that, I hope, will point to new directions and can start a dialogue about the threat war poses to humanity's future.

Perhaps *chaos* is a name we give to an order that as yet we do not understand. I hope that this book may bring some order to the chaos of modern war by presenting some original perspectives on its conduct. And such insight, I dare hope, may be a first step to liberation.

Rendezvous

Alan Seeger

I have a rendezvous with Death
At some disputed barricade,
When Spring comes back with rustling shade
And apple-blossoms fill the air—
I have a rendezvous with Death
When Spring brings back blue days and fair.

It may be he shall take my hand
And lead me into his dark land
And close my eyes and quench my breath—
It may be I shall pass him still.
I have a rendezvous with Death
On some scarred slope of battered hill,
When Spring comes round again this year
And the first meadow-flowers appear.

God knows 'twere better to be deep
Pillowed in silk and scented down,
Where love throbs out in blissful sleep,
Pulse nigh to pulse, and breath to breath,
Where hushed awakenings are dear . . .
But I've a rendezvous with Death
At midnight in some flaming town,
When Spring trips north again this year,
And I to my pledged word am true,
I shall not fail that rendezvous.

Alan Seeger, American poet and soldier, fought on the Allied side in the Battle of the Somme; he died July 4, 1916, at the age of twenty-eight.

In memory of my students who died in the wars I have seen.

J. G. S.

Map 1   Europe in 1914

1

The Iron Dice: World War I

If the iron dice must roll, may God help us.
Theobald von Bethmann-Hollweg
German chancellor, August 1, 1914

The emperors and generals who sent their men to war in August 1914 thought in terms of weeks, not months, let alone years. "You will be home before the leaves have fallen from the trees," the German Kaiser told his troops in early August; at the same time, members of the czar's Imperial Guard wondered whether they should take along their dress uniforms for their victorious entry into Berlin or have them brought to the front by the next courier. Few foresaw the world catastrophe that would snuff out the lives of an entire generation and consign the next to disillusion and despair. When it was all over, no one was who he had been and, as D. H. Lawrence said, "all the great words were cancelled out." In one of history's consummate touches of irony, one of the few who did see the shadow of war lengthening into years was the chief of the German general staff, Helmuth von Moltke, who predicted "a long and wearisome struggle," but who also believed that sooner or later war was inevitable; on June 1 he saw fit to pronounce that Germany was "ready, and the sooner the better for us."

This theme of inevitability is a haunting and pervasive one. Most of the statesmen who made the crucial decisions behaved like actors in a Greek tragedy. The terrible dénouement was foreseen, but somehow it could not be prevented. Time and again, people shifted responsibility from themselves to an impersonal God or Providence that was deemed to be in ultimate control. In the words of German chancellor Theobald von Bethmann-Hollweg, on August 1: "If the iron dice must roll, may God help us," or in those of Emperor Franz-Joseph of Austria-Hungary: "We cannot go back now." Historians too have been affected by this fatalistic attitude. As one leading scholar has summed up his analysis of the outbreak of the war: "All the evidence goes to show that the beginning of the crisis . . . was one of those moments in history when events passed beyond men's control."[1]

The thesis of this chapter is that such a view is wrong: Mortals made these decisions. They made them in fear and in trembling, but they made them nonetheless. In most cases, the decision makers were not evil people bent on destruction but were frightened and entrapped by self-delusion. They based their policies on fears, not facts, and were singularly devoid of empathy. Misperception, rather than conscious evil design, appears to have been the leading villain in the drama.

In this analysis I shall not dwell on the underlying causes of the world war. Not only have these been discussed exhaustively by leading historians,[2] but I seriously question whether they can be related directly and demonstrably to the fateful decisions that actually *precipitated* the war. For example, historians are virtually unanimous in their belief that the system of competitive alliances dividing Europe into two camps in 1914 was a principal factor that caused the war to spread. This strikes me as a mechanistic view that undervalues psychological and personality considerations. On July 5 Germany fully supported her ally Austria-Hungary's desire to punish Serbia for the assassination of the Austrian crown prince. By late July, however, when Austrian policy threatened a general mobilization in Russia on Serbia's behalf, Germany attempted to restrain her ally. In this attempt she failed, and the result was world conflagration. But had the German Kaiser or his chancellor *succeeded* in restraining the Austrians, historians would have had to credit the alliance system with the *prevention* of a war. In other words, a study of the leading personalities of the time and the manner in which they perceived one another may be a more fruitful analysis than to postulate such abstractions as alliance systems, militarism, or nationalism.

The crucial events that led to—and over—the threshold of war are the German pledge of support to Austria in her policy toward Serbia; Austria's ultimatum to Serbia and rejection of the Serbian response; Germany's efforts to mediate and to restrain Austria; and the actual outbreak of general war on August 1, precipitated by Germany's declaration of war on Russia and the invasion of Luxembourg and Belgium.

The Kaiser's Fateful Pledge

Word of the assassination of the Austrian crown prince Franz Ferdinand on June 28, 1914, reached the German Kaiser on his yacht near Kiel. According to an eyewitness, Wilhelm II turned deathly pale as he heard the fatal news from Sarajevo.[3] He had been drawn to the Austrian archduke and his wife and had just returned from visiting the couple at their castle. Franz Ferdinand's intention to marry a lady-in-waiting had aroused the sullen opposition of the aged emperor, Franz-Joseph, who had consented only on the condition that the marriage be a morganatic one, that is, that the couple's children would be deprived of the right of succession to the throne. This act of renunciation had embittered Franz Ferdinand, a condition further aggravated by the condescension of the Austrian court toward his wife, Sophie.

Kaiser Wilhelm was a moody man with a mercurial temper. The romantic predicament of his Austrian friend had appealed to him, and he had formed a deep and apparently genuine personal attachment to him. He was deeply shaken when he heard that the archduke's last words to his wife were, "Sophie, Sophie, do not die, live for our children,"[4] before death claimed them both, and his fury and indignation toward the Serbians were thoroughly aroused; he described them as "bandits" and "murderers." In addition to his personal grief, he believed that the assassination represented a profound threat to the monarchical principle. Therefore it is not surprising that Admiral Alfred von Tirpitz reported in his *Memoirs* the Kaiser's conviction that the Russian czar would not support "the assassins of royalty."[5] The crowned heads of Europe would have to take a common stand against the threat of regicide.

With characteristic impetuosity, the Kaiser wanted Austria to punish Serbia as quickly as possible. He was convinced that the entire civilized world, including Russia, would be sympathetic. He put it in no uncertain terms: "Matters must be cleared up with the Serbians and that soon. That is self-evident and the plain truth."[6] On July 5 he took the fateful step of assuring Austria that she could count on Germany's "faithful support" even if the punitive action she was planning to take against Serbia would bring her into conflict with Russia. In other words, the Kaiser issued Austria-Hungary a blank check. Before he left on a vacation cruise the next morning, he exclaimed confidently: "I cannot imagine that the old gentleman in Schönbrunn will go to war, and most certainly not if it is a war over the Archduke Franz Ferdinand."[7]

The incredible fact is that the German Kaiser had not the slightest idea of what the Austrians would do. Impelled by a generous impulse of loyalty to his dead friend, he offered what he thought would be moral support to the aggrieved party. That this guarantee would entail military support never seriously occurred either to him or to the German military and governmental apparatus that fully supported his move. Even more important, the Kaiser believed that a common loyalty to monarchy would be a stronger bond than the links of ethnic kinship; in other words, that the czar would support the Kaiser against his fellow Slavs in Serbia. On both these counts Wilhelm II proved to be terribly mistaken.

The Kaiser used a special term for his pledge to Austria: *Nibelungentreue*. There is no adequate English translation for this term. The *Nibelungenlied* was a collection of German sagas peopled with heroes whose highest virtues were honor, courage, and loyalty. The pledge of a *Nibelung* is a blood bond that is sacred and irrevocable; once given, it can never be retracted. Wilhelm's cousin Ferdinand I of Bulgaria understood its significance when he observed: "I certainly do not like my cousin Kaiser Wilhelm, but I feel sorry for him all the same. Now he will be dragged into the whirlpool, be entangled, and he will have to fight, whether he wants to or not. That is all he gets out of his *Nibelungentreue*."[8]

The Kaiser's decision to support Austria-Hungary under any circumstances demonstrated an extraordinary confusion of personal ethics and political judgment. His friendship with the archduke prompted him to place the fate of his nation in the hands of another power. His view of the Russian czar as a kindred-spirited fellow monarch led him to assume that such a relinquishment of control carried no risk whatsoever. And his romanticism robbed him of all flexibility in the emerging crisis.

It is not true, as many historians have stated, that the Kaiser wanted war. Nor is it true, as his definitive biographer has said, that he "succumbed to a power he had not reckoned with: the power of Fate; had it not been for that, the war would never have started."[9] Such thinking is guilty of blind determinism. The Kaiser was indeed to blame. His flaw was both moral and political, for his form of loyalty demanded sacrifice beyond himself. It offered up the German nation, and it emboldened the senile monarchy of Austria-Hungary to take a desperate gamble. The cliché of the saber-rattling Kaiser is misleading. What is closer to the truth is that he permitted others to rattle and ultimately use the saber for him.

The Austrian Ultimatum to Serbia

During the tense days of July 1914, the fate of Austria-Hungary was in the hands of three men: Emperor Franz-Joseph, his foreign minister, Count Leopold von Berchtold, and the chief of staff, Conrad von Hötzendorff.

At the time of the Sarajevo assassination Franz-Joseph was an exhausted old man. The wars he had waged in the past had ended in defeat or loss of territory. In his declining years he was embittered by personal disasters: the murder of his wife, the tragic death of his son, and now the murder of his nephew. "Everyone is dying around me," he said mournfully. There is little doubt that above all he wished his life to end in peace. Shortly after the assassination of Franz Ferdinand, he spoke of plans for a summer respite needed to regain his strength. Evidently he had no expectation of even a local war with Serbia. When Hötzendorff urged mobilization measures, after receiving Kaiser Wilhelm's promise of support on July 5, the emperor refused to approve them, pointing out the danger of an attack from Russia and the doubtfulness of German support. During the next three weeks, however, Franz-Joseph's strength began to fail, and his signature affixed to the crucial documents laid before him by his foreign minister revealed a trembling and uncertain hand. More important, the marginal annotations no longer showed the probing mind of earlier years. One distinguished historian even maintains that the foreign minister dispatched the crucial ultimatum to Serbia "without the knowledge or approval of Franz-Joseph."[10] While this is difficult to prove, it is likely that the aged sovereign no longer fully grasped the consequences of the policies that Count Berchtold and his chief of staff were now pursuing.

Hötzendorff, who was also head of the militarist party in Vienna, believed passionately in the need to preserve his nation's status as a great power. Even before Sarajevo he feared the disintegration of the Habsburg empire from either internal decay or violent overthrow by its enemies. If Austria-Hungary accepted this final insult, then the dual monarchy would indeed become a "worm-eaten museum piece." Therefore Serbia had to be dealt a punishing blow quickly, before the situation deteriorated even further. Hötzendorff's own words are illuminating:

> For this reason, and not as vengeance for the assassination, Austria-Hungary must draw the sword against Serbia. . . . It [is] not a question of [a] knightly duel with "poor little" Serbia, as she like[s] to call herself, nor of punishment for the assassination. It [is] much more the highly practical importance of the prestige of a Great Power. . . . The Monarchy ha[s] been seized by the throat, and ha[s] to choose between allowing itself to be strangled and making a last effort to prevent its destruction.[11]

In the view of Austria-Hungary's chief of staff, then, the monarchy's status as a great power was in desperate peril. Both pride and prestige motivated his policy.

Count Berchtold was said by Sidney B. Fay to be "as helpless and incompetent a person as was ever called to fill a responsible position in time of danger."[12] The record of his behavior during the critical weeks of July 1914 reveals a striking difference between his attitude toward Serbia before July 5, the date of the Kaiser's blank check to Austria, and his approach to the problem after that date. When informed of the tragedy of Sarajevo, Berchtold vacillated. He hesitated to take military action against Serbia for fear that the Kaiser would not support him, but he shared Hötzendorff's conviction that something had to be done to preserve Austria's great power status. The Kaiser's pledge served to resolve Berchtold's indecision, and the promise of German support enabled him to use the Sarajevo assassination as the final justification for clearing up Austria's Serbian problem once and for all. He drafted an ultimatum that he was certain Serbia would reject. Protected by Germany, he could then deal a mortal blow without fear of Russian intervention.

Count Berchtold's outstanding character trait seems to have been his duplicity. Though outraged by Sarajevo, he took no action until he received the German guarantee, and then went a great deal further than the Kaiser could possibly have wanted. Austria-Hungary's failing prestige could now be buttressed by a German guarantee. With the German *Nibelungentreue* translated into an ironclad commitment, Germany could thus be made to pay the price of Austria-Hungary's last and fateful effort to remain a world power.

Berchtold appears to have been the main, possibly even the sole, author of the Serbian ultimatum. He communicated its general tenor to Berlin, and the Kaiser, incredibly enough, did not demand to see the precise text. Thus, when Berchtold transmitted the note to Serbia, Wilhelm was faced with a fait accompli. The terms of the ultimatum were stern and unyielding: they included demands for the dissolution of Serbian nationalist groups, the dismissal of key military officers, the arrest of leading political figures, and the right for Austria-Hungary to implement these measures to her complete satisfaction. Serbia was given forty-eight hours to respond or else face the consequences.

The Serbian prince regent Peter and his ministers were deeply shaken by the harshness of the ultimatum. They suspected that it was a pretext to eliminate Serbia as a sovereign state. After all, even though the assassins were Slav nationalists with Serbian ties, they were subjects of the empire, and the assassination itself had taken place on Austro-Hungarian soil. In desperation, the prince regent cabled the following plea to the Russian czar: "We are unable to defend ourselves and beg your Majesty to come to our aid as soon as possible. The much-appreciated goodwill which your Majesty has so often shown toward us inspires us with the firm belief that once again our appeal to your noble Slav heart will not pass unheeded."[13]

The Serbian ministers then began to work around the clock on their reply. They argued bitterly over the intent of the ultimatum. A minority felt that the demands were honestly calculated to exact punishment for the assassination and to guarantee Austria's future security, but the majority was convinced that the document had been framed deliberately to elicit a rejection. The final reply was actually conciliatory and accepted most of the Austrian demands. Only those that would virtually have abrogated Serbia's sovereignty were treated somewhat evasively. The consensus was reached within minutes of the deadline. To add to the tension, the only remaining typewriter broke down, and the final text was copied out in a trembling hand by a secretary.

Just before the deadline of 6 P.M. on July 25, Nikola Pashich, the Serbian interior minister, arrived at the Austrian embassy in Belgrade with the reply. Baron W. Giesl, the Austrian ambassador, was under strict instructions from Berchtold to break off diplomatic relations unless Serbia yielded on every point. He hurriedly glanced at the document, noted the Serbian qualifications on some of the demands, and immediately dispatched a note to Pashich informing him that Austria-Hungary had severed diplomatic relations with Serbia. The note overtook Pashich during his return to the ministry, and he found it there on his arrival. So great was Giesl's eagerness that he and the entire staff of the Austrian legation managed to catch the 6:30 P.M. train from Belgrade.

The news reached Emperor Franz-Joseph two hours later at his summer villa in Ischl. According to an eyewitness, the old man looked at the message, sank into a chair, and muttered in a choked voice: *"Also doch!"* (What did I tell you!).[14] Berchtold then convinced the broken man of the need to order partial mobilization. On July 28 Austria-Hungary officially declared war on Serbia. One day later Belgrade was under bombardment.

During these fateful days the Kaiser was cruising on his yacht in the North Sea. He showed so little interest in the matter that he did not even ask to see the text of the Serbian reply until the morning of July 28, a few hours before Austria declared war. After reading it, he jotted the following words in the margin: "A brilliant performance for a time-limit of only 48 hours. This is more than one could have expected! A great moral success for Vienna; but with it every reason for war drops away, and Giesl ought to have remained quietly in Belgrade! After such a thing I should never have ordered mobilization."[15] To his secretary of state, Gottlieb von Jagow, Wilhelm issued the following instruction: "I propose that we say to Austria: Serbia has been forced to retreat in a very humiliating manner and we offer our congratulations; naturally, as a result, every cause for war has vanished."[16] A few hours later, however, when Austrian bombs fell on Belgrade, Kaiser Wilhelm was compelled to face the dreadful consequences of the heedless pledge to Austria he had made less than a month before.

The Closing Trap

The war that broke out on July 28 was a localized conflict between Serbia and Austria-Hungary. The Austrians gambled that it would remain so. Count Berchtold was convinced that there was nothing to fear from Russia; after all, the czar, who lived in fear of assassination himself, was sure to sympathize with a determined

Austrian move against Serbia for the cause of monarchy. And even if this assumption were incorrect, then a swift and decisive military victory over Serbia would confront the czar with a fait accompli. But most important, Berchtold was sure that the Kaiser's guarantee to Austria would prevent Russian intervention and that therefore the war would remain localized and could safely be brought to a quick and successful conclusion.

It now becomes essential to this analysis to consider the actual situation in Russia at the time of Sarajevo. Russia's foreign policy rested on the shoulders of three men: Czar Nicholas II, the foreign minister, Sergei Sazonov, and the minister of war, Vladimir Sukhomlinov.

The czar, though kind and considerate in personal relations, was the epitome of apathy and indifference in matters of public policy. Barbara Tuchman offers a devastating vignette describing the czar's reaction to the news of Austrian and German plans for mobilization. "Nicholas listened," she writes, "and then, as if waking from a reverie, said gravely, 'God's will be done.'"[17] His main conception of government was to preserve intact the absolute monarchy bequeathed to him by his father. The czarina had fallen under the spell of the magnetic personality of Rasputin, and the imperial court was totally out of touch with the people whom the monarchy was supposed to govern.

Sazonov, the czar's foreign minister, was a highly emotional man who had entered the diplomatic service when frail health forced him to abandon his original intention to become a monk. The German ambassador at St. Petersburg described him as "filled with glowing patriotism bordering on chauvinism. When he talk[ed] of past events in which he thought Russia suffered injustice, his face assumed an almost fanatical expression."[18] According to another eyewitness, his lips trembled with emotion when he once remarked that he could not survive another defeat such as Russia had suffered in her war with Japan.[19]

The man responsible for Russia's preparations for war was Sukhomlinov, a pleasure-loving man in his sixties. Sazonov, who disliked him intensely, said that "it was very difficult to make him work but to get him to tell the truth was well-nigh impossible."[20] He held office at the whim of the czar and through the artful cultivation of Rasputin. Naturally lazy, he left his work largely to subordinates and, in the words of the French ambassador, Maurice Paléologue, kept "all his strength for conjugal pleasures with a wife 32 years younger than himself," whom he had married after a sensational divorce scandal. The evidence for the divorce was supplied by an Austrian named Altschiller, who then became a close friend of the minister. In January 1914 Altschiller was exposed as Austria's chief espionage agent in Russia. Totally unreceptive to new ideas, Sukhomlinov prided himself on not having read a military manual in twenty-five years. The phrase "modern war" irritated him. "As war was," he said, "so it has remained." As a result, he clung stubbornly to obsolete theories and ancient glories and believed unquestioningly in the supremacy of the bayonet over the bullet.

This, then, was the trio of men to whom the prince regent of Serbia appealed for help against Austria-Hungary. The popular response in Russia to the Austro-Serbian rupture was extremely heated. On July 26 crowds chanting, "Down with Austria," and, "Long live Serbia," marched through the streets of St. Petersburg. Hostile demonstrations were held in front of the Austrian embassy, and the police had to protect the diplomatic staff from being attacked by the incensed crowd. The czar, when informed of the ultimatum, displayed mild irritation and requested Sazonov to keep him informed. Sazonov's own reaction, however, was explosive: *"C'est la guerre européenne."* He was convinced that the ultimatum was a pretext for Austrian aggression against Serbia. When Count S. Szápáry, the Austro-Hungarian ambassador at St. Petersburg, attempted to defend his country's action by emphasizing the need for a common stand against revolutionary agitation and regicide, Sazonov shouted heatedly: "The fact is, you want war and you have burned your bridges. You are setting Europe on fire."[21] Sazonov was particularly infuriated by Berchtold's methods: the shortness of the time limit, the humiliating demands, and the infringements on Serbia's sovereignty. By the time the German ambassador, Count Friedrich von Pourtalès, called on Sazonov in support of his Austrian colleague, the Russian foreign minister had worked himself into a towering rage. His fury was such that Pourtalès expressed the fear that he was blinded by his hatred of Austria. "Hate," replied Sazonov, "is foreign to my nature. I do not hate Austria; I despise her." And then he exclaimed: "Austria is seeking a pretext to gobble up Serbia; but in that case Russia will make war on Austria."[22]

General Sukhomlinov too had no doubt that Austria would invade Serbia after the time limit expired. He felt that war between

Austria and Serbia would mean war between Austria and Russia and therefore between Germany and Russia. As one of his aides put it: "One does not send such an ultimatum except when the cannons are loaded."[23] These Russian perceptions of Austrian intentions produced the next logical step for Russia: mobilization.

In conjunction with its declaration of war against Serbia, Austria-Hungary had mobilized eight out of a total of sixteen army corps. By this action Berchtold hoped not only to administer a decisive military defeat to Serbia but also to frighten off Russia from intervening. Sazonov, however, viewed this partial mobilization as directed against Russia and so decided to order a partial mobilization of his own. He hoped that quick Russian action would deter Austria from attacking Serbia in the first place. Thus, both the Austrian and Russian decisions to mobilize a part of their armies were essentially bluffs designed to deter the other side.

When the Kaiser was informed of the Austrian declaration of war and the partial Russian mobilization, his indifference gave way to growing panic. The implications of his blank check policy now became painfully clear. He decided to make a determined effort to localize the Austro-Serbian war and to act as mediator between Austria and Russia. In this attempt he was encouraged by Sir Edward Grey, the British foreign secretary, who was becoming increasingly nervous as tensions grew with every passing hour.

The Kaiser took the most direct possible route: He sent a telegram to his cousin Czar Nicholas II. The following excerpt reveals his conciliatory intent:

> It is with the gravest concern that I hear of the impression which the action of Austria against Serbia is creating in your country. . . . With regard to the hearty and tender friendship which binds us both from long ago with firm ties, I am exerting my utmost influence to induce the Austrians to deal straightly to arrive at a satisfactory understanding with you. I confidently hope you will help me in my efforts to smooth over difficulties that may still arise.
>
> Your very sincere and devoted friend and cousin.
>
> Willy[24]

In the past, direct personal messages of this kind had been helpful in steering the Russian and German ships of state through troubled waters. At the same time, Bethmann-Hollweg, acting on the Kaiser's instructions, dispatched to Berchtold another telegram asking him to halt the Austrian armies in Belgrade and not spread the war.

The Russian leadership too was eager to prevent the Austro-Serbian conflict from escalating into a Russo-German war. Sazonov told General von Chelius, the German military plenipotentiary in St. Petersburg, that "the return of the Kaiser has made us all feel easier, for we trust in His Majesty and want no war, nor does Czar Nicholas. It would be a good thing if the two Monarchs should come to an understanding by telegraph."[25] Accordingly, Nicholas sent to his German cousin the following telegram, which crossed that sent by Wilhelm:

> Am glad you are back. In this most serious moment, I appeal to you to help me. An ignoble war has been declared on a weak country. The indignation in Russia shared fully by me is enormous. I foresee that very soon I shall be overwhelmed by the pressure brought upon me and be forced to take extreme measures which will lead to war. To try and avoid such a calamity as a European war, I beg you in the name of our old friendship to do what you can to stop your allies from going too far.
>
> Nicky[26]

Wilhelm's response to this telegram was another wire asking his cousin not to take military measures that "would be looked upon by Austria as threatening."[27] Nicholas wired back the following message:

> Thank you heartily for your quick answer. The military measures which have now come into force were decided five days ago for reasons of defense on account of Austria's preparations. I hope from all my heart that these measures won't in any way interfere with your part as mediator which I greatly value. We need your strong pressure on Austria to come to an understanding with us.[28]

This last communication, which was received by the Kaiser on July 30, completely destroyed his sense of balance. In growing panic, he wrote the following comments in the margins of the czar's wire:

> According to this the Czar has simply been tricking us with his appeal for assistance and has deceived us. . . . Then I must mobilize too. . . . The hope that I would not let his mobilization measures disturb me in my role of mediator is childish, and solely intended to lure us into the mire. . . . I regard my mediation action as brought to an end.[29]

In short, the Kaiser believed that the czar had used the German mediation effort to get a five-day head start in his own military preparations behind Wilhelm's back. The "Willy-Nicky" telegrams had simply bought time for the Russians. By the afternoon of July 30 the Kaiser's panic took on a quality of paranoia. At 1 P.M. a telegram arrived from Lord Grey, who warned that "if war breaks out, it [would] be the greatest catastrophe that the world has ever seen."[30] Wilhelm's response was to scribble in the margin: "This means they will attack us. Aha! The common cheat."[31] In the Kaiser's view, England was combining threat with bluff "to separate us from Austria and to prevent us from mobilizing, and to shift responsibility of the war."[32]

Wilhelm's response to both Austrian and Russian general mobilization was to place the blame on England. At the very moment when Lord Grey was desperately attempting to avert a general war, the Kaiser saw the British at the head of a plot to attack and destroy Germany. In an extraordinary and revealing marginal comment on one of Lord Grey's diplomatic notes, Wilhelm wrote:

> The net has been suddenly thrown over our head, and England sneeringly reaps the most brilliant success of her persistently prosecuted, purely anti-German world policy, against which we have proved ourselves helpless, while she twists the noose of our political and economic destruction out of our fidelity to Austria, as we squirm isolated in the net.[33]

This British plot, which included Russia and France, to exterminate Germany was absolutely real to the Kaiser. The time to strike back had come. "This whole business must now be ruthlessly uncovered," the Kaiser exclaimed to Bethmann, "and the mask of Christian peaceableness publicly and brusquely torn from its face in public, and the pharisaical hypocrisy exposed on the pillory."[34] The entire world must unite against "this hated, lying, conscienceless nation of shopkeepers; for if we are to be bled to death, England shall at least lose India."[35]

This was the basis on which Kaiser Wilhelm made his decision to strike first. On July 31 the Kaiser proclaimed a "state of threatening danger of war" and issued a twelve-hour ultimatum to Russia demanding demobilization. When the Russian leadership refused to comply, Wilhelm promptly ordered full mobilization. The iron dice had begun to roll.

The Iron Dice

As emperors and statesmen on all sides gradually lost control over the deepening crisis, generals and military staffs began to dominate the scene. During the final period before the outbreak of general war, one appalling fact becomes terrifyingly clear: the unrelenting rigidity of military schedules and timetables on all sides. All these had been worked out in minute detail years before, in case war should come. Now that it was imminent, each general was terrified lest his adversary move first and thus capture the initiative. Everywhere, then, military staffs exerted mounting pressure on their chiefs of state to move schedules ahead so as to strike the first blow. What each plan lacked to an astonishing degree was even a small measure of flexibility. In the words of the chief of the mobilization section of the Russian general staff, for example, "the whole plan of mobilization is worked out ahead to its final conclusion and in all its detail . . . once the moment is chosen, everything is settled; there is no going back; it determines mechanically the beginning of war."[36] This was not only an accurate description of the situation in Russia, but also of that in Austria, France, and, most particularly, Germany.

In Russia, the czar vacillated between full mobilization, which would make retreat very difficult, and partial mobilization, which left some room for maneuver. When informed of the Austrian bombardment of Belgrade on the afternoon of July 29, he decided to order full mobilization. That evening, however, Wilhelm's telegram arrived in which he pleaded with the czar not to take the military measures that would precipitate a calamity. Pondering the telegram, the czar now felt that he had made a mistake in signing the ukase for general mobilization. He decided to cancel the order and substitute another one for partial mobilization. At this point the Russian generals became extremely alarmed. Minister of War Sukhomlinov, Chief of Staff General Ianushkevich, and Chief of Mobilization General Dobrorolski all were convinced that a suspension of general mobilization would give the enemy the opportunity to mobilize more quickly than Russia. The czar nonetheless remained firm, and toward midnight of July 29 the order for partial mobilization was released.

The three generals, however, refused to yield. On the following morning they won Sazonov over to their point of view. The foreign minister in turn promised to win over the czar. The chief of staff asked Sazonov to telephone him at once from Peterhof to let him know whether or not he had succeeded. If Sazonov's news was positive, the chief of staff would convert the partial mobilization to a general one and immediately thereafter "retire from sight, smash my telephone and generally take all measures so that I cannot be found to give any contrary orders for a new postponement of general mobilization."[37]

It took Sazonov approximately one hour to convince the czar. The arguments he used were essentially those of the generals. The foreign minister telephoned the chief of staff as promised and added: "Now you can smash the telephone. Give your orders, General, and then—disappear for the rest of the day."[38]

We have already seen Berchtold's role in persuading Emperor Franz-Joseph to agree to partial mobilization against Serbia. Berchtold, in turn, was under the influence of the Austrian chief of staff, Hötzendorff, who hoped to deter Russia through a quick military victory and thus keep the war localized. Hötzendorff was ready, however, to risk intervention by Russia, and so he insisted on the mobilization of eight army corps, or approximately half the Austrian armed forces. He also worked out a plan to convert partial to full mobilization with a minimum of delay, which in fact he did when the news of Russian general mobilization reached Vienna. Encouraged by a telegram from Moltke, the German chief of staff, urging general mobilization, Hötzendorff decided to push the button on July 31 instead of on August 1, the date agreed upon in an audience with Emperor Franz-Joseph. As head of Austria's militarist party, Hötzendorff had great faith in the ability of his army to deliver a crushing blow to Serbia and, if necessary, to capture the initiative in a military campaign against Russia.

In Germany the Kaiser waited anxiously for a Russian reply to his ultimatum. When the deadline of noon on August 1 passed without word, Wilhelm's remaining balance collapsed and paranoia again took over. Hearing the news of the Russian mobilization, Wilhelm burst into a tirade without any connection to reality:

> The world will be engulfed in the most terrible of wars, the ultimate aim of which is the ruin of Germany. England, France, and Russia have conspired for our annihilation . . . that is the naked truth of the situation which was slowly but surely created by Edward VII. . . . The encirclement of Germany is at last an accomplished fact. We have run our heads into the noose. . . . The dead Edward is stronger than the living I![39]

A short time before he decreed general mobilization at 5 P.M. on August 1, the Kaiser confided to an Austrian officer: "I hate the Slavs. I know it is a sin to do so. We ought not to hate anyone. But I can't help hating them."[40]

Wilhelm's hatred of the Slavs kept his mind attuned to a war with Russia. But his general staff, in particular Moltke, its chief, thought differently. For several years, the German generals had been committed to the Schlieffen Plan—the product of Count Alfred von Schlieffen—one of the most illustrious disciples of the nineteenth-century Prussian strategic thinker Karl von Clausewitz. The Schlieffen Plan envisaged a German attack on France through Belgium as the most promising first strike in the event of the outbreak of a general European war. The fact that such a move would violate the neutrality of Belgium hardly bothered the German generals. Caught between his personal desire to begin a military campaign with a devastating blow against Russia and the plan of his general staff to invade Belgium and France, the Kaiser, like Bismarck before him, began to dread the specter of a two-front war. In the meantime, however, mobilization had been ordered, and the gigantic German war machine, prepared for years for this day, had begun to roll. Barbara Tuchman paints a vivid picture of this machine:

> Once the mobilization button was pushed, the whole vast machinery for calling up, equipping, and transporting two million men began turning automatically. Reservists went to their designated depots, were issued uniforms, equipment, and arms, formed into companies and companies into battalions, were joined by cavalry, cyclists, artillery, medical units, cook wagons, blacksmith wagons, even postal wagons, moved according to prepared railway timetables to concentration points near the frontier where they would be formed into divisions, divisions into corps, and corps into armies ready to advance and fight. One army corps alone—out of the total of 40 in the German forces—required 170 railway cars for officers, 965 for infantry, 2960 for cavalry, 1915 for artillery and supply wagons, 6010 in all, grouped in 140 trains and an equal number again for their supplies. From the moment the order was given, everything was to move at fixed times according to a schedule precise down to the number of train axles that would pass over a given bridge within a given time. Confident in his magnificent system, Deputy Chief of Staff General Waldersee had not even returned to Berlin at the beginning of the crisis but had written to Jagow: "I shall remain here ready to jump; we are all prepared at the General Staff; in the meantime there is nothing for us to

do!" It was a proud tradition inherited from the elder, or "great" Moltke who on mobilization day in 1870 was found lying on a sofa reading *Lady Audley's Secret.*[41]

With the momentum of mobilization directed toward the French frontier, the Kaiser's fear of a two-front war rose to a frenzy. Desperately he looked for a way out, and indeed it seemed that at the last minute the opportunity was offered to him. A colleague of Bethmann's suggested the proposal of autonomy for the French province of Alsace in exchange for a pledge of French neutrality. With France neutral, England would remain neutral as well, and the Kaiser could turn his forces against Russia. Prince Karl Max Lichnowsky, the German ambassador in London, did indeed report that England would observe neutrality if Germany refrained from attacking France.

The Kaiser seized this chance for a one-front war and immediately sent for Moltke, who had just put the mobilization order into effect. The trains had already begun to roll toward France as a car, sent out specially to fetch Moltke, brought the perplexed chief of staff to the imperial palace. Wilhelm quickly explained the situation and then announced to Moltke: "Now we can go to war against Russia only. We simply march the whole of our army to the East."[42]

Moltke, the successor of Schlieffen, had planned for this day for a decade. In 1914, at the age of sixty-six, he was still living in the shadow of his illustrious uncle, the victor over France in 1870. This burden had taken its toll: The younger Moltke tended toward melancholy, was a poor horseman, and was a follower of Christian Science. Introspective by nature, he carried Goethe's *Faust* in a pocket of his military tunic and was an ardent reader of contemporary literature. Military decisions were agonizing for him, and he reached them only after searing self-doubt. The emotional cost of making them was so great that he found it next to impossible to alter them, let alone reverse them. In short, he totally lacked flexibility.

When the Kaiser told Moltke of his plan, the chief of staff was aghast. "Your Majesty," he exclaimed, "it cannot be done." When pressed for a reason, Moltke explained: "The deployment of millions cannot be improvised. If Your Majesty insists on leading the whole army to the East it will not be an army ready for battle but a disorganized mob of armed men with no arrangements for supply. Those arrangements took a whole year of intricate labor to complete and once settled, it cannot be altered."[43] The vision of 11,000 trains wrenched into reverse was simply too much for Moltke to bear. He refused the Kaiser point-blank. "Your uncle would have given me a different answer," Wilhelm said bitterly. This statement, Moltke wrote afterward, "wounded me deeply," but did not change his opinion that the job "could not be done."[44] In fact, it could have been done, as Barbara Tuchman reveals in *The Guns of August:* "The German General Staff, though committed since 1905 to a plan of attack upon France first, had in their files, revised each year until 1913, an alternative plan against Russia with all the trains running eastward." General von Staab, the chief of the German Railway Division, was so shocked by Moltke's "it cannot be done" that he wrote a book about it after the war. In this work von Staab showed painstakingly how, given notice on August 1, he could have turned most of the armed forces around and deployed them against Russia by mid-August.

Be that as it may, Moltke convinced the Kaiser on that fateful August 1 that the German machine that had begun to roll toward the west could no longer be either stopped or turned around. The Kaiser made one final effort: He dashed off a telegram to King George of England informing him that due to "technical reasons" mobilization could no longer be countermanded; he also stated that if both France and England would remain neutral, he would "employ [his] troops elsewhere." Simultaneously, Wilhelm ordered his aide-de-camp to telephone German headquarters at Trier, a point near the Luxembourg border where German troops were scheduled to cross the frontier at any moment. Moltke, according to his memoirs, thought that his "heart would break."[45] The railways of Luxembourg were essential to his timetable, since they ran into Belgium and from there into France. He "burst into bitter tears of abject despair" and refused to sign the order countermanding the invasion of Luxembourg. While he was sulking, another call came from the Kaiser, summoning him to the palace. Upon his arrival there, Moltke was informed by the Kaiser that a negative response about the prospects of English neutrality had been received from Prince Lichnowsky. "Now you can do what you like," the Kaiser said to Moltke. The chief of staff later reported that he "never recovered from the shock of this incident. Something in me broke and I was never the same thereafter."[46]

As it turned out, the Kaiser's final effort had been too late. His phone order to Trier had not arrived in time. German soldiers had already crossed the border into Luxembourg and had entered the little town of Trois Vierges, named for the three virgins who symbolized faith, hope, and charity.

At the same time, Count Pourtalès, the German ambassador at St. Petersburg, presented the Kaiser's declaration of war to Sazonov. According to Paléologue, the French ambassador, Sazonov responded by exclaiming: "The curses of the nations will be upon you!" to which the German replied: "We are defending our honor."[47] The night before, Admiral Tirpitz had wanted to know why the Kaiser had found it necessary to declare war on Russia at all since no immediate invasion of Russia was planned and the entire thrust of the German strategy was directed westward. To this question the naval minister never received a satisfactory answer. Nor can we know with certainty what would have happened if Moltke had acquiesced to the Kaiser's order to turn the army around and march toward the east. At the very least, however, valuable time would have been gained. Quite possibly, the outbreak of general war might have been postponed or even averted. But the unrelenting logic of a military schedule foreclosed that possibility.

In France a similar confrontation between a statesman and a general occurred. Premier René Viviani, haunted by the fear that war might erupt by accident, through "a black look, a brutal word, a shot," took an extraordinary step on July 30 and ordered a 10-kilometer withdrawal along the entire French-German border, from Switzerland to Luxembourg. In Viviani's words, France took a chance "never before taken in history." The French commander in chief, General Joseph Joffre, agreed but reached the opposite conclusion. Trained to seize the offensive, he regarded the withdrawal as suicidal and pleaded with the premier to mobilize. By the morning of August 1, he had declared that since each twenty-four-hour delay before general mobilization would mean a 15- to 20-kilometer loss of territory, he would refuse to take the responsibility as commander. Several hours later, he had his way and the premier authorized full mobilization.

England was the only major European power that had no military conscription. The cabinet hoped to keep the nation out of war, but it also realized that England's national interest was tied to the preservation of France. As Sir Edward Grey put it in a typical understatement: "If Germany dominated the continent, it would be disagreeable to us as well as to others, for we should be isolated."[48]

As the tension mounted, the cabinet became increasingly divided. The man who most clearly saw the imminent outbreak of war on the continent was Winston Churchill, first lord of the admiralty. On July 28 Churchill ordered the fleet to sail to its war base at Scapa Flow, and thus prepared it for possible action and probably saved it from a surprise torpedo attack. When Germany declared war on Russia on August 1, Churchill asked the cabinet to mobilize the fleet instantly. Encountering no opposition, he went to the Admiralty and promptly issued the order to activate the fleet.

We see, then, that the chiefs of state of every European nation involved in a military alliance were pressed by their general staffs to mobilize. The generals, under the relentless pressure of their self-imposed timetables, stridently demanded action lest even one crucial hour be lost to the enemy. The pressure on the brink was such that ultimately the outbreak of war was experienced not as a world tragedy but as a liberating explosion.

Conclusion

It is my conviction that during the descent into the abyss, the perceptions of statesmen and generals were absolutely crucial. For the sake of clarity and precision, I should like to consider the following dimensions of this phenomenon: (1) a leader's perception of himself, (2) his perceptions of his adversary's character, (3) his perceptions of the adversary's intentions, (4) his perceptions of the adversary's power and capabilities, and (5) his capacity for empathy with his adversary.

All the participants suffered from greater or lesser distortions in their images of themselves. They tended to see themselves as honorable, virtuous, and pure, and the adversary as diabolical. The leaders of Austria-Hungary probably provide the best illustration of this. Berchtold and Hötzendorff perceived their country as the bastion of European civilization. They saw an Austria-Hungary fighting not only for its national honor but for its very existence against an enemy who had it "by the throat." The possibility of losing prestige and sinking to the status of a second-class power was anathema to the two Austrian leaders. Therefore, they deemed it essential to take a firm and fearless stand that, in their minds, would make a potential enemy back down. The fact that not only Serbia, but Russia too, perceived the Austrian action as aggression never seriously perturbed either Berchtold or his chief of staff. If aggression is defined as the use of force against the territory of another nation in violation of the wishes of that nation's people, then indeed the Austrian move against Serbia fits that definition. Yet the Austrians never saw their action in that light, and charges of aggression were simply ignored. In their zeal to defend Austria's honor and to ensure her status as a major power, Berchtold and Hötzendorff stepped over the edge of a precipice. Their sights were so set on their goal that they failed to pay attention to the world around them; they virtually ignored the reactions of their ally, Germany, and those of their potential adversaries, Russia, England, and France. In their eagerness to vindicate the image of Austria as a virile nation, they led their country to destruction.

Diabolical enemy images were rampant during the crisis, but probably the clearest and most destructive of these were entertained by Kaiser Wilhelm. Before the crisis had reached the boiling point, the Kaiser's efforts to mediate between Austria and Russia were carried out fairly rationally and constructively. But when the czar decided to mobilize, Wilhelm's deep-seated prejudices against the Slavic peoples broke through and sent him into a frenzy. As tensions mounted, this frenzy assumed paranoid proportions and was finally redirected, of all things, toward England, which at that very moment was making every effort to preserve the peace. Wilhelm saw devils in both Russia and England; this perception, more than any other, led to his decision to strike first.

All the nations on the brink of the disaster expected the worst from their potential adversaries. The Russian leadership provides a case in point. Because the czar and his generals felt themselves to be threatened by Austria, Sazonov, who "did not hate Austria, but despised her," responded with threats of hostile action. As Berchtold and Hötzendorff, and later the Kaiser, perceived the Russians' hostility, they too escalated their hostile behavior. These acts convinced the Russians that their initial perceptions had been correct. Thereafter, the diplomatic exchanges became increasingly negative and threatening, and not even the "Willy-Nicky" telegrams were able to save the situation. When a nation designates another nation as its enemy and does so emphatically enough and long enough, the perception will eventually come to be true.

Perceptions of power during the crisis were particularly revealing. During the early phases, leaders notoriously tended to exaggerate their own power and describe their enemies as weaker than they really were. Wilhelm's pledge to Austria, for example, displayed a fundamental contempt for Russia's military power and an exaggerated confidence in his influence on the Russian leadership. Similarly, the Austrians had contempt for Russia's military machine, which they perceived as more cumbersome and weaker than it actually was. As stress mounted, however, these perceptions gradually changed and were soon replaced by acute fears of inferiority. Interestingly enough, these fears did not deter any of the participants from actually going to war. At the boiling point, all leaders tended to perceive their own alternatives as more restricted than those of their adversaries. They saw their own options as limited by necessity or "fate," whereas those of the adversary were characterized by many choices. This may help explain the curiously mechanistic quality that pervaded the attitudes of statesmen everywhere on the eve of the outbreak: the "we cannot go back now" of Franz-Joseph; the "iron dice" of Bethmann; and the absolute determinism and enslavement to their timetables of the military leaders, who perceived the slightest advantage of the enemy as catastrophic.

Everywhere, there was a total absence of empathy; no one could see the situation from another point of view. Berchtold did not see that, to a Serbian patriot, Austria's action would look like naked aggression. He did not see that, to the Russian leadership, war might seem the only alternative to intolerable humiliation; nor did he see the fateful mood swings of his ally, the German Kaiser, from careless overconfidence to frenzied paranoia. Wilhelm's growing panic and total loss of balance made any empathy impossible. And the Russians' contempt for Austria and fear of Germany had the same effect.

Finally, one is struck with the overwhelming mediocrity of the people involved. The character of each of the leaders, diplomats, or generals was badly flawed by arrogance, stupidity, carelessness, or weakness. There was a pervasive tendency to place the preservation of one's ego before the preservation of peace. There was little insight and no vision whatsoever. And there was an almost total absence of excellence and generosity of spirit. It was not fate or Providence that made these people fail so miserably; it was their own evasion of responsibility. As a result of their weakness, a generation of Europe's young men was destroyed. The sins of the parents were truly visited on the sons, who forfeited their lives. Of all the cruelties that people have inflicted on one another, the most terrible have always been brought by the weak against the weak.

I should like to conclude this chapter with one of the most enduring true vignettes that have emerged from World War I. On Christmas Day 1914, German and British troops put up banners to wish each other season's greetings, sang "Silent Night" in both languages, and eventually climbed out of their opposing trenches to play a Christmas Day football match in No Man's Land and share German beer and English plum jam. After Christmas, they went back to killing each other.

After the failure of the Christmas Truce of 1914, the chivalry that still prevailed in the early months of the Great War was soon cast aside by all sides. And then, the road was open, straight and wide, to the abyss of the twentieth century.

NOTES

1. F. H. Hinsley, *Power and the Pursuit of Peace* (London: Cambridge University Press, 1963), p. 296.

2. See, for example, Sidney Bradshaw Fay, *The Origins of the World War,* 2 vols. (New York: Free Press, 1928–1930); Luigi Albertini, *The Origins of the War of 1914,* 3 vols. (London: 1952–1957); or Fritz Fischer, *Griff nach der Weltmacht* (Hamburg: 1961).

3. René Recouly, *Les Heures Tragiques d'Avant-Guerre* (Paris: 1923), p. 19.

4. *Origins of the World War,* Vol. 2, p. 126.

5. Alfred von Tirpitz, *My Memoirs* (London: Hurst & Blackett, 1919), pp. 241–242.

6. *Origins of the World War,* Vol. 2, p. 209.

7. Joachim von Kürenberg, *The Kaiser* (New York: Simon & Schuster, 1955), p. 293.

8. Ibid., p. 295.

9. Ibid., p. 430.

10. *Origins of the World War,* Vol. 2, p. 253.

11. Ibid., pp. 185–186.

12. *Origins of the World War,* Vol. 1, p. 469.

13. *Les Pourparlers Diplomatiques* (Serbian Blue Book) 16/29 juin–3/16 août (Paris: 1914), p. 37.

14. Freiherr von Margutti, *Vom Alten Kaiser* (Vienna: 1921), p. 404.

15. Karl Kautsky (ed.), *Die Deutschen Dokumente zum Kriegsausbruch* (Berlin: 1919), p. 271.

16. Ibid., p. 293.

17. Barbara Tuchman, *The Guns of August* (New York: Macmillan, 1962), pp. 59–60.

18. Pourtalès to Bethmann, August 23, 1910, cited in *Origins of the World War,* Vol. 1, p. 265.

19. Mühlberg, German ambassador in Rome, to Bülow, June 11, 1909, cited in *Origins of the World War,* Vol. 1, p. 265.

20. *Diplomatische Aktenstücke zur Vorgeschichte des Krieges* (Austrian Red Book of 1919) (Vienna: 1919), p. 16.

21. Ibid., p. 19.

22. Ibid.

23. *Die Deutschen Dokumente,* p. 291.

24. Ibid., p. 335.

25. Ibid., p. 337.

26. Ibid., p. 366.

27. Ibid., p. 359.

28. Ibid., p. 390.

29. Ibid.

30. Ibid., p. 321.

31. Ibid.

32. Ibid.

33. Ibid., p. 354.

34. Ibid., p. 350.

35. Ibid.

36. S. Dobrorolski, *Die Mobilmachung der russischen Armee, 1914* (Berlin: 1921), p. 9.

37. Cited in *Origins of the World War,* Vol. 2, p. 470.

38. Ibid., p. 472.

39. Cited in *Guns of August,* p. 75.

40. Ibid., p. 74.

41. Ibid., pp. 74–75.

42. Ibid., p. 78.

43. Ibid., p. 79.

44. Ibid.

45. Ibid., p. 81.

46. Ibid.

47. Ibid., p. 83.

48. Ibid., p. 91.

SELECTED BIBLIOGRAPHY

BRANDS, H. W. *Woodrow Wilson.* New York: Times Books, 2003.

CHURCHILL, WINSTON. *The World Crisis, 1911–1914.* New York: Scribner, 1928.

EARLE, EDWARD M., Ed., *Makers of Modern Strategy.* Princeton, N.J.: Princeton University Press, 1943.

FAY, SIDNEY B. *The Origins of the World War.* 2 vols. New York: Free Press, 1966.

GOERLITZ, WALTER. *History of the German General Staff.* New York: Praeger, 1955.

HERMANN, CHARLES F., Ed., *International Crisis: Insights from Behavioral Research.* New York: Free Press, 1972.

HOLSTI, OLE R. *Crisis, Escalation, War.* Montreal and London: McGill-Queen's University Press, 1972.

KEEGAN, JOHN. *The First World War.* New York: Knopf, 1999.

KURENBERG, JOACHIM VON. *The Kaiser.* New York: Simon & Schuster, 1955.

MACMILLAN, MARGARET. *Paris 1919: Six Months That Changed the World.* New York: Random House, 2002.

ROUZEAU-AUDOIN, STEPHANE, and ANNETTE BECKER. *14–18: Understanding the Great War.* Trans. CATHERINE TEMERSON. New York: Hill & Wang, 2002.

TUCHMAN, BARBARA T. *The Guns of August.* New York: Macmillan, 1962.

ICELAND

ATLANTIC
OCEAN

NORWAY

SWEDEN

FINLAND

North
Sea

ESTONIA

LATVIA

LITH.

SOVIET
UNION

DENMARK

IRELAND

GREAT
BRITAIN

NETH.

BELG.

GERMANY

POLAND

CZECH.

LUX.

FRANCE

SWITZ.

AUS.

HUNGARY

ROMANIA

Black
Sea

ITALY

YUGOSLAVIA

BULGARIA

PORTUGAL

SPAIN

CORSICA

SARDINIA

ALB.

TURKEY

GREECE

Mediterranean Sea

SICILY

CRETE

USSR before the War

Soviet Annexations

Soviet Influence

Soviet Occupation Zones

U.S. Occupation Zones

- - - Iron Curtain (1947)

MAP 2   Europe in 1945

2

Barbarossa:
Hitler's Attack on Russia

You will never learn what I am thinking. And those who boast most loudly that they know my thought, to such people I lie even more.
Adolf Hitler, to Lieutenant General Franz Halder,
August 1938

The most distrustful persons are often the biggest dupes.
Cardinal de Retz (1614–1679), *Mémoires* (1717)

Sigmund Freud once remarked that if a little child had the physical strength to do so, it would smash everything in its path that aroused its displeasure. The key to an understanding of Adolf Hitler's invasion of Russia is more likely found in the realm of psychology than in political science or strategic thought. Hitler was not interested in just defeating Russia; it was not even important to him to conquer and incorporate her into the grand design of his Third Reich that was to last for a thousand years. What he really yearned to do, with all the passion of his demonic nature, was to destroy Russia altogether—to crush her government, pulverize her economy, enslave her people, and eliminate her as a political entity. His determination to destroy Russia was unalterable regardless of Joseph Stalin's policy toward Germany; the German assault would have been unleashed sooner or later.

It was this childlike single-mindedness that made Hitler's attack on Russia so utterly destructive and so difficult to comprehend. Stalin was indeed afraid that Hitler might attack some day, but he believed that the Führer would first present him with an ultimatum to which a rational response might be made. The Soviet leader did not believe that Hitler would attack no matter what, nor was he alone in this belief. The great majority of world leaders and intelligence services had misperceived Hitler's intentions just as badly.[1] As a result, Hitler achieved almost complete strategic and tactical surprise in his attack on Soviet Russia. Stalin—that least trusting, most cunning, and devious of men—had actually placed his trust in the rationality of Hitler, the least rational of men. The mystery of this war lies therein. What led Hitler to this utterly self-destructive decision to invade? What was the basis of Stalin's trust in a man who had broken every promise and violated every pledge? What psychological interplay between these two evil geniuses pitted them against each other in mortal combat? The answers to these questions unlock some of the mysteries that continue to surround the outbreak of one of the bloodiest and most terrible wars in modern history.

Hitler and Russia

Hitler's intention to conquer Russia was first made public in his memoirs, *Mein Kampf,* which were published in 1924, the year of Lenin's death. Here he made known his ambition to acquire *Lebensraum* in the east:

> We terminate the endless German drive to the South and West of Europe, and direct our gaze towards the lands in the East. . . . If we talk about new soil and territory in Europe today, we can think primarily only of Russia and its vassal border states. The colossal empire in the East is ripe for dissolution, and the end of the Jewish domination in Russia will also be the end of Russia as a state.

To understand Hitler's growing hatred of Russia, one must appreciate the fact that he paved his road to power with Communist blood. As the German population grew polarized between right and left because of the deepening economic crisis and a wave of unemployment, Hitler began to perceive the Communists as his only serious obstacle and, next to the Jews, his worst enemies. His storm troopers confronted them in innumerable street battles, beer hall skirmishes, and fistfights in crowded meeting halls. Since Russia was the citadel of the Communist movement, Hitler's fury against the Soviet Union became an obsession. What began as a desire merely to conquer Russia changed over the years to a deep emotional need to destroy her.

As a young artist in Vienna, Hitler had accumulated a fair amount of knowledge of English, French, and Italian history and culture, but there is no evidence that he had the slightest acquaintance with Russian civilization or that he ever read a book by a Russian writer. To him, Russia was a vast land beyond the pale of civilization, inhabited by ignorant peasants and their savage Bolshevik masters. Shortly after beginning the invasion of Russia, he said: "The Bolsheviks have suppressed everything that resembles civilization, and I have no feeling at all about wiping out Kiev, Moscow, and St. Petersburg."[2] This attitude crystallized during the years of his struggle for power. By the time he became chancellor, it had congealed into an idée fixe.

Hitler's first years in power brought him into gradually escalating conflict with the Soviet Union, and with every confrontation his fury against Bolshevism soared to new heights. One of his first acts on becoming chancellor in 1933 was to abrogate a long-standing mutual rearmament agreement that had strengthened both the German and the Soviet armies. Three years later, Hitler persuaded Japan to sign the Anti-Comintern Pact, which contained a number of secret military provisions directed against Russia. Late in 1936 Hitler confronted Stalin on the field of battle for the first time, albeit indirectly, by sending thousands of airmen, artillerymen, and tank crews, thinly disguised as volunteers, to fight in the Spanish Civil War. But it was the annexation of Czechoslovakia in 1939 that revealed for the first time Hitler's mindless hatred for the Slavic peoples in all its merciless brutality.

In Operation Green, the blueprint for the invasion of Czechoslovakia, Hitler had written: "It is my unalterable decision to smash Czechoslovakia in the near future." To his generals, he explained this move as the first step toward a larger "reckoning with the East." Much has been written about Hitler's interview with Dr. Emil Hácha, the hapless president of Czechoslovakia, that took place shortly before the German armored columns entered Prague. During the conversation Hácha fainted and had to be revived with a hypodermic needle. But what many historians generally fail to consider is the fierceness of Hitler's rage against the Czech statesman. Dr. Paul Schmidt, the interpreter who was present at the time, was struck by Hitler's ferocious hatred and commented on it afterward.[3] This hatred seems not to have been manufactured just for the purpose of intimidating Hácha; it evidently sprang from deep and genuine emotional wellsprings. Its very intensity apparently had a profound psychological impact on Hácha and contributed to his political capitulation.

Arthur Schopenhauer, in his book *The World as Will and Idea,* advanced the argument that blind, unreasoning will is the most powerful human force. Reason is simply a "light that the will had kindled for itself" in order better to attain the object of its drive. Perhaps this may explain the paradox of Hitler's decision in 1939 to ally himself temporarily with Stalinist Russia, the country that, above all others, he passionately wanted to destroy. After Czechoslovakia, the next Slavic country on his timetable of destruction was Poland. But to crush Poland quickly and without risk Hitler needed the acquiescence of Stalin. An alliance with Stalin would also enable Hitler to complete his conquest of Western Europe without the risk of a two-front war. With the resources of all Europe at his command, the task of annihilating Russia would then be simple. In short, Hitler allied himself with Stalin in order to crush him more effectively later in a war of total annihilation.

In August 1939 Hitler instructed his foreign minister, Joachim von Ribbentrop, to explore with Stalin the possibility of a nonaggression pact, complete with a "supplementary protocol" that would divide up and apportion Poland between the two dictators. When, after a week, no response had arrived from the Kremlin, Hitler himself took the initiative and wrote Stalin a letter in which he in effect asked the Soviet leader to hurry, as a German invasion of Poland was imminent:

> The tension between Germany and Poland has become intolerable. . . . A crisis may arise any day. Germany is at any rate determined from now on to look after the interests of the Reich with all the means at her disposal.[4]

On August 21, in a letter addressed to "The Chancellor of the German Reich, A. Hitler," Stalin replied that he would receive Ribbentrop in Moscow on August 23. On the following day, in a state of euphoria, Hitler addressed his generals and announced his plans for the imminent destruction of Poland:

> I shall give a propagandist cause for starting the war. Never mind whether it is plausible or not. The victor will not be asked, later on, whether we told the truth or not. In starting and waging war, it is not Right that matters but Victory. Have no pity. Adopt a brutal attitude. . . .

Complete destruction of Poland is the military aim. To be fast is the main thing. Pursue until complete annihilation. The start will be probably ordered for Saturday morning.[5]

Saturday was August 26, and the attack on Poland was to take place only two days after the signing of the Nazi-Soviet pact. Hitler was in no mood to lose time in his plans to destroy another Slavic country.

The Hitler-Stalin pact was duly signed in Moscow on August 23. The attached Secret Additional Protocol divided up Poland and assigned to the Soviet sphere of influence Finland, Estonia, Latvia, and part of Romania. Nine days later Hitler invaded Poland, and England and France declared war on Germany. Stalin now hoped that his three enemies would exhaust each other in a long and bloody war and that he could simply sit by and watch their agonizing deaths.

To Stalin's growing dismay, however, Hitler's armies made short shrift of most of Western Europe. The goal of annihilating Russia lay in Hitler's mind like bedrock, and not for a moment did he consider abandoning it. In fact, a mere three months after signing the nonaggression pact with Stalin, Hitler informed a group of high military officers that he would move against the Soviet Union immediately after the conquest of Western Europe. General Franz Halder, who kept a copious diary, recorded on October 18, 1939, that Hitler had instructed his generals to regard conquered Poland as "an assembly area for future German operations."

As Hitler observed that Stalin's attitude toward territorial conquest began to resemble his own, his rage against Bolshevik Russia gradually assumed frantic proportions. Stalin's attack on Finland in late 1939 sparked an emergency meeting with Hitler's generals in Berlin at which he demanded that an attack on Russia be launched by the autumn of 1940. The desperate protestations by the entire general staff that such a short schedule would pose insuperable logistical problems made Hitler postpone the projected assault until the spring of 1941. To make matters worse, while Hitler was busy conquering Denmark and Norway in the spring of 1940, Stalin imposed Red Army bases on the three Baltic states of Estonia, Latvia, and Lithuania. In June Stalin took the provinces of Bessarabia and Bukovina away from Romania, and one month later, on July 21, he simply annexed the three Baltic states. That same day, in a raging speech to his generals, Hitler ordered immediate feasibility studies for the conquest of Russia.

Hitler's obsession with the Soviet Union now began to color his view of Britain. So desperate was he to destroy Russia that he told his generals in July 1940 that Britain's stubborn determination to continue the war could only be explained by its hope that Russia would enter the war. Therefore, Hitler argued, Russia had to be destroyed first, since the road to London passed through Moscow: "If Russia is smashed, Britain's last hope will be shattered. . . . In view of these considerations Russia must be liquidated, spring 1941. The sooner Russia is smashed, the better."[6] In early August Hitler ordered *Aufbau Ost* (Buildup East), his plan "to wipe out Russia's very power to exist."[7] The destruction of the Soviet Union came first. Operation Sea Lion, the planned invasion of Britain, had to wait.

Hitler's hatred of Russia blinded him completely to the strategic realities that prevailed in the summer of 1940. Stalin had absolutely no intention of helping Britain in her plight. It is quite conceivable that Hitler could have dealt Britain a fatal blow had he not been mesmerized by his need to annihilate the Soviet Union at all costs. Winston Churchill recognized this only too well when he wrote to Franklin D. Roosevelt at the time that the continuation of the war "would be a hard, long, and bleak proposition." Thus Hitler's boundless hatred for the Slavic peoples was responsible for one of the greatest blunders of his career.

In the autumn of 1940 Hitler issued a directive to transfer large segments of the Wehrmacht to the east. Strict orders were given to keep these transfers secret so as not to arouse Stalin's suspicions. Accordingly, the German military attaché in Moscow was instructed to inform the Soviet government that the massive troop transfers were merely efforts to replace older men who were being released to industry. In the words of General Alfred Jodl, "these regroupings must not create the impression in Russia that we are preparing an offensive in the East."[8]

Hitler was so infuriated by Stalin's annexation of the two Romanian provinces that in late August 1940 he ordered five panzer and three motorized divisions plus airborne troops to seize the Romanian oil fields. Moscow was not consulted, and in late September Soviet foreign minister Vyacheslav Molotov warned Hitler that the Soviet Union still had interests in Romania. He also complained that the Germans had sent reinforcements to Norway by way of Finland, countries he considered to be in the Soviet sphere of influence. In October Ribbentrop asked Stalin to send Molotov to Berlin so that "the Führer could explain personally his views regarding the future molding of relations between the Reich and the Soviet Union." He hinted that Hitler intended to propose a scheme that would in effect divide up the world among the four leading dictatorships. As he put it euphemistically: "It appears to be the mission of the Four Powers—the Soviet Union, Italy, Japan, and Germany—to adopt a long-range policy by delimitation of their interests on a world-wide scale."[9] Stalin accepted the invitation on behalf of Molotov, and on November 12 the Soviet foreign minister, eager for a more advantageous division of the spoils, and apparently quite unaware of *Aufbau Ost,* arrived at Berlin's main railroad station, which was decorated for the occasion with the hammer and sickle flying side by side with the swastika. It was this meeting between Hitler and Molotov that provided the final spark to Operation Barbarossa, the invasion of Russia.

Dr. Paul Schmidt, Hitler's interpreter, left a vivid account of the Berlin meeting. It seems that during the morning of November 12 Ribbentrop was given the task of explaining Hitler's conception of the "new order" to Molotov. The Führer, he said, had concluded that all four allies should expand in a southerly direction. Japan and Italy had already done so, and Germany would seek new *Lebensraum* in Central Africa. The Soviet Union too might "turn to the South for the natural outlet to the open sea which was so important to her." "Which sea?" Molotov asked laconically. Ribbentrop had no answer. In the afternoon it was Hitler's turn. In Schmidt's words, "the questions hailed down upon Hitler; no foreign visitor had ever spoken to him in this way in my presence."[10] The precise Bolshevik with the pince-nez wanted to know what Hitler was up to in Finland and demanded that German troops be pulled out. In addition, he wanted clarification regarding Soviet interests in Bulgaria, Romania, and Turkey. Hitler was too taken aback to answer and proposed to adjourn the meeting until evening. At the dinner meeting, the Führer did not make an appearance, leaving Ribbentrop to entertain the Russian. This he did by expounding at length on the imminent collapse of Britain and the great opportunity, in which the Soviet Union would share, to divide up the remnants of the British Empire. At almost that very moment, according to Dr. Schmidt, the air-raid sirens began to sound and Ribbentrop and his guest were forced to run for shelter somewhat unceremoniously. British bombers had raided Berlin. When Ribbentrop, sitting in the air-raid shelter, repeated again that the British were finished, Molotov asked: "If that is so, why are we in this shelter, and whose are these bombs which fall?"[11]

The next day, after Molotov's departure, Hitler was beside himself with rage. "Stalin is clever and cunning," he told his generals. "He demands more and more. He is a cold-blooded blackmailer. A German victory has become unbearable for Russia. Therefore: she must be brought to her knees as soon as possible."[12] On December 18 Hitler dictated the secret directive that became the basis for Operation Barbarossa:

> The German Armed Forces must be prepared, even before the conclusion of the war against England, to crush Soviet Russia in a rapid campaign. . . . I shall issue orders for the deployment against Soviet Russia eight weeks before the operation is timed to begin. Preparations . . . will be concluded by May 15, 1941. It is of decisive importance that our intention to attack should not be known.[13]

May 15, then, became the date for the destruction of Russia. Throughout the winter Hitler was preoccupied with the military planning for Barbarossa. He decided to penetrate the Soviet Union with two gigantic armies, one to conquer Leningrad in the north and the other to attack Kiev in the south. Moscow, in Hitler's view, would inevitably fall once the rest of Western Russia had been conquered. Only nine copies of this directive were made, one for each of the three armed services, the others to be kept under guard at Hitler's headquarters. The Führer demanded that the number of officers privy to the secret be kept as small as possible. "Otherwise the danger exists that our preparations will become known and the gravest political and military disadvantages result."[14] There is no evidence whatsoever that any of the generals who were taken into Hitler's confidence objected to Barbarossa. Halder, the chief of the general staff, noted in his diary in December 1940 that he was full of enthusiasm for the Russian campaign. Several weeks later, in February 1941, Halder submitted such an optimistic assessment of German chances to annihilate the Red Army in short order that Hitler exclaimed jubilantly: "When Barbarossa commences, the world will hold its breath and make no comment."[15] He then called for the operation map in order to put the finishing touches on his plans for the massacre that was to begin on May 15.

During this crucial period two events took place that prompted Hitler to postpone the invasion of Russia by five weeks. It is of the utmost importance to consider these events, since the postponement of the invasion probably spelled the difference between victory and defeat.

In October 1940 Mussolini, eager for martial glory of his own, decided to invade Greece in a surprise attack. When Hitler visited his fellow dictator in Florence on October 28, Mussolini met him at the railroad station and announced triumphantly: "Führer, we are on the march! Victorious Italian troops crossed the Greco-Albanian frontier at dawn today!"[16] According to Schmidt, who was present, Hitler managed to control his rage. Shortly thereafter, however, the Italian campaign turned into a rout, and by January 1941 Mussolini had to ask Hitler humbly for military assistance. Hitler complied, and by April 1941 Nazi tanks rattled into Athens and the swastika flew from the Acropolis. The price of this diversionary maneuver, however, amounted to twelve German divisions mired down in Greece.

The second and even more pivotal event was a coup d'état that took place in Yugoslavia on March 26, 1941. During that night the government of the regent, Prince Paul, who had come close to being a puppet of Hitler, was overthrown. Peter, the young heir to the throne, was declared king, and the Serbs made it quite clear on the following day that Yugoslavia's subservience to Germany had ended.

According to William L. Shirer, the Belgrade coup threw Hitler into one of the wildest rages of his life.[17] He took it as a personal affront from a Slavic nation that existed only at his whim. Calling his generals into immediate session, Hitler announced that "no diplomatic inquiries [would] be made, and no ultimatum presented."[18] Yugoslavia would be crushed with "unmerciful harshness." He ordered Goering to "destroy Belgrade in attacks by waves" and also ordered the immediate invasion of Yugoslavia. Then he announced to his generals the most fateful decision: "The beginning of the Barbarossa operation will have to be postponed by up to four weeks."[19]

Once again, none of the generals present objected. But six months later, when German troops were hit by deep snows and Arctic temperatures in front of Moscow, three or four weeks short of what General Halder thought they needed for final victory, the chief of staff was to recall with deep bitterness that the postponement of

Barbarossa was probably the most catastrophic military decision of the entire war. In order to vent his personal revenge on a small Slavic nation, the Nazi leader had thrown away the opportunity to annihilate the Soviet Union. Hitler himself realized this shortly before his death. Like the Roman emperor Augustus, shouting to a pitiless sky, "Varus, give me back my legions," Hitler, in the underground bunker of the Reich chancellery with the Russians only blocks away, was said to have screamed in anguish at a portrait of Frederick the Great: "Give me back my four weeks!"

On March 30, 1941, the number of Wehrmacht officers fully apprised of Barbarossa suddenly jumped to approximately 250. The occasion was a long speech delivered by Hitler in the new Reich chancellery in Berlin. The subject was the coming massacre of the Soviet Union, now rescheduled to begin on June 22, 1941. The basic purpose of the speech was to prepare the generals for a war of total annihilation. Hitler described the coming campaign as a war to the death between two opposing ideologies. The struggle would be conducted with merciless harshness, and no quarter would be given. Breaches of international law would be excused since Russia had not participated in the Hague Conference and therefore had no rights under it. Soviet commissars who surrendered were to be executed. Hitler stated in conclusion, "I do not expect my generals to understand me, but I shall expect them to obey my orders."[20] None of the generals in Hitler's audience asked any questions, nor was there any discussion. Five years later at the Nuremberg war crimes trials, when the question of the notorious Commissar Order was brought up, several generals confessed that they had been horrified but had lacked the courage to object.

During the final weeks before the invasion, Hitler alternated between detailed military planning and indulgence in fantasies of what he would do to the hated Russians. "In a few weeks we shall be in Moscow," he declared, "there is absolutely no doubt about it. I will raze this damned city to the ground and I will make an artificial lake to provide energy for an electric power station. The name of Moscow will vanish forever."[21] Russian tradition, history, and culture would cease to exist. No Russian books, except perhaps agricultural handbooks, would be published, and Russian children would be given just enough instruction in their schools to understand the orders of their German masters. All Russian Jews would perish, and the population of Russia would be drastically reduced through starvation and mass executions. On the morning after the summer solstice, the German army would smash into Russia. Long before the winter solstice, Russia would disappear from the map.

Hermann Goering was placed in charge of the economic exploitation of the Soviet Union. On May 23, 1941, Goering issued a directive in which he announced that most of Russia's food production would go to Germany, and the Russian population would be left to starve:

> Any attempt to save the population from death by starvation . . . would reduce Germany's staying power in the war. As a result, many millions of persons will be starved to death if we take out of the country the things necessary for us. This must be clearly and absolutely understood.[22]

Once again, there is no evidence that any of Goering's subordinates who prepared the spoliation of Russia during that pleasant German spring of 1941 voiced any protest.

When the order to invade the Soviet Union was finally given at 3 A.M. on June 22, Hitler was the absolute master of the most formidable fighting machine the world had ever seen: 154 German divisions, not to mention Finnish and Romanian detachments, were massed on the Russian border; 3,000 tanks and 2,000 airplanes were ready for battle; generals fresh from a succession of victories were in command of the Wehrmacht. It seemed that nothing could prevent Hitler's entry into Moscow before the end of the summer.

In addition, the attack was a complete surprise, due not so much to Hitler's discretion as to Stalin's stubborn refusal to believe that a surprise attack was imminent. During the night of the invasion, Moscow slept peacefully. As dawn broke, the commander of a small Soviet frontier post was awakened by artillery fire. When he called the general in command to report the shelling, the reply was: "You must be insane." By this time, the Germans had overrun the post and advanced deep into Russia.

Examining these events, one is struck by Hitler's private and personal involvement in the war against Russia. The need to destroy the hated Slavic nation was an oppressive presence that blinded him completely to the strategic realities in Russia, both before and after the invasion. Perhaps the most revealing document on this subject is a letter that Hitler wrote to Mussolini on June 21, a few hours before the German troops poured into Russia. As Hitler wrote:

> Since I struggled through to this decision, I again feel spiritually free. The partnership with the Soviet Union . . . was nevertheless often very irksome to me, for in some way or other it seemed to me to be a break with my whole origin, my concepts and my former obligations. I am happy now to be relieved of these mental agonies.[23]

Thus German soldiers, sure of a summer victory, entered Russia wearing their light uniforms. No provisions had been made to procure winter clothing, nor had preparations been made to cope with the Russian winter. Men and machines were tooled to perfection, but only for another blitzkrieg. The lessons of Charles XII of Sweden and of Napoleon Bonaparte, who had met their doom in the snows of Russia, were ignored. Yet Hitler chose for his greatest military venture two symbols, the murky significance of which is strange indeed. Barbarossa, after whom he named the campaign, had been a crusader of the Holy Roman Empire who had failed in his mission to the East and had drowned. His corpse and the site of his burial were lost. Even more peculiar was the choice of June 22 as the day of reckoning. As Hitler never mentioned the fate of the Grand Armée in its retreat from Moscow in 1812, it has never been established whether he knew that this was the anniversary of Napoleon's invasion of Russia almost a century and a half before.

Stalin and Germany

Today, when one thinks of the Russo-German war, the images that come most quickly to mind are the Soviet victory at Stalingrad and the ultimate triumph of Soviet arms in Berlin in 1945. What is remembered less readily is that "the scale of the disaster wrought by the German invaders in the first hours, days, weeks, and months of the war can be considered unprecedented in the history of modern warfare."[24] One month after the beginning of the invasion, the German Army Group Center was within 200 miles of Moscow; Army Group North was moving toward Leningrad; and Army Group South was approaching Kiev, the capital of the Ukraine. Most of the Soviet air force had been destroyed, much of it on the ground during the first five days. More than half a million prisoners had been taken by the advancing German armies. By midsummer of 1941 German troops controlled Soviet territory amounting to more than twice the size of France. While there can be no doubt about the determined resistance and dogged fighting spirit of the Red Army, it is likely that in the last analysis the Soviet Union was saved by her immense space, manpower, resources, and, perhaps most important, the Russian winter.

The haunting question that arises when one contemplates the disaster of June 1941 is: How was it possible for Hitler to achieve such complete strategic and tactical surprise when Stalin had received an abundance of intelligence information warning of the imminent attack? Without a doubt, Stalin "received more and better information on the approaching danger, even on specific details of date and hour of invasion, than did any other leadership of an attacked country in the history of modern warfare."[25] Winston Churchill, who personally warned Stalin several times, was so appalled by the Russian's heedlessness that he reached the conclusion that "Stalin and his commissars showed themselves to be the most completely outwitted bunglers."[26]

Soviet prewar predictions of the likely course of a Nazi-Soviet war were separated from reality by an unbridgeable gulf. In the summer of 1939 there appeared in the Soviet Union a novel by N. Shpanov, entitled *The First Strike—The Story of a Future War*, in which a Fascist air attack on the Soviet Union was repulsed by Soviet fighters within half an hour. Ten hours later the Soviet air force reported the destruction of the entire German war-making potential. Considering that this fictional war story seems to have been widely believed in the Soviet Union, one can appreciate that the reality of the summer of 1941 took on the dimensions of a colossal nightmare and produced a "mental vacuum and a terror of the unexplainable."[27] Yet an explanation must be sought in the personality of the absolute ruler of the Soviet Union—Joseph Stalin.

Probably the single most important reason for the disaster was the Great Purge of the 1930s. Although all sectors of Soviet society were crippled by the unprecedented terror unleashed by Stalin after the death of Sergei Kirov in 1934, the officer corps of the Red Army was virtually decimated. General Shmushkevich, chief of the Soviet air force and senior military officer before the Nazi invasion, was executed a mere two weeks before the German assault.

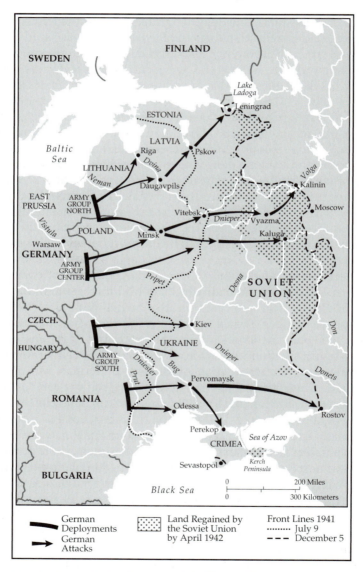

Map 3   **Operation Barbarossa and the Eastern Front, 1941–1942**

It is likely that even if Stalin had heeded the numerous intelligence warnings of the Nazi attack, he could not have averted the disaster completely. The Great Purge was a horrible bloodletting; many more senior officers were killed during those years than during four years of war against Nazi Germany.[28] Arrests of senior officers in 1936 began the assault. In 1937 a group of the highest-ranking officers of the Red Army, including General Tukhachevsky, were arrested, tried as "foreign agents," and shot. A crescendo of executions took place under the direction of the head of the Secret Police, N. I. Yezhov, until that "lord high executioner" was himself executed in 1939 and replaced by Lavrenti Beria. During these years the Soviet military establishment sustained terrible and irreplaceable losses. Moreover, the professional competence of the Red Army, not to speak of its morale, deteriorated to dangerously low levels. By 1940 about one-fifth of the positions of unit and subunit commanders were vacant; military schools could neither fill vacancies nor provide reserves.[29] At the time of the invasion, only 7 percent of all Soviet officers had received higher military education, and 37 percent had not even completed military training; 75 percent had occupied their posts for less than a year.[30] Careers were made and broken with dizzying speed, and inexperienced men often reached the apex of command, not out of professional competence but because of political favor and the personal whim of the supreme commander, Joseph Stalin.

The purge produced an atmosphere of overwhelming fear; the knowledge of the possible consequences of a single misstep gave rise to a situation in which decisions on trivial as well as grave matters ultimately gravitated to the center of all power—Stalin. By 1941 military policy had in effect been reduced to preparing proposals for Stalin, asking permission from Stalin, appealing for help to Stalin, and, above all, executing the orders of Stalin.[31] Even after the invasion, the Soviet generals feared Stalin more than they feared the Germans. Top field commanders, responsible for the lives of close to 700,000 troops almost certain to be annihilated in the trap at Kiev in 1941, refused to risk Stalin's anger by requesting permission to withdraw. Very much like Field Marshal Friedrich von Paulus at Stalingrad, who feared Hitler's anger more than Soviet guns, the Russian generals preferred to take their chances with the Nazis rather than run the risk of Stalin's wrath. The Soviet leader's control over the Red Army in 1941 was as complete as Hitler's dominance over the Wehrmacht.

What compelled Stalin to these purges, which almost broke the backbone of Russia's fighting forces in her hour of supreme trial? The evidence suggests that Stalin placed the security of his power within the Soviet state above all else, including the security of the nation from foreign attack. Essentially, the purges were designed to eliminate not only all actual but also all potential opposition to Stalin's absolute rule. Conveniently enough, many victims of the purge, some of whom were made to testify at the trumped-up Moscow Trials, were depicted as "paid agents of the capitalist powers." The attention of the Russian people was thus deflected from their real domestic problems to imaginary dangers that lurked outside Soviet borders. Stalin stopped the engine of destruction only when it threatened, in its mad momentum, to get out of hand completely, but not before it had almost destroyed the very fabric of society.

In his famous "secret speech" to the Twentieth Party Congress in 1956, Nikita Khrushchev accused Stalin of empty boasts about Russia's fighting ability in 1941 and chastised him for failing to heed the many clear warnings of Nazi intentions in word and deed that were made available to him before the invasion. He challenged Stalin's qualifications as a military commander, and citing his nervousness and hysteria, Khrushchev noted that for two weeks after the invasion Stalin had been in a state of nervous collapse and "ceased to do anything whatever" except sulk. But he reserved his strongest words for Stalin's disastrous annihilation of military cadres during the years of the Great Purge. This, said Khrushchev, almost cost the Soviet Union its existence as a sovereign nation.

Stalin's role as war leader was elevated after Khrushchev's ouster in 1964, but condemnation of the purge remained official Soviet policy. As a more balanced picture of the man who ruled Russia for a quarter of a century slowly emerges, his role in the "Great Patriotic War" will almost surely remain controversial. The Great Purge, however, will probably continue to be regarded both inside and outside the former Soviet Union as Stalin's greatest crime and worst blunder.

A second major cause for the disaster of June 1941 was Stalin's decision to ally himself with Hitler in 1939. Stalin justified the pact on the occasion of his first broadcast to the Soviet people after the invasion. In this message, delivered on July 3, he said: "We secured peace for our country for one and a half years, as well as an opportunity of preparing our forces for defense if fascist Germany risked attacking our country in defiance of the pact. This was a definite gain for our country and a loss for fascist Germany."[32] In short, Stalin argued that his deal with Hitler had given Russia the same breathing spell that Czar Alexander had secured from Napoleon at Tilsit in 1807 and that Lenin had wrested from Germany at Brest-Litovsk in 1917. This argument merits detailed and objective consideration.

During the early 1930s Stalin began to cast about for allies to counter the rising threat of Hitler. He sought mutual security pacts and promoted popular front alliances between Communist parties and other anti-Fascist groups within other nations. By 1938, however, Stalin felt increasingly insecure in his temporary alliance with Britain and France. He may even have suspected that Britain aimed at encouraging Hitler to strike to the east in order to provoke a death struggle between the Soviet Union and Germany. In any event, the Anglo-French fiasco at Munich confirmed the Soviet leader's suspicion that an alliance with Hitler might be highly advantageous. Stalin calculated that such a pact would safeguard the Nazi dictator's eastern flank and thus give him the green light to launch an offensive against the West. Since, in Stalin's view, Nazi Germany and Western Europe were approximately equal in strength, a mutually exhausting war would give the Soviet Union an opportunity to grow stronger in peace and ultimately absorb both adversaries. In addition, a pact with Hitler would buy time, an essential commodity since the Great Purge had seriously weakened the Soviet military machine. Moreover, the Soviet Union would at last be able to make some territorial gains: half of Poland and the three Baltic states of Latvia, Lithuania, and Estonia. Thus, in 1939, Stalin decided to sacrifice Marxism-Leninism on the altar of Machiavelli.

As it turned out, Stalin's premises included one fundamental miscalculation: It took Hitler not years but weeks to conquer most of Western Europe. By 1940 Stalin was dismayed to find himself confronted with a Nazi colossus with the resources of most of Western Europe at its disposal. Throughout 1941, 1942, and 1943 Stalin was to complain bitterly that there was no second front in Europe against Hitler and that Russia was forced to bear the sole burden of containing the German army. In 1939 there was still a western front in Europe that could have drawn off the German forces. Poland would not have been overrun in two weeks if Stalin had supported her instead of carving her up with Hitler. And most important, there might not have been any war if Hitler had known that he would have had to face the Soviet Union in alliance with England and France. Even his timid generals had warned him at the time that Germany's chances of winning were slim against such a formidable coalition.

Stalin's pact with Hitler was also the result of his contempt for the policies of Britain and France. He argued that he had only done what the two capitalist powers had done the year before at Munich: bought peace and the time to rearm at the expense of a small state. Chamberlain had bought time by sacrificing Czechoslovakia; Stalin could do the same and sacrifice Poland. By the time Ribbentrop visited Moscow on August 23, 1939, to sign the pact, Stalin had become so anti-British that he exchanged confidences with his German guest. "The British military mission in Moscow," he told Ribbentrop, "had never told the Soviet government what it really wanted." Ribbentrop responded by saying that Britain had always tried to disrupt good relations between Germany and the Soviet Union. "England is weak," he declared, "and wants to let others fight for her presumptuous claim to world dominion." Stalin eagerly concurred and added: "If England dominated the world, that was due to the stupidity of the other countries that always let themselves be bluffed."[33] After signing the pact, Stalin spontaneously proposed a toast to Hitler: "I know how much the German nation loves its Führer. I should therefore like to drink to the Führer's health."[34] As Ribbentrop was leaving, Stalin took him aside and said: "The Soviet Government takes the new pact very seriously. I can guarantee on my word of honor that the Soviet Union will not betray its part- ner."[35] In short, Stalin wanted to convey to Hitler that he trusted him more than he had ever trusted the British and French. Less than four weeks later he absorbed his share of Poland.

The Soviet population appears to have been utterly confused by Stalin's *volte-face.* In the following excerpt, a pilot in the Soviet air force, writing after the war, looked back on those "twenty-two strange and incomprehensible months" when the pact was in force:

> The fascists were no longer called fascists—one could not find any trace of this word in the press or in official reports and speeches. Things which we had become accustomed to seeing as hostile, evil, and dangerous . . . had somehow become virtually neutral. This was not stated directly in

words but rather crept into our consciousness from the photograph showing Hitler standing beside Molotov, from reports of Soviet oil and Soviet grain flowing from us to fascist Germany, and even from the introduction of the Prussian parade step at that time. Yes, it was difficult to understand what was what![36]

There is little doubt that at the time the pact was signed Stalin had more faith in Hitler than in "Anglo-American capitalism." In this exaggerated trust in his fellow dictator and his equally exaggerated suspicion of Britain and the United States lies yet another key to the riddle of the disaster of June 1941.

During the year preceding the invasion, eighty-four separate warnings about Barbarossa were conveyed to the Soviet Union,[37] and presumably a great number were brought to Stalin's attention. The strongest warning, however, emanated from British and American sources. Because of its source, Stalin in most cases discounted the information rather than considering it on its merits. He received with suspicion, or even rejected outright, all information about Hitler's actions that came from the British or the Americans. Since he believed that Britain wanted him to go to war with Germany, he was convinced that all British intelligence about the possibility of imminent war was a fabrication designed to provoke a Russo-German war. When he finally realized the veracity of this "capitalist" intelligence, the time for effective countermeasures had almost passed. A fair sample of these warnings will suffice to demonstrate the depths of Stalin's self-delusion.

The British government attempted to warn Stalin on six separate occasions. On June 25, 1940, Churchill wrote a personal letter to Stalin in which he pointed out that Hitler's insatiable lust for conquest posed a common problem. Ambassador Stafford Cripps delivered Churchill's note and added his own concurring remarks. Stalin, who, according to Cripps, was "formal and frigid," never bothered to reply to Churchill's note. In late February 1941 Cripps, on his own initiative, again warned Molotov, stating that he was convinced that Hitler would attack the Soviet Union before the end of June. Stalin not only dismissed the warning but passed it on privately to the German ambassador. On June 13 a Tass release branded Cripps an *agent provocateur.* On March 30, 1941, Churchill was dismayed by the growing eastward deployment of German forces and again instructed Cripps to warn Stalin with an urgent personal message. Once more, there was no reply from the Kremlin. On June 10 British intelligence had become convinced that Hitler was about to attack and that an explicit warning to Stalin was in order. Accordingly, on that day Under Secretary Sir Alexander Cadogan summoned Soviet ambassador Ivan Maisky to the Foreign Office and proceeded to document a detailed inventory of Germany's recent eastward deployment, giving specific dates and places of movement of division after division.[38] He then announced that "the Prime Minister asked that these data be communicated immediately to the Soviet Government."[39] Maisky recalls in his memoirs that he conveyed this warning to Moscow immediately, adding his own impression to the effect that the report "should give Stalin serious food for thought and lead him urgently to check it and, in any case, give strict instructions to our Western frontier to be on guard."[40] Maisky further recalls his "extreme amazement" when the only apparent response to his own warning was a Tass communiqué issued on June 14 publicly denouncing "the British and foreign press rumors about the imminence of war between the USSR and Germany."[41] On June 13 Anthony Eden, together with Victor Cavendish-Bentinck, the chairman of Britain's Joint Intelligence Committee, saw Maisky once again to warn him. Cavendish-Bentinck added that "he would put his money on 22 June."[42] Finally, at 1 P.M. on Saturday, June 21, Cripps telephoned Maisky to inform him that he now had reliable information that the attack would take place on the following day. Maisky sent a telegram to Moscow and nervously awaited the outcome. By daybreak he had his answer.

No wonder that Churchill, on his first wartime trip to Russia, August 15, 1942, asked Stalin why he had chosen to ignore these repeated warnings. Stalin shrugged and replied: "I did not need any warnings. I knew war would come, but I thought I might gain another six months or so."[43] We know from the memoirs of General Georgi Zhukov, however, who worked closely with Stalin at the time, that the Soviet leader was "strongly prejudiced against information coming from imperialist circles, particularly from Churchill."[44] Ideological blinders prompted Stalin to trust Hitler rather than Churchill.

The Americans too were generous with their intelligence information. On March 1, 1941, Cordell Hull and Sumner Welles tried to warn Soviet ambassador Konstantin Umansky in Washington.

According to Hull, Umansky "visibly blanched, averred that he fully realized the gravity of the message and promised to forward it to Moscow immediately."[45] But instead of heeding the warning, Molotov instructed Umansky to inform the German ambassador in Washington that the Americans had evidence of a German plan to attack Russia. Stalin was so fearful of "Anglo-American provocations" that he decided to tattle to the Nazis in order to maintain the precariously balanced Russo-German relationship. What he did not know was that Hitler had already decided to end the entire balancing act.

Britain and the United States, of course, were not the only sources from which Moscow received its information. Stalin had his own man in Tokyo, Dr. Richard Sorge, who conveyed repeated warnings about the imminence of Barbarossa. Leopold Trepper, *le grand chef* of Soviet espionage in Europe, also communicated vital information. Finally, the countless flights by German reconnaissance planes over Soviet territory and unmistakable firsthand reports about German troop movements toward the Soviet border disturbed Stalin's monumental complacency. His response, however, was not to take military defense measures but to engage in special demonstrations of friendliness toward Hitler, to bribe history as it were, in order to postpone what he now began dimly to feel would be a catastrophe. On April 13, 1941, for example, Stalin threw his arm around the German military attaché, Colonel Krebs, at the Moscow railroad station, and said to him: "We will remain friends with you— through thick and thin!"[46] Two days later, Stalin unconditionally accepted Hitler's proposals for the settlement of the border between the two countries. In addition, Stalin continued to supply grain, petroleum, manganese ore, and rubber to blockaded Germany. This compliant attitude struck Hitler as "very remarkable," and indeed it was. In a supreme gesture of conciliation, Stalin closed the embassies of countries conquered by Hitler and proceeded to recognize the pro-Nazi government of Iraq.

On June 14, 1941, the very day that Hitler convened his final military conference for the planning of Barbarossa, Stalin authorized Tass to broadcast a communiqué stating that "rumors of Germany's intention to break the pact and open an attack on the USSR are devoid of all foundation; the recent transfer of German troops is . . . it must be assumed, connected with other reasons which have no bearing on Soviet-German relations."[47] Thus, one week before the invasion, Stalin still refused to face squarely the accumulating evidence.

This evidence suggests the following conclusions about Stalin's failure to prepare for the disaster. First, he perceived British and American warnings as "capitalist provocations" and simply dismissed them. In no case did he bother to examine the evidence on its own merits. When, however, under the weight of irrefutable facts coming in from Soviet sources, Stalin began to realize in early 1941 that Hitler might indeed attack, this realization was too terrifying for him to bear. He then began to engage in appeasing Hitler. As Admiral N. G. Kuznetsov of the Soviet navy recounts: "Stalin acted so as to avoid giving Hitler the slightest pretext for an attack in order not to provoke a war. As a result, when German planes photographed our bases, we were told: Hold your fire! When German air intelligence agents were caught over Soviet fortifications and made to land at our airports, the order was: Release them at once!"[48] Finally, Stalin believed that if Hitler did decide to attack, he would first present the Soviet Union with an ultimatum. What he did not perceive at all was Hitler's childlike, single-minded determination to destroy Russia regardless of the Soviet leader's actions. Therefore Stalin erred in three fundamental ways: He was too blinded by his own ideological biases to credit the veracity of truthful Anglo-American information; he attributed to Hitler a basically rational view of Russo-German relations and was unable to understand the nature of Hitler's irrational and mindless hatred for Russia; and, finally, when the dreadful truth became clear, Stalin found its implications so horrendous that he was simply unable to face the consequences.

Thus, when Hitler struck, Stalin became paralyzed and suffered a nervous breakdown. According to Khrushchev's "secret speech," as well as the memoirs of leading Soviet military men, it took repeated proddings by members of the Politburo to shake Stalin out of his lethargy. But he did finally emerge, and on July 3, with élan restored, he broadcast his first war speech to the Russian people. In the end, despite the horrors of the purges, the blunders of the pact with Hitler, and his blindness toward Hitler's true intentions, Stalin triumphed over Nazi Germany. His hold on reality, though precarious at times, nevertheless remained firm on the field of battle. Hitler, on the other hand, behaved like a compulsive gambler unable to cut his losses, living more and more in fantasy until, when overtaken by reality, he was face-to-face with doom.

Conclusion

How was it possible for Hitler to inflict himself on the German people, to mesmerize them, and to take them with him to disaster in the wastes of Russia?

I am convinced that Hitler's charismatic grip on Germany can best be explained by the authoritarian structure of the German family. Erik Erikson paints a convincing portrait of the typical German father, whose frequent remoteness and tyranny over his children make their maturation process excessively difficult:

> When the father comes home from work, even the walls seem to pull themselves together. . . . The children hold their breath, for the father does not approve of "nonsense"—that is, neither of the mother's feminine moods nor of the children's playfulness. . . .
>
> Later, when the boy comes to observe the father in company, when he notices his father's subservience to superiors, and when he observes his excessive sentimentality when he drinks and sings with his equals, the boy acquires the first ingredient of *Weltschmerz:* a deep doubt of the dignity of man—or at any rate of the "old man." . . .
>
> The average German father's dominance and harshness was not blended with the tenderness and dignity which come from participation in an integrating cause. Rather, the average father, either habitually or in decisive moments, came to represent the habits and ethics of the German top sergeant and petty official who—"dress'd in a little brief authority"—would never be more but was in constant danger of becoming less; and who had sold the birthright of a free man for an official title or a life pension.[49]

This kind of father, of course, makes the son's adolescence an unusually difficult period of "storm and stress" that becomes a strange mixture of open rebellion and submissive obedience, of romanticism and despondency. For each act of rebellion the boy suffers profound guilt, but for each act of submission he is punished by self-disgust. Hence, the search for identity frequently ends in stunned exhaustion, with the boy "reverting to type" and, despite everything, identifying with his father. The excessively severe superego implanted by the father in his son during childhood has entrenched itself like a garrison in a conquered city. The boy now becomes a "bourgeois" after all, but he suffers eternal shame for having succumbed.

During the 1930s the catalytic agent that offered the possibility of escape from this vicious cycle was Adolf Hitler. In the Führer's world the adolescent could feel emancipated. The motto of the Hitler Youth, "Youth shapes its own destiny," was profoundly appealing to a youth whose psychological quest for identity was often thwarted. Erikson points out that Hitler did not fill the role of the father image. Had he done so, he would have elicited great ambivalence in German youth. Rather, he became the symbol of a glorified older brother, a rebel whose will could never be crushed, an unbroken adolescent who could lead others into self-sufficiency—in short, a leader. Since he had become their conscience, he made it possible for the young to rebel against authority without incurring guilt. Hermann Goering echoed the sentiments of the Hitler Youth when he stated categorically that his conscience was Adolf Hitler. It was this complete official absolution from guilt that made the German pattern of authoritarianism unique.

Parents were to be silenced if their views conflicted with the official doctrines of the Third Reich: "All those who from the perspective of their experience and from that alone combat our method of letting youth lead youth, must be silenced."[50] The young Nazi was taught that he was destined by Providence to bring a new order to the world. Young Nazi women too felt a surge of pride to learn that childbirth, legitimate or illegitimate, was a meaningful act because "German women must give children to the Führer." I recall how, on numerous occasions, large groups of young women would march through the streets chanting in chorus: "We want to beget children for the Führer!" National socialism made it possible for the young to rid themselves of their deep-seated personal insecurities by merging their identities with the image of a superior and glorious German nation. This image of a common future was well expressed in the famous Nazi marching song sung by the German soldiers as they advanced into Russia: "Let everything go to pieces, we shall march on. For today Germany is ours; tomorrow the whole world!"

Gregor Strasser summed up Hitler's appeal concisely:

> Hitler responds to the vibrations of the human heart with the delicacy of a seismograph . . . enabling him, with a certainty with which no conscious gift could endow him, to act as a loudspeaker proclaiming the most secret desires, the least permissible instincts, the sufferings, and personal revolts of a whole nation.[51]

It apparently was Hitler's gift to suspend the critical faculty of others and to assume that role for himself alone. He appealed to the deepest unconscious human longings. His premium on harshness and brutality and his rejection of all things civilized and gentle caused those who were victimized by him to strive constantly to be what they were not and to exterminate that which they were. In the end, in fighting for Hitler in Russia, his soldiers and his generals were fighting unconsciously for what appeared to them to be their own psychological integrity. To face themselves and what they had done honestly and without rationalization would have meant the collapse of their entire world view and complete psychological disintegration. The only way for the German people to break this fatal bond with Hitler was to drink the cup of bitterness to the end and go down with him to destruction.

What was Stalin's role in the Soviet recovery from the initial disaster? No doubt, the Soviet leader received a great deal of help from Hitler. The Nazi leader's policy of treating Russians as subhumans to be shipped as slaves to the German Reich soon encountered fierce resistance. Early Russian defections to the German side quickly ceased, and the Nazi invaders found themselves confronted by a nation fighting for its survival.

Even more important, Stalin immediately perceived that the Russian soldier would not give his life for Communism, the party, or its leader, but that he would fight to the death for his Russian homeland. In his first broadcast after the invasion on July 3, Stalin appealed to "Comrades, citizens, brothers and sisters, fighters of our Army and Navy" to repel the invaders in a "great patriotic war." This was something new. Stalin had never spoken like this before. He conjured up images of Napoleon and Wilhelm II, who also had been smashed by a people fighting for their motherland. This war, Stalin said, was not an ordinary war between two armies; it was a war of the entire Soviet people fighting against the Nazi hordes. In short, Stalin appealed to the national loyalties, rather than to Communist loyalties, of the Russian population. It was going to be 1812 all over again.

The effect of this speech was electric. Until that time there had always been something artificial in the public adulation of Stalin. After all, he had been associated with forced collectivization and the terror of the Great Purges. But now, after this patriotic appeal, which greatly resembled Churchill's famous "blood, toil, tears, and sweat" speech just before Dunkirk, the Russian people felt that they had a strong and able war leader. Konstantin Simonov, in his novel *The Living and the Dead,* wrote a poignant description of the impact of Stalin's address on soldiers in a field hospital:

> There was a discrepancy between that even voice and the tragic situation of which he spoke; and in this discrepancy there was strength. People were not surprised. It was what they were expecting from Stalin. They loved him in different ways, wholeheartedly, or with reservations; admiring him and yet fearing him; and some did not like him at all. But nobody doubted his courage and his iron will. And now was a time when these two qualities were needed more than anything else in the man who stood at the head of a country at war.[52]

This passage is particularly remarkable since it was written in 1958, at the height of Khrushchev's "de-Stalinization" drive. But evidently the author was unwilling to distort the truth on this cardinal point. Most Western observers who heard the speech also testified to its critical, even decisive, importance.

After the story of the outbreak of this terrible war is told, one final truth emerges with striking clarity: Hitler ultimately lost the war because he despised everything and everybody including the German people whom he professed to love. In the end, Stalin emerged triumphant despite his blunders and his purges because he was able to convince the Russian people that he was committed to the preservation of their homeland. Hitler never learned from his mistakes when the fortunes of war began to go against him in Russia. He compounded them again and again until disaster became a certainty. Stalin, on the other hand, did learn from his initial errors and thus was able to turn a rout into a final victory. The war in Russia became the supreme character test for both men and revealed them to the core. In Stalin, madness never gained the upper hand; in Hitler, madness conquered.

NOTES

1. Barton Whaley, *Codeword Barbarossa* (Cambridge, Mass.: MIT Press, 1973), p. 7.

2. Robert Payne, *The Life and Death of Adolf Hitler* (New York: Praeger, 1973), p. 430.

3. Ibid., p. 336.
4. Documents on German Foreign Policy, Files of the German Foreign Office, VII, pp. 156–157.
5. Cited in *Life and Death of Adolf Hitler,* p. 361.
6. Cited in William L. Shirer, *The Rise and Fall of the Third Reich* (Greenwich, Conn.: Fawcett, 1960), p. 1047.
7. Ibid.
8. Ibid., p. 1048.
9. Ibid., p. 1053.
10. Paul Schmidt, *Hitler's Interpreter* (New York: Heinemann, 1951), p. 212.
11. *Rise and Fall of the Third Reich,* p. 1061.
12. Ibid., p. 1062.
13. Ibid., p. 1063.
14. Ibid., pp. 1064–1065.
15. Ibid., p. 1078.
16. *Hitler's Interpreter,* p. 220.
17. *Rise and Fall of the Third Reich,* p. 1080.
18. Ibid.
19. Oberkommando der Wehrmacht (OKW), Minutes of the Meeting, *Trials of War Criminals before the Nuremberg Military Tribunals,* Vol. 4 of 15 vols. (Washington, D.C.: Government Printing Office, 1951–1952), pp. 275–278.
20. *Life and Death of Adolf Hitler,* p. 419.
21. Ibid., p. 431.
22. *Rise and Fall of the Third Reich,* p. 1093.
23. Cited in *Rise and Fall of the Third Reich,* pp. 1114–1115.
24. Severin Bialer, ed., *Stalin and His Generals* (New York: Pegasus, 1969), p. 181.
25. Ibid., p. 180.
26. Winston S. Churchill, *The Second World War* (London: Cassell, 1950–1955), Vol. 3 of 6 vols., p. 316.
27. *Stalin and His Generals,* p. 179.
28. Ibid., p. 63.
29. Ibid.
30. Ibid.
31. Ibid., p. 89.
32. Cited in *Rise and Fall of the Third Reich,* p. 721.
33. Ibid., p. 718.
34. Ibid., p. 719.
35. Ibid.
36. Cited in *Stalin and His Generals,* pp. 128–129.
37. *Codeword Barbarossa,* pp. 24–129.
38. Ibid., p. 107.
39. Ibid., p. 108.
40. Ivan Maisky, *Memoirs of a Soviet Diplomat: The War, 1939–1943* (New York: Scribners, 1968), p. 149.
41. Ibid.
42. *Codeword Barbarossa,* p. 115.
43. *Second World War,* Vol. 4, p. 493.
44. Georgi K. Zhukov, *Memoirs* (New York: Delacorte, 1971), p. 224.

45. Cordell Hull, *Memoirs* (New York: Macmillan, 1948), p. 968.
46. Cited in *Rise and Fall of the Third Reich,* p. 1100.
47. *Codeword Barbarossa,* p. 207.
48. *Stalin and His Generals,* pp. 199–200.
49. Erik Erikson, *Childhood and Society* (New York: Norton, 1950), p. 289.
50. Ibid., p. 300.
51. Cited in Walter C. Langer, *The Mind of Adolf Hitler* (New York: Basic Books, 1972), p. 205.
52. Alexander Werth, *Russia at War* (New York: Avon Books, 1964), pp. 173–174.

SELECTED BIBLIOGRAPHY

BEEVOR, ANTONY. *The Fall of Berlin 1945.* New York: Viking, 2002.
BEEVOR, ANTONY. *Stalingrad: The Fateful Siege, 1942–1943.* New York: Viking, 1998.
BESCHLOSS, MICHAEL. *The Conquerors: Roosevelt, Truman and the Destruction of Hitler's Germany 1941–1945.* New York: Simon & Schuster, 2002.
BIALER, SEVERIN, Ed. *Stalin and His Generals.* New York: Pegasus, 1969.
BULLOCK, ALAN. *Hitler and Stalin: Parallel Lives.* New York: Knopf, 1992.
CARLEY, MICHAEL JABARA. *1939: The Alliance That Never Was and the Coming of World War II.* Chicago: Ivan Dee, 1999.
CHURCHILL, WINSTON S. *The Second World War.* Boston: Houghton Mifflin, 1948–1954, 6 vols.
ELON, AMOS. *The Pity of It All: A History of the Jews in Germany, 1743–1933.* New York: Metropolitan Books, 2002.
ERIKSON, ERIK. *Childhood and Society.* New York: Norton, 1950.
GILBERT, MARTIN. *The Second World War.* New York: Henry Holt, 1989.
HAFFNER, SEBASTIAN. *Defying Hitler.* New York: Farrar, Straus & Giroux, 2002.
HAMANN, BRIGITTE. *Hitler's Vienna: A Dictator's Apprenticeship.* New York: Oxford University Press, 1999.
HERF, JEFFREY. *Divided Memory: The Nazi Past in the Two Germanys.* Cambridge, Mass.: Harvard University Press, 1997.
IRVING, DAVID. *Hitler's War.* New York: Viking, 1977.
JACKSON, JULIAN. *The Fall of France: The Nazi Invasion of 1940.* New York: Oxford University Press, 2003.
KATZNELSON, IRA. *Desolation and Enlightenment: Political Knowledge After Total War, Totalitarianism, and the Holocaust.* New York: Columbia University Press, 2003.
LANGER, WALTER C. *The Mind of Adolf Hitler.* New York: Basic Books, 1972.
ODOM, WILLIAM. *The Collapse of the Soviet Military.* New Haven, Conn.: Yale University Press, 1998.
PAYNE, ROBERT. *The Life and Death of Adolf Hitler.* New York: Praeger, 1973.

SERVICE, ROBERT. *A History of Twentieth-Century Russia.* Cambridge, Mass.: Harvard University Press, 1998.

WAITE, ROBERT G. L. *The Psychopathic God: Adolf Hitler.* New York: Basic Books, 1977.

WERTH, ALEXANDER. *Russia at War.* New York: Avon Books, 1964.

ZHUKOV, GEORGI K. *Memoirs.* New York: Delacorte, 1971.

MAP 4   The Korean War, 1950–1953

3

The Temptations of Victory: Korea

This was the toughest decision I had to make as President.　　Harry S Truman, June 26, 1950

The reasons for the outbreak of the Korean War remain a mystery; we can only speculate about the motivations for the North Korean attack of June 1950. Four possible explanations, given here in descending order of probability, suggest themselves.

The most likely explanation of the attack is that it was a probing action by Stalin against the West. With the establishment of the North Atlantic Treaty Organization (NATO) in 1949, Soviet advances into Western Europe had begun to meet determined resistance. It appeared that the absorption of Czechoslovakia in 1948 might be Stalin's final European triumph. The time had arrived to turn to Asia. Conveniently enough, Secretary of State Dean Acheson, in a speech before the National Press Club in Washington on January 12, 1950, had outlined the "military defense perimeter" of the United States. There was one notable omission: Korea. It is reasonable to assume that Stalin, thus encouraged, ordered the North Koreans to attack the South.

A second possibility is that Stalin sought to create problems not for the United States but for China. Since Mao Zedong had come to power in China without the help of Stalin, who at the time was engaged in major purges of Communist parties everywhere, it is likely that the Soviet leader was troubled by Mao's ascendancy. It might be argued that Stalin's pact with Mao in February 1950 was merely a facade and Stalin's order to absorb South Korea an attempt to place China in a Soviet nutcracker. In short, Stalin might not have told the Chinese about the imminent attack. It might have been as much of a surprise to them as it was to the Americans. And if the war did involve the United States, then Stalin would succeed in ruining any possibility of reconciliation between mainland China and America. A Machiavellian plan indeed, but certainly not one that was beyond the Soviet leader's capabilities.

A Chinese initiative in North Korea presents a third, though unlikely, possibility. Mao Zedong had been in power for less than a year and was fully occupied with problems of domestic consolidation. Besides, North Korea was clearly in the Soviet orbit, and China had little, if any, influence there.

Finally, it is possible, though not very likely, that the North Korean attack was an internal affair, initiated by an independent decision of Premier Kim Il Sung, as the Soviet Union would contend. According to this argument, Kim Il Sung, clearly a second-rater next to such powerful Communist leaders as Tito, might have advanced to the front rank with a successful attack on South Korea.

Though the causes of the offensive remain uncertain, it does appear probable that Stalin was behind the North Korean attack. His motives are not so clear. In any event he was sure of a speedy military victory. The North Korean leadership announced that it would win the war before V-J Day in September. Once again a war launched in early summer was to end in victory before the leaves had fallen from the trees.

The focus of this chapter will be the response to the North Korean assault by the United States and the United Nations. The evidence here is abundant, and empirical analysis is possible. The following crucial phases of the American and UN responses will be examined: (1) President Truman's decision in June 1950 to commit American forces and the role of the United Nations in initiating the "police action"; (2) General Douglas MacArthur's crossing of the thirty-eighth parallel; (3) his drive toward the Chinese border at the Yalu River that precipitated China's military intervention; and (4) the significance of the Korean War in the larger perspective of recent history.

President Truman's Decision

At 4 A.M. on Sunday, June 25, 1950, more than 100,000 North Korean troops charged across the thirty-eighth parallel into South

Korea. This event presented the United States with two classical challenges of a genuine crisis: danger and opportunity.

At the time of the North Korean attack, Harry S Truman was sixty-six years old and had served as president for more than five years. Truman had always admired "strong liberal Presidents" and had singled out for his particular affection Thomas Jefferson, Andrew Jackson, Abraham Lincoln, Theodore Roosevelt, and Franklin D. Roosevelt. He saw himself as the champion of the common person and was deeply committed to the liberal tradition in American politics.

Perhaps most significant for the Korean decision was Truman's belief in a strong chief executive. In his view, whenever a president weakly deferred to Congress, the public interest was the real loser. A decade of experience as senator had made Truman wary of the power of special interests in the passage of legislation. Certain decisions, particularly those pertaining to foreign policy, could be made only by the president in a strictly bipartisan manner. His readiness to accept full responsibility for crucial decisions was expressed by the motto inscribed on the triangular block that was always prominently displayed on his desk: "The buck stops here."

Harry Truman was blessed with the capacity to make extremely tough decisions without tormenting afterthoughts. As he wrote in a letter to his mother shortly after he assumed office: "I have to take things as they come and make every decision on the basis of the facts as I have them and then go on from there; then forget that one and take the next."[1] At the time he made the decision to drop the atomic bomb on Japan, he wrote to his sister: "Nearly every crisis seems to be the worst one, but after it's over, it isn't so bad."[2] Critics of President Truman have never asserted that his "resolution [was] sicklied o'er with the pale cast of thought." His advisers admired his readiness to accept full responsibility, though historians for decades to come will undoubtedly regard most of the Truman foreign policy decisions as controversial. In addition, Truman was deeply committed to the United Nations: "As long as I am President," he declared on May 10, 1950, "we shall support the United Nations with every means at our command."[3]

Secretary of State Dean Acheson, fifty-seven years old at the time of the Korean crisis, had been in office for almost a year and a half. Acheson's relationship with Truman was excellent; he thought of himself as "the senior member of the Cabinet" and was completely loyal to the president. Truman, in turn, had great confidence in Acheson's judgment, and in disagreements between the secretary of state and other members of the cabinet he almost always ruled in Acheson's favor.

The secretary of state also admired his president's ability to make difficult decisions. "The decisions are his," wrote Acheson; "the President is the pivotal point, the critical element in reaching decisions on foreign policy. No good comes from attempts to invade the authority and responsibility of the President."[4] A secretary of state, in Acheson's view, should be the "principal, unifying, and final source of recommendation" on foreign policy matters to the president. Acheson's admiration for Truman was rooted in his belief that the more difficulty a problem presented, the less likely it was that one decision was right. As he put it: "The choice becomes one between courses all of which are hard and dangerous. The 'right' one, if there is a right one, is quite apt to be the most immediately difficult one. . . . In these cases the mind tends to remain suspended between alternatives and to seek escape by postponing the issue."[5] Acheson saw it as his duty to give the president the "real issues, honestly presented, with the extraneous matter stripped away,"[6] but the decision was the president's: "Ultimately, he must decide."[7] Finally, like his chief, Acheson was committed to the United Nations. On June 22, 1950, only two days before the North Korean attack, he had declared before a Harvard commencement audience that the United States would give its "unfaltering support to the United Nations."[8]

At 11:20 P.M. on Saturday, June 24, Acheson telephoned President Truman at his home in Independence, Missouri, where he was spending a quiet weekend with his wife and daughter. "Mr. President, I have very serious news," the secretary of state reported, "the North Koreans have invaded South Korea."[9] He explained that a few minutes earlier a cable had been received from John J. Muccio, the United States ambassador to South Korea, advising that North Korean forces apparently had launched "an all-out offensive against the Republic of Korea."[10]

Acheson recommended an immediate emergency meeting of the UN Security Council. The president concurred and expressed his strong conviction that the matter must be brought before the United Nations. A few minutes later, Assistant Secretary of State John D. Hickerson telephoned the home of Ernest A. Gross, the United States deputy representative to the United Nations, and, failing to reach him, telephoned the secretary-general of the United Nations, Trygve Lie.

Trygve Lie, the first secretary-general, had been active in Norwegian labor politics for many years before his election to the United Nations post. He was known as a man of strong convictions who did not hesitate to take positions on explosive issues. Only a few months before the Korean crisis, he had provoked the extreme displeasure of the American government by publicly supporting the application of the People's Republic of China for membership in the United Nations. By summer, his relations with the host country had deteriorated even further because of Senator Joseph McCarthy's search for disloyal Americans in the UN Secretariat.[11] Upon hearing of the invasion, Lie reproached the Soviet Union. "My God," he exclaimed, "that's a violation of the United Nations Charter!"[12] He immediately decided to cable a request for full information to the United Nations Commission on Korea, whose observers were actually on the scene. In the meantime, Acheson and a small group of State Department officials in Washington considered possible courses of action.

What is most striking about these early American responses is the unanimous agreement that the United States would have to respond to the North Korean challenge through the United Nations. Ambassador Philip C. Jessup summarized these first reactions: "We've got to do something, and whatever we do, we've got to do it through the United Nations."[13] At 2 A.M. on Sunday, Secretary Acheson again telephoned the president and informed him that a group of officials in the State Department had drafted a resolution charging North Korea with a "breach of the peace" and an "act of aggression" and asking the UN Security Council to put an end to the fighting. President Truman approved the draft, and at 3 A.M. Ambassador Gross telephoned Secretary-General Lie requesting a meeting of the Security Council by early afternoon.

During the early hours of Sunday morning, top officials at the United States Mission to the United Nations, under the guidance of Ambassador Gross, planned the American strategy for the Security Council meeting. Gross, greatly worried about a possible Soviet veto that would paralyze the council, made contingency plans for initiating an emergency session of the General Assembly within twenty-four hours. The delicate problem of whether the operative paragraph of the resolution should take the form of an "order" or a "recommendation" to the Security Council was sidestepped when Gross suggested that the phrase "call upon" be employed. This language was diplomatically strong, but kept the precise legal status of the resolution somewhat in doubt. Another problem was resolved by midmorning when a message from the United Nations Commission on Korea became available. The commission reported a "serious situation which [was] assuming the character of full-scale war." Since sole reliance on American sources might have created difficulties in the Security Council, this United Nations source provided a most welcome basis for factual information. By noon the Americans were ready for the meeting.

Shortly after 11 A.M. Acheson arrived coatless at the State Department. This was unusual behavior for Acheson, who had been named "Best-Dressed Man of the Year" in 1949. Reporters thus deduced that the situation was most serious. Indeed, Acheson had just learned from military intelligence sources at General MacArthur's headquarters in Tokyo that the North Korean attack appeared to be an "all-out offensive" and that "the South Koreans seemed to be disintegrating."[14] At 2:45 P.M. he telephoned the president, who now decided to return to Washington without delay. At the Kansas City airport, the president was described by reporters as "grim-faced," and one of his aides privately told a reporter: "The boss is going to hit those fellows hard."[15]

According to his *Memoirs,* Truman spent most of the journey to Washington alone in his compartment, reflecting on the "lessons of history." The North Korean attack, in his view, was only another link in the chain of aggressive acts by the German, Italian, and Japanese military adventurers that had led to World War II. There was no doubt in the president's mind that a Soviet probing action was behind the North Korean invasion. Unless Communist belligerency was deterred promptly and effectively, a third world war between Communist and non-Communist states was inevitable. In addition, the principles of the United Nations, ratified with such high hopes in 1945, would have to be affirmed through a collective response to aggression.[16] Therefore Truman was determined to act through the United Nations if possible, but without it if necessary. While still airborne, the president sent a message to his secretary of state instructing him to arrange a dinner conference at Blair House to which leading State and Defense Department officials were to be invited. At that very moment, the UN Security Council was beginning its emergency session. Present in the council chamber were the representatives of China, Cuba, Ecuador, Egypt, France, India, Norway, the United Kingdom, the United States, and Yugoslavia. The Soviet Union, conspicuous by its absence, was boycotting the Security Council to express its opposition to the presence of Nationalist China.

Secretary-General Lie informed the council that, judging from information submitted by the United Nations Commission on Korea, he believed that North Korea had violated the charter. He then went on to say that he considered it "the clear duty of the Security Council to take steps necessary to re-establish peace and security in that area."[17] Immediately after the secretary-general had made his statement, Ambassador Gross proceeded to read the American draft resolution to the assembled delegates. He "called upon" North Korea to cease hostilities and to withdraw to the thirty-eighth parallel; he also "called upon" all member states "to render every assistance to the United Nations in the execution of this resolution."[18] Though no mention was made of the Soviet Union, American officials were convinced that it was behind the North Korean move. As Edward W. Barrett, assistant secretary of state for political affairs, put it, "the relationship between the Soviet Union and the North Koreans [was] the same as that between Walt Disney and Donald Duck."[19] At 5:30 P.M. the council was ready to vote on the American draft resolution. The final vote would have been unanimous save for a single abstention: Yugoslavia. Several delegates, believing that the United Nations was fighting for its very life, actually risked their political futures by deciding to vote in the absence of instructions from their governments.[20] Independent voting of this nature was most unusual.

In spite of strong UN support, neither President Truman nor his secretary of state had any illusions about the situation. Both men knew that the United States would have to take unilateral military initiatives if the North Korean attack was to be stemmed successfully.

President Truman landed in Washington "in a grim mood." "That's enough," he snapped at reporters who crowded around him to take pictures; "we've got a job to do!"[21] Before departing for Blair House, he stated that he was not going to let the North Korean attack succeed and that he was going to "hit them hard."[22] Thirteen of the nation's top diplomatic and military leaders, including the

Joint Chiefs of Staff, awaited the president at Blair House, and by dinnertime Truman and Acheson were in complete agreement on the main proposals to be presented at the meeting.

After dinner the president opened the discussion by calling on the secretary of state to advance suggestions for consideration by the conference. He encouraged all those present to voice their opinions freely. Acheson then proceeded to make four specific recommendations: (1) that General MacArthur be authorized to furnish South Korea with generous supplies of military equipment; (2) that the air force be authorized to cover and protect the evacuation of American civilians; (3) that consideration be given to strengthening the role of the UN Security Council; and (4) that the Seventh Fleet be interposed between Formosa (Taiwan) and the Chinese mainland.[23]

There was complete agreement on Acheson's first recommendation. As General Omar Bradley put it: "This is the test of all the talk of the last five years of collective security."[24] In view of the sparsity of information from the battle area, however, no one recommended that American ground forces be committed at that moment. "No one could tell what the state of the Korean army was on that Sunday night," the president later noted in his *Memoirs.*[25] Accordingly, as an interim measure, General MacArthur was authorized to give the South Koreans whatever arms and equipment he could spare. There was no disagreement whatsoever over the second recommendation, which was Ambassador Muccio's main concern. As Defense Secretary Louis A. Johnson put it, the measure was more of an "assumption" than a "decision." So far as the role of the United Nations was concerned, the president emphasized that in this crisis the United States was "working for" the world organization. He added that he would wait for the Security Council resolution to be flouted before taking any additional measures, though he instructed the Chiefs of Staff to "prepare the necessary orders" to make American forces available should the United Nations request them.[26] Finally, there was full agreement that the Seventh Fleet be used to restrain the Chinese Communists as well as the Chinese Nationalists from military operations that might widen the theater of war. The conference closed with a strong sense of resolve that the United States was prepared, under the United Nations banner, to take whatever measures were required to repel the invasion.

By Monday morning the situation had hardened. Ambassador Gross reported from the United Nations that there appeared to be growing support among the delegates for sterner measures to enforce North Korean compliance with the Security Council Resolution of June 25. Meeting with reporters in Washington, President Truman pointed to Korea on a large globe in his office and said to an aide: "This is the Greece of the Far East. If we are tough enough now, there won't be any next step."[27] Members of the White House staff commented on the president's mood of grim resolution. By 2 P.M. the military situation in Korea had grown so desperate that President Syngman Rhee placed a personal telephone call to Washington to plead with President Truman to rescue his government from complete disaster. The president and secretary of state met in seclusion during the afternoon to plan the next steps. By evening they had agreed that the situation had become serious enough to warrant another full-scale conference at Blair House at 9 P.M.

"There was no doubt! The Republic of Korea needed help at once if it was not to be overrun," Truman recalled in his *Memoirs* about the second conference.[28] Unless such help was immediately forthcoming, no further decisions regarding Korea would be necessary. Accordingly, the president proposed that the navy and air force be instructed to give the fullest possible support to the South Korean forces south of the thirty-eighth parallel. In addition, the president recommended stepped-up military aid to the Philippines and the French forces engaged in fighting Communist Vietminh troops in Indochina. No mention was made of ground troops in Korea, but it was clear that American sea and air cover were logical preludes to such a commitment. It was thought unlikely that strong naval and air support would give the South Koreans sufficient superiority to render a ground commitment unnecessary. Ambassador Gross believed that the Security Council resolution could be "stretched" to cover the president's recommendations. The problem of possible Soviet or Chinese countermoves was discussed and the conclusion reached that neither the Soviet Union nor China was likely to intervene directly in Korea. Once again, the conferees drew historical parallels, this time from the Greek crisis of 1947 and the Berlin crisis of 1948, when resolute American resistance had been successful. Support for the president's position was unanimous. As Defense Secretary Johnson was to recall later: "If we wanted to oppose it, then was our time to oppose it. Not a single one of us did. There were some pointing out the difficulties . . . and then the President made his decision which . . . I thought was the right decision."[29]

Ambassador Jessup recalled that he "felt proud of President Truman," and General Bradley explained that "we did it so we wouldn't have one appeasement lead to another and make war inevitable."[30] The president confided to Acheson that "everything I have done in the last five years has been to try to avoid making a decision such as I had to make tonight."[31] In his *Memoirs* he later recalled that "this was the toughest decision I had to make as President."[32]

By Tuesday, June 27, General MacArthur had been notified of the president's decision. He reacted with pleasant surprise, since he had not expected such forceful action. At noon the president and Acheson briefed a group of congressional leaders on the most recent developments. The responses in both the Senate and House were overwhelmingly favorable. Although a few congressmen and senators questioned the president's authority to make these decisions without prior congressional approval, not a single legislator openly doubted the wisdom of the decision.

During the afternoon attention shifted from Washington to the United Nations. At 3 P.M. the Security Council met in one of the most dramatic sessions of its short history. There was considerable apprehension in the United States Mission that Ambassador Yakov A. Malik of the Soviet Union would be present in order to cast a veto. A great deal of thought had been given to this possibility, and various contingency procedures that would mobilize the General Assembly were under active consideration. Just before the Security Council meeting Ambassadors Gross and Malik were lunching with Secretary-General Lie and other UN delegates. As the delegates rose from the table, Lie approached Malik and told him that the interests of the Soviet Union demanded his participation in the meeting. "No, I will not go there," the Soviet delegate replied. Outside the restaurant Ambassador Gross heaved a huge sigh of relief.[33]

The Soviet absence from the council on that fateful afternoon has been the subject of a great deal of speculation. Most likely, it was a blunder. The cumbersome Soviet processes for making decisions probably had left Malik without instructions on what to do in the Security Council. Hence his only option was to be absent from the council altogether.

Chief delegate Warren R. Austin read the text of the American resolution, which had been approved personally by President Truman. Its operative paragraph recommended "that Members of the

United Nations furnish such assistance to the Republic of Korea as may be necessary to repel the armed attack and to restore international peace and security in the area."[34] The council had before it another report from the UN Commission on Korea stating that the North Korean regime was carrying out a "well-planned, concerted, and full-scale invasion of South Korea."[35] The council postponed a vote twice because the delegates of India and Egypt were waiting for instructions. Finally, just before midnight, the Security Council passed the American-sponsored resolution, with the United Kingdom, France, China, Cuba, Ecuador, and Norway in support; Egypt and India abstaining; Yugoslavia in opposition; and the Soviet Union absent. The Security Council had recommended that military measures be taken to stem the North Korean assault. At almost precisely the time of the voting, Seoul, the capital of South Korea, was taken by the North Korean army.

On the following morning President Truman chaired a meeting of the National Security Council in Washington. Before the council was a report from General MacArthur stating that "the United States would have to commit ground troops if the thirty-eighth parallel were to be restored."[36] The president signed a bill to extend the Selective Service Act but stopped short of ordering American ground forces into combat in Korea. That afternoon, with the loud acclaim of the press, General MacArthur flew to Korea to conduct a personal reconnaissance of the military situation. The *New York Times* commented editorially that:

> Fate could not have chosen a man better qualified to command the unreserved confidence of the people of this country. Here is a superb strategist and an inspired leader; a man of infinite patience and quiet stability under adverse pressure; a man equally capable of bold and decisive action.[37]

The president decided to wait for the general's report from the scene of battle before taking the crucial step of committing ground forces.

MacArthur, with a small group of advisers, surveyed "the dreadful backwash of a defeated and dispersed army" during a convoy ride toward Seoul. The roads were clogged with thousands of southbound refugees, who were probably unaware that MacArthur was passing through. The South Korean army seemed to be in a state of complete and disorganized rout.[38] During his flight back to Tokyo the general drafted a report to the president in which he made his position absolutely clear:

> The only assurance for holding the present line and the ability to regain the lost ground is through the introduction of United States ground combat forces into the Korean battle area. . . . Unless provision is made for the full utilization of the Army-Navy-Air team in this shattered area, our mission will at best be needlessly costly in life, money, and prestige. At worst, it might even be doomed to failure.[39]

Specifically, the general declared that if the president gave the authorization, he could "hold Korea with two American divisions."[40]

At the same time that MacArthur was drafting his report the president held a press conference in Washington. One reporter wanted to know whether the United States was at war or not. "We are not at war," the president replied. When another reporter queried the president whether "it would be possible to call the American response a police action under the United Nations," Truman responded that this was exactly what it was. The action was being taken to help the United Nations repel a raid by a "bunch of bandits."[41] Later that evening, Truman and Acheson considered President Chiang Kai-shek's offer to send 33,000 Chinese Nationalist troops to Korea. The president was not inclined to accept the offer but delayed making a final decision.

MacArthur's urgent recommendation to commit American ground forces in Korea reached Washington at dawn on June 30. "Time is of the essence and a clear-cut decision without delay is essential," the general insisted. At 5 A.M. Secretary of the Army Frank Pace, Jr., communicated MacArthur's recommendation to the president. Without hesitation, Truman approved the commitment of one regimental combat team. During the morning he met with the secretary of state and top military officials. At that conference it was decided to decline politely the Chinese Nationalist troop offer and to give MacArthur "full authority to use the troops under his command."[42]

On the afternoon of June 30 Ambassador Austin informed the UN Security Council of the latest American decision. He emphasized again that the American action was being taken under the United Nations banner. Other members, however, would have to contribute if the Korean police action was to be a genuine collective security measure. The United States had taken the lead in protecting the UN Charter; now it was up to the others to assume their share of the responsibility.

In response to the Security Council Resolution of June 27, Secretary-General Lie had sent a cable to all member states asking for information on the nature and amount of assistance each member state was prepared to give. Of the fifty-nine replies, he felt fifty-three were generally favorable.[43] In concrete and specific terms, however, actual military contributions were slow to arrive. Within two weeks of the request, naval and air units from the United Kingdom, Australia, and New Zealand were actively involved, and units from the Netherlands and Canada were on their way. By the middle of September Lie had reported that fourteen members other than the United States had contributed ground forces. From the beginning, the United States had borne the main brunt of the fighting, with the Republic of Korea in second place. By services, the American contribution was 50.32 percent of the ground forces, 85.89 percent of the naval forces, and 93.38 percent of the air forces. The respective contributions of South Korea were 40.10 percent, 7.45 percent, and 5.65 percent.[44] From these figures it is clear that the contributions of other UN members were small indeed. Though military contributions from member nations remained disproportionate throughout the Korean War, it must be noted that thirty governments did render supplementary assistance in the form of field hospitals, blood plasma, rice, and soap. Iceland, for example, made a contribution of cod-liver oil for the troops.

In view of the predominant role played by the United States, the Security Council decided on July 7 to establish a "Unified Command" under the leadership of the United States and authorized this command to use the UN flag. On the following day President Truman designated General MacArthur as supreme commander of the UN forces. However, the general also retained his title of commander in chief of United States Forces in the Far East; MacArthur viewed his connection with the United Nations as nominal and continued to receive his instructions directly from the president. On August 1, when Malik, the Soviet delegate, returned to the Security Council and assumed the presidency of that body, the council went into eclipse. On September 6 the Soviet Union cast its first veto on the Korean problem and thus removed any further possibility of using the Security Council to direct the UN action in Korea.

When the UN General Assembly met in mid-September, it was confronted with a dramatic change in the military situation in Korea. On September 15 General MacArthur had executed a daring amphibious landing at Inchon that had taken the North Koreans by complete surprise. Two weeks later the North Koreans were in full retreat, and the UN forces, in hot pursuit, had reached the thirty-eighth parallel. The question now facing the United States and the UN General Assembly was whether the UN forces should cross into North Korea. Suddenly a desperate crisis had been resolved, and an attractive new opportunity had arisen: The invader was on the run and could now be taught a lesson. This prospect, however, raised serious tactical as well as policy questions that had to be resolved quickly. The relationship between the United States and the United Nations needed to be clarified, especially the role of the supreme commander, General MacArthur. The possible responses of the two great Communist powers, China and the Soviet Union, to a UN crossing of the parallel had to be weighed. In short, the sudden successes of MacArthur's forces presented entirely new challenges. But these events were to precipitate a massive military intervention by China only a few weeks later, and—in MacArthur's words—an "entirely new war."

General MacArthur's Gamble

Two explosive events brought the UN forces face-to-face with China on the battlefields of Korea: first, the crossing of the thirty-eighth parallel in October and, second, the drive toward the Chinese border at the Yalu River in November. Crucial to both events was the personality of General MacArthur, who was widely acclaimed as, and probably believed himself to be, America's greatest living soldier. The startling success of his Inchon landing had made the general's confidence in his own military genius unshakable. President Truman and Secretary of State Acheson had full confidence in America's most honored soldier and believed the armed might of the United States to be invincible. Nevertheless, UN Unified Command was badly mauled in its first encounter with Chinese troops, and MacArthur suffered the worst defeat in his entire military career. An analysis of the outbreak of this "entirely new war" may help to explain this paradox.

As the UN forces approached the parallel, the problem of whether to cross it presented the Unified Command with an acute dilemma.

On the one hand, it was impossible to achieve total defeat of the North Korean invaders if the UN forces were not allowed to cross the parallel. It could be argued that the North Korean attack destroyed the sanctity of the thirty-eighth parallel as a boundary and that the "hot pursuit" of the invader was therefore perfectly in order. On the other hand, if the mission of the Unified Command was merely to "repel the armed attack," then the case could be made that the UN forces should not be permitted to cross into territory that was not a recognized part of the Republic of Korea before the North Korean attack. Moreover, there was the important question: Who was to decide whether UN forces should cross the parallel, and if so, for what purpose and within what limits? Finally, there was on record an explicit warning that had been made by Indian Ambassador K. M. Panikkar in Peking. If UN forces crossed the parallel, China probably would enter the war.[45]

In view of these conflicting considerations, there was considerable initial confusion over the matter. Truman's first response on September 22 was to let the United Nations make the decision.[46] Less than a week later, however, he apparently changed his mind and instructed Acheson to declare that the resolutions passed by the Security Council in June and July gave the Unified Command the necessary authority to cross the parallel. This was also the position taken by MacArthur and the Joint Chiefs of Staff. MacArthur, in particular, was of the opinion that the resolution of June 27 extended ample authority to cross the parallel. He felt that he required broad and flexible powers and that any restrictions placed on him would be rendered ineffective by the need to ensure the safety of his troops. This view evidently impressed the president and his top advisers. As it turned out, it was never seriously disputed by most of the other member states of the United Nations.

When the UN General Assembly met in late September, most delegations were quite willing to follow the leadership of the United States. In view of the fact that the United States had been the first to come to the assistance of South Korea, and had now apparently reversed the scales of battle in favor of the UN forces, this willingness to accept the American lead was considered quite natural. Ambassador Austin set forth the American position in a major speech before the General Assembly on September 30. He argued the case for crossing the parallel in the strongest possible terms: "The artificial barrier which has divided North and South Korea has no basis for existence either in law or in reason. Neither the United Nations, its Commission on Korea, nor the Republic of Korea recognizes such a line. Now, the North Koreans, by armed attack upon the Republic of Korea, have denied the reality of any such line."[47] The United States took the lead in drafting an eight-power resolution calling for the taking of appropriate steps "to insure conditions of stability throughout Korea" and "the establishment of a unified, independent and democratic Government in the sovereign State of Korea."[48] Apart from the Soviet bloc, there was little opposition, and the final vote on October 7 was 47 in favor, 5 opposed, and 7 abstentions.[49] The UN General Assembly had now placed its seal of approval on the twin American objectives: to destroy the North Korean forces and to unify the entire country under the flag of the UN command.

On October 8 MacArthur, speaking as UN commander in chief, called on the North Korean army to surrender and "cooperate fully with the United Nations in establishing a unified, independent, democratic government of Korea."[50] He informed the North Korean authorities that, unless a favorable response was immediately forthcoming, he would "at once proceed to take such military action as may be necessary to enforce the decrees of the United Nations." The ultimatum was drafted personally by MacArthur, and the style and phraseology were unmistakably his own.

There is no evidence to suggest that Truman's position on the question of crossing the thirty-eighth parallel differed from MacArthur's. The president and his top aides felt that by its aggression North Korea had forfeited any right that it might previously have had to prevent the execution of the UN's decree by force. Neither the fact that the UN General Assembly lacked the legal authority to legislate decrees nor the fact that its recommendation of October 7 had been only partially accepted deterred the American leadership from declaring its own military objectives to be identical with those of the United Nations. And neither the presence of Soviet advisers with the North Korean army down to the battalion level nor the stern warning issued by China deterred MacArthur from crossing the parallel and initiating a rapid advance toward the Chinese border at the Yalu River.

South Korean troops crossed the parallel into the North on October 1, and the first American forces, the First Cavalry Division, followed suit on October 7. Ambassador Panikkar issued his warning on October 2, and on October 10 China's Foreign Minister Zhou

En-lai announced that "the Chinese people [would] not stand idly by in this war of invasion." These warnings received only passing attention in Washington and Tokyo. The tendency among American government officials was to dismiss them as Chinese bombast.

On October 15, however, Truman and MacArthur met on Wake Island. As a result of the increasing frequency of Chinese warnings, the president had become sufficiently concerned to ask the general for a professional assessment about the possibility of Chinese intervention. MacArthur considered this possibility remote:

> Had they interfered in the first or second month, it would have been decisive. We are no longer fearful of their intervention. We no longer stand hat in hand. The Chinese have 300,000 men in Manchuria. Of these, probably not more than 100 to 125,000 are distributed along the Yalu River. They have no Air Force. Now that we have bases for our Air Force in Korea, if the Chinese tried to get down to Pyongyang, there would be the greatest slaughter.[51]

Four days later, when MacArthur's forces entered Pyongyang, the State Department also came to the conclusion that Chinese intervention in Korea was "unlikely." In the opinion of one leading authority:

> This assessment was by no means confined to the department over which Acheson presided. It was shared alike by the President, the Joint Chiefs of Staff, members of the National Security Council, General Walter Bedell Smith, Director of Central Intelligence, prominent senators, congressmen, and political pundits of all hues. If questioned, that amorphous character "the man in the street" would have expressed the same opinion.[52]

Nevertheless, at the very time that the American leadership denied the possibility of Chinese intervention, the Chinese Fourth Field Army crossed the Yalu and penetrated the ragged mountain terrain of North Korea.

Truman and MacArthur were convinced that China neither would nor could intervene in Korea and believed that their frequent pronouncements of America's nonaggressive intentions would reassure the Chinese leaders. On November 16 the president declared that the United States had "never at any time entertained any intention to carry hostilities into China."[53] He added that "because of the long-standing American friendship for the people of China, the

United States [would] take every honorable step to prevent any extension of the hostilities in the Far East."[54] Thus American policy-makers chose to view the tension between America and China as a passing phenomenon and felt that assurances of goodwill toward China would suffice to insulate the Korean conflict from Chinese intervention. Operating on the assumption of long-standing Sino-American friendship, both Truman and MacArthur were deeply astonished at the rising tone of violence in Chinese statements during the month of October. They simply did not see the intervention coming. That the illusion of a firm Sino-American friendship underlying a Communist veneer persisted in the face of growing evidence to the contrary suggests that the United States was not yet prepared to take the new China seriously. Her statements were not as yet considered credible. So far as Panikkar's warning was concerned, neither Truman nor MacArthur took it seriously. Truman viewed it as "a bold attempt to blackmail the United Nations" and later observed in his *Memoirs,* "Mr. Panikkar had in the past played the game of the Chinese Communists fairly regularly, so that his statement could not be taken as that of an impartial observer."[55]

On the other side of the Yalu, the Chinese leaders regarded the United States as the heir to Japan's imperialist ambitions in Asia. They became increasingly convinced that only a powerful intervention in Korea would prevent the United States from invading China. As one scholar of Chinese-American relations has noted:

> While Secretary Acheson was talking about the traditional friendship of America, the Chinese Communists were teaching their compatriots that from the early nineteenth century onward the United States had consistently followed an aggressive policy toward China which culminated in her support for Chiang Kai-shek in the civil war and her present actions in Korea and Taiwan. The Chinese people were told to treat the United States with scorn because she was a paper tiger and certainly could be defeated.[56]

Truman, MacArthur, and the State Department perceived a China that no longer existed. The conviction that China would not intervene represented an emotional rather than an intellectual conclusion, an ascription to the enemy of intentions compatible with the desires of Washington and Tokyo.[57] This misperception laid the groundwork for a military disaster of major proportions.

If the Americans misperceived Chinese intentions by refusing to take them seriously, the Chinese erred in the opposite direction. The world, as viewed in Peking, was rife with implacable American hostility. Not only were American troops marching directly up to the Chinese border at the Yalu River, but the United States was protecting the hated Nationalist regime in Taiwan and was aiding the French against the revolutionaries in Indochina. In addition, the United States was rehabilitating and rearming Japan. With this outlook, the Chinese leaders not surprisingly regarded verbal protestations of goodwill on the part of the United States as a mockery.

Basic to an understanding of MacArthur's drive to the Yalu was his peculiar misperception of China's power. Even though he characterized China as a nation lusting for expansion, MacArthur had a curious contempt for the Chinese soldier. He equated the thoroughly indoctrinated, well-disciplined Communist soldier of 1950 with the demoralized Nationalist soldier of 1948. To be blunt, he did not respect his enemy, and this disrespect was to cost him dearly. Far from regarding the Chinese as military equals, MacArthur insisted that "the pattern of the Oriental psychology [was] to respect and follow aggressive, resolute and dynamic leadership, to quickly turn on a leadership characterized by timidity or vacillation."[58] This paternalistic contempt for the military power of the new China led directly to disaster in October and November 1950. The story is worth examining in some detail.

On October 26, to the accompaniment of fierce bugle calls, shrill whistles, and blasts from shepherds' horns, the Chinese launched a surprise attack on South Korean and American forces some 50 miles south of the Chinese border. The results were devastating. Several UN regiments were virtually decimated. Nevertheless, Major General Charles A. Willoughby, MacArthur's main intelligence officer, voiced the opinion on the following day that "the auspicious time for Chinese intervention [had] long since passed" and that "there [was] no positive evidence that Chinese Communist units, as such, [had] entered Korea."[59] On November 1 the Chinese initiated a massive attack against the United States Third Battalion and virtually tore it apart. Then, after shattering the United States Eighth Cavalry, the Chinese abruptly broke contact and withdrew.

MacArthur's reaction to these events demonstrates how difficult it is for an old but stubbornly entrenched misperception to yield to reality. On the day of the Chinese disengagement, his estimate of total

Chinese strength in Korea was between 40,000 and 60,000 men.[60] In fact, as of October 31, the Chinese had deployed, with utmost secrecy and within short distances of the American forces they were about to strike, almost 200,000 men.[61] Some of these had crossed the Yalu before the Wake Island meeting between Truman and MacArthur.

The Chinese troops had done what MacArthur had deemed impossible. They had moved by night in forced marches, employed local guides and porters, and used the barren and hostile terrain of the North Korean hills to their advantage. They had then launched their assault on MacArthur's unsuspecting army. When the Chinese temporarily withdrew, MacArthur immediately ascribed this turn of events to the heavy casualties the enemy had sustained. In MacArthur's view, the Chinese needed to rest, and so a golden opportunity was at hand for a second and victorious American drive to the Yalu.

In retrospect, it is clear that:

> The Chinese withdrawal in early November was designed to encourage the enemy's arrogance; to lure the UN forces deeper into North Korea, where their tenuous supply lines could be interdicted and where units separated from one another by the broken terrain could be isolated and annihilated. This was the nature of the deadly trap which P'eng, at his Shenyang headquarters, was setting for the overconfident general in the Dai Ichi Building in Tokyo.[62]

MacArthur, then, believing that he was faced with 40,000 instead of 200,000 Chinese soldiers whom he believed to be badly in need of rest after their encounter with the American army, advanced north-ward again for the "final offensive." The Chinese watched for three weeks until finally, on November 27, they attacked in overwhelming force, turning the American advance into a bloody rout. Thus a peasant army put to flight a modern Western military force commanded by a world-famous American general. In one bound China had become a world power, and the image of the Chinese ward, almost half a century in the making, was finally shattered at a cost of tens of thousands of battle casualties on both sides. MacArthur, incredibly enough, did not learn much from the experience. In the words of his aide-de-camp, Major General Courtney Whitney, the general "was greatly saddened as well as angered at this despicably surreptitious attack, a piece of treachery which he regarded as worse even than Pearl Harbor."[63] The stark truth was that MacArthur had fallen blindly into the trap of his own misperceptions.

The paternalistic attitude of American leaders toward Communist China died hard. It remained extremely difficult for the United States to admit that the new China was growing in power and was fiercely hostile, and that this attitude was more than a passing phenomenon. Many rationalizations were invoked to explain this disturbing new presence on the world scene. Communism was viewed as somehow "alien" to the "Chinese character." It would pass, leaving the "traditional friendship" between China and America to reassert itself—although the paternalism implicit in this traditional relationship was never admitted.[64] At other times, Chinese hostility to the United States was explained as the result of the evil influence of the Soviet Union:

> On November 27, immediately following Mr. Vyshinsky's statement of charges of aggression against the U.S., the United States representative in this Committee [one of the United Nations], Ambassador Dulles . . . with a feeling of sadness rather than anger, said one could only conclude that the Soviet Union was trying to destroy the long history of close friendship between China and the United States and to bring the Chinese people to hate and, if possible, to fight the United States.[65]

One of the more bizarre examples of this attempt to maintain old attitudes in the face of bewildering new facts was the brief flurry of articles in the press during December 1950 reporting the possibility of a UN military action in China—directed not against the Chinese people but against the Mao faction, which was presumed to be their oppressor. A headline in the *New York Herald Tribune* proclaimed, "Declaration of State of War Against Mao's Faction Urged"; the text of the article read, "So far as can be determined now, the action of the UN will not be one of war against China or the Chinese people but against one faction in China, namely the Communists."[66] How this distinction was to be put into effect on the battlefield was never made clear, and apparently the utterly unrealistic nature of the proposal led to its early death. Nevertheless, the distinction between the Chinese people and their Communist leaders persisted for some time. On December 29, 1950, in a statement for the Voice of America, Dean Rusk, then assistant secretary of state for Far Eastern affairs, accused the Chinese Communists of having plotted the

North Korean assault. The press reported, "As all American officials have done consistently, Mr. Rusk drew a distinction between the Chinese people, for whom the United States has a long tradition of friendliness, and their Communist rulers."[67] By denying that the new government of China had a power base and a measure of popular support, the United States tried to maintain intact its old illusions about the historical relationship between the two nations. But it had been the relationship between predator and hunted, a fact that had never been admitted.

Indian Ambassador Panikkar detected this blind spot in the American picture of China. He noted that in the early days of the Korean War the Western military attachés in Peking had been utterly confident that Chinese troops could not possibly stand up to the Americans. He noted further that the defeat in late November came as a profound shock to the Americans, and their attitude thenceforth was very different.[68] In a good summation of the problem, he stated: "China had become a Great Power and was insisting on being recognized as such. The adjustments which such a recognition requires are not easy, and the conflict in the Far East is the outcome of this contradiction."[69]

The Chinese intervention in the Korean War provides a good illustration of the practical, operational consequences of divergent perceptions in world affairs. These perceptions are in effect definitions of the situation at hand. Once the situation has been defined, certain alternatives are eliminated. One does not conciliate an opponent who is perceived as implacably hostile; therefore, the Chinese Communists felt in the end that they had no resort but to intervene in Korea. One does not credit the threats of an opponent whose powers one perceives as negligible; the United States viewed even specific Chinese warnings as bluffs. One does not compromise with an opponent whose ideology is perceived as antithetical to one's own values; the United States and China remained poised on the brink of potentially disastrous conflict, neither one accepting the other's perception of its world role as legitimate. This was the central significance of the "entirely new war" that was to ravage the peninsula for another eighteen months.

Conclusion

The outbreak of the Korean War may be divided into three separate and distinct phases: the decision to repel the North Korean attack; the decision to cross the thirty-eighth parallel; and MacArthur's drive to the Yalu River that provoked the Chinese intervention. In my judgment, the first decision was correct, the second dubious, and the third disastrous.

When President Truman made his decision to commit American ground forces in Korea, Stalin was still alive and the global Communist movement still intact. China and the Soviet Union had just concluded an alliance. Korea was a test of whether the Communist movement could, by direct invasion, impose itself on the territory of another political entity, or whether that attack could be stemmed through collective action led by the United States.

The president's early decisions were firm, yet graduated: A full week elapsed between his initial response and the infantry commitment. During that week his top advisers were fully heard on several occasions, and their support remained virtually unanimous throughout. The North Koreans had ample opportunity to stop their invasion and thus avoid a full-scale collision with American power. Instead, they pressed the attack and escalated the ferocity of the initial encounter. Finally, even though the president "jumped the gun" on the United Nations by twenty-four hours, he genuinely perceived his action as taken on behalf of the principle of collective security set forth in the UN Charter.

Temptation beckoned when the tide of battle turned decisively in favor of the Unified Command. Initially, neither Truman nor MacArthur contemplated the seizure of North Korea, but the success of the Inchon landing provided the opportunity to turn the tables and invade the invader. At this critical juncture, the general, now speaking as a "United Nations commander," insisted on forging ahead, and the president gave his permission. The United Nations was treated rather cavalierly, as little more than an instrument of American policy, and although the UN secretary-general and most member nations accepted their role rather meekly, they had serious inner doubts. A United Nations victory, had it occurred, would clearly have been a victor's peace.

Disaster struck at the Yalu largely because of the hubris of General MacArthur. The UN commander lacked all respect for the new China and preferred instead to act out of hopes and fears rather than realities and facts. By provoking the Chinese intervention, MacArthur probably prolonged the war by another two and a half years, and it turned into one of the bloodiest conflicts in recent history. Aside from the 34,000 American dead, South Korea suffered over 800,000 casualties, and North Korea more than 500,000. The Chinese suffered appalling losses of 1.5 to 2 million men. The war ended indecisively in a draw in June 1953, with the two Koreas remaining fully armed and bitterly hostile to one another.

Yet, paradoxically, the violent clash between the United States and China at the Yalu River might in one sense have contributed in the long run to improved relations between the two countries, for the effectiveness of China's intervention in Korea established her as a power to be reckoned with. It shattered once and for all the condescension that had previously characterized the American view of China. One cannot, of course, answer with certainty the question of whether China and America would have gone to war over Vietnam in the 1960s if they had not fought in Korea. But it is highly probable that the Korean War served as a powerful corrective and thus as a restraining memory.

In the Korean War the victim of aggression was tempted by aggression and succumbed to the temptation. The United Nations became a party to the war and remained identified with one side in the conflict to the end. Since its identity became fully merged with the American cause, it lost the power to be a truly neutral mediator in Korea. This is perhaps the clearest lesson of the outbreak of this war: As the United Nations was captured by one of the parties to the conflict and made into its instrument, all sides suffered in the long run, and particularly the United Nations itself. No objective entity could now be called on to serve as referee or buffer. Hence, the fighting stopped only through exhaustion, when both sides finally despaired of victory.

Afterthoughts: Fifty Years Later

Kim Il Sung, the man who launched the North Korean attack in 1950, died in 1994. His son, Kim Jong Il, succeeded him. The younger Kim and President Bill Clinton signed an "Agreed Framework" in 1994, in which North Korea pledged to freeze and, eventually, to dismantle its nuclear weapons program in exchange for international aid to build two light-water, power-producing nuclear reactors.

The Bush administration's new doctrine of preemptive war and its inclusion of North Korea in the "axis of evil" precipitated a series of responses in North Korea, which tended to view the new doctrine as a direct threat. After all, if Washington was willing to attack Iraq, another nation with a suspected nuclear program, might it not also be willing, even likely, to do the same to North Korea?[70] This fear may explain why Kim Jong Il not only decided to restart his nuclear plutonium program, but also threatened first to withdraw from the Nuclear Non-Proliferation Treaty (NPT) in January 2003 and then, one month later, threatened to declare the Panmunjon Truce Agreement of 1953 null and void. In April 2003, North Korea became the first country to withdraw as a state party in the NPT's thirty-two-year history. Indeed, the North Korean ambassador to the United Nations went so far as to say he considered President Bush's "axis of evil" speech a declaration of war against North Korea.

We have here a classic example of two nations in confrontation, with each expecting the worst from the other. As we have seen from our analysis of World War I, such a condition may easily precipitate a war through miscalculation.

Even though Secretary of Defense Donald Rumsfeld declared that waging war against Iraq and North Korea simultaneously would not be a problem, the administration thought better of that plan and decided instead to engage North Korea in multilateral negotiations including other interested parties, such as Japan, China, Russia, and obviously, South Korea. After repeated statements by Bush that he was not prepared to reward North Korea's "bad behavior," he nonetheless promised to extend food and oil assistance to the impoverished nation if it would build down its nuclear arsenal.

The double standard applied by the administration must be apparent even to a casual observer. In effect, the United States was saying to one member of the "axis of evil"—Iraq—"If you build nuclear weapons we will go to war with you," but to another—North Korea—"Since you already have nuclear weapons we are willing to negotiate with you." To complete the paradox, Saddam Hussein was removed from power and no nuclear weapons or any other weapons of mass destruction were found, whereas Kim Jong Il was allowed to possess at least some nuclear weapons and had become a negotiating partner with his neighbors in Asia and the United States.

In June 2003, in order to reduce the risk of war with the North, the United States and South Korea agreed to gradually reposition American troops far away from the demilitarized zone that separates North and South Korea. Seoul, South Korea's capital with 17 million people, was within easy artillery range of the demarcation line separating the two Koreas. Such a redeployment, in the opinion of the United States and South Korea, would reduce the chances of war by accident with a country that had a standing army of more than 1 million troops on constant alert. North Korea's response to this initiative was to declare that it was seeking to develop nuclear weapons so that it could reduce the size of its huge army that it could no longer afford.[71] This new gambit, presenting the quest for nuclear weapons as a cost-saving measure, took Secretary of State Colin Powell by surprise. "I'll have to reflect on that for a while," he said.[72]

To complicate the situation further, strong evidence came to light in July that North Korea had built a second secret plant for producing weapons-grade plutonium, possibly to ensure second-strike capability if the United States were to attack first. In late July, North Korea "blinked" and decided to accept an American offer of multilateral talks involving China, Japan, Russia, South Korea, and the United States, on the issue of the North's nuclear weapons programs. From another perspective, of course, it could be argued that the United States "blinked" by agreeing to negotiate with an "evil axis" member over its weapons of mass destruction instead of resorting to military force.

The first set of meetings of the six nations took place in Beijing in August. North Korea used the occasion to announce that it was a nuclear power and that it planned to test an atomic bomb in the near future to prove it. The United States responded that it would not tolerate a nuclear North Korea. China, backed by the other negotiating countries, made an attempt to calm the rising temperature between North Korea and the United States by urging the six powers to reconvene within two months.

Clearly, the United States and North Korea greatly feared each other's intentions. Given this mindset, mere procedural concessions did not bring the crisis to an end. The only way to induce North Korea to terminate its nuclear programs was for the United States to give it a guarantee that it would not strike first. Given the vast military superiority of the United States, such a proposal was worth the risk, especially when it was combined with offers from the other negotiating powers to help rescue North Korea's foundering economy. During his visit to Asia in October 2003, President Bush made just such an offer. This decision to return from confrontation to diplomacy was welcomed by America's negotiating partners, and placed the ball squarely in North Korea's court. Indeed, China, Russia, Japan, and South Korea had exerted their influence on the president to change direction and Bush, beset by guerrilla warfare in Iraq, decided not to risk a two-front war. Thus, another major crisis was narrowly averted.

In January 2004, in another breakthrough, a private delegation of American experts on nuclear weapons traveled to North Korea to visit one of that nation's nuclear plants. Upon their return to the United States, the delegates reported that North Korea seemed open to further dialogue. It was a beginning.

NOTES

1. Harry S Truman, *Memoirs* (Garden City, N.Y.: Doubleday, 1955), Vol. 1 of 2 vols., p. 293.
2. Ibid., p. 433.
3. Raymond Dennett and Robert R. Turner, eds., *Documents on American Foreign Relations* (Princeton, N.J.: Princeton University Press, 1951), p. 4.
4. Dean G. Acheson, "Responsibility for Decision in Foreign Policy," *Yale Review* (Autumn 1954), p. 12.
5. Ibid., p. 7.
6. Ibid.
7. Ibid.
8. *Department of State Bulletin*, 23, 574 (July 1950), p. 17.
9. *Memoirs*, Vol. 2, p. 332.
10. Department of State, *United States Policy in the Korean Crisis*, Far Eastern Series, No. 34 (Washington, D.C.: Government Printing Office, 1950), p. 1.
11. For a full treatment of this subject, see John G. Stoessinger, *The United Nations and the Superpowers*, 3rd ed. (New York: Random House, 1973), chap. 3.
12. Cited in Glenn D. Paige, *The Korean Decision* (New York: Free Press, 1968), p. 95.
13. Ibid., p. 100.
14. *New York Herald Tribune*, June 26, 1950.
15. *New York Times*, July 2, 1950.
16. *Memoirs*, Vol. 2, pp. 332ff.
17. United Nations Security Council, Fifth Year, *Official Records*, No. 15, 473rd Meeting (June 25, 1950), p. 3.
18. *New York Times*, June 26, 1950.
19. Ibid.
20. *Korean Decision*, p. 120.
21. *Chicago Tribune*, June 26, 1950.
22. Ibid.
23. *Korean Decision*, p. 127.
24. *Memoirs*, Vol. 2, p. 334.
25. Ibid., p. 335.
26. Ibid.
27. Beverly Smith, "The White House Story: Why We Went to War in Korea," *Saturday Evening Post* (November 10, 1951), p. 80.
28. *Memoirs*, Vol. 2, p. 337.
29. Cited in *Korean Decision*, p. 179.
30. Ibid.

84   *Why Nations Go to War*

31. "White House Story," p. 80.
32. *Memoirs,* Vol. 2, p. 463.
33. *Korean Decision,* p. 203.
34. United Nations Document S/1508, June 26, 1950.
35. United Nations Document S/1507, June 26, 1950.
36. Roy E. Appleman, *South to the Naktong, North to the Yalu* (Washington, D.C.: Government Printing Office, 1960), p. 34.
37. *New York Times,* June 29, 1950.
38. Courtney Whitney, *MacArthur: His Rendezvous with History* (New York: Knopf, 1956), p. 327.
39. Ibid., pp. 332–333.
40. Marguerite Higgins, *War in Korea* (Garden City, N.Y.: Doubleday, 1951), p. 33.
41. *Korean Decision,* p. 243.
42. *Memoirs,* Vol. 2, p. 343.
43. *United Nations Bulletin* (July 15 and August 1, 1950), pp. 50–53, 95, 99.
44. Leland M. Goodrich, *Korea: A Study of U.S. Policy in the United Nations* (New York: Council on Foreign Relations, 1956), p. 117.
45. K. M. Panikkar, *In Two Chinas* (London: Allen & Unwin, 1955), p. 110.
46. *New York Herald Tribune,* September 22, 1950.
47. UN General Assembly, *Official Records,* Fifth Session, First Committee (September 30, 1950), p. 39.
48. Ibid.
49. The negative votes were cast by Byelorussia, Czechoslovakia, Poland, the Ukraine, and the USSR. Abstaining were Egypt, India, Lebanon, Saudi Arabia, Syria, Yemen, and Yugoslavia.
50. *New York Times,* October 9, 1950.
51. U.S. Senate, *Military Situation in the Far East,* Hearings before the Committee on Armed Services and the Committee on Foreign Relations, 82nd Cong., 1st sess. (1951), p. 3483.
52. Samuel B. Griffith II, *The Chinese People's Liberation Army* (New York: McGraw-Hill, 1967), p. 124.
53. *New York Times,* November 17, 1950.
54. Ibid.
55. *Memoirs,* Vol. 2, p. 362.
56. Tang Tsou, *America's Failure in China, 1941–1950* (Chicago: University of Chicago Press, 1963), p. 578.
57. *Chinese People's Liberation Army,* p. 124.
58. Douglas MacArthur, Message to Veterans of Foreign Wars, August 28, 1950.
59. *Military Situation in the Far East,* p. 3427.
60. *Chinese People's Liberation Army,* p. 134.
61. Ibid., p. 129.
62. Ibid., p. 134.
63. *MacArthur,* p. 394.
64. Allen S. Whiting, *China Crosses the Yalu* (Stanford, Calif.: Stanford University Press, 1960), pp. 169–170.
65. United States Mission to the United Nations, Press Release No. 1129, February 2, 1951.

66. *New York Herald Tribune,* December 6, 1950.
67. *New York Herald Tribune,* December 30, 1950.
68. *In Two Chinas,* p. 117.
69. Ibid., pp. 177–178.
70. James T. Laney and Jason Shaplen, "How to Deal with North Korea," *Foreign Affairs* (March/April, 2003).
71. *New York Times,* June 10, 2003.
72. *Ibid.*

SELECTED BIBLIOGRAPHY

BLAIR, CLAY. *Forgotten War: America in Korea 1950–1953.* New York: Anchor Books, 1989.

BUZO, ADRIAN. *The Guerrilla Dynasty: Politics and Leadership in Korea.* Boulder, Colo.: Westview, 1999.

DE RIVERA, JOSEPH. *The Psychological Dimensions of Foreign Policy.* Columbus, Ohio: Merrill, 1968.

DUJARRIE, ROBERT, Ed. *Korea: Pivot in Northeast Asia.* Indianapolis, Ind.: Hudson Institute, 1998.

EBERSTADT, NICHOLAS. *The End of North Korea.* Washington, D.C.: American Enterprise Institute Press, 1999.

FINKELSTEIN, DAVID M., and MARYANNE KIVLEHAN, eds. *China's Leadership in the 21st Century: The Rise of the Fourth Generation.* Armonk, N.Y.: M. E. Sharpe, 2003.

GOODRICH, LELAND M. *Korea: A Study of U.S. Policy in the United Nations.* New York: Council on Foreign Relations, 1956.

HARRISON, SELIG S. *Korean Endgame: A Strategy for Reunification and U.S. Disengagement.* Princeton, N.J.: Princeton University Press, 2002.

HASTINGS, MAX. *The Korean War.* New York: Simon & Schuster, 1987.

LANEY, JAMES T., and JASON T. SHAPLEN. "How to Deal with North Korea." *Foreign Affairs,* March/April 2003.

PAIGE, GLENN D. *The Korean Decision.* New York: Free Press, 1968.

SALISBURY, HARRISON E. *The New Emperors: China in the Era of Mao and Deng.* Boston: Little, Brown, 1992.

SIGAL, LEON V. *Disarming Strangers: Nuclear Diplomacy with North Korea.* Princeton, N.J.: Princeton University Press, 1998.

STOESSINGER, JOHN G. *Nations at Dawn: China, Russia, America.* 6th ed. New York: McGraw-Hill, 1993.

STUECK, WILLIAM. *Rethinking the Korean War: A New Diplomatic and Strategic History.* Princeton, N.J.: Princeton University Press, 2002.

TERRILL, ROSS. *The New Chinese Empire: Beijing's Political Dilemma and What It Means for the United States.* New York: Basic Books, 2003.

TRUMAN, HARRY S. *Memoirs.* 2 vols. Garden City, N.Y.: Doubleday, 1955.

WHITING, ALLEN S. *China Crosses the Yalu.* Stanford, Calif.: Stanford University Press, 1960.

WHITNEY, COURTNEY. *MacArthur: His Rendezvous with History.* New York: Knopf, 1956.

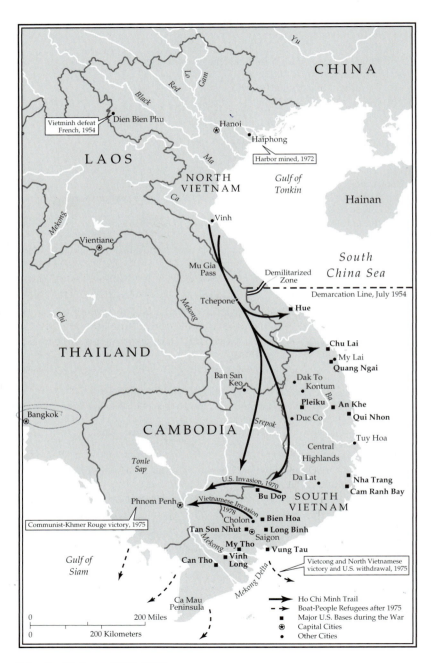

Yu

CHINA

Lo

Red

Gam

Black

Vietminh defeat
French, 1954

Dien Bien Phu

Hanoi ⊛

Haiphong

LAOS

Ma

Harbor mined, 1972

**NORTH
VIETNAM**

*Gulf of
Tonkin*

Ca

Hainan

Vinh

Mekong

Vientiane ⊛

**Mu Gia
Pass**

Demilitarized
Zone

*South
China Sea*

Tchepone

Mekong

Hue

Demarcation Line, July 1954

Chi

THAILAND

Chu Lai

My Lai

Quang Ngai

**Ban San
Keo**

Dak To

Kontum

Pleiku

An Khe

Ba

Duc Co

Qui Nhon

Bangkok ⊛

CAMBODIA

Srepok

Tuy Hoa

*Tonle
Sap*

Central
Highlands

Da Lat

Nha Trang

U.S. Invasion, 1970

Bu Dop

Cam Ranh Bay

Phnom Penh ⊛

Vietnamese Invasion, 1978

**SOUTH
VIETNAM**

Communist-Khmer Rouge victory, 1975

Cholon

Bien Hoa

Tan Son Nhut ⊛

Long Binh

Saigon

My Tho

Vung Tau

Mekong

Can Tho

**Vinh
Long**

*Gulf of
Siam*

Mekong Delta

Vietcong and North Vietnamese
victory and U.S. withdrawal, 1975

**Ca Mau
Peninsula**

| 0 | | 200 Miles |

| 0 | | 200 Kilometers |

→ Ho Chi Minh Trail

- - → Boat-People Refugees after 1975

■ Major U.S. Bases during the War

⊛ Capital Cities

• Other Cities

MAP 5   Vietnam, 1954–1975

4

A Greek Tragedy in Five Acts: Vietnam

If you look too deeply into the abyss, the abyss will look into you.
                                    Friedrich Nietzsche

Vietnam was the Thirty Years' War of the twentieth century. In the course of a single generation five American presidents misperceived reality in Indochina and substituted their own phantoms, first called fear and later called hope. These fears and hopes obscured reality until they produced a nightmare that could not be denied: the longest war in American history and the most divisive conflict domestically since the Civil War.

I do not believe that history will show that five evil men deceived their people and led them into war in Indochina. I do believe, however, that each of these five men, in his own particular way, made a concrete policy decision that escalated the war and contributed to the ultimate disaster. It is for this reason that this chapter will deal with the Vietnam war in five "acts," each to be seen as a quantum leap in a gradually escalating conflict.

In retrospect, the tragedy of the American encounter with Vietnam is plain. But the question remains whether it was an example of Greek tragedy, the tragedy of necessity, in which the feeling aroused in the spectator is "What a pity it had to be this way" or of Christian tragedy, the tragedy of possibility, in which the feeling aroused is "What a pity it was this way when it might have been otherwise." The main thesis of this chapter is that in Vietnam the misperceptions of five presidents transformed a tragedy of possibility into a tragedy of necessity.

Act One: Truman—Asia Was Not Europe

President Truman's perception of Indochina underwent profound changes between 1945 and 1952. In 1945, when hostilities erupted between France and Ho Chi Minh, the president was decidedly sympathetic to the latter. He regarded the war as France's problem and what France deserved for her colonial ambitions. An American OSS officer who had worked closely with Ho Chi Minh for several months before V-J Day had described him as an "awfully sweet guy whose outstanding quality was his gentleness."[1] This perception was much like that of President Franklin D. Roosevelt during World War II. Roosevelt had openly opposed the return of French power to Indochina and had advocated some form of international trusteeship for the area. If the fighting in Indochina was a colonial war, it followed that the United States should disapprove of France. This remained American policy under Roosevelt's successor. In 1947 President Truman urged France to end the war and resisted all French appeals for assistance, insisting, for example, that American-produced propellers be removed from the British aircraft given by Britain to the French troops fighting against Ho Chi Minh.[2]

When President Truman's perception, and that of the American leadership in general, did change, the reversal was based not on actual events in Indochina but on developments completely outside the area. In 1948 America's concept of its world role changed profoundly. Crisis followed crisis, from Berlin, to Greece, and to Czechoslovakia, and the division between East and West crystallized and hardened. The concepts of an "iron curtain" and "containment" came to pervade the entire American view of foreign affairs. The chasm between East and West appeared deeper by the day, and President Truman, architect of the North Atlantic Treaty, began to see himself as the leader of an embattled "free world" resisting the expansion of a ruthless totalitarianism.

The threat in Europe was undeniable, and President Truman's response to it was, on the whole, not exaggerated. The Truman Doctrine probably saved Greece and Turkey from Soviet conquest, and the North Atlantic Treaty in all likelihood stopped Stalin from overrunning Western Europe. The new American definition of the European situation, however, spilled over to encompass the entire globe. Having recognized a mortal threat in the heart of Europe, the American leadership soon came to redefine *all* conflicts throughout the world as part of the same struggle. Truman, in effect, decided to transplant the containment policy from Europe to Indochina.

Inexorably, the United States came to believe that the "frontiers" of the free world included Asia as well. In October 1948 the House Foreign Affairs Subcommittee on World Communism issued a report calling China the active theater of the Cold War. The report said that the Communists were using China as a testing ground for tactics they might employ to take over the world and recommended a "guarantee of territorial and political integrity" to the Chinese Nationalists.[3]

This shift in outlook implied an American redefinition of the "true" nature of Ho Chi Minh as well:

> In this country, it is only now beginning to be understood that in any Asiatic nationalist movement connected with Moscow through its leadership, the totalitarian-imperialist trend must inevitably kill native nationalism. . . . His [Ho Chi Minh's] Indochinese independence has become the means to another end: Russian conquest of the Southeast Pacific.[4]

On June 17, 1949, the *New York Herald Tribune* stated flatly that "Ho Chi Minh is a Comintern agent whom the French rate as an authentic political genius." This redefinition did *not* coincide with any objective developments in the Indochinese conflict. It coincided instead with an extraneous event: the Communist victory in China. The sense of betrayal that the American public felt over the loss of China intensified the anxieties arising from the Cold War. Thus peril in Europe, compounded by betrayal in China, produced a strongly emotional reevaluation of the United States' relationship to Southeast Asia.

Hence American failure in China was attributed to the machinations of a worldwide conspiracy. From 1949 onward the American press reflected a shift in attitudes such that the perceptual grid of Cold War categories was ultimately superimposed on the older conflict in Indochina. This grid gradually eclipsed all awareness of the nationalist origins of the Ho Chi Minh insurgency. It even erased American recollections of the colonial conditions that had sparked the revolt until finally, the original disapproval of France as an imperial power disappeared altogether in a redefinition of the French as "defenders of the West."

One by one the ambiguities disappeared. "Nationalist rebels" were steadily amalgamated with the Communist threat. Bao Dai, once referred to as the "nightclub emperor" and described as a man irretrievably tainted by his close association with the French colonial regime, was now officially considered as "offering more opportunity to the Vietnamese people to develop their own national life than a leader who must obey the orders of international Communism."[5] On February 2, 1950, the *Department of State Bulletin* asserted that the recognition of Ho Chi Minh by the USSR, China, North Korea, and the East European nations ended any speculation as to the fate of Vietnam under Ho, who was now described as a lifelong servant of world Communism.

Since the definition of what was going on in Indochina had changed, it was only natural that there should be a closely related shift in ideas of what should be done. Now that the deadly enemy was seen at work in Southeast Asia, President Truman was eager to keep the French in Indochina. In May 1950 the Griffin mission recommended an aid program of $23 million in economic assistance and $15 million in military aid to the French in Indochina.[6] A few days after the outbreak of the Korean War President Truman authorized the first shipments of aircraft to Indochina. In addition, $119 million in military aid was made available to France under the Mutual Defense Assistance Program. This aid increased to $300 million in 1952. Thus before he left the presidency in 1953 Harry Truman had underwritten the French war effort in Indochina.

By 1951 the American leadership and large segments of the American public perceived France as the free world's frontline ally in the fight against Communism in Southeast Asia. "That the French are making a tremendous effort to hold Indochina for the free world is better understood now than it was a short time ago," stated the *New York Times* in an editorial on September 24, 1951. The reevaluation was even made retroactive: "A bitter and bloody struggle between Communist forces and French Union troops has been racking Indochina for six years," declared the State Department's Office of Public Affairs in 1951.[7] And in March 1952, a State Department official stated that "in this battle to preserve their country from Communism, France is contributing financially and militarily. . . . French soldiers and resources have borne the brunt of this brutal attack."[8]

By early 1952 the Cold War grid was firmly in place. No longer was Southeast Asia viewed as the arena of an anticolonial revolt; it had now become part of the global East-West power struggle. On January 25, 1952, the *Christian Science Monitor* stated in an editorial that "no one planned that, after a stalemate in Korea, there should be a new trial of strength in the southward projection of Asia," implying that the Indochinese conflict had begun *after* the outbreak of the Korean War. The editorial concluded by imposing the Cold War dichotomy in full force: "Indochina is a place which is bound to be occupied eventually either by East or West. The strategic prizes are so great that the issue must be joined and eventually settled."

While President Truman's attention in Asia was, of course, focused primarily on Korea, by 1950 he believed that the French were fighting for the free world in Indochina just as the United Nations was fighting for it in Korea. He never committed combat troops to Southeast Asia as he did to Korea, but he authorized material aid in 1950 and raised the level of this assistance steadily until he left office in 1953. By that time the United States was paying almost one-third of the total cost of the French war effort in Indochina. President Truman had transferred his Cold War images from Europe to Southeast Asia and based his policies there on facile analogies rather than specific Asian realities. But Asia was not Europe, and what had worked in Europe would turn out to be a disaster in Indochina.

Act Two:
Eisenhower—The Lesson of France Ignored

President Dwight D. Eisenhower and Secretary of State John Foster Dulles were absolutely convinced that China would intervene in the Indochina war on the side of Ho Chi Minh against France, just as it had intervened on the side of North Korea against the United States. To forestall such an intervention, Eisenhower and Dulles had increased American military aid to France to $500 million by 1953. By 1954 this assistance had reached the $1 billion mark. The United States was now paying over one-half the cost of the Indochina war.[9]

The American expectation of a Chinese invasion was so powerful that it defied all evidence to the contrary. Neither the fact that the anticipated invasion failed to materialize nor the lack of evidence that it was actually planned lessened American apprehensions. Instead, the very strength of the expectation produced its own substantiation. Time and again, unfounded rumors were accepted as proof of impending intervention. The result was a recurrent pattern of false alarms. These began as early as April 11, 1951, with a headline in the *New York Times* reporting that a "Chinese Unit [was] Said to Join [the] Vietminh." Secretary Dulles repeatedly stated that the Chinese were directly engaged in battlefield operations. On April 5, 1954, during the siege of Dien Bien Phu, he claimed that Chinese troops were actually participating in the battle for the French fortress.[10] President Eisenhower, looking back upon this period in his memoirs, declared that "the struggle . . . began gradually, *with Chinese intervention* [italics mine], to assume its true complexion of a struggle between Communist and non-Communist forces rather than one between a colonial power and colonists who were intent on attaining independence."[11]

By 1954, largely as a result of these perceptions, the Americans were fighting a proxy war in Indochina. The battle for Dien Bien Phu almost changed this into a direct American war of intervention. Dien Bien Phu was France's last stand in Indochina. France had fought for almost a decade and had committed an army of 400,000 men. On March 20, 1954, with the fortress already under siege, General Paul Ely, commander of the French forces in Indochina, informed President Eisenhower that unless the United States intervened, Indochina would be lost. Admiral Arthur W. Radford, chairman of the Joint Chiefs of Staff, recommended military intervention, and Vice President Richard M. Nixon backed him, saying on April 16 that "if the United States cannot otherwise prevent the loss of Indochina, then the Administration must face the situation and dispatch troops."[12] President Eisenhower overruled his vice president and the chairman of the Joint Chiefs of Staff and decided not to intervene. He feared that the French had engendered too much popular antagonism to win the war and also felt that his administration would get little backing from the Congress for a military intervention in Asia so soon after the conclusion of the Korean War. Consequently, on the American side the war remained a war by proxy for a little while longer, but by a narrow margin.

The facts, in all cases, were strikingly different from Eisenhower's and Dulles's perceptions. So far as Ho Chi Minh's relations with

China were concerned, the North Vietnamese leader was always somewhat suspicious of China. In Bernard Fall's words, he was "probably equipped with an instinctive Vietnamese fear of Chinese domination, no matter what its political coloration, just as to a Russian, *any* Germany might be slightly suspect."[13] His policy was essentially one of balance, of maintaining the independence and integrity of his movement, vis-à-vis both China and the Soviet Union, while accepting as much aid as could safely be accepted from both.

Chinese aid to Ho Chi Minh was at times considerable, but never decisive. It consisted mostly of light weapons, trucks, and radios, largely of American manufacture, that had been captured from the Chinese Nationalists some years before.[14] In view of economic needs at home and the burdens imposed by the Korean War, China could hardly afford to become a bottomless reservoir of military assistance for the Vietminh forces. The best analysis of the Chinese relationship with Ho Chi Minh has probably been provided by Robert Guillain, the frontline correspondent for *Le Monde* in Indochina: "China adheres to a very simple principle: that the balance of power never inclines in any permanent direction toward the French side. There is no need—and this is the difference from what has happened in Korea—of direct intervention, of an invasion."[15] Thus, when France received more American aid following the outbreak of the Korean War, the Chinese stepped up their own aid program just enough to reestablish a rough equilibrium. As Melvin Gurtov put it: "The Indochina campaign eventually became a crude game in which the French could never permanently regain the high ground."[16] Thus Chinese military intervention on the side of the Vietminh never materialized. Instead, the Chinese used the Vietminh as their proxy.

The Geneva Conference of mid-1954 and the formation soon thereafter of the Southeast Asia Treaty Organization (SEATO) marked the end of French military involvement and the beginning of an American military presence in Indochina. The Geneva Conference resulted in the signing of several agreements to cease hostilities in Indochina and to establish the three independent sovereign states of Laos, Cambodia, and Vietnam. The accords on Vietnam provided for a "provisional military demarcation line" at the seventeenth parallel. Vietminh forces were to regroup north of the line, while the forces of the French Union were to regroup to the south. The line was to have military significance only, and the political unification of Vietnam was to be brought about through a general election two years hence under the supervision of a neutral three-power International Control Commission consisting of Canada, India, and Poland.

France had little choice in the matter, but her exit was made relatively gracefully. Ho Chi Minh's Vietminh forces were dominant in more than three-quarters of Vietnam and were poised to overrun considerably more. To Ho, the terms of the accords were acceptable because he was convinced that the general election of 1956 would win him all of Vietnam. From his point of view, the certainty of a military victory was simply replaced by the certainty of a political victory. Both the Soviet Union and China, reflecting their recently adopted line of "peaceful coexistence," applied pressure on Ho to accept the terms of the accords, reassuring him that his victory at the polls was certain.

The United States never signed the Geneva Accords. But in a unilateral decision at the end of the Geneva Conference the United States government pledged to "refrain from the threat or the use of force to disturb" the settlement and added that it would view any violation of the accords with grave concern.

The general American position at the conference remained ambivalent, since on the eve of a congressional election campaign the maintenance of Eisenhower's domestic appeal as peacemaker in Asia was of great importance. Moreover, to block a peaceful settlement of the Indochina war would also have jeopardized French participation in European defense plans. These conflicting considerations led the Eisenhower administration to dissociate the United States from the Geneva Accords and to seek another solution that would prevent any further territory in Asia from falling under Communist control. The answer was the creation of SEATO. Secretary of State Dulles declared that now that the war had ended, the United States could make arrangements for collective defense against aggression and build up "the truly independent states of Cambodia, Laos, and South Vietnam." On the day the treaty was signed in Manila, its eight signatories designated in an additional protocol the states of Cambodia and Laos and "the free territory under the jurisdiction of the state of Vietnam" to be under SEATO protection. The United States thus created SEATO to offset the results of Geneva. It also decided to consider South Vietnam a separate state.

The Vietminh, on the other hand, regarded SEATO as a clear violation of the spirit of the Geneva Accords. Ho Chi Minh saw the American position as an effort to deprive the Vietminh in the political arena of what it had gained militarily on the battlefield. Nevertheless, Ho withdrew his forces from the South, assuming that he would get enough votes there in 1956 to emerge with a clear national majority at election time. His electoral strength in the North was certain, and if only a minority supported the Vietminh in the South, his election would be ensured. President Eisenhower also thought that elections, if held on the basis of the Geneva Accords, would lead to a Communist victory. As he put it in 1954: "Had elections been held as of the time of the fighting, possibly 80 percent of the population would have voted for the Communist Ho Chi Minh as their leader rather than Chief of State Bao Dai."[17]

In the meantime, Ngo Dinh Diem, an American-backed Roman Catholic from a Mandarin family, began to challenge Emperor Bao Dai in the South. The United States strongly supported Diem in his bid for power, and in October 1955 Diem proclaimed the establishment of a Republic of Vietnam, with himself as president.

Hence Geneva and the SEATO treaty meant the end of French power in Indochina and the beginning of the American effort to enter the struggle with its own military presence. As yet, there had been no significant military encounters between Vietminh and American forces. But the path had become continuous. The Vietminh saw the Americans as following the course of French imperialism, and the Americans perceived Geneva as a well-laid Communist trap to engulf all of Vietnam. The end of a colonial war merely signified the beginning of a war between Americans and Communists.

As the East-West conflict superseded the colonial war, the tenor of battle gradually intensified. A pattern of escalation emerged in which every failure at diplomatic negotiations paved the way for yet another upward step on the scale of violence.

The first such discernible moves after Geneva were the American effort between 1954 and 1956 to strengthen President Diem's military establishment, and Ho Chi Minh's visits to Moscow and Peking in 1955 to negotiate aid and friendship treaties with the two Communist powers. Diem declared in July 1955 that since South Vietnam had not signed the Geneva Accords, he was not prepared to permit elections under the conditions specified by them. He also added that there was no freedom in the North to campaign for any opposition to Ho Chi Minh. President Eisenhower supported this view, and July 1956, the date scheduled for general elections in the accords, passed without any elections being held. Ho, in retaliation, began to train Communist cadres for guerrilla warfare in the South.

During the remaining years of the Eisenhower administration the United States continued to support the increasingly unpopular President Diem with military advisers, and by 1960 almost 1,000 Americans were serving in South Vietnam in that capacity. Thus Eisenhower and Dulles, ignoring the terrible lesson of the defeat of France, nevertheless decided to take on the burden of Vietnam. Communism had to be stopped, even though in this particular case "Communism" was an obscure Asian peasant country that by no stretch of the imagination could have posed a threat to the United States. Once again, fear rather than facts determined policy.

Act Three: Kennedy—The Military

During his brief presidency of a thousand days John F. Kennedy deepened the American involvement in Vietnam considerably. By the time of his death, the United States had greatly increased the number of military advisers in Vietnam; napalm and other antipersonnel weapons had been authorized for limited use against the enemy; and the United States had become identified with the highly unpopular regime of President Diem. The Vietnamese leader's violent death preceded Kennedy's own by only three weeks.

Even though Kennedy felt compelled to demonstrate his toughness in the international arena, after the disaster at the Bay of Pigs and his abrasive meeting with Nikita Khrushchev in Vienna, he was deeply skeptical about the possibility of a decisive American victory in Vietnam. In a revealing moment, he exclaimed: "In the last analysis, it is *their* war; it is they who must win it or lose it." He was pressed relentlessly by the military to commit combat troops to Vietnam but refused to do so to the end. Yet under his leadership the United States entered a crucial period of transition, from a marginal commitment to a fateful and direct involvement. The reason for this tragedy was that most of the men around the president, including his secretary of defense and the chairman of the Joint Chiefs of Staff, perceived Vietnam essentially as a military rather than political problem. In their view, greater quantities of more sophisticated weapons would guarantee victory in a relatively short period of time. Kennedy's instincts told him that this assumption was probably wrong, but he permitted the facts and figures of the military experts to sway him. Shortly before his death, his doubts prevailed, but by then it was too late. Close to 17,000 Americans were serving as advisers in Vietnam by the end of 1963.

Kennedy's first response to stepped-up Vietcong guerrilla activity in South Vietnam was to emphasize the need for antiguerrilla warfare training in the United States. The result was the creation of the Special Forces, which enjoyed the president's particular favor. In October 1961, according to David Halberstam, the entire White House press corps was transported to Fort Bragg to watch a demonstration put on by the Special Forces:

> It turned into a real whiz-bang day. There were ambushes, counterambushes and demonstrations in snakemeat eating, all topped off by a Buck Rogers show: a soldier with a rocket on his back who flew over water to land on the other side. It was quite a show, and it was only as they were leaving Fort Bragg that Francis Lara, the Agence France-Presse correspondent who had covered the Indochina war, sidled over to his friend Tom Wicker of the *New York Times*. "All this looks very impressive, doesn't it?" he said. Wicker allowed that it did. "Funny," Lara said, "none of it worked for us when we tried it in 1951."[18]

In 1961 Walt Rostow drew the president's attention to Brigadier General Edward Lansdale. Lansdale had made a reputation for himself by helping Philippine president Ramon Magsaysay defeat the Huk rebellion. He seemed to be just the man to defeat the Vietcong. Lansdale recommended that the number of American military advisers in Vietnam be increased to 3,000 men. Kennedy rejected the recommendation but authorized the dispatch of 400 men from the Special Forces to Vietnam. This would give him the opportunity to see how his favorites would acquit themselves in real action.

In March 1961 Kennedy appointed Frederick E. Nolting, Jr., ambassador to Vietnam. As head of the political section of NATO, Nolting had earned a good, solid reputation but had never been to Asia, and his ideas about Communism had been filtered through the prism of his European experience. Nolting requested as his deputy William Trueheart, another man who had never visited Asia. This was the price that Kennedy paid for the mistakes of the past. Since the days of Senator Joseph McCarthy most experts on Asia had been considered possible security risks, whereas specialists on Europe like Nolting and Trueheart were above suspicion. The fact that they were totally ignorant about Asian realities did not seem to be a serious concern.

In April 1961, in order to boost President Diem's morale, Kennedy decided to ask Vice President Lyndon Johnson to visit Vietnam on his Asian tour. Johnson was less than enthusiastic, but the president coaxed him into accepting: "Don't worry, Lyndon," he said. "If anything happens to you, Sam Rayburn and I will give you the biggest funeral Austin, Texas, ever saw."[19]

Johnson was favorably impressed with Diem. He hailed him publicly as "the Winston Churchill of Southeast Asia," though when asked by a reporter for the *Saturday Evening Post* whether he really believed that about Diem, Johnson answered: "Shit, man, he's the only boy we got out there."[20] In his official report to the president, Johnson declared that: "The battle against Communism must be joined in Southeast Asia with strength and determination to achieve success there. Vietnam can be saved if we move quickly and wisely. . . . The most important thing is imaginative, creative American management of our military aid program."[21] Thus, Johnson committed the president more deeply to Vietnam and in addition committed himself personally to the war.

The most crucial single event that escalated the American commitment during the Kennedy administration was the Rostow-Taylor Report. In October 1961 the president decided to send two of his own special representatives to Vietnam for an on-site fact-finding trip. He chose Walt Rostow and Maxwell Taylor because of the interest these two men had shown in Kennedy's own favorite approach to the Vietnam problem: limited antiguerrilla warfare.

The report came as a profound shock to Kennedy. Rostow and Taylor recommended the introduction of 8,000 American combat troops into Vietnam and stated flatly that without such a commitment Vietnam could not be saved. It was their position that American air power could save Vietnam at any time and that Hanoi and Peking would face serious logistical difficulties if they attempted to counter American power. So far as fighting conditions for the proposed American combat troops were concerned, Taylor and Rostow declared that they found South Vietnam "not an excessively difficult or unpleasant place to operate." They thought it comparable to Korea, where American troops had learned to fight efficiently and well.

Kennedy's own misgivings about this report were echoed by George Ball, the under secretary of state for economic affairs, who had observed the French disaster in Indochina and noted the parallels. Ball warned the president that even a small combat commitment of 8,000 men would change the nature of the commitment and the nature of the war. Within five years, he warned, the commitment would be escalated to 300,000 men. Although Kennedy had his own doubts about the Rostow-Taylor recommendations, he nevertheless expressed his belief in the ability of rational men to control irrational commitments. He was reported to have laughed at Ball's warning and to have said: "George, you are crazier than hell."[22]

In a conversation with Arthur Schlesinger, Jr., the president expressed his own reservations very clearly: "They want a force of American troops. They say it is necessary in order to restore confidence and maintain morale. But it will be just like Berlin. The troops will march in, the bands will play, the crowds will cheer, and in four days everyone will have forgotten. Then we will be told we have to send in more troops. It's like taking a drink. The effect wears off and you have to take another."[23] Finally, the president compromised. Instead of 8,000 combat troops, he authorized 15,000 military advisers and support units. In making this crucial decision, he made any future withdrawal from Vietnam that much more difficult. Yet by doing less than he was called on to do, the president maintained the illusion that he was holding the line rather than taking the United States deeper into the war. The commander of the American advisory and support team was to be Lieutenant General Paul D. Harkins, an officer described by David Halberstam as "a man of compelling mediocrity."[24]

The performance of the South Vietnamese army did not improve despite the presence of the new American advisers. The Vietcong had escalated their own guerrilla activities, and by late 1962 the situation had become desperate. Generals Taylor and Harkins persisted in transmitting overly optimistic military reports to the president. As one firsthand observer succinctly put it: "It became increasingly a policy based on appearances; Vietnamese realities did not matter, but the *appearances* of Vietnamese realities mattered because they could affect American realities. More and more effort went into public relations because it was easier to manipulate appearances and statements than it was to affect reality on the ground."[25] Harkins argued fiercely for the unlimited use of napalm and crop defoliation. Kennedy hated these weapons because of their particularly inhumane character. Harkins persisted, however, and finally Kennedy approved the use of napalm in battles where there were no population centers and reluctantly authorized limited defoliation on lines of communications, but not on crops. Again, by authorizing less than Harkins and the military wanted, the president felt that he was limiting, rather than expanding, the use of American power.

Robert McNamara, Kennedy's secretary of defense, was also certain of an American victory. He visited Vietnam frequently, but he was so much the prisoner of his own limited experience that he constantly tried to apply American production techniques to an Asian political revolution. His relentless emphasis on quantifiable data and statistics blinded him to the essential quality of his Vietcong enemy: a total commitment to the task of expelling the Americans, who by now had become identified as the successors of French colonialism.

In mid-1963 Kennedy was jarred by reports about the growing unpopularity of President Diem. Increasingly he felt that the United States would have to dissociate itself from the repressive harshness of the South Vietnamese ruling family. The new United States ambassador, Henry Cabot Lodge, advised that if a coup d'état materialized against Diem, the United States should not attempt to thwart it. During September and October the Diem regime resorted to particularly brutal measures to crush Buddhist dissidents. More and more the United States looked like the ally of a reactionary government because that government had the single virtue of being anti-Communist. In November Diem was killed, and three weeks later John Kennedy was murdered. Lyndon Johnson, who admired Diem and always opposed the planned coup against him, allegedly said in an almost mystical way after the president's death, that "the assassination of Kennedy was a retribution for the assassination of Diem."[26]

Kennedy and his military advisers never took seriously the statement made by many Vietcong soldiers that it was the duty of their generation to die for their country. They believed that the Vietcong, in their "black pajamas," were a fake army and that the South Vietnamese had the real and legitimate army. In reality, the reverse was closer to the truth. Taylor and Rostow, in their crucial report, had equated Vietnam with Korea. They had ignored the all-important difference that the Korean conflict had been a conventional war with a classic border crossing by an enemy in uniform, whereas in Vietnam there was a political struggle conducted by guerrillas feeding on subversion and taking advantage of a jungle terrain where front lines became virtually meaningless.

Thus President Kennedy—essentially a man of reason with a profoundly skeptical bent—became the victim of that particularly American form of hubris that blithely assumed that technology, computerlike efficiency, production, air power, and, above all, competent American management could overcome any adversary. This mind set ignored the reality of an army of guerrillas who were quite prepared to die for their cause, would match the American escalation man for man, if not weapon for weapon, and were prepared to fight for a generation or more. At the time of President Kennedy's death, 17,000 Americans were serving in Vietnam, but only seventy had died by the end of 1963.

Act Four: Johnson—The Catastrophe

"I can't get out. I can't finish it with what I have got. So what the hell can I do?"[27] Shortly after he made this remark to his wife in March 1965 President Johnson authorized sending massive combat troops to the war in Vietnam. By taking this step, he involved the United States deeply and consciously in a war that he could not win but that he also felt he could not afford to lose.

The record of the Johnson presidency in Vietnam is a story of self-delusion and misperception so vast that it turned into a national catastrophe. Despite relentless bombing raids on both North and South Vietnam and the introduction of more than half a million American troops, the enemy was not defeated. Instead, Johnson's ego, stubbornness, and pride destroyed his presidency and divided his people in a spiritual civil war.

At no single point when he made his decisions to escalate the bombing or the ground commitment did Johnson realize that he had crossed the Rubicon and unleashed a major American land war in Asia. He always hoped that one more bombing raid or a few more troops would bring the enemy to the conference table. As a consequence, he misperceived his enemy, misled his people, and ultimately deceived himself.

It all began in January 1964 with a memorandum to the president from the Joint Chiefs of Staff, urging him to increase the commitment in order to win the war more quickly: "The United States must be prepared to put aside many of the self-imposed restrictions which now limit our efforts, and to undertake bolder actions which may embody greater risks."[28] Specifically, the Joint Chiefs were of the opinion that aerial bombing would bring North Vietnam to its knees. Rostow stated in support of this recommendation that "Ho Chi Minh has an industrial complex to protect; he is no longer a guerrilla fighter with nothing to lose."[29]

In the meantime, Robert Johnson, head of the Policy Planning Council and deputy to Rostow, undertook a careful study of the probable effects of bombing. The study concluded that the bombing would not work and predicted, prophetically, that it would imprison the American government. Economic growth was not a major Hanoi objective, the study said, challenging one of Rostow's favorite theses; rather, it was the unfinished business of throwing the foreigners out of the country. Hanoi had two formidable pillars of strength: the nationalist component of unity and the Communist component of control, which made for a well-organized, unified modern state. Bombing would not affect such a regime. On the contrary, it might even strengthen it.

This remarkable study was ignored. Rostow, who was totally committed to bombing, never brought it to the president's attention. More and more, the president's advisers, both civilian and military, moved toward a consensus on the bombing policy. Robert McNamara, McGeorge Bundy, Maxwell Taylor, and Dean Rusk—all of them perceived a chain of aggression emanating from China that urged North Vietnam onward. Ho Chi Minh, in turn, was the source of the Vietcong aggression in the South. Therefore bombing would stop aggression at the source—in the North—and would convince China of American determination. No more dominoes would be permitted to fall to Communism. In a revealing "Pentagon Papers" memorandum to McNamara, John McNaughton, a former Harvard law professor and then assistant secretary of defense, set forth American goals in South Vietnam in terms of the following priorities:

70 percent—To avoid a humiliating U.S. defeat.
20 percent—To keep South Vietnamese territory from Chinese hands.
10 percent—To permit the people of South Vietnam to enjoy a better, freer way of life.[30]

One notes that the official reason given to the American people for the intervention in Vietnam with air power and ground troops made up only one-tenth of the government's actual rationale.

The specific incident that triggered the bombing of North Vietnam was the encounter of the two American warships *C. Turner Joy* and *Maddox* with North Vietnamese patrol boats in the Gulf of Tonkin. The administration maintained that the ships had been fired upon in neutral waters and that retaliation was mandatory. Subsequent studies have cast serious doubts on this official version. After painstaking research, one scholar reached the dramatic conclusion that there had been no attack on the *Maddox* and the *Turner Joy* at all, that the president had misled Congress and the people and through that deception had been able to obtain congressional authorization for a war that he had decided on months before while promising the voters peace.[31] Whether or not one regards this conclusion as too harsh, there can be little doubt about the fact that the American retaliation was disproportionate. On August 4, 1964, American bombers destroyed twenty-five North Vietnamese patrol boats and blew up the oil depot at Vinh in North Vietnam. McNamara reported to the president that, at Vinh, "the smoke was observed rising to 14,000 feet." Johnson was overheard to say to a reporter, "I didn't just screw Ho Chi Minh; I cut his pecker off."[32]

During the next few days Senator William Fulbright served as floor sponsor of the Tonkin Gulf Resolution that would give the president broad authority for military action in Indochina. When Senator John Sherman Cooper asked whether this resolution would enable the president "to use such force as could lead into war," Fulbright answered in the affirmative. Two years later, he remembered this episode with deep regret and bitterness.

During his campaign for reelection in 1964 Johnson tried to keep Vietnam out of the public eye as much as possible. When later asked why, he answered: "If you have a mother-in-law with only one eye and she has it in the center of the forehead, you don't keep her in the living room."[33] Vietnam decisions were closely guarded secrets and were made by half a dozen men. Escalation proceeded by stealth.

Only one man in Johnson's inner circle openly voiced his doubts about Vietnam: George Ball. Ball challenged the assumption made by the others that the United States necessarily controlled the scale and intensity of the war. Once on the tiger's back, one could not be sure of picking a safe place to dismount. Moreover, nothing that could be truly effective against North Vietnam could be tried without risking a much larger war. Ball did not oppose the war because he was a "dove." He simply did not believe in the dissipation of American power through misuse.

On February 7, 1965, the Vietcong attacked the American barracks at Pleiku. Eight Americans were killed and sixty were wounded. Bundy, after a quick visit to Pleiku, recommended a reprisal policy of sustained bombing against the North that would cease only if the Vietcong ended their insurrectionist activities. An old Eisenhower aide, Emmett John Hughes, asked Bundy what he would do if the North Vietnamese retaliated by matching the American air escalation with their own ground escalation. "We can't assume what we don't believe," Bundy replied.[34]

Thus Lyndon Johnson began the relentless bombing campaign that was to devastate North Vietnam for the next three years. Though he probably had his own reservations about its effectiveness, his enormous ego and machismo played a considerable role. Moreover, his inner circle was supportive: McNamara considered victory through air bombardment technologically feasible; Bundy made it intellectually respectable; and Rusk thought it historically necessary.

The bombing campaign, or "Operation Rolling Thunder," as it was referred to in The Pentagon Papers, did not produce the desired effect. Ho Chi Minh did exactly what Bundy had thought impossible: He matched the American air escalation with his own escalation, through infiltration on the ground. Since withdrawal was unthinkable, there was now only one possible response: to meet the Vietcong challenge head on with American combat troops on the ground.

In March 1965 General William Westmoreland, the commander of United States forces in Vietnam, requested only two marine corps. By April the Joint Chiefs were recommending a commitment of 50,000 men. Some senators became a trifle uneasy but were quickly reassured by Vice President Hubert Humphrey, who said: "There are people at State and the Pentagon who want to send three-hundred thousand men out there. But the President will never get sucked into anything like that."[35] In May the figure was revised upward to 80,000. George Ball was appalled but could not reverse the trend. He was alone in his resistance. In June Westmoreland demanded 200,000 men. This would cross the Rubicon and turn Vietnam into a major American war. Johnson reluctantly assented, sensing the terrible trap that was closing in on him. As one reporter wrote of the occasion: "The President is a desperately troubled man resisting the awful pressures to plunge deeper into the Vietnam quagmire—resisting them as instinctively as an old horse resists being led to the knackers. The President bucks, whinnies and shies away, but always in the end the reins tighten—the pressures are too much for him."[36] The White House gradually became a fortress. Doubters became enemies and ultimately traitors. Only unreserved and unquestioning loyalty was acceptable to the president.

Westmoreland demanded, and received, more and more men for Vietnam. Yet Hanoi met every American escalation with an escalation of its own. In November 1965 Westmoreland projected American troop levels that would reach 600,000 men by 1967. This too was of no avail. A great power of 200 million people fighting a limited war found itself stalemated by a small Asian nation of 17 million fighting a total war.

Failure took its toll. One by one the intellectuals departed. Bundy and McNamara left. Rostow remained. Of him, Johnson would say: "I'm getting Walt Rostow as my intellectual. He is not Bundy's intellectual. He is not Schlesinger's intellectual; he is going to be my goddam intellectual."[37] The president refused to give in. "A bombing halt," he would say, "I'll tell you what happens when there is a bombing halt: I halt and then Ho Chi Minh shoves his trucks right up my ass. That's your bombing halt."[38] What became clear in 1967, however, even to a self-deluded Johnson, was the fact that Ho Chi Minh did not have to run for reelection in 1968.

A few months before he left the Department of Defense, McNamara authorized a comprehensive study of all materials pertaining to Vietnam, going back to the 1940s. When he read the first chapters of these "Pentagon Papers," he told a friend that "they could hang people for what's in there."[39] His successor was Clark Clifford, who assumed the role thus far played unsuccessfully by George Ball. He finally succeeded in making the president face, slowly and in agony, the true dimensions of the catastrophe.

The North Vietnamese Tet offensive that began in January 1968 underscored the disaster. Americans at home were now able to see that, despite three years of bombing and a commitment of half a million men, the enemy was still able to mount offensives. It now became clear that the United States suffered much more from the war of attrition than did the enemy. The North Vietnamese manpower pool was far from depleted, and there was always the possibility of an intervention by Chinese "volunteers." There was to be no light at the end of the tunnel for Lyndon Johnson. In March 1968 he announced a bombing halt and withdrew from the presidential race. Vietnam had made the man elected by the largest landslide in American history into a one-term president.

Lyndon Johnson, totally ignorant of Asia in general and of Vietnam in particular, was governed exclusively by his own misperceptions of Asian reality. In his view, aggression had to be stopped "at the source" and the "source" was Communism in North Vietnam and China. The fact that Communism had broken up into numerous diverse political and ideological fragments appears to have been lost on him. He never understood that this was a revolutionary war in which the other side held title to the revolution because of the colonial war that had just ended. Revolution and antirevolution were the real issues, not Communism and anti-Communism. That is why the Vietcong were willing to fight and die and the South Vietnamese were not. That is why McNamara's statistics were valueless: They overlooked the fact that even if the South Vietnamese forces outnumbered the Vietcong by a ratio of ten to one, it did no good because the one man was willing to fight and die and the ten were not.

And then there was Ho Chi Minh—a man totally unlike anyone Lyndon Johnson had ever met. The president dealt with his adversary by means of all the time-honored American political techniques; when force did not work, he tried manipulation. But neither bombs nor dollars would tempt Ho Chi Minh. Johnson, unable to understand an adversary who was unwilling to bargain, resorted to the use of military force, the only instrument of compulsion he had.

Because he believed he could not lose, Johnson dropped still more bombs and sent still more men to their death. He shielded himself with the belief that America was fighting in Vietnam for selfless and idealistic reasons. A credibility gap had become a reality gap: The myth of false innocence enabled the United States to wreak destruction on a grand scale in Indochina, all in the name of kindliness and helpfulness. Gradually, the means became so horrible that it became increasingly difficult to justify the ends. The war in Vietnam finally became a lost crusade.

Ho Chi Minh the man was very different from Lyndon Johnson's image of him as Mao Zedong's puppet. True, the North Vietnamese leader was an old Bolshevik who had been one of the founders of the French Communist Party in 1920. But he was a more senior member of the Communist world than Mao and was a unique figure in his own right. He was as much a Vietnamese nationalist as a Communist. David Halberstam described him as "part Gandhi, part Lenin, all Vietnamese."[40] After his victory over the French at Dien Bien Phu in 1954, Ho not only enjoyed the veneration of his people but was also treated with a special respect throughout the Third World. Mao Zedong had simply defeated other Chinese, but Ho Chi Minh had defeated a powerful Western nation.

Ho Chi Minh's most distinctive quality, however, was his incorruptibility. In a country whose leaders invariably reached a certain plateau and then became more Western and less Vietnamese, corrupted by money and power, Ho Chi Minh remained a Vietnamese Everyman. The higher he rose, the less he sought the trappings of authority. He shunned monuments, marshal's uniforms, and general's stars, always preferring his simple tunic. The "black pajamas" that Lyndon Johnson mocked were in fact his source of strength, for they symbolized his closeness to the peasants, who both loved and obeyed him. The secret of his success was his ability to walk humbly among his own people; he was never separated from the people by police motorcades and foreign advisers.

What made Ho so effective was the contempt with which he was viewed by the West. For example, *Time* magazine once referred to him as a "goat-bearded agitator who learned his trade in Moscow." By remaining a Vietnamese, a peasant like his ancestors, he became the only leader with title to the revolution: to drive the French, and then the Americans, from Vietnam. The Soviet Communists recognized his strength; the Communist Party of Vietnam survived the Stalin years without the slightest touch of purge. The leadership of Ho Chi Minh was such that even Stalin decided not to interfere. Ho even had a sense of humor. "Come on, you will have dinner with the President of the Republic," Ho announced to Robert Isaacs, an old American friend and dinner guest in 1945, after the defeat of Japan. As they passed through a corridor, two young Vietminh guards snapped to attention and then, their revolvers showing, followed Ho to his car. Ho laughed. "How funny life is!" he exclaimed. "When I was in prison, I was let out for fifteen minutes in the morning and fifteen minutes in the evening for exercise. And while I took my exercise in the yard, there were always two armed guards standing right over me with their guns. Now I'm President of the Vietnam Republic, and whenever I leave this place, there are two armed guards right over me with their guns."[41] In his fundamental human qualities, Ho Chi Minh was the very opposite of Lyndon Johnson.

With Ho Chi Minh, Johnson followed the principle of the strong overpowering the weak. He believed that he could bend the enemy to his will and so avoid inflicting pain, death, and material destruction on the North Vietnamese. This strategy was feasible to someone who was rich, loved life, and feared pain. But in the Vietcong Johnson confronted the power of the weak. The weak defied the American president by their willingness to struggle, suffer, and die on a scale that seemed beyond reason. Interrogations of prisoners repeatedly revealed this phenomenon. When asked what would happen if more and more Americans came and bigger and bigger bombs dropped, the prisoners very often showed a fatalistic and dispassionate attitude: "Then we will all die." Such defiance brought Lyndon Johnson face-to-face with the threat of ultimate escalation—in the parlance of the time, to bomb North Vietnam into the Stone Age, or put more simply, to commit genocide. Looking into the abyss, Johnson hesitated, remembering Hitler and Hiroshima. The only alternative was withdrawal. Withdrawal meant losing, but massive escalation also meant losing, because the soul of the United States would have been lost and our social fabric completely destroyed. Thus Ho Chi Minh's strategy of weakness prevailed over Johnson's strategy of strength. Ho had progressively less to lose by continuing to fight, while the stakes grew more costly for his American opponent. Time was always on the side of Ho Chi Minh.

Perhaps the essential truth about Lyndon Johnson and the men who made Vietnam policy during his presidency was that they had never experienced the kind of pain or tragedy that is the source of empathy. These men had only been successful, and their vision was limited to the American experience. None knew, until it was too late, that nations, like people, can die. None knew that intelligence alone, without wisdom and empathy for suffering, is hollow.

One postscript to this analysis may be of relevance. In 1988

Richard N. Goodwin, an aide to Lyndon Johnson during the 1960s, published a memoir entitled *Remembering America*. The most fascinating part of this book was Goodwin's analysis of Johnson's personality during the height of the Vietnam War. Briefly put, the author argued, the president was probably clinically paranoid.

Like many paranoids, Johnson managed to live for most of his life with this affliction. But under the increasing strain of the war, he began to be consumed by irrational resentments and fears of conspiracy. Goodwin revealed that as early as 1965 he had grown so alarmed by Johnson's erratic behavior that he consulted several psychologists about his concern that the president was experiencing "sporadic paranoid disruptions."[42] The author also reported that his fellow White House aide, William Moyers, shared many of these worries. Goodwin's belief that Johnson was becoming unbalanced helped persuade him to oppose the president publicly on the war and finally to work for his defeat in 1968.

Goodwin's thesis is, of course, unprovable. But the fact that a thoughtful contemporary of Lyndon Johnson painted a chilling and convincing portrait of a president at war, descending into something approaching madness, is enough to give one pause and cannot be dismissed lightly. It merely deepens one's concern at the awesome power that a single individual can hold in the American democracy, for better or for worse.

Act Five: Nixon—Full Circle

The presidency of Richard Nixon brought a painful groping for extrication and "peace with honor." Nixon and Henry Kissinger, his main architect of foreign policy, devised a formula known as "Vietnamization," whereby the war would gradually be turned over to the Vietnamese as American combat troops were withdrawn. The American hope was to leave behind a viable anti-Communist South Vietnam with a friendly government firmly installed in Saigon. The central issue of the war remained the same: Who should rule in Saigon?

The withdrawal of American ground troops began in June 1969, when the peak figure of 541,500 men was reduced by 25,000. As withdrawal gathered momentum, a serious weakness became increasingly apparent in the "Vietnamization" strategy: As American strength was slowly ebbing, Communist forces became better able to attack and try to topple the South Vietnamese regime, to which American prestige remained committed. President Nixon's response to this challenge was twofold: the destruction of Communist sanctuaries by ground incursions into Laos and Cambodia, and increasing reliance on air power through bombing. Thus, as American participation in the ground fighting gradually diminished, the air war reached levels of unprecedented ferocity. This policy reflected the dilemma of a president who still believed in the essential mission of the United States in Vietnam but who wanted to attain his goal without incurring additional American casualties. Kissinger, in response to a question posed by an Asian diplomat as to whether President Nixon was going to repeat the mistakes of the Johnson administration, said, half in jest: "No, we will not repeat their mistakes. We will not send 500,000 men. We will make our own mistakes and they will be completely our own."[43] Quite unintentionally, this proved to be a prophetic statement.

In July 1969 the president announced the "Nixon Doctrine," to the effect that, in the future, the United States would avoid entanglements like Vietnam by limiting its support to economic and military aid rather than active combat participation. Peace negotiations had begun in earnest in Paris, and a moratorium against the war drew huge crowds in Washington demanding a rapid withdrawal of American troops. In January 1970, however, under the euphemism of "protective reaction" to cover air reconnaissance missions over North Vietnam, the United States renewed the bombing of the North. The Vietcong once again increased infiltration on the ground.

On April 30, 1970, in a nationally televised address, President Nixon announced an American-led South Vietnamese "incursion" into Cambodia to demonstrate that the United States was "no pitiful, helpless giant." In the same speech he declared that since 1954 the United States had "respected scrupulously the neutrality of the Cambodian people," but the discovery of Vietcong supply depots and sanctuaries had made this latest incursion necessary. It would shorten the war, the president explained. Three years later, in the midst of the Watergate hearings, it was revealed that in more than 3,500 raids during 1969 and 1970 American B-52s had dropped over 100,000 tons of bombs on Cambodia and Laos. In Tom Wicker's words, the April 30 speech was "a deliberate and knowing lie broadcast in person to the American people by their president."[44] When confronted with this contradiction, the president's spokesman at the Pentagon, Jerry Friedheim, said: "I knew at the time it was wrong and I am sorry."[45]

In May 1970 Nixon announced the end of large-scale bombing raids against the North, and in June he pronounced the Cambodian incursion a success. The Senate repealed the Tonkin Gulf Resolution and barred future military operations in Cambodia without congressional approval. American combat troops now stood at 400,000 men. The year 1971 saw protracted peace negotiations in Paris, while the fighting continued in South Vietnam between the Vietcong and the dwindling American forces and their South Vietnamese allies. By the end of the year another 200,000 Americans had returned home.

In March 1972 the North Vietnamese launched a major offensive with massed tanks and artillery in the most impressive show of force since the Tet assault of 1968. The North Vietnamese leadership had decided to make an all-out effort to seize what it could in the South at a time when it was facing the danger of a new form of diplomatic isolation. The latest American overtures to China and the Soviet Union threatened to separate North Vietnam from its two major Communist allies. The offensive began shortly after Nixon's visit to Peking in February but before his trip to Moscow, scheduled for May.

In April and May 1972 Nixon took two gambles that escalated the war to new levels of violence. In April B-52 bombers struck Hanoi and Haiphong in saturation bombings that far surpassed the ferocity of the Johnson raids. And on May 8 the president took a step that his predecessor had always ruled out as too perilous: He ordered the mining of North Vietnam's harbors to cut off the flow of tanks, artillery, and other offensive weapons supplied to Hanoi by the Soviet Union and other Communist nations. At the same time, however, he offered a total troop withdrawal from South Vietnam four months after an Indochina-wide cease-fire and the return of prisoners of war. The risk of a Soviet-American confrontation at sea dominated world attention for several days, but only verbal denunciations emanated from Moscow and Peking. The Soviet Union by now placed a higher priority on its own vital interests, which it perceived to lie in the growing détente with the United States, than on the interests of North Vietnam. The Soviet-American summit took place on schedule, and the president's gamble paid off. North Vietnam now realized that it had been virtually abandoned by its own allies. The United States suddenly found itself in the anomalous position of having reached détente with 1 billion Communists—800 million Chinese and 200 million Russians—while it pursued a relentless war against a small peasant country precisely because it was Communist.

In July the Paris peace talks resumed and troop withdrawal continued. On October 26, in a dramatic announcement, Kissinger predicted that "peace was at hand." This preelection optimism proved premature. Early in December Kissinger's "final talks" with the North Vietnamese were broken off, and he reported a stalemate.

On December 18 Nixon ordered all-out bombing attacks on Hanoi and Haiphong. Millions of tons of explosives were dropped on the North. The fierce intensity and relentlessness of the attacks produced an outcry of protest against "terror bombings" from many parts of the world. The raids were halted on December 30, and the Paris talks once again resumed. On January 23, 1973, after almost three decades of war in Indochina, a cease-fire was finally reached. The Paris Accords provided for the withdrawal of all American troops and military advisers, an exchange of prisoners, consultations between South and North Vietnam on general elections, new supervisory machinery, and the withdrawal of all foreign troops from Laos and Cambodia.

Essentially, what was achieved in Paris in 1973 was Vietnam's reversion to its status at the time of the 1954 Geneva Accords. The United States had come full circle in Vietnam, and the clock was turned back twenty years. There was an Orwellian irony to the situation. Progress was regress: 1954 by 1973.

The hope, after the withdrawal of American troops, was that South Vietnam would be able to defend itself against the North with military and financial assistance from the United States. For two years that American hope seemed justified, but then the dam broke. In the spring of 1975 the Khmer Rouge, the Communist insurgents in Cambodia, marched into the capital, Phnom Penh, and forced Marshal Lon Nol, Cambodia's American-supported president, to flee the country. Thus the American "incursion" of 1970 finally produced the opposite of what it had intended: a Communist instead of neutralist Cambodia. At the same time, the South Vietnamese army lost its fighting spirit and collapsed entirely. In a matter of weeks almost all of South Vietnam fell to the Communists. In the United States a test of wills took place between the administration of President Gerald R. Ford, who favored continued military aid to Cambodia and South Vietnam, and the Congress, which became increasingly reluctant to cooperate. Ultimately, the United States was left with the humanitarian responsibility of rescuing terror-stricken refugees who were fleeing the advancing North Vietnamese armies. In April Saigon surrendered to the Communists and was renamed Ho Chi Minh City. Twenty years of American effort had ended in failure. As Rusk, one of the main architects of American Vietnam policy during the 1960s, put it in April 1975: "Personally, I made two mistakes. I underestimated the tenacity of the North Vietnamese and overestimated the patience of the American people."[46]

By the mid-1970s both the supporters and the critics of the Vietnam war in the United States tended to regard the second Indochina war as one of the most terrible episodes in the history of American foreign policy. There was a general consensus that it would take a long time for the wounds to heal, both in Indochina and in the United States.

Conclusion

The American involvement in Indochina began almost imperceptibly, rather like a mild toothache. At the end, it ran through Vietnam and America like a pestilence. Each president based his policies on exaggerated fears and, later, on exaggerated hopes. Consequently, each president left the problem to his successor in worse shape than he had found it.

The United States dropped more than 7 million tons of bombs on Indochina. This is eighty times the amount that was dropped on Britain during World War II and equal to more than three hundred of the atomic bombs that fell on Japan in 1945. The bombs left 20 million craters that ranged from 20 to 50 feet wide and 5 to 20 feet deep. After the bombardments much of Vietnam looked like a moonscape. Nothing will grow there for generations.

America too was in anguish over the war. The country's leadership lost the respect of an entire generation, and universities were disrupted, careers blighted, and the economy bloated by war inflation.

The metal caskets in which 58,000 Americans returned from Vietnam became the symbol of the war's ultimate and only meaning.

In historical perspective, the great unanswered question about Vietnam will probably be: Which would have been less costly, an earlier Communist victory or the agony of this war? One cannot help but wonder what might have happened if not one American soldier had reached Indochina. Since history does not present alternatives, one cannot know where this road not taken might have led. Vietnam might well have gone Communist much earlier. But its form of Communism would probably have been of the Titoist variety, combining a strong dose of nationalism with a fierce tradition of independence vis-à-vis both Moscow and Peking. The United States could certainly have lived with that outcome. Its postponement was hardly worth the sacrifice of more than 58,000 American lives, hundreds of thousands of Vietnamese lives, and $150 billion.

The Khmer Rouge Communist government of Cambodia, led by Pol Pot, posed a different challenge. After this regime came to power in 1975, an estimated 1 million Cambodians were systematically murdered. Cities were emptied and some 4 million people were forced into the countryside on long marches. Survivors were herded into agricultural communes, and all vestiges of previous Cambodian society were eradicated. Money, wages, and commerce were abolished, and travel and contact with the outside world were forbidden. The slightest infraction was punishable by torture and death.

The end of this story was not without irony. In 1978 Vietnam, now a Communist nation backed by the Soviet Union, invaded and virtually dismembered Cambodia, which was receiving the support of China. The genocide of the Cambodian killing fields thus was ended not through moral pressures brought to bear by an outraged humanity, but through the power interests of the Sino-Soviet conflict. Very soon after the American withdrawal from Vietnam the only wars in Asia were fought by Communists against other Communists. As the twentieth century drew to a close, Communism the world over was in full retreat. Even Communist Vietnam was busy trading with the United States, and Ho Chi Minh City was full of Americans looking for new business opportunities. The reasons for the outbreak of the Vietnam war had become almost irrelevant. History had simply passed it by. When considered in this perspective, the awesome truth about Vietnam is clear: It was in vain that combatants and civilians had suffered, the land had been devastated, and the dead had died.

NOTES

1. Bernard B. Fall, *The Two Vietnams* (New York: Praeger, 1964), p. 82.
2. Victor Bator, *Vietnam: A Diplomatic Tragedy* (Dobbs Ferry, N.Y.: Oceana Publications, 1956), p. 206.
3. U.S. House Foreign Affairs Subcommittee on World Communism, *China and U.S. Far East Policy, 1946–1966,* 80th Cong., 2nd sess. (1967), p. 45.
4. Andrew W. Green, "Are You a Middle of the Roader?" *Plain Talk* (April 1949), p. 35.
5. Policy statement by Ambassador Loy W. Henderson, *Department of State Bulletin* (April 10, 1950), p. 565.
6. Miriam S. Farley, *United States Relations with Southeast Asia with Special Reference to Indochina* (New York: Institute of Pacific Relations, 1955), p. 4.
7. U.S. Department of State, Office of Public Affairs, *Background* (Washington, D.C.: Government Printing Office, October 1951).
8. U.S. Department of State, Statement by Robert E. Hoey, officer in charge of Vietnam-Laos-Cambodia affairs, Press Release No. 178, March 8, 1952.
9. *United States Relations,* p. 4.
10. John Foster Dulles, cited in *Vietnam,* p. 210.
11. Dwight D. Eisenhower, *Mandate for Change 1953–1956* (Garden City, N.Y.: Doubleday, 1963), p. 167. Italics added.
12. Richard M. Nixon, quoted in Chalmers M. Roberts, "The Day We Didn't Go to War," *The Reporter,* September 14, 1954.
13. *Two Vietnams,* p. 90.
14. Melvin Gurtov, *The First Vietnam Crisis* (New York: Columbia University Press, 1967), p. 14.
15. Robert Guillain, *La Fin des Illusions: Notes d'Indochine* (Paris: Centre d'Etudes de Politique Etrangère, 1954), p. 39.
16. *First Vietnam Crisis,* p. 15.
17. *Mandate for Change,* p. 372.
18. David Halberstam, *The Best and the Brightest* (New York: Random House, 1972), p. 124.
19. Ibid., p. 133.
20. Ibid., p. 135.
21. Ibid.
22. Ibid., p. 174.
23. Arthur Schlesinger, Jr., *A Thousand Days* (Boston: Houghton Mifflin, 1965), p. 371.
24. *Best and the Brightest,* p. 183.
25. Ibid., p. 207.
26. Ibid., p. 292.

27. Max Frankel, "The Lessons of Vietnam," in *The Pentagon Papers* (New York: Quadrangle, 1971), p. 644.
28. *Best and the Brightest,* p. 350.
29. "Lessons of Vietnam," p. 249.
30. Ibid., p. 263.
31. Anthony Austin, *The President's War* (Philadelphia: Lippincott, 1971), passim.
32. *Best and the Brightest,* p. 414.
33. Ibid., p. 424.
34. Ibid., p. 528.
35. Ibid., p. 572.
36. Stewart Alsop, cited in "Lessons of Vietnam," p. 650.
37. *Best and the Brightest,* p. 627.
38. Ibid., p. 624.
39. Ibid., p. 633.
40. David Halberstam, *Ho* (New York: Random House, 1971), p. 12.
41. Ibid., p. 83.
42. Richard N. Goodwin, *Remembering America* (Boston: Little, Brown, 1988).
43. *New York Times,* July 24, 1973.
44. Ibid.
45. *Washington Post,* January 28, 1973.
46. Interview on ABC television, April 3, 1975.

SELECTED BIBLIOGRAPHY

BERMAN, WILLIAM C. *William Fulbright and the Vietnam War.* Kent, Ohio: Kent State University Press, 1988.
BUI, TIN. *From Enemy to Friend: A North Vietnamese Perspective on the War.* Annapolis, Md.: Naval Institute Press, 2002.
ELLSBERG, DANIEL. *Secrets: A Memoir of Vietnam and the Pentagon Papers.* New York: Viking, 2002.
FALL, BERNARD B. *The Two Vietnams.* New York: Praeger, 1964.
FITZGERALD, FRANCES. *Fire in the Lake.* Boston: Little, Brown, 1972.
GOODWIN, RICHARD N. *Remembering America.* Boston: Little, Brown, 1988.
HALBERSTAM, DAVID. *The Best and the Brightest.* New York: Random House, 1972.
HANNAH, NORMAN B. *The Key to Failure: Laos and the Vietnam War.* Lanham, Md.: Madison Books, 1987.
KARNOW, STANLEY. *Vietnam.* New York: Penguin, 1984.
KISSINGER, HENRY. *Crisis: The Anatomy of Two Major Foreign Policy Crises.* New York: Simon & Schuster, 2003.
KISSINGER, HENRY. *Ending the Vietnam War: A History of America's Involvement in and Extrication from the Vietnam War.* New York: Simon & Schuster, 2003.
KISSINGER, HENRY. "The Long Shadow of Vietnam," *Newsweek,* May 1, 2000.
KISSINGER, HENRY. *White House Years.* Boston: Little, Brown, 1979.
LAMB, DAVID. *Vietnam, Now: A Reporter Returns.* New York: PublicAffairs, 2002.
MCALISTER, JOHN T. *Vietnam: The Origins of Revolution.* New York: Knopf, 1969.
MCNAMARA, ROBERT S. *In Retrospect.* New York: Times Books, 1995.

NGUYEN, CAO KY, and MARTIN J. WOLF. *Buddha's Child: My Fight to Save Vietnam.* New York: St. Martin's, 2002.

ROTTER, ANDREW J. *The Path to Vietnam: Origins of the American Commitment to Southeast Asia.* Ithaca, N.Y.: Cornell University Press, 1988.

SHEEHAN, NEIL. *A Bright Shining Lie: John Paul Vann and America in Vietnam.* New York: Random House, 1988.

STOESSINGER, JOHN G. *Henry Kissinger: The Anguish of Power.* New York: Norton, 1976.

STOESSINGER, JOHN G. *Crusaders and Pragmatists: Movers of Modern American Foreign Policy.* New York: Norton, 1985.

Republics Still Part of Yugoslavia

Secessionist Republics

Autonomous and Formerly Autonomous Areas in Serbia

Areas with Serbian Majorities in 1991

MAP 6   Yugoslavia and the Breakaway Republics, 1991

5

From Sarajevo to Kosovo: The War over the Remains of Yugoslavia

In June 1914, a Serb nationalist, Gavrilo Princip, steps out of the shadows of a side street in Sarajevo and shoots to death Franz Ferdinand, the successor to the throne of the Austro-Hungarian empire. This shot lights the fuse that starts World War I. Eighty years later, two young lovers meet on a bridge in Sarajevo to plan their escape from the besieged and war-torn city in order to marry and live a normal life. Two shots ring out. A Serb sniper has hit his target. The youngsters die, entwined in each other's arms.

To hell with the future! Let's get on with the past!
Overheard in a Belgrade café, August 1999

The Yugoslav tragedy frames the twentieth century like bookends. The country rose from the ashes of Austro-Hungary as the Kingdom of the Serbs, Croats, and Slovenes, later changed to Yugoslavia by King Alexander. The king, unable to resolve the rivalries among his three nationalities, was killed by an assassin's bullet in 1934. In 1941 the Nazis occupied Yugoslavia, and during their rule, three resistance movements sprang up which fought each other with as much ferocity as they fought the Nazis: Croat nationalists called "Ustashes," who engaged in massacres of non-Croatians; Serb nationalists called "Chetniks," who committed similar atrocities against non-Serbs; and finally, the Communist partisans who, while killing their political opponents, concentrated mainly on fighting the

German occupiers. Their leader, Josip Broz, was a locksmith. He was half-Serb, half-Croat, and in 1945, under the name of Tito, he emerged as undisputed victor and dictator of Yugoslavia. Tito was to rule Yugoslavia until his death in 1980. His solution to his country's endless ethnic rivalries was simple: Loyalty to him was all that mattered. He was a charismatic person, a mixture of guerrilla leader, rebel against Stalin, and ultimately world-renowned statesman. He simply papered over ethnic strife with the slogan "Brotherhood and Unity." Nationalism, whether Croat or Serb, or any other for that matter, was punishable with exile, prison, or even death.

Under his "Tito Constitution" of 1974, Yugoslavia was a federal state consisting of six equal republics and two autonomous regions within the republic of Serbia. The six republics were Slovenia, a Catholic Slavic region in the northwest; Croatia in the west, the second-largest republic and also Slavic and Catholic; Bosnia and Herzegovina (hereinafter called Bosnia), multiethnic with a Moslem plurality; Montenegro, a small Slavic Orthodox Christian entity; Macedonia, multiethnic and Orthodox Christian; and Serbia, Slavic and Orthodox Christian and the largest republic in the nation. The two Serb autonomous regions were Kosovo in the south, which had a Moslem Albanian majority, and Vojvodina in the north with a strong Hungarian minority. Tito conducted this ethnic and religious cacophony with a blend of diplomatic skill and occasional brutality. His leadership remained unquestioned throughout his long reign. As long as his subjects remained loyal to his vision of Yugoslavia, they could travel freely, enjoy the most prosperous economy in the Communist orbit, and thumb their noses at Stalin, Khrushchev, and Brezhnev, a not inconsiderable privilege in those days of Soviet power.

The lava erupted from the Yugoslav volcano almost immediately after Tito's death. It began, not surprisingly, in the Serb region of Kosovo, one of the autonomous regions. In March 1981 Albanian Moslem students touched off demonstrations demanding a larger political role for their compatriots. Anti-Serb rallies became so massive that the Yugoslav army had to intervene. Unrest continued to simmer until it boiled over again in 1987, this time much more fiercely. The Yugoslav president at the time was Ivan Stambolic, a conciliatory figure who abhorred the confrontations with the Albanians. He presided over an unwieldy collective federal presidency left behind by Tito. It consisted of the presidents of the six republics and the leaders of the two autonomous regions. Stambolic had been in Kosovo before, but this time he decided to send in his place his friend and protégé of twenty-five years: Slobodan Milosevic. "Be careful, keep a cool head," he advised his younger friend.[1] This cavalier decision was to cost Stambolic his job and launch Milosevic on a career of conquest and aggression in the name of a Greater Serbia.

Slobodan Milosevic had grown up during World War II in the shadow of death and betrayal. Both of his parents had committed suicide. He found refuge with his wife Mira and in the cause of Serbian nationalism.

In 1389 Kosovo was the site of an epic battle between Serbs and Ottoman Turks. The Serbs lost and lived for five centuries under Ottoman domination. To a Serb nationalist like Milosevic, Kosovo was sacred ground despite, or perhaps because of, the large number of Albanians living there. After all, the Albanians were Moslems, only a step removed from the hated Turkish oppressors. Now, almost six hundred years later, Slobodan Milosevic stepped on the balcony of Kosovo's city hall and saw Albanians hurling rocks at Serbs. "No one should dare to beat you," he screamed. "This is your land; these are your houses, your memories. You should stay here for the sake of your ancestors and descendants."[2] The Serbs below started chanting, "Slobo, Slobo," and began to attack the Albanians, who fled from the square in disarray. Milosevic returned to Belgrade a changed man. The Yugoslav Communist had become a Serb nationalist. "Milosevic was transformed, set afire by Kosovo," said Ivan Stambolic, shaking his head.[3] The Serb president's concern was justified: He would be ousted from the presidency by his best friend within six months.

Milosevic was gradually becoming the most visible and most dynamic political figure in Yugoslavia. Like other demagogues before him, he used the weapon of the mass rally. As he traveled throughout Serbia seeking support for his Kosovo policy, Serbs turned out to cheer him by the hundreds of thousands. When the Albanians organized rallies of their own, Milosevic broke them up with riot police. By late 1988, the Kosovo Assembly was firmly under Milosevic's control. Encouraged by this successful act of subjugation, Milosevic took on the Hungarian minority in the northern region of Vojvodina. Using the time-honored technique of agents provocateurs, he had his followers splash the Vojvodina Assembly with bottles of yogurt, a popular Hungarian food. Shortly after this "Yogurt Revolution," Vojvodina's autonomy, like that of Kosovo's before it, was ended.

Next on Milosevic's agenda was Montenegro, Yugoslavia's smallest republic. Three huge rallies broke the back of the Montenegro regime. Serb sympathies ran deep in the Montenegro mountains and, besides, Milosevic was a native of Montenegro. By now, his power extended beyond the borders of Serbia, and for the first time, the leaders of the other republics became concerned. By abolishing the autonomy of Kosovo and Vojvodina and by bringing Montenegro under his control, the Serb leader now controlled half the votes of post-Tito Yugoslavia's collective head of state. In effect, he had a veto power over any decision to be taken by the federal government of Yugoslavia. By 1989 Slobodan Milosevic was the most powerful political figure in the federation.

The Dismemberment of Yugoslavia Begins

Milosevic's rise to power was watched by the other republics with growing apprehension. Not only was there increasing concern over Serbia's roughshod treatment of its own provinces and of neighboring Montenegro, but even more concern over Milosevic's creeping infiltration of Yugoslav federal institutions. By 1989, for example, most of the generals in the Yugoslav army were Serbs. And Yugoslavia's prime minister, Ante Markovic, a competent economist who managed to bring the Yugoslav currency to the threshold of convertibility, was driven to complete exasperation by Milosevic's hysterical mass rallies. It had become clear that the Serb leader's ambitions extended far beyond Serbia. His goal was to take over all of Yugoslavia, as a successor to Tito.

Slovenia was the first to respond. The northwestern republic was the most prosperous in Yugoslavia. Sharing a border with Austria and Italy, it was also the freest. Its capital, Ljubljana, was a center of open political and intellectual debate. While Slovenes did not look for secession right away, they did reject a Serb-dominated Yugoslavia. They were also deeply affected by the collapse of Communism in the rest of Eastern Europe. Hence, a Communist-dominated Yugoslavia was equally repugnant. What they yearned for was a democratic Slovenia on the model of Austria or Italy.

Milosevic tried to apply his strong-arm methods in Slovenia. In December 1989 he organized a mass rally of Serbs in Ljubljana, but Slovene authorities canceled it at the last minute. Milosevic, infuriated, forced a showdown with the Slovenes in January 1990 at a hastily convened Communist Party Congress in Belgrade. There, the Slovenes, following Gorbachev's lead in the disintegrating Soviet Union, demanded pluralism and democracy throughout Yugoslavia. When Milosevic, who was now officially president of Serbia, rejected these proposals out of hand, the Slovene delegates simply walked out. They never returned. Instead, they announced an election in sovereign Slovenia for April 1990. Thus the Slovene republic, frightened and repulsed by Milosevic's Serbia, was the first to secede from the federation. A defiant opponent of Milosevic, Milan Kucan, became Slovenia's first president and promptly gave up his Communist party membership. The dismemberment of Tito's Yugoslavia had begun.

Croatia was next, but its process of secession was far more complex. Unlike Slovenia, Croatia descended into violence and war. There is a reason for this difference. Slovenia's population was relatively homogeneous with no large ethnic minorities in active opposition. Croatia, on the other hand, was home to a large minority of Serbs, most of whom were concentrated in the Krajina, an area which constituted almost one-third of Croatia's territory. Milosevic reminded the Krajina Serbs of atrocities committed by the Ustashe Croats during World War II and whipped them into a nationalist frenzy. By late 1990, the Krajina Serbs demanded autonomy from Croatia and union with Serbia.

The leader of Croatia, Franjo Tudjman, was an ardent nationalist with no love lost for the Serbs. Under Tito's dictatorship, he had been jailed for speaking out publicly in favor of an independent Croat state. And in 1990, when the Serbs announced a referendum on autonomy, Tudjman promptly declared it illegal. The showdown between the Serbs and Croats in Croatia took place in Knin, a Serb township in the center of the Krajina. When the Serbs surrounded the Croat-controlled police station, the chief of police lost his nerve. "Let's promise them anything," he said, "as long as we get out of here alive. These are Chetniks! You don't know what that means—they'll hang us!"[4]

Milosevic, who had masterminded the showdown, emerged triumphant once again. But Knin was to be his last bloodless victory. The Krajina Serbs, emboldened by their success, now began a process that has already gone down in history as "ethnic cleansing." Their first victim was Kijevo, a Croat village in the Serb-held Krajina, an enclave within an enclave. It was an irritant to the Serbs who decided to erase it from the map.

The power behind this first experiment in "ethnic cleansing" was a Serb lieutenant who had been posted to Knin in the summer of 1991. His name was Ratko Mladic. Like his role model Slobodan Milosevic, Mladic had been shaped by World War II and was orphaned at the age of two. His father had been killed while participating in a partisan raid on the home village of a Croat Ustashe leader. Mladic's enthusiasm for the Serbian cause inspired the Krajina Serbs with a fanatical loyalty. On August 26, 1991, the village of Kijevo was leveled in a brutal artillery bombardment. Serb troops tore down the signpost in Latin script at the entrance of the village. Four years later, Croats would rip down the same signpost.[5] (The Serbo-Croatian language is written by the Serbs in Cyrillic script.)

A few weeks later, the Krajina Serbs tried to "cleanse" a larger Croat community, the town of Vukovar. But here they encountered fierce resistance: It took thousands of troops brought in from Serbia proper to finish the job. And when the Serbs tried to annex the ancient port city of Dubrovnik, the Croat defenders of the medieval fortress were able to stand their ground. Thus by the end of 1991, Tudjman's Croatia had withstood the Serb assault and gained its independence, but a Serb fifth column now controlled one-third of his country. It was a heavy price to pay for sovereignty. Almost forgotten in the ruins of the Serbo-Croat war, the nation called Yugoslavia had virtually ceased to exist.

The atrocities of the war in Croatia also triggered the first of many interventions from abroad. First, the European Community (EC), under German pressure, recognized Croatia's sovereignty in order to enhance its status vis-à-vis Serbia. But the EC was unable to negotiate a truce. Second, the United Nations intervened under the aegis of former United States Secretary of State Cyrus Vance, who achieved a short-lived truce. This enabled the UN Security Council to authorize a UN Protection Force (UNPROFOR), which, in early 1992, acted as a buffer between the warring parties. But by the time the UN troops arrived, the deed was done and the UN was unable to turn back the clock. All the blue helmets could do was to patrol the new boundaries resulting from the Serbian incursions into Croat territory. Hence, in a tragic and unintended way, the UNPROFOR, far from protecting the victim, all but ratified the acts of the aggressor. Under President George Bush, the United States remained out of the fray in the belief that the collapse of Yugoslavia was a European, not American, problem.

The War in Bosnia

After Slovenia and Croatia had achieved their independence, the situation in Bosnia grew ever more precarious. Unlike Slovenia and Croatia, Bosnia was a truly multiethnic state with close to half its population Moslem, one-third Serb, and the remainder Croat. The three groups were completely intermingled, which made the drawing of any border almost impossible. The capital, Sarajevo, host city to the 1984 Olympics, was famous for its mixture of different cultures and religions. Bosnia's president Alija Izetbegovic, a prominent intellectual with a law degree, liked to compare Bosnia to the skin of a leopard, with each spot a different group.

Bosnian Moslems had converted during the Ottoman era and, because of their culture and religion, considered themselves a separate people.[6] Croat and Serb nationalists, however, claimed that the Bosnians were in effect Serbs or Croats who, in the course of five centuries of Ottoman occupation, had decided to convert to Islam. After all, their language was Serbo-Croatian. This latter view became a welcome rationale for aggression against Bosnia's Moslems. When Serbs and Croats were on speaking terms, their favorite topic was the partition of Bosnia between them.

With Slovenia and Croatia both independent, Bosnian President Izetbegovic faced a terrible choice of either following in Croatia's footsteps and seeking EC recognition of its sovereignty or remaining in a Serb-dominated rump Yugoslavia. Both roads would lead to the same disastrous end: conflict with Serbia. Izetbegovic chose to cast his lot with the EC in the desperate hope that the Western Europeans would guarantee Bosnia's independence by force of arms. On April 6, 1992, the EC did indeed recognize Bosnia as a sovereign state. The United States followed suit the next day. Neither, however, extended guarantees of any kind. The new state was on its own.

For the Bosnian Serbs this meant war. Their leader, Radovan Karadzic, had a Montenegro peasant background and was the first in several generations of his family to receive an education. He became, of all things, a psychiatrist, but this accomplishment did not prevent him from falling under the spell of Slobodan Milosevic. If Bosnia were recognized as a sovereign state, he threatened, it would be stillborn. Karadzic proclaimed a new state called the Serbian Republic of Bosnia, with Sarajevo—for the moment under enemy occupation—as its capital. He himself would serve as president.

Karadzic was as good as his word. Almost overnight Sarajevo was transformed from a luminous European capital into a labyrinth of roadblocks and barricades, haunted by masked gunmen and murderous snipers. There was a glimmer of hope in the air, however, on that fateful April morning. Thousands of ordinary Sarajevo citizens of all nationalities walked toward the city center in protest against the ethnic division of a city that for hundreds of years had been a symbol of tolerance and coexistence. A young journalist from Reuters news agency was among them, and his recollections of the first casualty of war in Sarajevo are worth quoting in full:

> We were there because we thought there was still time to change people's minds, to save Sarajevo and Bosnia as a place where Muslims, Serbs and Croats could live together as they had for 500 years.
>
> Late in the morning several thousand of us decided to make our way to one of the barricades on the other side of the Vrbanja bridge, behind the parliament tower.
>
> The idea was to cross the bridge to Grbavica, to show that the city still belonged to the people—all the people.
>
> Many people will tell you now that they saw the war coming then, but I didn't and I don't think Suada did either. For Suada, a Muslim from the lovely city of Dubrovnik on Croatia's Adriatic Coast, the issue was more than abstract.
>
> Her parents had been trapped in Dubrovnik since October of 1991 when Serbs laid siege to the city during their war with Croatia. Refugees in their own town, they had been driven from their home by relentless Serb shelling and were living in an hotel.
>
> As a medical student scheduled to graduate in May Suada could easily have stayed away from the demonstration that day. She wasn't from Sarajevo. She wasn't even Bosnian. But my friend was outraged by the division of a city she had come to know and love over five years of schooling. And her family was already paying a price for the kind of ethnic hatred that lay behind the barricades.

It was not an angry crowd. I remember Suada standing there that morning with her blonde hair and sparkling blue eyes, laughing. The people around us, most of them young, were good-humored and eager to make their point in a peaceful way.

I was about fifty meters from the bridge when a few shots—maybe five or six—rang out. Everybody began to run.

Once we got to cover behind a building I was incredibly angry. It had never occurred to me that someone would open fire on a group of unarmed demonstrators.

Strange to say, war still didn't seem inevitable. It was only a few days later that there seemed no turning back, that we began to speak of Suada as the person killed in the Bosnian war.

What had seemed a random act of violence, a great personal tragedy, slowly took shape in our minds as the first incident in a far greater drama: Europe's worst war in fifty years.[7]

At this critical juncture, the world was witness to a remarkable individual initiative. Elie Wiesel, the Nobel Peace Prize laureate, went to Sarajevo and called for a peace conference there with the leading heads of state as well as the presidents of the former Yugoslavia. In addition, he approached the Bush administration with the recommendation to convene an International War Crimes Tribunal to bring war criminals to justice. His proposals were prophetic and were to be adopted in their essence three years and tens of thousands of lives later in Dayton, Ohio, and at the Hague.[8] But for the moment, his pleas for peace were ignored by the combatants. Instead, the Serbs began their siege of Sarajevo.

The long Serbian siege of Sarajevo was without a doubt the most widely publicized event of the war in Bosnia. In the words of a leading journalist, "a European city was being reduced to nothing: Carthage in slow motion, but this time with an audience and a videotaped record."[9] This might have been a deliberate strategy thought out by Radovan Karadzic and his military counterpart, Ratko Mladic. While the attention of the media was focused on Sarajevo, the two men pursued a relentless policy of "ethnic cleansing" all over Bosnia that, by the end of 1992, had cost 100,000 Bosnian lives and had driven 2 million people—almost half the population of Bosnia—from their homes.[10]

The brutality of this operation compels comparison with the Nazis' treatment of the Jews. Concentration camps, starvation, physical and mental torture, and mass executions were commonplace throughout Bosnia. Even rape of Bosnian women was policy because it made them unacceptable to their men; hence there would be no Bosnian progeny. An enormous refugee exodus overwhelmed a stunned UN High Commissioner for Refugees (UNHCR) that tried desperately to provide minimal aid to the legions of homeless people. Since the United Nations was unable to reverse or even stop the "cleansing" operation, it frequently found itself in the role of a reluctant collaborator.

By early 1993 Karadzic and Mladic had brought two-thirds of Bosnia under Serb control. Only Sarajevo was holding out and, with it, two enclaves in eastern Bosnia: the towns of Srebrenica and Gorazde. With this unfinished business out of the way, most of Bosnia, with the exception of territory under Croat control, would be ethnically "pure" for the Serbs. "We are the winners," Milosevic exclaimed triumphantly on a flight to London, where he planned to attend a conference on Bosnia hastily arranged by Lord Peter Owen of Great Britain, a top mediator, and Secretary-General Boutros Boutros-Ghali of the United Nations.[11]

While Milosevic was in London, Karadzic and Mladic, his two minions in Bosnia, began to apply pressure on Srebrenica, once a lovely city in the Drina Valley. In March UNPROFOR commander Phillipe Morillon was informed that the "Serb offensive was about to begin and that the Moslems in Srebrenica were virtually defenseless, with thousands dying of starvation." Morillon, in a futile gesture, made his way to the besieged town and made a public promise which he never had the power to keep: "I will never abandon you."[12] The guilt over this empty promise was to haunt him for years. In April Mladic extended an ultimatum to the 30,000 Moslems of Srebrenica via the UNHCR. "Either they surrender or you get all the Moslems out of Srebrenica. Else we take the town in two days."[13] The top UNHCR official in the town acquiesced with deep repugnance. "I prefer thirty thousand evacuees to thirty thousand bodies; we have to save their lives," he said helplessly.[14] Thus the most extensive single act of "ethnic cleansing" in Bosnia was carried out by the United Nations, under the moral blackmail of the Bosnian Serb leadership. On April 5, 1993, Srebrenica surrendered. Larry Hollingworth, a British UNHCR field officer gave vent to his feelings, which were broadcast and printed all over the world.

My first thought was for the commander who gave the order to attack. I hope he burns in the hottest corner of hell. My second thought was for the soldiers who loaded the breaches and fired the guns. I hope their sleep is forever punctuated by the screams of the children and the cries of their mothers. My third thought was for Dr. of Medicine, Karadzic, the Professor of literature, Koljevic, the Biologist, Mrs. Plavsic, and the geologist, Professor Lukic. And I wonder, will they condemn this atrocity? Or will they betray their education and condone it? And I thought of the many Serbs that I know around this country, and I wondered: do they want the history of the Serb nation to include this chapter, a chapter in which their army drove innocent people from village to village to village until finally they are cornered in Srebrenica, a place from which there is no escape, and where their fate is to be transported out like cattle, or slaughtered like sheep?[15]

Apparently, as the Nazis had demonstrated, education was no barrier to inhumanity.

On April 16, in a classic example of closing the stable door too late, the UN Security Council declared Srebrenica, Tuzla, Zepa, Gorazde, and Sarajevo as "safe areas." This was a misnomer, to put it mildly. The "safe areas" were probably among the most dangerous places on earth. Many of the Moslem refugees "cleansed" by the Serbs sought refuge in the Croatian part of Bosnia and even in Croatia itself. This led to desperate fighting between Moslems and Croatians. General Mladic was, of course, delighted. "I will watch them destroy each other and then I will push them both into the sea," he commented gleefully.[16]

It was a bomb that landed in Sarajevo's market square on February 5, 1994, that finally prompted the international community to rouse itself from its inertia and try to intervene. The mortar, most likely of Serbian origin, killed sixty-nine people and left over two hundred wounded. Given the fact that over 10,000 Sarajevans had died as victims of Serb bombardment, the "marketplace bomb" was just another disaster in a seemingly endless chain. But this one was highly visible and hence of great symbolic value. It finally made the Western powers stand up to the Bosnian Serbs, albeit with agonizing slowness. The NATO powers, led by the United States and France, issued an ultimatum to the Serbs, requiring them to withdraw their heavy weapons from the outskirts of the city within ten days or be subject to air strikes by NATO warplanes. The Serbs dragged their feet but finally complied when President Boris Yeltsin of Russia promised to send Russian peacekeepers under UN auspices to the areas from which the Serbs had withdrawn. Thus NATO hardly scored a victory, but Yeltsin scored a diplomatic triumph. Yet, Karadzic remained unfazed. Although his big guns were silent for the moment, the Serb encirclement of Sarajevo remained intact. He knew he held a trump card in his pocket: Gorazde.

The city of Gorazde was the final enclave to be "cleansed" of Moslems. Since it separated two chunks of Serb-held territory, it was of greater strategic importance than Srebrenica. Mladic began a tank assault on April 10, 1994, hoping for a rerun of Srebrenica, but he encountered stiffer resistance. Sir Michael Rose, commander of UNPROFOR, warned Mladic to stop or face NATO air strikes. Undeterred, Mladic pressed on. After securing approval from both NATO and UN Headquarters, Rose authorized the first NATO air assault. Mladic was still persistent. Rose ordered yet more strikes, but Mladic was now at the outskirts of Gorazde. He called Rose and screamed that no UN official would leave Serb territory alive. On April 15 the Serbs began their final assault and captured the strategic heights around Gorazde. Ratko Mladic had achieved his own war aims in Bosnia.

The NATO council squabbled in Brussels with the Americans demanding more air strikes, which the British found incompatible with the neutrality of UNPROFOR. Instead, they chided the Americans for refusing to commit ground troops.

President Izetbegovic wrote a desperate letter to UN Secretary-General Boutros Boutros-Ghali: "The so-called safe area has become the most unsafe place in the world. . . . If Gorazde falls, I think that a sense of responsibility would commend you to leave the post of UN Secretary-General. This is the least you can do."[17] And in a speech to a crowd in Sarajevo he spoke of self-reliance. "We have learned our lesson," he exclaimed. "And the lesson is: we have to be strong because in the world only force is respected."[18]

Boutros Boutros-Ghali never responded. He had been to Sarajevo only once, on December 31, 1992. On that occasion, he had astonished the Sarajevans by admonishing them: "I understand your frustration, but you have a situation that is better than ten other places in the world. . . . I can give you a list."[19] Fred Cuny, a dedicated relief worker from Texas with vast experience in Bosnia, had formed a very low opinion of UNPROFOR by 1994. "If the

UN had been around in 1939," he quipped, "we would all be speaking German."[20]

It is no doubt true that Bosnia was not one of the UN's proudest moments. Yet one should not confuse the UN workers in Bosnia, many of whom were tireless and dedicated, with the UN Security Council in New York. For two years the great powers, including the United States, refused to act. And when they finally did, it was almost too late.

The Tide Turns against the Serbs

By the summer of 1994, Slobodan Milosevic had run out of worlds to conquer. He was the undisputed leader of Serbia as well as Montenegro and, through his faithful henchmen Karadzic and Mladic, had carved out huge areas of Croatia and Bosnia for "ethnically pure" Serbs to settle in. The time had come to consolidate his victories and perhaps even make peace, provided, of course, it was on his own terms.

The latest peace plan on the table was proposed by the so-called Contact Group, comprising the United States, Great Britain, Russia, France, and Germany. The five powers advanced a plan that would earmark 51 percent of Bosnia for a Moslem-Croat Federation and 49 percent for the Serbs. Milosevic, convinced that Karadzic and Mladic would find the proposal unacceptable, pretended to be flexible in his negotiations with the Contact Group. This, predictably, infuriated the two Bosnian Serbs, who promptly fell into Milosevic's trap. They now looked like warmongers while he appeared as a peacemaker. Milosevic had reached the conclusion after Gorazde that Karadzic and Mladic had outlived their usefulness; it was time for them to step into the shadows so that he could shine in the limelight. But his action was widely perceived among Bosnian Serbs as a dagger in their back. To get rid of his political rivals, Milosevic was demoralizing the Bosnian Serbs as a military fighting force. This proved to be a fatal blunder.

There were two other new developments that helped to turn the tide of war against the Serbs. While the United States itself was still unwilling to enter the war officially, retired American army officers under contract to the Croatian government taught the Croats military strategy and tactics from NATO staff college texts. This initiative greatly enhanced the combat effectiveness of the Croatian army.

The newly confident President Tudjman of Croatia now applied the old dictum that the enemy of my enemy is my friend and decided to enter into a military alliance with the Bosnians. President Izetbegovic accepted, perceiving the Croats clearly as a lesser evil than the Serbs. Help for Bosnia also came from another quite unexpected source. Iran, sensing the possibility of gaining a foothold in Europe, decided to send arms shipments to its fellow Moslems in Bosnia. With the tacit acquiescence of the United States, Iranian arms began to flow into Bosnia in late 1994 and continued to do so for a year.

Thus it came about that, in the summer of 1995, the Croats, and then the Bosnians, turned the tables on the Serb invaders. Beginning in May, a revitalized Croat army swept into the Krajina region and put the Serbs to flight. Tens of thousands of them formed endless columns of refugees, fleeing in their tractors toward Serbia. By the time the city of Knin was recaptured—four years after the Serbs had conquered it—Europe witnessed the largest forcible displacement of people since World War II.[21] Croats lined the roads, throwing rocks and spitting on the fleeing Serbs. By August the Krajina was back in Croat hands. Its fall tilted the fortunes of war decisively against the Serbs.

Throughout all this, Milosevic did nothing. He was prepared to sacrifice the Serbs in Croatia so that he could hold on to the Serb conquests in Bosnia. The strategy did not work, however. Karadzic and Mladic, in an open letter, accused Milosevic of treason and betrayal. Their army, like that in the Krajina, was overextended and their state, abandoned by their former patron, was eroding from within. A newly invigorated Bosnian army pushed the Serbs out of one-third of the territory they had occupied for three years. By the end of summer the war had come full circle.

Perhaps the most significant result of this reversal in the fortunes of war was that it brought peace nearer. In a horrible sort of way, "ethnic cleansing" had created partitions that were acceptable to the combatants. When the tide of war turned decisively in 1995, and Serbs fled toward Serbia from their enclaves in Croatia and Bosnia, the outlines of a peace settlement came into view. Croatia was now the biggest winner, and Bosnia was still the biggest loser, with Serbia somewhere in between. But all three states had managed, more or less, to "cleanse" their territories of unwelcome intruders. This, in one of the great ironies of history, made possible the peace accords of Dayton, Ohio.

The Dayton Peace Accords

In October 1995 the Bosnian army, led by its brilliant commander, Atif Dudakovic, in concert with his Croatian allies, was in hot pursuit of the fleeing Serbs. The coalition forces were only days, possibly hours, away from overrunning Banja Luka, the last significant Bosnian city still under Serb control. The allies were preparing to force the Serbs into unconditional surrender and then throw them out of Bosnia. Then on October 12, without warning, the United States demanded an immediate cease-fire. The coalition, dependent on the goodwill and support of the Americans, grudgingly complied.

Historians will long debate the wisdom of this action. General Dudakovic has much in common with General Norman Schwarzkopf, who, in 1991, was prepared to march on Baghdad but was stopped from doing so by President Bush, who believed that such a move would have exceeded the UN's mandate in Iraq. One cannot help but wonder whether private citizen George Bush may have had moments of regret when he saw television images of an arrogant Saddam Hussein ruling Iraq with an iron fist for the next decade.

In October 1995 the American argument was symmetry. The Clinton administration believed that a lasting peace was more likely to hold in Bosnia if none of the combatants was totally opposed to it and if all of them were relatively unhappy, but none unhappy enough to overturn a settlement. Hence the Bosnian Serbs had to be rescued from complete annihilation. After weeks of cajoling by the indefatigable United States Assistant Secretary of State Richard Holbrooke, the presidents of Serbia, Croatia, and Bosnia met in Dayton, Ohio, to sign a peace accord. Witnesses were officials from the United States, Britain, France, Germany, Russia, and the European Union.

The main provisions were the following: First, the accord envisioned a reconstituted single state of Bosnia with a temporary "Inter-Entity Boundary" between the Bosnian-Croat Federation and the Bosnian Serb Republic. Second, free elections throughout all of Bosnia were planned for no later than September 1996. Third, persons indicted by a Special International War Crimes Tribunal in the Hague would not be allowed to participate. Fourth, a NATO implementation force (IFOR) consisting of 60,000 men, 20,000 of whom were to be Americans, would ensure compliance and have unimpeded freedom of movement throughout Bosnia. Finally, all persons were granted the right to move freely throughout the country.

Unfortunately, the Dayton Accords were badly flawed from the beginning. The American hope to re-create a multiethnic Bosnia and a free and open Sarajevo did not reflect the realities. The terrible events of the war had left scars too deep to heal quickly. The lines of separation did not blur; they hardened. The Moslem authorities of Sarajevo, for example, confiscated tens of thousands of apartments that had belonged to Serbs and assigned them to Moslem tenants. When the returning Serbs tried to reclaim their apartments, they were told to go back to Serbia. Serbs who had remained in their homes during the war were beaten and frequently expelled. It was ethnic cleansing in reverse.[22] The Moslems also threatened to boycott the elections for the understandable reason that Karadzic and Mladic were still at large and free to affect the outcome. In the opinion of one journalist, it was as if the United States and its allies had decided to hold elections in postwar Germany with Heinrich Himmler and Adolf Eichmann still in charge of a large zone, suppressing and murdering opponents.[23] Moreover, to the dismay of the Moslems, Srebrenica was packed with Serb refugees from Sarajevo who would no doubt elect a Serb mayor and a Serb city council. They too in the Moslems' view should go back to Serbia.[24] The Croat-Moslem Federation was also fragile. Too many animosities lay buried underneath a superficial unity that was largely the result of a wartime coalition against the Serbs. The Croats in Bosnia wanted out of Bosnia and to be reunited with Croatia. In the face of all this instability and growing unrest, the Americans nonetheless insisted that elections be held on schedule. The reason was obvious: Without the presence of IFOR, the Bosnian elections would probably be a farce, and the 20,000 American troops were scheduled to be withdrawn before the end of the year. Without an American military presence on the ground, the accords were certain to unravel.

In June 1996, under American and European pressure, Serbia and Croatia, as well as the Bosnian Serbs, Croats, and Moslems, signed an agreement to limit armaments, in particular, tanks, artillery, combat vehicles, and aircraft.[25] As an additional incentive, the Americans promised that some of their troops would remain in Bosnia beyond the deadline. Despite these positive developments, however, the chances of reconstituting a truly multiethnic Bosnia remained remote.

The UN War Crimes Tribunal

Perhaps the most hopeful result of the war in Bosnia was the effort to hold murderers and rapists individually accountable for their crimes before a UN War Crimes Tribunal. As in Nuremberg in 1945, however, the judges would have to wrestle with the all-too-familiar "I took orders" defense. In the first trial before the Tribunal, a twenty-four-year-old Croat murderer of dozens of Moslem men in Srebrenica declared that "if I hadn't killed them, they [the Serbs] would have killed me."[26]

In July 1996, one year after the Serbian conquest of Srebrenica, the UN War Crimes Tribunal in the Hague issued international arrest warrants for Radovan Karadzic and Ratko Mladic. These warrants obliged member states of the United Nations to arrest the two men if they entered their countries. In addition, the Tribunal also demanded an investigation to determine whether President Slobodan Milosevic shared the responsibility for war crimes in the Bosnian conflict. In a related case, the World Court of the United Nations ruled that it had jurisdiction in the genocide case brought by Bosnia against Serbia, clearing the way for a full hearing as to whether Serbia was the aggressor in the Bosnian war.[27]

Apparently, the mounting evidence of Serb culpability in the war triggered the initiatives of these two judicial organs. In a scathing summary, Judge Claude Jorda, the chief prosecutor of the UN War Crimes Tribunal, charged that "in addition to the killing of thousands of civilians, Bosnian Serbs had destroyed 1,123 mosques, 504 Roman Catholic churches, and 5 synagogues and had also targeted cemeteries and monasteries in their effort to create purely Serbian regions."[28] The judge declared that, while some Croats and Moslems had also committed atrocities, the Serb crimes were more systematic and centrally directed. "Ethnic cleansing," the judge concluded, "was not the byproduct of the war but rather its aim."[29]

On the very day the arrest warrants were issued, investigators from the War Crimes Tribunal were working to exhume hundreds of bodies of Moslem men and boys from more than a dozen mass graves near Srebrenica. Next to the graves were spent cartridges and bullet-scarred trees, clearly showing that the victims had been lined up and shot, and then their bodies covered with dirt. A mile or so away in Srebrenica, the town's Serb residents were celebrating the first anniversary of their victory with singing and alcohol, while thousands of Moslem women whose sons and husbands had been shot were living hopelessly among the rubble. Karadzic and Mladic were at large in Pale, the Bosnian Serb capital, avowing their innocence. Karadzic sent a lawyer to the Hague and granted an interview to Barbara Walters of the American Broadcasting Company, during which he denied all the accusations of the Tribunal.

The Clinton administration tended to hold the Serbs responsible for the war from the beginning. Some American military leaders, however, disagreed. General Charles G. Boyd, the former deputy commander in chief, U.S. European command, for example, believed that all three factions were pursuing the same objective: not to be a minority. His observations in Bosnia led him to the conclusion that all parties were equally guilty of inhumanity, and that the United States was prejudiced against the Serbs. "Ethnic cleansing," in his words, "evoked condemnation only when it was committed *by* Serbs, not *against* them."[30] The commander's statement does not take into account who had started the war. By the summer of 1996, the War Crimes Tribunal, after extensive investigations, agreed with the Clinton administration's assessment and targeted Slobodan Milosevic. Not only had the Serbian president started the war, but four years later he refused or was unable to persuade his former henchmen in Bosnia, Karadzic and Mladic, to stand trial before the UN War Crimes Tribunal in the Hague. Not unlike Hitler, Milosevic had been the driving engine of aggression. And not unlike Hitler's *Gauleiters,* Karadzic and Mladic had carved out fiefdoms of their own in conquered territories.

Finally, by late July 1996, with the elections in Bosnia less than two months away, the Clinton administration had had enough. Richard Holbrooke, the architect of the Dayton Accords, went to Belgrade and threatened Milosevic with economic sanctions if he did not use his influence to remove Karadzic from power and, if possible, from Bosnia. The seasoned American diplomat came back with a somewhat hollow victory. Karadzic agreed to give up both the presidency of the Bosnian Serb Republic as well as the leadership of his political party. He flatly refused, on the other hand, to leave Bosnia, let alone give himself up to the Hague Tribunal. Most important, however, in order to ensure his continuing influence over the coming Bosnian elections, the wily Karadzic transferred his presidency to Biljana Plavsic and his party post to Momcilo Krajisnik, both of whom were as ardently nationalist and separatist as he himself was. But because these two politicians had not been indicted for war crimes, they passed, in the words of a senior White House official, "[t]he pornography test of decency."[31] Mladic had retreated into his military headquarters in Eastern Bosnia since the signing of the Dayton Accords. The form of Dayton had thus been preserved—the substance was another matter.

With Karadzic out of power, at least officially, political campaigning for the elections began immediately. No fewer than forty-seven parties and 25,000 candidates presented themselves for office. But this appearance of an almost Athenian kind of democracy was misleading. In the only precedent to date, people clearly voted along ethnic lines in a municipal election held in June in Mostar, a Bosnian city divided between Moslems and Croats. A moderate multiethnic coalition of Moslems, Croats, and Serbs led by a popular former mayor had received only 1,900 out of 58,000 votes.[32] Separation, not unity, seemed to be the voters' preference. When Momcilo Krajisnik, Karadzic's successor, was asked about the chances of restoring a multiethnic unitary Bosnia, he responded with biting sarcasm: "You can't grow bananas here," he said, "bananas may grow in Africa but not here."[33] He was not alone. His hard-line Croat and Bosnian counterparts also did their best to intimidate and even terrorize their more liberal opponents in the weeks leading up to the September elections in Bosnia.

The presidential and legislative elections scheduled for September 14, 1996, yielded no surprises. Hard-line nationalist candidates won handily in all three Bosnian enclaves—Moslem, Serb, and Croat. Momcilo Krajisnik, the Serb winner, stood for union with Serbia just as fiercely as his indicted predecessor, Radovan Karadzic, had done. His Croat counterpart, Kresimir Zubak, a disciple of Croat president Franjo Tudjman, was equally adamant about union with Croatia. And Alija Izetbegovic, the Moslem candidate, led an almost exclusively Moslem party, determined to turn Sarajevo into a Moslem city. These three men formed the joint presidency of Bosnia, envisioned under the Dayton Accords. They met stiffly and perfunctorily on September 30 for the first time in a hotel in Sarajevo, chaired by the Bosnian member of the trio. Their main achievement was an agreement to set up telephone lines among themselves, but not among the general populations of the three enclaves. Local elections were postponed until November because of "irregularities" observed by UN and European election monitors. The three-headed Bosnian presidency seemed like a throwback to the multiheaded Yugoslav presidency of the post-Tito era that had given rise to the crisis in the first place. As Henry Kissinger astutely observed, "None of the three religious groups—the Serb, Croat and Moslem—had ever accepted domination by one of the others. Occasionally obliged to yield to superior outside forces—Turkish, Austrian or Communist—they have never submitted to each other."[34] To this list of outside forces must be added IFOR, under American leadership, and its follow-up, a force of roughly 15,000 American troops authorized by the Clinton administration in 1997 to succeed IFOR and keep the peace in Bosnia.[35]

The fact remained that the United States, despite its determined effort to reconstitute a multiethnic Bosnia, ran counter to the will of most of Bosnia's population. That will still pointed toward partition, and only a massive military intervention by the United States and NATO—an unlikely event in any case—might be able to prevent it in the short run. Bosnia in the end will be much more likely to resemble Cyprus, with its clearly drawn lines of ethnic demarcation between its Greek and Turkish populations. This may be tragic, but far less so than the outbreak of yet another war.

In April 2000, at long last, NATO took a stand for justice and arrested Mr. Krajisnik, the fanatical Serb separatist, in the Bosnian town of Pale. He was immediately flown to the Hague to stand trial for genocide.

Kosovo:
The War against Europe's Last Dictator

When the tide of war turned against the war lovers of the twentieth century, they showed nothing but contempt for their own peoples. "Germany does not deserve me!" Hitler had exclaimed as the Nazi state went down in flames in 1945. When Saddam Hussein was roundly beaten in the ground war against the UN coalition in 1991, he turned his fury against the Kurdish and Shi'ite minorities inside Iraq; and when Slobodan Milosevic was chased out of Croatia and Bosnia and then lost an election in Belgrade in 1996, he decided to shore up his own power in Serbia by expelling over 1 million Albanians from

Kosovo. This was the place where he had first embarked on his course of aggression ten years earlier. It was also the place where it came to a fiery end.

The "ethnic cleansing" campaign against the Albanians in Kosovo, which Milosevic planned after his military defeats, made the earlier campaign in Bosnia look like a dress rehearsal for the main event in barbarism. Only in retrospect, after seventy-eight days of NATO air strikes had forced him to capitulate, did the ferocity and scale of his policy become clear to a world numbed by a century of inhumanity. The Serb leader's goal was the forcible expulsion of Kosovo's Albanians from homes they had occupied for generations. The exodus was to be accelerated by looting, murder, rape, arson, and terror on so vast a scale that it invited comparisons with Nazi Germany. All identification papers were to be confiscated in order to turn the Albanians into stateless nonpersons and render their return to Kosovo impossible. The only thing that Milosevic did not copy from Hitler were the gas chambers of Auschwitz. Instead, his destitute victims were to be driven into the neighboring states of Albania, Montenegro, and Macedonia. Kosovo was to be emptied of the hated Moslems and the defeat at the battle of Kosovo in 1389 was to be avenged once and for all. Surely, Milosevic calculated, this "final solution" would not only enhance his status with the Serbian people but also guarantee his continued hold on political power. The technique was all too familiar. Only the identity of the victims changed. This time they were to be the Moslems rather than the Jews.

The first victim of Serb brutality was an Albanian schoolteacher shot in his classroom near Pristina in November 1997. Twenty thousand Albanians attended his funeral. It was on that occasion that members of the Kosovo Liberation Army (KLA) made their first appearance. By February 1998, the Serb forces had escalated their campaign by burning down dozens of villages after engaging in looting and killing sprees all over the province. The desperate survivors became homeless fugitives, the forerunners of a floodtide of refugees. Not surprisingly, with every atrocity, the ranks of the KLA grew in numbers and momentum. In historical perspective, Milosevic may well appear as the unwitting chief recruiter for the KLA.

The Western response to the Serb assault at first was hesitant, if not inept. Throughout the remainder of 1998, the Contact Group, now including Italy, alternated between negotiations and the threat of NATO air strikes. Milosevic, sensing NATO's ambivalence, stepped up the ferocity of his own campaign. During that period, more than three hundred Albanian villages were destroyed and their inhabitants either killed or driven from their homes.

The West's leading negotiator was Richard Holbrooke, the same diplomat who had persuaded Milosevic to sign off on the Dayton Accords of 1995. Under these accords, Serbia had been allowed to retain its overall control of Kosovo while recognizing the region's local self-government. But as Serb atrocities became more and more outrageous, the KLA demanded complete independence for Kosovo, an option Holbrooke was unprepared to support. As the Western powers began to threaten Serbia with air strikes, this contradiction became more and more apparent. It was the tragic flaw of Holbrooke's Rambouillet peace accord, which finally fell apart in early 1999 because it still affirmed ultimate Serb control over Kosovo even though it restored its local autonomy which had been revoked by Milosevic. By then it had become illogical, not to say absurd, that NATO should threaten Serbia with air strikes while simultaneously declaring that the most it could guarantee the Kosovars was local autonomy with Milosevic continuing to rule as their ultimate master. Not surprisingly, the Serb leader perceived the Western position as a bluff, which he was quite prepared to call by escalating his own terror campaign. What he did not realize was that this decision would harden the West's determination ultimately to stand up to him and to go to war for the freedom of the Kosovars.

The immediate catalyst for NATO to begin a campaign of air strikes against strategic targets in Serbia was twofold. First, the discovery of numerous massacres of Albanians, including women and children, by the Serb forces hardened NATO's resolve. Second, the Western powers discovered Milosevic's overall strategic plan to "solve" the Albanian problem, known as Operation Horseshoe. In accordance with its code name, Milosevic planned to encircle the Albanians inside a giant horseshoe and then force them to exit Kosovo. The destruction of their property and all identification papers would ensure that they could never return. In short, Kosovo would be "cleansed" of Moslems in order to provide lebensraum for Serb settlers. Adolf Eichmann, the man in charge of the deportation of Jews during the Nazi regime, would likely have appreciated the scale of Operation Horseshoe.

The nineteen members of the NATO alliance did not expect a long war. They believed that a short bombing campaign would bring Milosevic to his knees. None of them believed that a ground war would be necessary. Incredibly enough, NATO even announced that no deployment of ground forces was contemplated. This turned out to be a serious misjudgment. First, it signaled to Milosevic that NATO's ranks were divided and that its resolve might weaken quickly. Indeed, there was some basis for such a conclusion. Not only did Russia and China attack the NATO strikes savagely, but several alliance members expressed concern that the UN Security Council had not been consulted about the bombing campaign. Second, Serbia was no Iraq. The Serbs were tough fighters who had put up stiff resistance to the Nazis, so stiff in fact that Stalin had never dared to invade Yugoslavia in the late 1940s. It is very likely that Milosevic concluded the opposite of what NATO expected: He decided to escalate his terror campaign in Kosovo by a quantum leap into total savagery in order to achieve his aims. While this decision would spell disaster for more than a million Albanians, it would also hasten Milosevic's own defeat.

Operation Horseshoe kicked into high gear during the night of March 24, 1999, when NATO began its air strikes on Yugoslavia. Its terrible course of destruction was documented by hundreds of eye-witnesses in a special report by the *New York Times* on May 29, 1999, aptly entitled "Horror by Design."[36] Apparently, groups of men with black masks appeared in the middle of the night, took women and children out of houses, raped the women, killed the men, cut up their bodies, and then burned the houses. The speed and scale of the Serbian campaign was without precedent, even by the violent standards of the war in Bosnia, as wave upon wave of masked men spread terror throughout the villages, and then the towns, of Kosovo. Ethnic Albanians moved from house to house, moving in with relatives and friends and fleeing again, to stay ahead of the advancing Serbs. Since many of the houses were built close together, the Albanians broke holes through the walls so that they could escape from one home to another should the Serbs break down the doors. As word of the terror spread throughout Kosovo, fear became the Serbs' most effective ally, and as the campaign progressed, all it took was a handful of armed masked Serbs to drive thousands of people from their homes, rob them, and send them off in caravans, their houses in flames. Fear was compounded with humiliation and dehumanization. The Serbs made every effort to ensure that those who fled would not come back. The refugees were stripped of all identity papers and even the license plates on their cars were methodically unscrewed at the borders. "This is not your land—you will never see it again," the Serbs screamed at the helpless Albanians before they were thrown out of Kosovo. "Go to your NATO—go to your Clinton."[37]

By late May, close to 1 million Albanians had been driven out of Kosovo. Half of them were huddled in makeshift refugee camps on the Albanian border, one-quarter in Macedonia, and the rest in Montenegro. In addition, hundreds of thousands more were hiding in forests and mountains inside Kosovo, their fate unknown.

In retrospect, it has become clear that Milosevic's brutal campaign had three major goals: first, to crush the KLA; second, to change permanently the ethnic balance of Kosovo in favor of the Serbs; and finally, to overwhelm NATO with an unmanageable relief crisis, calculating that the task of caring for a million refugees would divert the Western alliance from its air strike campaign. As it turned out, Milosevic failed on all three counts because he made one colossal miscalculation.

As the adage goes, one picture speaks louder than a thousand words. When photographs of thousands of Albanians herded like cattle into trains leaving Pristina for the Macedonian border reached Western television screens, the response was electric. Packed with helpless people screaming in despair, the trains were all too reminiscent of the Nazi Holocaust. Western resolve hardened almost overnight and the result was a renewed determination by the alliance members to see the air war through to a successful conclusion. One cannot help but wonder what might have been if Milosevic had not escalated the terror to such unspeakable heights. NATO's consensus on continuing the air war might well have dissipated under mounting criticism from China and Russia, and even within its own ranks.

Milosevic's gamble did seem to work for a few weeks. This was largely due to NATO's policy of protecting its pilots from Serb antiaircraft fire by instructing them to fly at safe altitudes of 15,000 feet or more and then only under near-perfect weather conditions. As a result, "far beneath the high-flying planes, small groups of Serb soldiers and police in armored vehicles were terrorizing hundreds of thousands of Albanian Kosovars."[38] Hence, in the view of at least

MAP 7   Crisis in Kosovo

one military analyst, "The immediate possibility of saving thousands of Albanians from massacre and hundreds of thousands from deportation was obviously not worth the lives of a few pilots."[39] This may well be true, but it is no less true that NATO's policy of protecting the lives of its pilots may have made it possible to stay the course until the Serbs were forced to surrender after seventy-eight days. Not even numerous civilian casualties on the ground, including the unfortunate mistaken bombing of the Chinese embassy in Belgrade, could deter the allies from their ultimate objective. In the end, it was the ghost of Adolf Hitler that made the alliance stand fast.

Not surprisingly, the main architect of NATO's air campaign was an American whose childhood had been spent in Serbia during the Holocaust. Madeleine Albright had spent two years in Belgrade as a child when her father, the Czechoslovak diplomat Josef Korbel, served there as ambassador during World War II. Only after she had become secretary of state did she discover that several members of her family were of Jewish descent and had perished under the Nazis. Her heritage came to the fore when Milosevic began to terrorize the Albanians in 1998. "History is watching us," she told a meeting of foreign ministers. "In this very room our predecessors delayed as Bosnia burned, and history will not be kind to us if we do the same." When the French and Italian ministers proposed a softening in the language they would use to threaten the Serbs, Albright's aide Jamie Rubin whispered to her that she could probably accept it. She snapped back, "Where do you think we are, Munich?"[40] Tirelessly, she kept wavering ministers in line, sometimes by persuading the British foreign minister to call them. No one was permitted to send mixed signals to Milosevic. So tenacious was she that the air strikes were described in several European capitals as "Madeleine's War." Perhaps for someone who had to flee from Hitler, and then Stalin, as a child, the war became a very personal mission. But in all of this, Albright enjoyed the full support of President Bill Clinton. After she had explained the war in Kosovo to American troops gathered at an air base in Germany, the president thanked her "for being able to redeem the lessons of (your) life by standing up for the freedom of the people in the Balkans."[41]

Secretary Albright had her critics, of course. One of them was her mentor, Peter Krogh, who had been dean of Georgetown's School of Foreign Service during her tenure there. Krogh accused Albright of basing American foreign policy on humanitarian principles while ignoring primary strategic interests such as integrating Russia and China into the international system. Albright responded by declaring that the stability of Europe was essential to the United States and that Kosovo, if left to Milosevic, could have destabilized Europe. And yet, one might ask, how should the United States choose where to become involved? Why Kosovo and not Rwanda? Albright responded that the three main criteria of involvement were the immensity of the crime, the importance of the region to the United States, and the presence of an organization capable of dealing with the crisis. All these factors were present in the case of Kosovo. Hence the United States decided to lead and most Europeans decided to follow, some like Britain with enthusiasm and others, more reluctantly. After seventy-eight days, Milosevic had finally had enough. He surrendered via the good offices of Viktor Chernomyrdin, Russia's special envoy, just when NATO leaders were contemplating the painful implications of a ground war.

NATO emerged victorious with air power alone and without a single combat casualty. It was a victory without precedent in military history. Yet, the magnitude of the fallout from the war was staggering: more than 1 million refugees living on three borders in hopelessness and squalor; the ignition of hatreds that would last for generations; and the death of thousands of men, women, and children. Europe's last dictator had been defeated, once again, but at a terrible price; moreover, like Saddam Hussein before him, he still ruled at war's end.

There appear to be two main reasons why Milosevic decided to give in. First, 20,000 bombs had been dropped on Yugoslavia and its war machine and infrastructure were beginning to fall apart. Second, on May 27 the International War Crimes Tribunal in the Hague indicted the Serb leader and four of his closest associates for war crimes and crimes against humanity. Louise Arbour, the Canadian chief prosecutor, announced that arrest warrants for the five men had been served on all member states of the United Nations and on Switzerland. "The world is now a much smaller place for these men," Ms. Arbour added; "we require these states, including Yugoslavia, to arrest the accused if they are within their jurisdiction and deliver them to the Hague for trial."[42] In effect, the charges branded the Milosevic regime as criminal and Milosevic himself as an international pariah. Negotiations with him would be extremely awkward, though not illegal, for any state respecting the UN Charter.

Almost immediately after the Tribunal action, Milosevic changed his stance and put out peace feelers to Viktor Chernomyrdin, who promptly embarked on another peace mission to Belgrade, this time a successful one. Quite clearly, Milosevic realized that his very life would be in jeopardy if he slipped from power and also understood that he could not prevail by continuing the war. His capitulation to NATO was driven by totally selfish motives: to stay in power and wrap himself in the mantle of sovereignty vis-à-vis the Hague Tribunal so it would not be able to touch him.

The Hague Tribunal based its indictment of Milosevic on a mountain of evidence, including eyewitness accounts from thousands of refugees who had seen killings, massacre sites, and mass graves. It concluded that Operation Horseshoe was a military plan designed by Belgrade's general staff under the direct control of Slobodan Milosevic. By the time NATO began its air strikes, the Serb armies were operating in concert across the towns and villages of Kosovo. The tactics were always the same, and the slaughter of civilians terrorized most Albanians into flight. Soon, Serb forces needed only to display a corpse or two to empty an entire village. Just to make sure that nobody remained behind, the Serbs would usually come back a second and even a third time. The chain of command clearly led to Milosevic himself. An analogy might help to show both the horror and the absurdity of this operation. It was as if the Joint Chiefs of the United States armed forces had planned and executed an operation to terrorize and then drive most Mexican-Americans out of Texas, from Laredo and Brownsville all the way up to San Antonio, in the name of avenging the Alamo.

By June 1999, Milosevic's dream of a Greater Serbia was dead. His tactics of mass killings and civilian evictions had forged a separate Croatia, a new Bosnian identity, and a devastated Kosovo. Serbia itself lay in ruins and even the Orthodox Church, which had supported Milosevic in the early years of conquest, now demanded that he step down.

NATO's surrender terms to Milosevic included three main demands: first, the withdrawal of all Serb military forces within a week; second, the return of all Albanian refugees to Kosovo; and third, the deployment of 50,000 peacekeepers, supplied by the nineteen alliance members, to oversee the transition from war to peace. The largest contingent of 17,000 soldiers would come from Britain, with the United States contributing 7,000. It quickly became apparent that making peace might be as daunting as making war. NATO's first priority was to assist the refugees in their safe return to Kosovo from dozens of camps that had sprung up on the borders of Albania, Macedonia, and Montenegro during the spring of 1999. Before relief workers managed to provide minimal emergency help, thousands of refugees slept in the mud. There they lived in makeshift overcrowded tents and waited in long lines for food and water. The workers were so overwhelmed by the sheer mass of homeless, desperate people that Macedonia even closed its border for several days. Conditions became so unsanitary that the outbreak of epidemics was a major concern. President Clinton, at war's end, visited one of these muddy refugee encampments and, standing on a crude wooden box, spoke words of hope to the homeless who feared finding ashes instead of their former homes in Kosovo.

The coordinating body overseeing relief work was the UNHCR, which, in collaboration with NATO, did a remarkable job providing minimal food and shelter for hundreds of thousands. The United Nations wisely decided not to wait till war's end to find homes for the refugees. Between April and June more than 75,000 found new homes in thirty countries. Germany admitted 13,000, with Turkey, Norway, Italy, Canada, France, Austria, and the United States absorbing more than 5,000 each. When the camp loudspeakers announced the end of the war, the refugees were at first extremely skeptical because Milosevic was still in power. Then, as word spread through the camps that NATO peacekeepers were pouring into Kosovo, they began to prefer repatriation to resettlement in foreign lands. On June 17, 1999, 12,000 cheering Albanians started their journey home in the first wave of a reverse exodus of refugees. Field workers from UNHCR began registering the names of the returning Kosovars, but they soon gave up when the process became too cumbersome and left it to the KLA to record the arrivals. No one asked the refugees for any proof of who they were. Plastic cards with numbers were handed out to each family head who was then instructed to use the card to register in the weeks ahead in his home village. In most cases, however, the refugees found nothing but cinders on their return. The following story describes the predicament of many returning Kosovars:

Standing on cinders, Mr. Kryeziu looked around and sighed deeply. "There is nothing," he said. The house was completely burned out, the rooms were empty, the only things left were some blackened wires. Like all the refugees, he remembered the moment the Serbs ordered him out two days after the NATO bombing began. The police came and said to the people, "You have two minutes to leave your houses." We grabbed our car and tractor and fled. We did not take anything.

He looked now around the family compound. His dog was shot dead, the place where the family stored the feed corn was smashed, along with the garage. The floor of every empty room was crunched with cinders and charcoal. There had been two cows, but he couldn't find them.

"Why did they have to burn all of them?" he said, looking at the charred buildings sadly. "Why didn't they leave one of them so that when we came back we could have a shelter?"[43]

What Mr. Kryeziu failed to mention was the fact that the departing Serbs had booby-trapped thousands of the burned-out houses they had left behind with powerful mines. Clearly, civilian casualties would continue to mount even after war's end.

In addition to NATO's main responsibility—the safe return of the refugees—it faced the daunting problem of rebuilding a viable infrastructure for the devastated province. In particular, what would be the role of the KLA in this process?

Even before it was able to tackle this problem, however, NATO had to deal with two hundred Russian troops who were the first to enter Kosovo and had entrenched themselves at the Pristina airport. Just how and why they had beaten NATO to the draw was never completely clarified, and it took weeks of intensive negotiations to devise a formula whereby the Russians, who had added another 3,600 troops in the meantime, became integrated into KFOR, the NATO peacekeeping force.

The KLA presented a far more complex problem. It had been persuaded to sign a disarmament agreement with NATO. The Albanian resistance fighters, who included 10,000 hard-core members and about 20,000 "irregulars" who had joined their ranks from Albanian minorities all over the world, were most reluctant to lay down their arms. After all, they had supplied NATO with target information during the bombing campaign, and their leader, Hashim Thaci, claimed that NATO had made the KLA into partners in the task of rebuilding Kosovo. NATO, wary of dissension within KLA's ranks and fearful of the KLA's thirst for revenge against the Serbs, at first insisted that the alliance remain the exclusive military presence in Kosovo. After considerable prodding from

KLA leaders, however, NATO reconsidered. In exchange for a pledge by the KLA to disband its guerrilla force, NATO in turn promised that it would allow the fighters to form a modest Kosovo Protection Force modeled after the National Guard in the United States.

As NATO moved its peacekeepers into Kosovo, the Serb forces pulled out, often leaving additional destruction in their wake. In rare cases Serb civilians stayed behind and tried to live side by side again with the returning Kosovars; in all but a very few cases, these experiments to recreate a multiethnic Kosovo were doomed to failure. Memories of horror made it next to impossible for the Albanians to tolerate any Serbs as their neighbors. Yet more myths of hate were bound to make reconciliation next to impossible.

It seems that in the larger perspective of history, the only logical outcome of the war over the remains of Yugoslavia will be partition. Bosnian Croats will join Croatia and Bosnian Serbs will reunite with Serbia, leaving an independent but smaller Moslem Bosnia. There have been at least three "temporary" demarcation lines in recent history that have congealed into permanence: the Greeks and Turks on the island of Cyprus in 1964; Korea in 1953; and Indochina in 1954. No national elections were ever held in Korea or in Vietnam; nationalist hatreds simply ran too deep. Americans tend to underestimate such hatred and continue to be hopeful that their model of multicultural tolerance may be exportable. Therefore they abhor partitions. But there are times when a partition is more merciful than artificial union. India and Pakistan reached this conclusion after a terrible war and the largest population exchange in history; Arabs and Israelis, despite heroic efforts at reconciliation, may be headed for separation. And millions of ordinary people all over the world prefer a divorce to a bad marriage.

In the case of Kosovo, at the dawn of the twenty-first century, most of the expelled Kosovars had returned, in many cases, to the rubble of their former homes. NATO peacekeepers did their best to prevent revenge by the outraged Albanians against their former Serb tormentors. A UN civil administration did its best to build the foundations for elections that would determine a future government. In this effort the United Nations agreed to share power with a four-member Albanian administrative council including members of a newly formed Kosovo Protection Corps. Continuing massive relief efforts remained the responsibility of the UNHCR.

One conclusion is already clear. The multiethnic Kosovo for which NATO went to war is gone, probably forever. As in the rest of the former Yugoslavia, the horrors of the war have made such a solution impossible. Instead, Kosovo will probably remain a NATO protectorate with UN assistance for quite some time and then may opt for independence. Yet, one overarching truth stands out: A brutal forced exodus of a million people was reversed by civilization outraged.

A word about myths and legends may be appropriate here. In Serbian history, they have assumed a formidable power over the minds and hearts of the people. Foremost among them, of course, is the myth about the great battle of Kosovo in 1389. According to it, that Turkish victory destroyed the medieval Serbian Empire and the defeated Serbs were promptly placed under Ottoman rule. The Serbian legend maintains that Tsar Lazar, addressing his troops before going into battle, allegedly declared: "It is better to die in battle than to live in shame. . . . we have lived a long time in the world; in the end, we seek to accept the martyr's struggle and to live forever in heaven."[44]

This Kosovo Covenant, in the view of most Serbs including Slobodan Milosevic, has assumed the power of an almost religious fanaticism.

In the view of a brilliant British historian, Noel Malcolm, both myths about the battle of 1389 are false. After exhaustive research from all available sources, the author concluded that Serbian statehood actually survived the crucial battle for another seventy years with only a limited degree of interference by the Ottoman Turks.[45] Malcolm effectively demolished numerous other myths, both Serbian as well as Albanian, but discovered that the more serious distortions prevailed on the Serbian side.

Myths are heady stuff and will not be easily dispelled by even the most conscientious historians. These legends tend to develop a life of their own and those who pass them on from one generation to another stubbornly refuse to be confused by historical facts.

New myths will now be fashioned by the Serbs departing from Kosovo, as well as by the returning Kosovars. It is very likely that the Serbs will elevate the ancient battle of 1389 to even greater heights, especially since the patriarchate of the Serbian Orthodox Church is located in the Kosovo town of Peć. And the returning Albanians now proudly point to their conviction that they are descendants of the ancient Illyrians who once inhabited the area that is Kosovo today. Once again, as so often in the past, misperceptions not only helped precipitate a war, but made its carnage, when it came, one of the most barbaric of the century.

Conclusion:
A New Dawn of Peace with Justice?

Despite the terrible story of this war, it is possible to conclude this chapter on a note of hope. In the first place, a war lover was beaten. Slobodan Milosevic's days of power over a shrinking Yugoslavia clearly were numbered. He had achieved "ethnic cleansing," not for the Serbs who had to abandon Kosovo, but for the Moslem Koso-vars who had returned. With its indictment of May 27, 1999, a UN War Crimes Tribunal had turned the would-be builder of a Greater Serbia into a pariah under international law. Milosevic at first scoffed at this indictment, but soon stopped laughing when he saw his dream of a Greater Serbia reduced to ruins. Protest movements against him grew to huge numbers all over Serbia after he lost a crit-ical election in Belgrade.

Milosevic was ousted as president in October 2000. His successor, Vojislav Kostunica, a constitutional lawyer, claimed victory from Belgrade's City Hall with the words "Good evening, dear liberated Serbia!"[46] After deafening applause from the crowd below he added: "Big beautiful Serbia has risen up just so one man, Slobodan Milo-sevic, will leave." Soon thereafter Kostunica ordered an investigation of Milosevic on corruption charges, which resulted in the arrest of Milosevic and his transfer to a Belgrade jail.

President Clinton had vowed that the United States would not contribute "one red cent" to the reconstruction of Serbia while Milosevic was still in power. Now, he offered a new regime a $5 mil-lion bounty if Milosevic were to be extradited to the Hague. Kostu-nica, a Serb nationalist, hesitated to take this drastic step, but his pro-Western prime minister, Zoran Djindjic, did not. On June 29, 2001, Milosevic was whisked into a police van from his Belgrade jail and flown by helicopter to an American airbase in Tuzla, Bosnia, and from there to a military airfield near the Hague. Shortly there-after, the chief prosecutor of the UN War Crimes Tribunal, Carla del Ponte of Switzerland, began to prepare for the trial of Europe's last dictator. Thus, within two years of his original indictment as a war criminal, Milosevic had gone from power to prison.

In July 2002 a new International Criminal Court (ICC) super-seded the War Crimes Tribunal when sixty-six countries ratified its statute. The United States was not among them. The Bush adminis-tration feared that the new court might engage in "political prosecu-tions" of Americans. These fears seemed unfounded; the court's judges were superb jurists with impeccable reputations, such as Richard May of the United Kingdom, before whom Milosevic appeared on charges of genocide.

The trial of Slobodan Milosevic before the ICC is surely a signifi-cant triumph for justice. It is the first time since the Nuremberg and Tokyo trials at the end of World War II that a head of state was held individually accountable for his actions. On the other hand, there is a great deal yet to be done. Karadzic and Mladic, the two perpetra-tors of murderous "ethnic cleansing" campaigns in Croatia and Bosnia, were still at large, even though del Ponte asserted that their arrest would "transform the two men from symbols of a lack of a backbone into symbols of the international community's resolve."[47] Some progress was made however, when in October 2003, it was revealed by eyewitnesses testifying before the ICC that the killings of unarmed Moslem men and boys in Srebrenica had been coldly planned by the Serbs, not improvised in chaos.[48] Unfortunately, the brave Serb prime minister, Zoran Djindjic, who had extradited Milosevic to the Hague had been assassinated in May 2003. His suc-cessor, Zoran Zivkovic, however, immediately pledged his support of his martyred predecessor's policies. It must also be noted that the opposition of the United States, while not crippling the ICC, has certainly weakened it. By June 2003, for example, even though 137 countries had signed the ICC's Statute and ninety had ratified it, the United States had succeeded in cajoling thirty-seven countries to sign agreements promising not to extradite U.S. citizens to the Court in the Hague.[49] But, on the other hand, in December 2003, the Serb commander of the cruel siege of Sarajevo was convicted of crimes against humanity and sentenced to 20 years in prison and another Serb war criminal was sentenced to 17 years for the massacre of 7,000 Moslems in Srebrenica. Moreover, during that month, Gen-eral Wesley Clark, former Supreme Commander of NATO, testified in the Hague against Milosevic, asserting that the former president of Serbia had guilty knowledge of the Srebrenica massacre before it occurred. Thus, in broad historical perspective, as one surveys the gradual evolution of global institutions such as the United Nations, the very existence of an International Criminal Court must be considered a milestone of progress for international law.

An encouraging showdown occurred just before New Year's Eve of 2003. In an absurd backlash against the Hague Court, the ultranationalist party in Serbia received enough votes for Milosevic to win him a seat in the Serb parliament. Nonetheless, the accused war criminal continued to remain in the Court's custody. It was international law, not nationalist extremism, that had the final word.

Finally, by its victory over Milosevic in his war against the Albanian Moslems of Kosovo, NATO had established a new principle of international law: Not only would the persecution of a dictator of his own people not be tolerated, it would be reversed. In this effort, the United States led and the rest of NATO followed. This new principle of humanitarian intervention was still far from universal, but it was a beginning. At the dawn of a new millennium, it was a ringing affirmation of the Universal Declaration of Human Rights, adopted more than half a century ago by the United Nations through the tireless efforts of the delegate from the United States, Eleanor Roosevelt.

NOTES

1. Laura Silber and Allan Little, *Yugoslavia: Death of a Nation* (New York: Penguin, 1996), p. 39.

2. Ibid., p. 38.

3. Ibid.

4. Ibid., p. 99.

5. Ibid., p. 172.

6. Gale Stokes, *The Walls Came Tumbling Down: The Collapse of Communism in Eastern Europe* (Oxford: Oxford University Press, 1993), p. 250.

7. Samir Koric, Reuters News Agency, April 4, 1992, as quoted in *Yugoslavia*, pp. 227–228.

8. Interview with Elie Wiesel, July 14, 1996.

9. David Rieff, *Slaughterhouse: Bosnia and the Failure of the West* (New York: Simon & Schuster, 1995), p. 216.

10. *Yugoslavia*, p. 252.

11. Ibid., p. 258.

12. Ibid., p. 267.

13. Ibid., p. 268.

14. *Slaughterhouse*, p. 208.

15. *Yugoslavia*, p. 270.

16. Ibid., p. 295.

17. Ibid., pp. 331–332.

18. Ibid., p. 334.
19. *Slaughterhouse,* p. 24.
20. Ibid., p. 140.
21. *Yugoslavia,* p. 350.
22. *New York Times,* June 1, 1996.
23. Anthony Lewis, "Bosnia Betrayed Again," *New York Times,* June 3, 1996.
24. *New York Times,* May 22, 1996.
25. Ibid., June 15, 1996.
26. Ibid., June 1, 1996.
27. Ibid., July 12, 1996.
28. Ibid.
29. Ibid.
30. Charles G. Boyd, "Making Peace with the Guilty," *Foreign Affairs* (September/October 1995), p. 23. (Italics mine.)
31. Ibid., July 21, 1996.
32. Ibid.
33. Ibid., August 9, 1996.
34. Henry Kissinger, "America in the Eye of the Hurricane," *Washington Post,* September 8, 1996.
35. *Wall Street Journal,* October 1, 1996.
36. John Kifner, "Horror by Design: How Serb Forces Purged One Million Albanians," *New York Times,* May 29, 1999.
37. Ibid.
38. Edward Luttwak, "Give War a Chance," *Foreign Affairs* (July/August 1999), p. 41.
39. Ibid.
40. *Time,* May 17, 1999.
41. Ibid.
42. *New York Times,* May 28, 1999.
43. *New York Times,* June 17, 1999.
44. Emmert, T.A., *Serbian Golgotha: Kosovo 1389,* New York, 1990, as quoted by Noel Malcolm, see Note 10.
45. Malcolm, Noel, *Kosovo: A Short History* (New York: HarperPerennial, 1999), p. 77.
46. *New York Times,* October 6, 2000.
47. *New York Times,* June 28, 2003.
48. *New York Times,* October 12, 2003.
49. *New York Times,* June 11, 2003.

SELECTED BIBLIOGRAPHY

ASMUS, RONALD D. *Opening NATO's Door: How the Alliance Remade Itself for a New Era.* New York: Columbia University Press, 2002.
BASS, GARY J. "Milosevic in The Hague." *Foreign Affairs,* May/June 2003.
BOYD, CHARLES G. "Making Peace with the Guilty." *Foreign Affairs,* September/October 1995.

BURG, STEVEN L., and SHOUP, PAUL S. *The War in Bosnia-Herzegovina: Ethnic Conflict and International Intervention.* Armonk, N.Y.: Sharpe, 1999.

CENTRAL INTELLIGENCE AGENCY. *Balkan Battlegrounds: A Military History of the Yugoslav Conflict, 1990–1995.* Washington, D.C.: CIA Office of Public Affairs, 2002.

COHEN, ROGER. *Hearts Grown Brutal: Sagas of Sarajevo.* New York: Random House, 1998.

DOBBS, MICHAEL. *Madeleine Albright: A Twentieth-Century Odyssey.* New York: Holt, 1999.

DRAKULIC, SLAVENICA. *The Balkan Express.* New York: Norton, 1993.

HOFFMANN, STANLEY. *The Ethics and Politics of Humanitarian Intervention.* South Bend, Ind.: University of Notre Dame Press, 1996.

HOLZGREFE, J. L., and ROBERT KEOHANE. *Humanitarian Intervention: Ethical, Legal, and Political Dilemmas.* New York: Cambridge University Press, 2003.

JOB, CVIJETO. *Yugoslavia's Ruin: The Bloody Lessons of Nationalism.* Lanham, Md.: Rowman & Littlefield, 2002.

JONES, DOROTHY. *Toward a Just World: The Critical Years in the Search for International Justice.* Chicago: University of Chicago Press, 2002.

LOYD, ANTHONY. *My War Gone By, I Miss It So.* New York: Atlantic Monthly Press, 1999.

MALCOLM, NOEL. *Kosovo: A Short History.* New York: HarperPerennial, 1999.

PERICA, VJEKOSLAV. *Balkan Idols: Religion and Nationalism in Yugoslav States.* New York: Oxford University Press, 2002.

RIEFF, DAVID. *Slaughterhouse: Bosnia and the Failure of the West.* New York: Simon & Schuster, 1995.

SHATZMILLER, MAYA, Ed. *Islam and Bosnia: Conflict Resolution and Foreign Policy in Multi-Ethnic States.* Montreal: McGill-Queens University Press, 2002.

SILBER, LAURA, and ALLAN LITTLE. *Yugoslavia: Death of a Nation.* New York: Penguin, 1996.

SIMMS, BRENDAN. *Unfinest Hour: Britain and the Destruction of Bosnia.* London: Penguin, 2002.

STOKES, GALE. *The Walls Came Tumbling Down: The Collapse of Communism in Eastern Europe.* Oxford: Oxford University Press, 1993.

TERRY, FIONA. *Condemned to Repeat? The Paradox of Humanitarian Action.* Ithaca, N.Y.: Cornell University Press, 2002.

THOMAS, ROBERT. *The Politics of Serbia in the 1990s.* New York: Columbia University Press, 1999.

VICKERS, MIRANDA. *Between Serb and Albanian: A History of Kosovo.* New York: Columbia University Press, 1998.

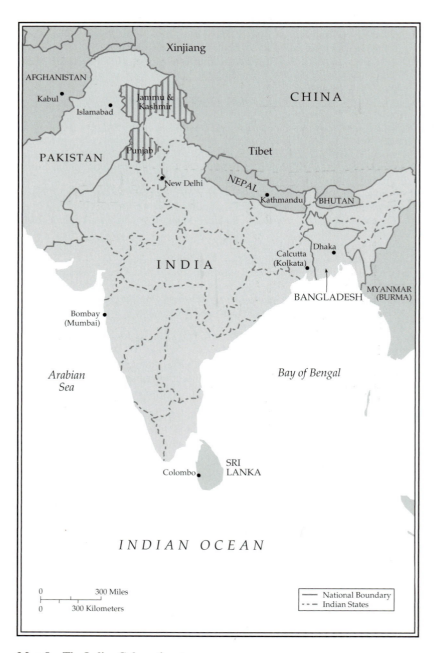

MAP 8   The Indian Subcontinent

6

Four Battles over God: India and Pakistan in 1947, 1965, 1971, and 1998

Man's body is so small, yet his capacity for suffering is so immense.   Rabindranath Tagore

The most savage religious war in history was neither the Christian Crusades against Islam nor the Thirty Years' War that pitted Catholic against Protestant. It was the war of Hindu against Moslem in the twentieth century.

So long as India remained under the British Crown, the conflict between Hindus and Moslems remained relatively dormant, but the two religions, fearing each other more than they feared their common colonial master, waged separate struggles for independence against Britain: the Hindus under Mahatma Gandhi and the Moslems under Mohammed Ali Jinnah. When the time for freedom approached, the Moslems insisted on their own sovereign entity, apart from the Hindu majority of colonial India. Therefore when the transfer of power took place in 1947, two new states were born, India and Pakistan.

Britain had hardly withdrawn when the two fledgling states turned on each other with a terrible ferocity. Millions of terror-stricken Hindus in Pakistan fled for their lives to India and millions of equally frantic Moslems in India sought refuge in Pakistan. The result was the most massive population exchange in history. It has always been clear to participants and observers alike that these two religious groups agree on virtually nothing and regard each other as anathema. The Moslem believes in one god and his prophet, whereas the Hindu worships a pantheon of gods. Moslem society is

157

not based on caste; Hindu society has been stratified into a rigid caste system. Moslems believe in actively making converts, whereas Hindus tend to be more passive and absorptive. Moslems observe strict silence in their mosques; Hindus play music in their temples. Hindus will not eat beef, and Moslems are enjoined from eating pork. Each has always regarded the other as a peril.

The three wars to be examined are the outgrowth of this religious conflict. The fact that the two hostile religions were represented by sovereign states made the conflict even more ferocious. Nationalism and religion now were fatefully fused with the modern nation-state serving as a handmaiden to religious warfare. The political forces of the twentieth century were mobilized to fight the battles of an earlier age. And so three times in quick succession India and Pakistan, each invoking its ancient gods, met on fields of battle under empty skies from which the gods had departed.

Colonialism, Partition, and War

Ancient Hinduism was an austere doctrine subscribing to the view that the cause of all evil in the world was human desire. The path toward redemption lay in an individual's capacity to extinguish personal desire through an act of will and thus reach a state of Nirvana. Hinduism conceived of life as a never-ending cycle, where death simply meant passage into another incarnation of life. The form this new incarnation would take depended on one's behavior in the previous one, or Karma; it was quite possible for an individual to pass into a lower or a higher form of life. The standard of excellence to which the Hindu was to aspire was Nirvana, or the renunciation of desire. Since people were by nature unequal, only a few could attain this goal. This concept of the inequality of people was expressed in the caste system, which formed the basic structure of ancient Indian society. Society consisted of four rigidly separated castes: the Brahmins, or priests, who had come closest to the Hindu ideal; the warriors, who were to defend the society; the merchants; and the laborers. Actually, the social system was even more complex since each caste had numerous subdivisions. At the bottom of the social pyramid were the outcasts, or pariahs, also known as "untouchables."

The great inroads made by Buddhism in ancient India may be explained largely in terms of the austerity of Hindu doctrine. Though

Buddhism too was directed toward an afterlife, its view of humanity was much more optimistic; under its influence the Nirvana concept gradually changed from a doctrine of extinction and renunciation to a goal not unlike the Christian paradise. The figure of the Bodhisattva gained prominence in Indian life—the priest who, though entitled to enter Nirvana, has decided to postpone his own entrance in order to show the way to others. Late Buddhism, in fact, moved further and further from the austerity of the Hindu faith. Sometimes only a few invocations would suffice to gain entrance to Nirvana, and Bodhisattvas frequently became deities who served as "social workers" assisting their less fortunate brethren. Despite this radical transformation of Hinduism it must be remembered that Buddhism was able to evolve from Hinduism because the latter lent itself to the absorption of new forms of faith quite readily.

Islam, the third major religion of ancient India, came to India around 1000 A.D. and stands in striking contrast to the other two. Unlike Buddhism, Islam was never absorbed by the Hindus. The only attribute that Islam shared with its predecessor was its emphasis on the hereafter; there the similarity ended. When the Moslems first came to India, they destroyed all the Hindu temples and sculptures they found because they considered them idolatrous. After sections of India in the northeast and the northwest were conquered by Moslems, the Hindus tended to regard them as another caste to be kept rigidly separate. The religious conflict between Hinduism and Islam is thus at the root of the struggle between India and Pakistan. By the time the West arrived there, India was a politically divided society in which two radically different ways of life competed for the allegiance of the population: Hinduism, which was tolerant of dissent and absorptive; and Islam, which was militant, exclusive, and dogmatic.

British rule over India was established in the early seventeenth century through the instrument of the East India Company. In their campaign to gain control of the subcontinent, the British employed a strategy of "divide and conquer." The many local rulers were played off against each other until, by the late eighteenth century, most of India was in British hands.

The administration of British India is a story of contradictions, compromise, and conflict. The coming of the British added yet another element to an already highly complex Indian society. Christianity was brought to India, and yet the materialism of the Christian colonizers stood in stark contrast to the spiritualism of the Hindu.

The individualism of the British differed sharply from the group-centered culture of India, and the democratic ideal of equality was alien to the caste-conscious Hindu. On the whole, the British tried very hard to reconcile these many conflicts and sometimes succeeded.

In the pattern of indirect rule initiated by the British, a viceroy was put in charge of colonial administration. Local customs were left intact so long as they did not present a direct threat to the British presence or radically offend the British social ethos. The British did not interfere much with the caste system, although they did insist on the abolition of the Hindu custom of suttee, or the immolation of widows on the funeral pyres of their husbands. They also outlawed infanticide and *thuggee,* the practice of sacrificing unsuspecting travelers in lonely mountain passes to the goddess Kali.

The British made every effort to teach British democracy to the Indians, thus planting the seeds of the Indians' demand for self-rule. British law and contractual relationships were often mingled with Indian culture, and efforts were made to use indigenous talent in the civil service, especially in the later colonial period. But the British also exhibited extreme insensitivity. For example, in 1857 the rumor was started that pig and cow fats were being used to grease cartridges in rifles to be employed by Hindu and Moslem recruits in the army. The Sepoy Rebellion of 1857, which was touched off by this incident, was crushed by the British with extreme cruelty.

The economic aspects of the Indian colonial experience present a similarly mixed record. The early profits made by the East India Company were enormous. By flooding India with manufactured goods, the British compelled the indigenous population to concentrate on the production of raw materials, thus causing an imbalance in the economy and a decline in Indian industry. On the other hand, the industrial development of India meant the development of modern roads, telegraphs, harbors, mails, and railroads. Some aspects of this industrialization did not conflict with traditional customs, and at times they even helped to revive them. For example, a modern network of railroads made religious pilgrimages easier for many Hindus. Another important by-product of British colonialism was the rise of a new class of professionals, bankers, traders, educators, and lawyers, who were to play a major role in the rise of the new India.

It is impossible to say whether modern India has benefited or suffered more from its experience with British colonialism. To be sure, colonialism had many unfortunate effects: exploitation of the labor force, overdevelopment of natural resources, and dislocation of the economy through exportation of wealth in the form of raw materials, a condition of economic colonialism that was to last much longer than its political counterpart. On the other hand, the British also did much to prepare India for the modern world: They bestowed on the country an enlightened health and education program; they provided at least the foundations for a higher standard of living; and they educated an elite of future leaders.

In sum, then, India's experience with Western colonialism was by no means entirely negative. If one considers this fact, combined with the tolerant faith of the Hindu religion, it is not surprising that when the nationalist reaction occurred in India it followed an essentially nonviolent and democratic path.

The Indian nationalist movement was marked by the overwhelmingly powerful personality of Mahatma Gandhi. Gandhi was the spiritual father of the Indian Congress, the nationalist resistance organization under the British that, without his unifying influence, would have been destroyed by factionalism. Indeed, without the charismatic leadership of Gandhi, Indian nationalism might well have run a far more violent course.

Gandhi's nationalism was rooted in the doctrine of *ahimsa*, or noninjury to any living being. This concept was translated into the political doctrine of passive resistance, or civil disobedience, a technique of nationalist assertion that the British found very embarrassing. Gandhi lived most unpretentiously. He used a spinning wheel to produce his few garments, and his example led to a widespread boycott of foreign cloth. He denied himself all comforts and often endured long fasts in order to gain support for his causes. When the British imposed a heavy tax on salt in 1930, Gandhi walked 165 miles to the sea to make his own salt. Rather than cooperate with the British, he exhorted the population to go to jail, and he himself was frequently imprisoned. But he always emphasized the nonviolent character of Indian nationalism. Indeed, his rejection of bloodshed as a deplorable aberration was the movement's basic moral and political principle. The steady advance toward independence made by India between 1900 and 1947 was due in large measure to Gandhi's insistence on spiritual rather than physical power.

It was Gandhi who turned Indian nationalism from an urban, elite movement into a mass movement that reached the smaller towns and captured the popular imagination. But it was also Gandhi who unwittingly magnified the differences between Indian Hindus and Indian Moslems, through his emphasis on mass participation, majority rule, and Indian (Hindu) tradition. Moslems became apprehensive that majority rule and Hindu revivalism would undermine their faith and dim their political future.

Therefore, despite his enormous influence, Gandhi was unable to forge Indian nationalism into a cohesive whole. The congress was always viewed with suspicion by the Moslems, who feared persecution at the hands of a Hindu majority once India became independent. Though he tried his utmost to do so, Gandhi never succeeded in resolving the differences between the two faiths. In the end, in 1948 he was assassinated by a Hindu fanatic who found his dogged attempts at reconciliation unbearable.

The Moslems developed their own nationalist organization, the Moslem League. Its leader, Mohammed Ali Jinnah, insisted on the creation of a separate state of Pakistan for the Moslem minority. The great chasm between Hinduism and Islam robbed the Indian nationalist movement of much of its effectiveness. Often the two antagonists feared each other more than they did Britain. The depth of the conflict is illustrated by the fact that not even the unparalleled prestige of Gandhi was able to persuade his Hindu followers to make common cause with Islam. Nor did the Moslems feel any less strongly. Their view was expressed by Jinnah:

> How can you even dream of Hindu-Moslem unity? Everything pulls us apart: We have no intermarriages. We have not the same calendar. The Moslems believe in a single God, and the Hindus are idolatrous. Like the Christians, the Moslems believe in an equalitarian society, whereas the Hindus maintain their iniquitous system of castes and leave heartlessly fifty million Untouchables to their tragic fate, at the bottom of the social ladder.[1]

It is quite possible that this intense communal strife would have enabled the British to maintain control over India for an indefinite period. But World War II forced the British to make their peace with the prospect of Indian sovereignty. As a condition of India's collaboration in the war, Gandhi demanded a promise of immediate independence. When the British hedged, the Indian leader said caustically that he was unwilling to accept "a post-dated check on a bank that was obviously failing." Even a British guarantee of speedy independence did not prevent some Indian nationalist leaders, like Subhas Chandra Bose, from throwing in their lot with the Japanese. After the conclusion of the war, it fell to the British Labour government, which had always been severely critical of Conservative policy toward India, to honor Britain's pledge. But in 1947, when Indian nationalism finally triumphed, the country was a house divided. Despite Gandhi's repeated fasts and prayer meetings against it, partition seemed the only practicable solution. Hence India and Pakistan emerged from British colonial rule as two separate sovereign states.

The triumph of nationalism in India was thus distinctly marred by the tragedy of partition. Three staggering problems were the direct result of this tragedy. The first disaster was the gigantic population exchange. Over 7 million Hindus, fearful of persecution in Pakistan, sought refuge in India, and a similar number of Moslems fled India for Pakistan. A vast amount of violence and bloodshed generated by religious hatred accompanied these migratory waves. Millions of people, of course, lost their homes in the process, and the integration of these refugees presented an almost insurmountable hurdle to both of the new states.

The second problem was economic. Colonial India had been an economic unit for centuries, and now it was suddenly divided into three parts: India, East Pakistan, and West Pakistan. East Pakistan, formerly East Bengal, was separated from West Pakistan by almost 1,000 miles of Indian territory. These two Moslem enclaves, dating from the Moslem conquest, had nothing but their religion in common, not even language. Regional jealousies and economic competition between the two Pakistans immediately rose to the surface. Even worse, however, an economic war broke out between Pakistan and India. India devalued her rupee, but Pakistan refused to follow suit. Jute, an important raw material grown mostly in Bengal, now became prohibitively expensive in India. In short, the three parts of the Indian subcontinent, which for centuries had worked well together, were now involved in a destructive economic feud.

Overshadowing all other disputes between the two new nations was the struggle over contested territory, especially the princely state of Kashmir. India demanded Kashmir on the ground that its ruler was a Hindu, but Pakistan claimed the state on the basis that over three-fourths of the population was Moslem.

Kashmir combines extraordinary scenic beauty with great strategic importance. Since ancient times, the beautiful and fertile Kashmir Valley had been the resting place for caravans traveling between the plains of India and the highlands of Central Asia. Both India and Pakistan considered Kashmir absolutely vital to their strategic and defense requirements. India's prime minister Jawaharlal Nehru wrote:

> India without Kashmir would cease to occupy a pivotal position on the political map of Central Asia. Strategically, Kashmir is vital to the security of India; it has been so since the dawn of history.[2]

But Pakistan's prime minister Liaquat Ali Khan justified his claim with similar emphasis:

> Kashmir is very important, is vital to Pakistan. Kashmir, as you will see from the map, is like a cap on the head of Pakistan. If I allow India to have this cap on our head, then I am always at the mercy of India.[3]

To make matters even more complicated, the British left three choices to the so-called princely states after their departure: accession to India, accession to Pakistan, or independence. Lord Mountbatten, as representative of the British Crown, advised the leaders of the 565 princely states that they were free "to accede to one or the other of the two new Dominions as the effective successive Powers to the British Raj, at their discretion, with due consideration to be given to geographical contiguity and communal composition."[4] If neither choice was acceptable, they could form independent states. Of the 565, whose sizes ranged from that of a European country to that of a small village, only three opted for independence: Junagadh, Hyderabad, and Kashmir. Of these, the first two did not present insuperable obstacles. But Kashmir, larger than England, with an area of almost 85,000 square miles, now became a vital object of competition, coveted with equal fervor by both new states.

The maharajah of Kashmir, Hari Singh, offered to enter into a "standstill agreement" with both states in order to buy time and ensure Kashmir a measure of autonomy. By now, however, communal strife had engulfed much of the subcontinent, and Kashmir was drawn in. Moslem tribesmen from the northwest, enraged by alleged atrocities against the Moslems of nearby Jammu, invaded Kashmir. They came close to overpowering Kashmir's defenses and carried out mass killing, looting, and arson. Pakistan described the situation as a popular revolt by the Moslem majority of Kashmir against the Hindu prince's autocratic rule. The maharajah, in desperation, asked India for military aid. India, seizing the opportunity, made military intervention contingent on Kashmir's formal accession to India. The hard-pressed maharajah signed the Instrument of Accession to India on October 26, 1947. On the following day, Lord Mountbatten accepted the accession, but transmitted an accompanying letter in which he stated:

> It is my Government's wish that as soon as law and order have been restored in Kashmir and her soil cleared of the invaders, the question of the State's accession should be settled by reference to the people.[5]

Indian forces were rushed to Kashmir, just in time to stop the Moslem invaders a few miles from Srinagar, the capital. Pakistan immediately dispatched troops so as to forestall the collapse of the Moslem invasion. Thus, by late 1947, the two nations found themselves locked in deadly combat over Kashmir. The war continued inconclusively with neither side able to win a decisive military victory.

Charging Pakistan with aggression, India brought the dispute before the United Nations Security Council in early January 1948. Pakistan in turn accused India of genocide and illegal occupation of Kashmir. The Security Council called on both states to refrain from doing anything "which might aggravate the situation." It also established a UN Commission for India and Pakistan that was to investigate the facts and mediate between the contending parties. In August 1948 the commission recommended a cease-fire, which went into effect on January 1, 1949.

Thus ended the first phase of a modern religious war that erupted in the aftermath of colonial rule. The human tragedy surrounding the partition of the subcontinent was a grim reminder that turbulence and war had not ended with the passing of the European order in India. On the contrary, with the colonial lid off, Hindus and Moslems were free to turn on each other with the pent-up ferocity of centuries.

The Kashmir War of 1965

The political structures of Hindu and Moslem nationalism diverged sharply after partition. India, under the leadership of Jawaharlal Nehru, Gandhi's successor, immediately embarked on the ambitious and unprecedented experiment of shaping an overwhelmingly illiterate country into an advanced democracy. The Indian national elections of 1951–1952 were indeed an impressive performance. The new Indian government spared no effort to make this election truly democratic and, on the whole, succeeded admirably. The Congress Party, now pursuing a policy of gradual socialism patterned after the example of the British Labour Party, became the dominant political power, with Nehru its undisputed leader. Pakistan set out on a totally different road and fashioned its political system along authoritarian lines. After a succession of politicians had demonstrated their inability to govern, the army seized power in 1951. Under the leadership of General Ayub Khan, Pakistan instituted its first effective government and embarked on an ambitious economic development program. Pakistan developed a formidable power base, but at the expense of the democratic process.

Far from resolving the Kashmir dispute, the 1949 cease-fire had provided merely a breathing spell. India and Pakistan now continued the struggle by diplomatic means. Their initial involvement in international affairs was determined by their overriding search for security vis-à-vis each other. In fact, their quest for friends and allies may be interpreted quite accurately as an outgrowth, first and foremost, of their fear of one another. All other considerations were secondary.

During the 1950s the military leadership of Pakistan committed the Moslem nation to the Western alliance system. Believing that meaningful negotiations with India over Kashmir could be undertaken only by making Pakistan a strong military state, General Ayub Khan led Pakistan into two American-sponsored regional alliances, the Southeast Asia Treaty Organization (SEATO) and the Central Treaty Organization (CENTO). But in 1962, when war erupted between China and India over disputed border territory, Pakistan quickly gravitated toward India's enemy. Relations between China and Pakistan grew increasingly cordial. By the mid-1960s Pakistan was in the unique position of being a member of two Western military alliances and at the same time enjoying the friendship of the People's Republic of China.

In India Nehru labored hard and long during the 1950s to develop a policy of nonalignment and economic advancement for his country. Nehru's policy was handed a severe setback in the decisive defeat India suffered in the 1962 border war with China. The Soviet Union, increasingly estranged from China, attempted to exploit the situation by consolidating its ties with India, while the American leadership, fearful of Communist expansion, extended large quantities of military aid to both India and Pakistan, ostensibly for purposes of defense against Communism. In reality, however, both India and Pakistan used the American military equipment to bolster their strength against each other. It was against this complex background of multidimensional maneuverings that the conflict between Hindus and Moslems erupted once again into open warfare.

The war began in an unlikely spot, the so-called Rann of Kutch, an uninhabited piece of territory of little value that was a virtual desert during the dry season but became a flooded marsh during the monsoon. In the spring of 1965 both India and Pakistan stepped up patrolling activity in that area, and soon serious clashes occurred. Pakistani forces quickly outmaneuvered Indian troops, winning an easy victory. Although a cease-fire was achieved through the mediation efforts of British prime minister Harold Wilson, and both parties agreed to a mutual withdrawal of forces, the Rann of Kutch encounter "left Pakistan dangerously overconfident and India dangerously frustrated."[6]

The Pakistani leadership began to feel that the Kutch strategy should be tried in Kashmir. A prominent Urdu newspaper openly recommended that "the Rann of Kutch prescription should be applied on the Kashmir front,"[7] and the *Pakistan Times,* in a burst of euphoria, predicted that, "In the event of war with India, Pakistani troops would march up to Delhi, would occupy the Red Fort, and hoist the Pakistani flag on it."[8]

In India, on the other hand, resentment was rampant. To be defeated by China was one thing; to be outfought by Pakistan was something that most Indians were unwilling to accept. Lal Bahadur Shastri, Nehru's successor, came under increasing pressure to redress the Kutch defeat. The *Times of India* warned that "Pakistan has put the fish into the water to measure the temperature and one

fine morning Pakistan will present the world with a fait accompli—
the occupation of Kashmir."⁹

Thus Pakistan's overconfidence and India's humiliation brought
the two nations to the brink of war:

> It was barely credible in 1962 that two great countries should be at the
> brink of full-scale war, as China and India were, over an almost inacces-
> sible stretch of barren and snow-bound track. It is no more credible
> today that India and Pakistan should fight over a piece of barren land
> that spends half its life under water; yet it has happened.¹⁰

In August 1965 Ayub Khan, convinced that his policy of "leaning
on India" was working, made the fateful decision of sending Pakistani-
trained guerrillas into Kashmir. The infiltrators blew up bridges, disrupted lines of communication, and raided army convoys and military
installations. Not surprisingly, Indian forces in Kashmir rounded up
the guerrillas and then proceeded to occupy the three main mountain passes that had served as supply routes for the Pakistanis. Ayub
Khan now faced a difficult dilemma. He could hardly sustain a guerrilla campaign in Kashmir with the key mountain passes in Indian
hands. He either had to back down or raise the stakes. Calculating
that Indian fear of China would deter her from a vigorous response
against Pakistan and confident of his own military superiority, the
Pakistani leader decided to escalate the conflict.

On September 1 Pakistani forces, supported by ninety Patton
tanks, crossed the cease-fire line into southern Kashmir and
advanced so rapidly that they threatened the vital road over the
mountains linking Srinagar with the plains of India. If Pakistan
captured this road, Indian forces in Kashmir would be encircled.
India was now left with the choice of yielding or expanding the war.

On September 5 India opened a new front and invaded West Pakistan in a massive attack. The two armies were now locked in large-
scale combat over a wide area. Despite superior weapons and greater
mobility, the Pakistani forces were unable to break through Indian
lines and advance on India's cities as their leaders had so confidently
predicted they would do. In several encounters the Indians even
managed to outmaneuver and outfight their opponents, thus revers-
ing the situation that had prevailed in the Rann of Kutch. The Pakistani leadership was badly shaken and resorted to desperate
fighting to hold the line. After several weeks of war, the battlelines

became relatively stationary, with both sides having fought each other to a virtual standstill.

The war finally ended through the efforts of Soviet premier Aleksei Kosygin, who invited both parties to the negotiating table at Tashkent to settle their differences. Reasoning that a continued conflict between India and Pakistan would probably benefit China, the Soviet leader decided to act the role of peacemaker. Edward Crankshaw, who was in Tashkent during the Soviet-sponsored negotiations, commented:

> Mr. Kosygin, whose ideology demands the fostering of chaos and disruption in non-Communist lands, finds himself doing his level best to calm down a Hindu under direct threat from China and a Moslem supposed to be on friendly terms with Peking, embroiled in a quarrel over the possession of the mountain playground of the late British Raj. And, except for China, nobody minds.[11]

And so the world was treated to the strange spectacle of a Communist state successfully fashioning a truce between two bourgeois nations. The Kashmir problem was not resolved, of course. Both sides merely agreed to set forth their "respective positions" on the issue. Nor were the deeper animosities removed, or even mitigated. Tashkent merely signified a pause in a protracted conflict that so far had proved inconclusive. The decisive encounter was to come five years later, when the flames of war erupted once again with terrible ferocity.

The Bloody Dawn of Bangladesh

New nations are seldom born without great pain. The scale of human suffering that marked the birth of Bangladesh, however, was so vast that it stands out starkly even against the grim and melancholy canvas of the twentieth century. First, a natural disaster of titanic proportions, followed by a fratricidal war, then a flood of refugees, and finally another war—these were the four horsemen of the apocalypse that ushered the state of Bangladesh into the world in 1971.

To understand the outbreak of the war between Moslem and Moslem, one must appreciate that, first and foremost, the two Pakistans had nothing whatsoever in common *but* Islam. For almost a quarter century, the two wings of Pakistan stood more than 1,000 miles apart, with Indian territory in between. Aside from this physical, and consequently psychological, distance, the two peoples spoke different languages, had different racial characteristics, and prided themselves on different cultural achievements. As one observer put it rather bluntly: "The only bonds between the diverse and distant wings of their Moslem nation were the Islamic faith and Pakistan International Airlines."[12]

As if this condition were not enough to weaken the union, a sequence of developments aggravated the situation and eventually plunged the two Pakistans into all-out war. First, the founder of Pakistan, Mohammed Ali Jinnah, died one year after the creation of the state, and his successor, Liaquat Ali Khan, was felled by an assassin's bullet two years later. The loss of these two charismatic leaders left a serious void and contributed to the declining popularity of the Moslem League, which had provided a semblance of unity throughout Pakistan. Second, and even more serious, was the flagrantly unequal distribution of economic resources between the two Pakistans. From the very beginning, the West Pakistanis were far more generously endowed than their coreligionists in Bengal. In addition, West Pakistan, six times the size of East Pakistan, had to support only 40 percent of Pakistan's entire population. Third, and perhaps most important, was the tendency of the West Pakistani leadership to treat the Bengalis as poor relations. The nation's capital was established in the West, first in Karachi and later in Islamabad. As Pakistan became a major recipient of American military and economic aid, the West remained the main beneficiary. Westerners were always richer than easterners, and between 1950 and 1970 this income gap more than doubled. The Bengali jute and tea supplied between 50 and 70 percent of the nation's revenue, but the Bengalis received only 25 to 30 percent of Pakistan's total income. Thus, there was a parasitic quality to the West's relationship to the East. As a leading Bengali spokesman put it:

> We are only a colony and a market. If the only reason for our ties with West Pakistan is that we are both Moslem, why shouldn't we join some other state, like Kuwait, from which we might get more money?[13]

Finally, the West had a virtual monopoly on Pakistan's power elite: 85 percent of all government positions were held by westerners; two-thirds of the nation's industry and fourth-fifths of its banking and insurance assets were controlled by the West; and only 5 percent of Pakistan's 275,000-man army were Bengalis.

East Pakistanis tried hard to compensate for this disparity with cultural arrogance. They were lovers of art and literature and regarded the westerners' respect for the martial virtues with contempt. But gradually, under the growing pressures of deprivation, pride gave way to a Bengal nationalism demanding that its case be heard. Still, violence might have been avoided had not nature visited upon Bengal one of the most terrible calamities of the century. In November 1970 a devastating cyclone struck the coast of Bengal and claimed the lives of almost half a million people. Those who survived suffered starvation and disease. The catastrophe was so awesome that it was described as "a second Hiroshima."

At the time of the disaster the president of Pakistan was Yahya Khan, a general who had assumed power in 1969 by virtue of his military status. Yahya had promised free elections by the end of 1970. Two weeks elapsed, however, before the president even managed to visit the scene of the catastrophe, and most Bengalis perceived this delay as an example of West Pakistan's callousness and indifference to the calamity that had befallen them. The Bengalis' outrage now vented itself at the ballot box.

The election results turned out to be a bitter surprise for the military leadership as well as for the People's Party, headed by Zulfikar Ali Bhutto, a westerner. To their dismay, Sheik Mujibur Rahaman's Awami League won a sweeping victory in East Pakistan. Whereas Sheik Mujibur had always favored Bengali civil liberties, Yahya Khan's apathy in the wake of the cyclone provoked the Sheik's followers into a genuine nationalist movement. The league's platform of complete regional autonomy for East Pakistan would have given control of only foreign affairs and defense matters to the central government. On the basis of the election returns in December 1970, East Pakistan, with its large Bengali population, was allotted 169 seats in the National Assembly, while Bhutto's People's Party won only 90 seats. The results left no doubt that the next prime minister of Pakistan would not be Bhutto but the Bengali leader Sheik Mujibur Rahaman.

The western leadership found this outcome simply unacceptable. It feared that the Awami League, with its absolute majority in the National Assembly, would vote itself a program for virtual self-government, thus removing East Pakistan from the control of the central government. The weeks following the election were marked by a feverish contest for power that finally erupted into bloody conflict.

President Yahya Khan triggered the crisis when he announced the postponement of the assembly session to a later, unspecified date. The Awami League, perceiving this as a deliberate attempt to disregard a popular mandate for Bengali autonomy, launched a campaign of civil disobedience. The Bengalis defied the central government by calling a massive strike and managed to bring government operations to a virtual standstill. In response to this pressure, Yahya Khan scheduled the date of the assembly session for March 26, but at the same time made arrangements for a massive airlift of West Pakistani troops to East Pakistan.

In such a climate, negotiations were doomed from the start. On March 25 private talks between Yahya Khan and Sheik Mujibur broke down, and on his return to Islamabad the president denounced the sheik's activities as "acts of treason." He ordered the immediate arrest of Awami League leaders and directed the army to crush the secessionist movement and restore full authority to the central government. This decision directly precipitated the civil war and led to the end of a united Pakistan. In view of its crucial importance in the sequence of events, it is worth examining in some detail.

Yahya's plan was to destroy all Bengali resistance centers in one massive strike, thereby crushing the rebellion once and for all. West Pakistan leaders never doubted their own military superiority nor expected the Bengalis to put up more than token resistance. As one high-ranking army officer put it: "Those little brown buggers won't fight," and another predicted confidently: "A good beating and these chaps will come around."[14]

This attitude was deeply rooted in the culture of West Pakistan. The light-skinned westerners had always extolled martial virtues and looked down on the dark-skinned Bengalis, who preferred the word to the sword. For this reason Yahya crucially underestimated the appeal of Sheik Mujibur, whom he had never regarded as a legitimate spokesman for Bengali aspirations; instead, he imprisoned the sheik as a traitor. The sheik's statement in March that the Bengalis were "prepared to sacrifice one million people to gain independence"[15] was dismissed as empty rhetoric. Yahya, in fact, was reported to have referred to the Bengalis as "mosquitoes" who could be killed with one determined slap of the hand. He ignored the possibility that the "mosquitoes" might soon become guerrillas. Moreover, he never recognized the charisma of the Bengali leader, whom he dismissed as a saboteur and mischief maker. And finally, he never took into account the enormous logistical difficulties of supplying an occupation army from bases that were a thousand miles away. Instead, Yahya Khan preferred a military solution of the most brutal kind that not only alienated the Bengalis from West Pakistan forever but plunged the entire subcontinent into open conflict.

The western crackdown on Bengal was marked by extreme brutality. Pillage, murder, and rape were so pervasive that by April a powerful guerrilla movement had sprung up that fought the West Pakistanis with a courage born of desperation. On April 17 the Bengali resistance fighters, or Mukti Bahini, as they quickly came to be known, established a provisional government of their own in a mango grove just inside the East Pakistan border. They gave their embryonic state the name of Bangladesh.

In terror, millions of Bengalis fled for their lives from the pitilessness of the West Pakistanis. They chose as their haven the neighboring province of West Bengal, which was a part of India. Thus it came about that Moslems, in order to save themselves from other Moslems, sought refuge in India, the country of their former arch-enemy. The growing influx of these panic-stricken people began to create a terrible burden on the overpopulated and impoverished neighboring Hindu nation. India had to draw upon its meager resources in order to provide food, medical assistance, and shelter for the refugees and as a result had to suspend its own economic development plans. To make matters worse, West Bengal also happened to be one of India's politically most volatile and unstable states, and the flood of refugees naturally exacerbated this instability.

In view of these developments, India could not remain a passive observer of the civil war in Pakistan for very long. On April 16 the government, under Prime Minister Indira Gandhi, accused the West Pakistan army of "planned carnage and systematic genocide."[16] By May Pakistani troops were chasing Bengali guerrillas across the Indian border, and armed clashes between Indian and Pakistani border patrols were becoming commonplace.

As the flood of Bengali refugees gathered momentum, the Indian government became increasingly alarmed. Its treasury was being drained of $2.5 million a day. In the spring Gandhi warned the parliament that the refugee problem was "going to be hell for us; we are not going to allow them to stay here."[17] By November the Indian estimate of Bengali refugees had reached the 10 million mark. If this figure is correct, then "the mass movement of humanity over eight months of 1971 was the most intensive, regionally concentrated large-scale migration in the history of man."[18]

By mid-July Gandhi had evidence that a war with Pakistan would be cheaper than the economic burden of coping with the refugee problem for a single year. This evidence was supplied by the Institute for Defense Studies and Analysis in New Delhi. The Indians concluded that the refugees would cost their country $900 million within a year, or more than thirteen times the cost of the entire Kashmir war with Pakistan in 1965. This report was widely circulated and resulted in a wave of popular emotion in favor of war. The Indian leadership had to respond forcefully to alleviate the pressure.

On August 9 Gandhi, with an eye toward Pakistan's friendship with China, abandoned India's traditional policy of nonalignment and signed a treaty of friendship with the Soviet Union. This twenty-five-year treaty had all the earmarks of a military alliance. Reflecting the popular mood, the Indian Parliament hailed the new "realism" in India's foreign policy and praised Gandhi for having "put some meat in our vegetarian diet of non-alignment."[19] The pact was intended as a clear warning to Pakistan and as a deterrent against the possibility of Chinese intervention. Several weeks later, Gandhi embarked on a tour of the United States, Britain, and Western Europe to underline the gravity of the situation and the need for a political solution. Specifically, she demanded the release of Sheik Mujibur, which she hoped would result in Bengali autonomy and the return of the refugees to their former homes.

On the home front Gandhi quietly took measures to prepare the Indian army for action in case her diplomatic efforts failed. During the months of October and November 1971 Indian forces began to help the Mukti Bahini more actively. Gandhi was still hopeful that a major war could be averted and that the Indians, as discreetly as possible, could secure enough territory within East Pakistan to establish a Bangladesh regime. However, this clandestine support for the Bengali guerrillas turned out to be insufficient. Moreover, another natural calamity forced the Indian government to become even more actively involved.

In early November another cyclone struck, this time spending its fury on Indian soil. The death of 20,000 Indians sharply increased public pressures on Gandhi. The parliament now demanded that priority be given to the Indian victims and that forceful measures be taken to effect the repatriation of the Bengalis. In response to these pressures, Gandhi made a crucial military commitment. She authorized Indian forces to engage Pakistani troops on the East Pakistan border. Her strategy was to hit the West Pakistanis with quick, limited strikes that would tie down the occupation troops and give the Bengali guerrillas more freedom to maneuver. This "hit and run" strategy was greeted with a chorus of approval in the parliament. The commander of the Indian forces in the area, General Jagjit Singh Aurora, was happy that his troops could now challenge the Pakistanis in open combat. As he put it:

> I had finished building up my force in September, and I really began to retaliate in mid-October, but it wasn't until the third week of November that I got permission to go in and silence their guns by pushing them back and giving them a bloody nose.[20]

Gandhi had confidence in her strategy for another reason. She was convinced that China would be deterred from intervening, not only because of India's new alliance with the Soviet Union, but also because the Himalayan passes were already blocked by snow. Her assumption proved to be correct.

On November 30 Gandhi ordered a blackout of Calcutta, and on the following day Indian troops penetrated five miles into Pakistan as a "defensive measure." On that day the United States began its "tilt" toward Pakistan by canceling an arms shipment to India, and Gandhi exploded:

> If any country thinks that by calling us aggressors it can pressure us to forget our national interests, then that country is living in its own paradise and is welcome to it. The times have passed when any nation sitting three or four thousand miles away could give orders to Indians on the basis of their color superiority. India has changed, and she is no more a country of natives.[21]

Tension also ran high in Pakistan. By late November it had become public knowledge that President Yahya Khan had taken to heavy drinking. On November 25, while entertaining a delegation of visiting Chinese, he exclaimed to a reporter:

If that woman thinks she can cow me down, I refuse to take it. If she wants a war, I'll fight her! In ten days, I might not be here. There might be a war. I'll be off fighting a war![22]

Indira Gandhi's demand that Yahya Khan release Sheik Mujibur enraged the Pakistani leader so much that he sentenced the Bengali nationalist to death. Not only did he resist all appeals and efforts to change his mind, but on November 26 he outlawed the entire Awami League on grounds of conspiracy against the government. The death sentence against Sheik Mujibur, however, was never carried out.

Yahya Khan also displayed an increasing tendency to reduce the conflict between India and Pakistan to a personal test of strength between himself and Gandhi. In an interview with a *Time* correspondent, his vanity broke through. Proud of his thick black hair, he exclaimed to the reporter, "My strength lies in it—like Samson's."[23] And to a *Newsweek* correspondent, who questioned him about the possibility of war with India, he confided: "The worst losers will be the Indians themselves. I hope to God that woman understands."[24] A week later, the same reporter interviewed Gandhi, who promptly returned the compliment:

"That woman!" I am not concerned with the remark, but it shows the mentality of the person. He is one man who could not get elected in his own country if there were a fair election. I would say he would not even get elected in his province if there were a fair election. What weight has his judgment on India? It is a world which is quite outside his ken.[25]

On December 1 Gandhi issued an ultimatum in which she demanded that Yahya Khan withdraw all his forces from East Pakistan. This was a hard blow under any circumstances, but for a man with Yahya Khan's fragile ego, such an ultimatum from a woman was psychologically unacceptable. Thus, even though he knew that the Indian forces outnumbered his own by a ratio of five to one, the president of Pakistan authorized a massive air strike against India on December 3. The decision was greeted with a chorus of approval. Bhutto, who had just assumed the post of deputy prime minister, exclaimed, "Pakistan is faced with a predatory aggressor who never reconciled itself to the establishment of this country."[26] And Lieutenant General Niazi, commander of Pakistan's forces in the East, got right to the heart of the matter: "We are Moslems and we don't like Hindus. One Moslem soldier is worth five Hindus."[27]

Yahya Khan's military strategy was based on the example of the Israeli surprise attack of June 1967. He hoped to cripple the Indian Air Force with a single devastating blow and then move with impunity into Kashmir, which he could use as a trump card in post-war bargaining.

The execution of the December 3 air attack, however, turned out to be a military disaster. Indian jet planes, unlike Egyptian planes in 1967, were well protected in concrete revetments and virtually immune to the Pakistani assault. In addition, since only thirty-two Pakistani planes participated in the attack, the offensive strike was very feeble indeed. India's air marshal claimed that India was hardly bruised, let alone hurt, by the attack, and another military expert commented, "In military terms, no one in his right mind would have attacked with three or four planes at each airfield. It was sheer madness."[28]

The failure of the air attack, far from forcing the Pakistanis to face reality, had precisely the opposite effect. Fervent appeals for a holy war against India increased in frequency. The *Pakistan Times* editorialized:

> Plainly Islam is the issue between India and Pakistan. . . . Only those qualify to fight the battle of Pakistan who are prepared to fight the battle of Islam. . . . For us there is no choice but to fight, if need be to the last man.[29]

As the conflict intensified in early December, the elements of a fierce religious war made their appearance. Gradually all restraint was lost, and the religious basis of the struggle was revealed in all its fanaticism and ferocity. As a Pakistani pilot put it: "Our one god makes our victory certain. The Indians are worshippers of idols, of many gods. Ours is the true strength."[30] And an army colonel took strength from the concept of jihad, or holy war, when he asserted confidently that there would be no Pakistani casualties on the field of battle since, "in the pursuit of jihad, nobody dies; he lives forever."[31]

When Pakistan was confronted with dismemberment and defeat in mid-December, the truth was so appalling that it was unacceptable. Even the conquering Indian generals were moved to compassion when they saw their former colleagues from the British colonial army under siege in Dacca. Major General Gandharv Nagra's appeal to General Niazi, the defender of Dacca, makes poignant reading: "My dear Abdullah, I am here. The game is up. I suggest you give yourself up to me and I'll look after you."[32]

Gandhi thus emerged as the undisputed victor. India agreed to a cease-fire at its own convenience, acquired 2,500 square miles of territory in West Pakistan, and detained some 93,000 prisoners of war for almost two years. Pakistan was dismembered and East Pakistan emerged as Bangladesh. A bitter political divorce and a bloody war had led to the emergence of a new state in the family of nations.

Strife between Hindus and Moslems continued to erupt periodically. In 1984, for example, major riots took place in several Indian cities. In addition, the Sikhs, followers of a monotheistic blending of Hinduism and Islam that began about 1500, waged a campaign for national self-determination against the Indian government. Prime Minister Gandhi ordered the military suppression of the Sikh insurrection. In November 1984, however, she was assassinated by Sikhs who resented her strong-arm methods. Her son Rajiv Gandhi who succeeded her was himself assassinated in 1991. The world's most populous democracy still had not learned how to govern itself without violence.

When one surveys the history of India and Pakistan since the end of British colonial rule, it is difficult to avoid the conclusion that a high price in human suffering has been paid for independence.

Nuclear Viagra

In 1974 India became a member of the world's exclusive nuclear club by exploding a powerful atomic device. Prime Minister Gandhi, not surprisingly, asserted that she had made the decision for purely defensive and peaceful purposes. Pakistan, still smarting from its defeat three years earlier, promptly embarked on a crash program aimed at matching India's nuclear arsenal. During the next two decades both nations quietly pursued their nuclear programs while occasionally testing their military prowess by forays into disputed areas of Kashmir. But then, in May 1998, India carried out a number of underground nuclear tests in rapid succession. An alarmed Pakistan promptly followed suit and the world watched in shock as the fifty-year-old conflict was raised to a new and highly dangerous level. India's prime minister, Hindu nationalist Atal Behari

Vajpayee, took a defiant stand accusing China of bolstering Pakistan's nuclear arsenal to unacceptable levels. Pakistan responded by pointing to the intensely anti-Moslem attitude of India's governing Hindu Nationalist Party.

The nuclear tests were extremely popular in both countries. Euphoric crowds filled the streets of New Delhi and Islamabad and celebrated their respective governments for restoring national pride. In the words of a popular Pakistani general, Perves Musharraf, "We have been saved from our status of eunuchs."

United States Secretary of State Madeleine Albright expressed her strong displeasure by declaring that both Indians and Pakistanis were far less secure now than they were even three weeks earlier. When the United States threatened both nations with economic sanctions, however, both India and Pakistan responded by condemning American "monetary blackmail." Moreover, India accused the United States of hypocrisy for dragging its feet on nuclear arms control.

Tensions escalated in the spring of 1999 when General Musharraf led a Pakistani incursion into Kargil, a part of Kashmir under Indian control. Two months of fierce fighting erupted in the mountains of Kargil until President Clinton persuaded Pakistan's Prime Minister Sharif to withdraw his troops. An outraged Musharraf responded by announcing, "If I had done this, I would have lost the right to be the army chief." To no one's surprise, General Musharraf staged a coup in October, toppling Sharif from power and thereby ending Pakistan's ten-year-old experiment in democracy. The generals had returned.

Within hours of the coup in Pakistan and perhaps not coincidentally, the United States Senate, by a vote of 51–48, defeated one of President Bill Clinton's most cherished foreign policy objectives: the Comprehensive Test Ban Treaty. Opponents, pointing to the actions of India and Pakistan, argued that the treaty was unenforceable. But Carl Levin of the Senate's Armed Services Committee defended the treaty. "We no longer have standing when we defeated this treaty, to tell India or Pakistan 'don't test nuclear weapons'," he exclaimed. The president concurred. "By this vote," he declared, "the Senate majority has turned its back on fifty years of American leadership against the spread of weapons of mass destruction."

Many observers compared the Senate vote to its defeat of the League of Nations eighty years earlier. Be that as it may, the game of

"Nuclear Viagra" being played out between India and Pakistan not only turned the Indian subcontinent into a potential nuclear war zone, but also had serious repercussions on the policies of the world's leading nuclear power and thus, on the safety and security of planet Earth.

It did not take long for the tensions between the two nuclear powers to reach a climax. In December 2001 a radical Islamic group mounted a deadly car bomb attack on the Indian parliament, killing fifteen parliamentarians and five policemen. President Musharraf denied any involvement in the attack, but India refused to accept this explanation. Indian prime minister Vajpayee decided to sever all rail and air links to Pakistan and began to mass tens of thousands of troops along the 1,800-mile border. Musharraf reciprocated in kind and, after a rapid escalation by both sides, each country had deployed one million troops along the border. In May 2002 a second terrorist attack in Kashmir killed thirty-one people including the wives and children of Hindu soldiers stationed in Jammu and Kashmir. Even though Musharraf decided to arrest several Islamic radicals and denied once again any involvement in the attack, the Indian government now began to feel that its credibility depended on punishing, rather than merely admonishing, Pakistan. It was at this juncture that both countries began to brandish their nuclear weapons, with Pakistan pointing to the destructive power of its Ghauri II missile and India's defense minister, George Fernandez, responding that if Pakistan were to attack, "India would suffer a little in a nuclear war but there would be no Pakistan after its retaliation"[33] with its Agni missiles. This nuclear saber rattling quickly attracted the attention of the United States, which by now was contemplating war with Iraq. President George W. Bush urged both leaders to "step back from the abyss." Jack Straw, the British foreign secretary, declared that "the situation was dangerous but war was not inevitable."[34] Despite these interventions, L. K. Advani, India's deputy prime minister, was reported as saying in London that "we are at war."[35] He further clarified his statement by adding that it was a war against infiltration and terrorism. To underline its determination, India fired at Pakistani army posts in response to yet another car bomb attack by Islamic militants that had killed thirty-eight people in Indian Kashmir.

Realizing that India and Pakistan could stumble into a nuclear war by miscalculation, Secretary of State Colin Powell visited both countries to calm tensions. In Islamabad Powell emphasized the "enduring commitment of the United States to the great Moslem nation of Pakistan." On the following day, in New Delhi, Powell described the friendship between India and Washington as one between "two great democracies that share common values."[36]

Despite this concerted American effort to lower the tension level, the game of nuclear chicken continued unabated. The Indian government made public a fascinating discussion among its top officials: Since Vajpayee was in charge of the nuclear trigger, what would happen if he was asleep when Pakistan launched an attack, given that Pakistan's nuclear weapons could reach New Delhi in 300 seconds? The answer was the creation of a Nuclear Command Authority that would provide a backup within less than 300 seconds if the seventy-nine-year-old Vajpayee was asleep or had been killed.

In May 2003, after sixteen months of nuclear standoff, Prime Minister Vajpayee stepped away from doomsday and surprised Parliament with plans to send a new ambassador to Pakistan, to resume air traffic, and to open peace talks with Islamabad. "The talks this time will be decisive," he declared. "At least in my lifetime this will be the last time I will be making an attempt" to resolve the India-Pakistan dispute. Hours later, Pakistan's foreign minister said that his country would also upgrade diplomatic relations to their normal status. Vajpayee's courageous decision to break the deadlock rapidly defused what had become one of the world's most dangerous standoffs.

In November 2003, at long last, Indian and Pakistani military commanders agreed to a formal cease-fire along their common border including the volatile and heavily militarized front line in the disputed territory of Kashmir. It was the first real breakthrough since an insurgency began in the Indian-controlled portion of Kashmir in 1989. In January 2004, both sides stepped back from the brink as India's prime minister set foot on Pakistani soil for the first time in four years and shook the hand of that nation's president. Shortly thereafter, the two leaders began serious discussions to reduce tensions between their countries.

The ultimate disposition of Kashmir is difficult to fathom. One possible outcome might be an interim UN protectorate as in Kosovo, followed by elections. Such elections might produce two Kashmiri entities, each with its own government and constitution. One of these would be associated with Pakistan, the other with India. The end result might be two independent non-hostile states. All this would have to be the culmination of a fairly lengthy process and the involvement of the United Nations would be indispensable at every stage.

The nuclear dimension has added a frightening element to the India-Pakistan equation. In a sense, it is more dangerous than the Cold War confrontation between the United States and the Soviet Union. The two superpowers had a whole array of safety procedures guarding against accidental war, especially since the near-catastrophe of the Cuban Missile Crisis. India and Pakistan have little experience in such procedures and, even on the brink, seemed to be in almost total denial of a possible holocaust that would destroy millions of lives. They never felt the icy terror that gripped President Kennedy and Premier Khrushchev as they stared into the nuclear abyss. Absent that experience, one can only hope that future leaders of India and Pakistan will never again treat nuclear weapons with such nonchalance.

Conclusion

The elements that produced the four armed conflicts between India and Pakistan constituted a veritable witches' brew. When one sorts out these elements, it seems difficult indeed to conceive of a more explosive mixture. The awesome list includes religious conflict, territorial claims, economic imbalance, natural calamity, nationalist aspirations, refugee migration, nuclear competition, and personality clashes.

The basic conflict, of course, was religious in nature. Had it not been for the long-standing and bitter enmity between Hindus and Moslems, a single state, rather than two hostile ones, would have emerged out of the British colony. The ambiguous status of Kashmir, the ruler of which had been a Hindu but whose population had been predominantly Moslem, injected the element of territorial conflict into the picture. To make matters even more complicated, Pakistan was not really one state but two, with the eastern part suffering deprivation while the western part enjoyed relative affluence. A natural disaster in the shape of a cyclone that devastated Bengal with the fury of an atomic bomb highlighted the economic imbalance between the two Pakistans even further and precipitated demands for equality. When these demands for equal rights were denied, they grew into a virulent nationalism that turned the two Pakistans against each other in a ferocious civil war. The result was the gigantic exodus of refugees from Bengal into India. When India decided that war with Pakistan was cheaper than the support of 10 million refugees, armed conflict became a distinct possibility. And when personal antagonisms and a leader's fragile ego were added to the mixture, war became a certainty. The dreadful circle was closed, with Hindu once more pitted against Moslem.

It is not easy, of course, to assess the relative weight of each link in this fateful chain. Yet the evidence suggests that of all the chapters in this tragic story, the religious one is the most awful and most desperate. It is not an accident that the conflict began and ended as a religious war; this was always its essential and most irreconcilable feature. When the situation is viewed from this perspective, one must question the confident assertion made so often in Western history books that the age of religious warfare came to an end in 1648, when Catholics and Protestants made peace and signed the Treaty of Westphalia. In our secular age, more than three centuries later, the battle over God continues unabated, though with more awesome weapons and under bleaker skies.

NOTES

1. Quoted in George M. Kahin, *Major Governments of Asia* (Ithaca, N.Y.: Cornell University Press, 1958), p. 268.

2. Jawaharlal Nehru, *Independence and After* (New Delhi: Government of India Publication Division, 1949), p. 95.

3. M. Gopal, "Considerations of Defence," *Caravan* (New Delhi: February 1967), p. 67.

4. Alan Campbell-Johnson, *Mission with Mountbatten* (London: Robert Hale, 1952), pp. 357–358.

5. P. L. Lakhanpal, *Essential Documents and Notes on the Kashmir Dispute* (New Delhi: Council on World Affairs, 1967), p. 57.

6. William J. Barnds, *India, Pakistan, and the Great Powers* (New York: Praeger, 1972), p. 200.

7. *Nava-I-Waqt* (Lahore), May 9, 1965, p. 4.

8. *Pakistan Times* (Lahore), July 11, 1965, p. 7.

9. *Times of India* (New Delhi), July 18, 1965, p. 7.

10. *The Economist* (May 1, 1965), pp. 502–503.

11. *London Observer,* January 9, 1966, p. 11.

12. Dan Coggin et al., "Pakistan: The Ravaging of Golden Bengal," *Time* (August 2, 1971), p. 26.

13. Khushwant Singh, "Why They Fled Pakistan and Won't Go Back," *New York Times Magazine,* August 1, 1971.

14. Wayne Wilcox, "Conflict in South Asia," Paper presented at the University of London Institute of Commonwealth Studies, February 1972.

15. "Another War in Asia: Who's to Blame?" *Newsweek* (December 20, 1971).

16. "Bangladesh Is over the Border," *The Economist* (April 24, 1971).

17. Singh, op. cit.

18. Louis Dupree, "Bangladesh" (Part I), *American Universities Fieldstaff Reports,* South Asia Series, Vol. 16, No. 5, p. 2, 1972.

19. Quoted by Sydney H. Schanberg, "Pact Said to Bury India's Non-Alignment," *New York Times,* August 14, 1971.

20. Robert Shaplen, "The Birth of Bangladesh" (Part I), *New Yorker* (February 12, 1972), p. 55.

21. *London Times,* December 3, 1971.

22. Shaplen, loc. cit.

23. "Good Soldier Yahya Khan," *Time* (August 2, 1971).

24. "A Talk with Pakistan's President Yahya Khan," *Newsweek* (November 8, 1971).

25. "A Talk with India's Prime Minister Indira Gandhi," *Newsweek* (November 15, 1971),

26. Radio Pakistan Broadcast, December 3, 1971.

27. Shaplen, loc. cit.

28. "Another War in Asia: Who's to Blame?" op. cit.

29. *Pakistan Times,* December 4, 1971.

30. Rosanne Klass, "Pakistan's Costly Delusion," *Saturday Review* (February 5, 1972).

31. "Bangladesh: Out of War, a Nation Is Born," *Time* (December 27, 1971).

32. "India: Easy Victory, Uneasy Peace," *Time* (December 27, 1971).

33. *Economist,* January 11, 2003.

34. *Economist,* June 8, 2002.

35. *Economist,* August 31, 2002.

36. *Economist,* October 20, 2002.

SELECTED BIBLIOGRAPHY

BAJPAI, SHANKAR K. "Untangling India and Pakistan." *Foreign Affairs,* May/June 2003.

BARNDS, WILLIAM J. *India, Pakistan, and the Great Powers.* New York: Praeger, 1972.

BHATIA, KRISHNAN. *Indira: A Biography of Prime Minister Gandhi.* New York: Praeger, 1974.

BROWN, JUDITH M. *Gandhi: Prisoner of Hope.* New Haven, Conn.: Yale University Press, 1989.

ERIKSON, ERIK. *Gandhi's Truth.* New York: Norton, 1969.

GANDHI, MAHATMA. *An Autobiography: The Story of My Experiments with Truth.* 2 vols. Ahmedabad: Navajihan, 1927–1929.

JACKSON, ROBERT. *South Asian Crisis: India, Pakistan, and Bangladesh.* New York: Praeger, 1975.

JAFFRELOT, CHRISTOPHE, Ed. *Pakistan: Nationalism Without a Nation?* New York: Zed Books, 2002.

JONES, BENNET. *Pakistan: Eye of the Storm.* New Haven, Conn.: Yale University Press, 2002.

KAUL, SUVIR, Ed. *The Partitions of Memory: The Afterlife of the Divisions of India.* Bloomington: Indiana University Press, 2002.

KHILNANI, SUNIL. *The Idea of India.* New York: Farrar, Straus & Giroux, 1997.

LALL, ARTHUR. *The Emergence of Modern India.* New York: Columbia University Press, 1981.

LAMB, ALASTAIR. *The Kashmir Problem.* New York: Praeger, 1967.

ROBB, PETER. *A History of India.* New York: Palgrave, 2002.

SHAPLEN, ROBERT. "The Birth of Bangladesh," *New Yorker,* February 12, 1972.

VARSHNEY, ASHUTOSH. *Ethnic Conflict and Civic Life: Hindus and Muslims in India.* New Haven, Conn.: Yale University Press, 2002.

WEAVER, MARY ANNE. *Pakistan: In the Shadow of Jihad and Afghanistan.* New York: Farrar, Straus & Giroux, 2002.

ZAKARIA, RAFIQ. *Communal Rage in Secular India.* Mumbai: Popular Prakashan, 2002.

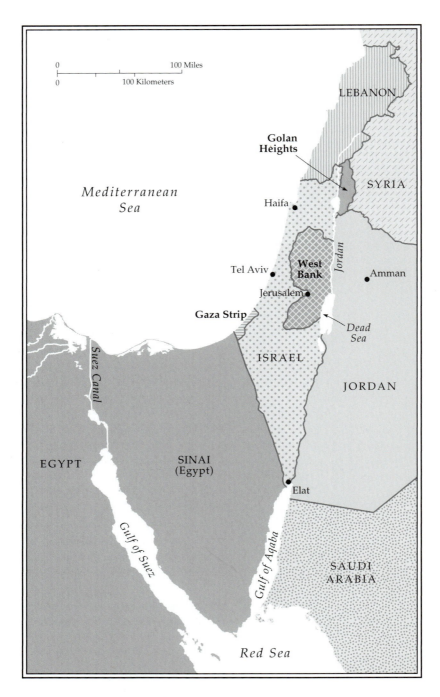

MAP 9   Israel and Its Neighbors

7

The Fifty Years' War in the Holy Land: Israel and the Arabs

War can protect; it cannot create.
Alfred North Whitehead

Historical tragedies do not arise from encounters in which right clashes with wrong. Rather, they occur when right clashes with right. This is the heart of the conflict between Israel and the Arab states in Palestine. A large number of Jews, responding to the horror of Hitler's systematic extermination of the Jews of Europe, attempted to save themselves by creating a state of their own. They established it in a land that had been occupied by Arabs for centuries, at the precise moment when the Arab peoples were emerging from the crucible of Western colonialism and were rediscovering their own national destinies. Thus Jewish nationalism clashed head-on with Arab nationalism in Palestine.

The four wars between Israel and her Arab neighbors have been the result of this collision. The modern Middle East has been the scene of both irreconcilable hopes and aspirations and bitter hatreds and violent passions. The wars were fought with the deepest emotion. Each side regarded its rights as self-evident and firmly based on the will of God, morality, reason, and law. As passions rose, irrationality became commonplace. Desperate deed was heaped on desperate deed until right and wrong, responsibility and guilt, could no longer be distinguished. Each side had done things that the other could neither forgive nor forget.

This tragic clash between two valid claims and two appeals for justice has not abated much with time. Nor has it been possible to break the impasse through a lasting peace settlement.

All this suggests that there is perhaps no solution to the Arab-Israeli problem outside the course of history. In the meantime, it is the scholar's duty to offer a diagnosis, even though it may not be possible to prescribe a cure for a "sickness unto death." The four Palestine wars were merely massive eruptions of a historical encounter that is nothing less than a protracted war spanning an entire generation. As such they offer us insight into, but not liberation from, some of the darkest recesses of the souls of nations and men.

The Palestine War of 1948

The Zionist movement was founded in 1897 with the publication of a book entitled *The Jewish State,* by Dr. Theodore Herzl, an Austrian journalist who urged the settlement of Jewish agriculturists and artisans in Palestine. These pioneers, Herzl hoped, would realize an ancient Jewish dream—the reestablishment of a Jewish homeland in the Promised Land and the gathering together of the Jewish people from their diaspora of 2,000 years. Responding to Herzl's vision and reacting to anti-Semitic pogroms in Russia and Poland, 60,000 Jews emigrated to Palestine between 1881 and 1914. The land that was used for the Jewish settlements was purchased from absentee Arab landlords by wealthy philanthropists like Baron de Rothschild of Paris or through funds collected by the Zionists abroad. By 1914 almost 100,000 acres of Palestinian land had been purchased by the Jews.

In 1917 Chaim Weizmann, a scientist of world renown and a fervent Zionist, persuaded British foreign minister Lord Arthur James Balfour to issue a proclamation that would convert Herzl's dream into a British pledge:

His Majesty's Government views with favor the establishment in Palestine of a national home for the Jewish people, and will use their best endeavors to facilitate the achievement of this object, it being clearly understood that nothing shall be done which may prejudice the civil rights of existing non-Jewish communities in Palestine, or the rights and political status enjoyed by Jews in any other country.

In 1922 Britain was given a League of Nations mandate over Palestine. The Palestinian Arabs, understandably enough, objected to the Balfour Declaration and became increasingly uneasy about the large influx of Jewish immigrants. During the 1930s, as Hitler's persecution of European Jews gathered momentum, Jewish immigration soared dramatically. By 1937 the Jews constituted almost one-third of the total population of Palestine. Between 1928 and 1937 their number had risen from 150,000 to 400,000. As the Zionist movement looked toward Palestine as the last refuge from the impending Nazi holocaust, Arab alarm grew accordingly. It was no longer a question of land purchased by individual settlers but the threat of an alien state in a land that had been inhabited by Arabs for over a thousand years. The British, caught in a vise between their pledge to the Jews on the one hand and to Arab oil and strategic interests on the other, tried to temporize, but finally placated the Arabs by imposing a ceiling on Jewish immigration. The Jews, in their plight, tried to run the British blockade. In most cases, the British intercepted the immigrant vessels and shipped the passengers to internment camps in Cyprus. In the particularly tragic case of the immigrant ship *Exodus,* the British sent the helpless Jews back to Germany. As one survivor put it, "The Germans killed us, and the British don't let us live."[1]

Despite the British blockade, tens of thousands of Jewish immigrants landed in Palestine illegally. The Arabs became increasingly restive, and bitter fighting erupted. The British, caught in the lines of fire, were unable to restore the peace. In 1947, in total frustration, Britain announced its intention to relinquish the mandate over Palestine and decided to place the entire problem before the United Nations.

The undisputed leader of the more than half a million Jewish settlers in Palestine in 1947 was David Ben-Gurion. Ben-Gurion's commitment to the Zionist ideal was total and unswerving. He had come to Palestine in 1906, had been a leading delegate to the World Zionist Congress, and by 1935 had become chairman of the Jewish Agency, which represented the World Zionist Movement. No single leader represented the Arab cause, but the most influential men were Haj Amin el-Husseini, the grand mufti of Jerusalem, Azzam Pasha, the secretary-general of the Arab League, King Abdullah of Transjordan, and Glubb Pasha, the commander of the British-trained Arab Legion. The grand mufti had been in Germany during the war and had helped the Nazis plan their "final solution" to the Jewish problem. He had designs to rule all Palestine and for this reason was distrusted by the other Arab leaders. Azzam Pasha was an Egyptian diplomat with relatively moderate views. King Abdullah of Transjordan, who had a reputation for compassion and humanity, met secretly once with Golda Meir to explore the possibility of an Arab-Jewish compromise. And Glubb Pasha's Arab Legion was the only Arab military force that was truly feared by the Zionists.

In early 1947 a specially constituted United Nations Committee on Palestine (UNSCOP) visited the area and examined the alternatives. After several months of highly charged debate, the committee finally recommended that Palestine, with its population of 1.2 million Arabs and 570,000 Jews, be partitioned into two states, one Arab and one Jewish, with Jerusalem held as trustee of the United Nations. The Jewish state would include 55 percent of the land and its population would be 58 percent Jewish, while the Arab state would encompass 45 percent of the land and have a 99 percent Arab population. This partition plan was eagerly welcomed by the Jews and denounced with equal fervor by the Arabs.

A number of meetings on the partition plan took place between Arab and Jewish leaders. In one such encounter Abba Eban, then an official of the Jewish Agency, met with Azzam Pasha to discuss the possibility of a compromise. Eban stated that "the Jews [were] a fait accompli in the Middle East and that the Arabs [would] have to reconcile themselves to that fact."[2] He then went on to propose an economic program for joint development of the Middle East. Azzam Pasha conceded that the plan was "rational and logical" but added that "the fate of nations [was] not decided by rational logic." "We shall try to defeat you," he said. "I am not sure we will succeed, but we will try. We were able to drive out the Crusaders, but on the other hand, we lost Spain and Persia. It may be that we shall lose Palestine. But it is too late for peaceful solutions."[3] When Abba Eban interrupted by pointing out that this left no alternative but a test of strength through force of arms, Azzam Pasha replied:

It is in the nature of peoples to aspire to expansion and to fight for what they think is vital. It is possible that I don't represent, in the full sense of the word, the new spirit which animates my people. My young son who yearns to fight, undoubtedly represents it better than I do. He no longer believes in the old generation. . . . The forces which motivate peoples are not subject to our control. They are objective forces. Nationalism, that is a greater force than any which drives us. We don't need economic development with your assistance. We have only one test, the test of strength.[4]

An eyewitness to this encounter detected no hatred in Azzam Pasha's tone. He referred to the Jews over and over as "cousins." Not once during the two-hour conversation did he express an unkind thought or use a hostile expression about the Jews. But he did confirm the character of the position of the Arab majority—a position based not on logic but "on a blind fatalism, ungovernable as the wind."[5] Sadly and without hatred, the two leaders took their leave of one another.

The lobbying for and against the partition resolution was the most intense that the United Nations had experienced in its short history. A two-thirds majority was required for passage of the resolution by the General Assembly. To offset the votes of just the Arab and Moslem nations, the Zionists needed twenty-two votes, and for each additional vote against partition they needed two in favor. While the Zionists were by no means certain that they could muster a two-thirds majority, they were encouraged by the fact that the two main antagonists in the Cold War, the United States and the Soviet Union, both supported them. In the United States President Truman was deeply sympathetic to the Jewish cause. Moreover, his political instincts told him that the Jewish vote might well be crucial to the presidential election of 1948. Overruling the objections of leading State Department officials over the Soviet threat and American access to military bases, Truman personally warned the United States delegate to the United Nations, Herschel Johnson, to "damn well deliver the partition vote or there will be hell to pay."[6] From the Soviet point of view, partition seemed the easiest way to oust Britain from the Middle East and to keep the United States at arm's length while playing the Arabs off against the Jews. Two days before the vote it became clear that the fate of Zionism was in the hands of a few small, remote nations, in particular Liberia, Haiti, the Philippines, and Ethiopia. The Zionists persuaded the United States to apply strong pressure to these countries. Nevertheless, on November 29, 1947, the outcome was very much in doubt. Moshe Sharett, the Jewish Agency's "foreign minister," solemnly warned the assembly that the Jewish people would never submit to any attempt to subjugate them to an Arab majority. On the other hand, Jamal Husseini, the acting secretary-general of the Arab League, declared that if the assembly did vote for partition, the Arabs of Palestine would go to war against the Jews as soon as the British left: "the partition line will be drawn in fire and blood."[7]

Two eyewitnesses have left a poignant account of that fateful vote on November 29:

> An aide set a basket before Aranha [the President of the General Assembly]. In it were fifty-six slips of paper, each bearing the name of one of the nations represented in the hall. Aranha extended his hand and slowly drew from the basket the name of the nation whose vote would begin the poll. He unfolded the piece of paper and stared an instant at the men ranged before him.
>
> "Guatemala," he announced. At his words, a terrible silence settled over the Assembly. Even the press gallery fell quiet. For an instant, the three hundred delegates, the spectators, the newsmen, seemed united in awe of the moment before them, in their awareness of the grave and solemn decision about to be taken.
>
> The delegate of Guatemala rose. As he did, suddenly, from the spectators' gallery, a piercing cry sundered the silence of the Assembly hall, a Hebrew cry as old as time and the suffering of men: "Ana Ad Hoshiya. O Lord, save us."[8]

With a vote of thirty-three in favor, thirteen against, and ten abstentions, the partition resolution was adopted. The Zionists were ecstatic, but the Arab delegates walked out of the General Assembly, declaring that their governments would not be bound by the United Nations decision.

Both Ben-Gurion, who had heard of the Zionist victory 6,000 miles away in Palestine, and the grand mufti of Jerusalem, who had followed every word of the Palestine debate in New York, knew that the vote was no guarantee that the Jewish state would actually come into being. Between the vote on that late November afternoon and the expiration of the British mandate in Palestine, scheduled for May of the following year, lay a span of time that might well be decisive. Both men immediately set out to strengthen their forces for the battle that loomed ahead. Violent Arab-Jewish clashes occurred in Jerusalem and other parts of the country the day after the United Nations vote. The Jews were fearful that Arab resistance would deprive them of the fruits of the partition vote. The Arabs were enraged at a decision that, in their view, deprived them of their patrimony. On both sides, there seemed to be no time to lose.

The search for arms now dominated the minds of Arab and Jewish leaders alike. In this vital quest, the Zionists were at a disadvantage. The right to buy arms openly on the international arms market was the prerogative of sovereign states. Lebanon and Syria, which had won their independence in 1943 and 1946, respectively, were legally free to purchase arms for the Arab cause. Syria's defense minister, for example, was able to place an order for 10,000 rifles with a leading arms manufacturer in Czechoslovakia. The Jews, on the other hand, had to resort to clandestine means. The Haganah, the underground Zionist army, bought up American surplus arms and machine tools that were destined to be converted into scrap metal. To bypass the British arms embargo, most of the equipment was broken down into its component parts, classified by code, and then shipped to Palestine in random bits and pieces under official import permits for such items as textile machinery. Another technique used by Ben-Gurion's men was to place an order on the stationery of a sovereign state. One such order, from "Ethiopia," reached the same Czech arms manufacturer who had served the Syrians. That order too was filled. Thus by late 1947 a jostling for territory between Arabs and Jews was threatening to erupt into organized warfare between two desperate peoples.

In December 1947 the seven members of the Arab League met in Cairo to discuss the threat of a Jewish state in their midst. The states that were represented at this historic meeting were Egypt, Iraq, Saudi Arabia, Syria, Yemen, Lebanon, and Transjordan. Together, their leaders ruled some 45 million people and had at their command five regular armies. Azzam Pasha, the secretary-general of the Arab League, had labored patiently to reach a consensus among the seven Arab leaders, whose only common bond was their hostility to Zionism but who were otherwise deeply divided by historic rivalries and future ambitions. After protracted debate, the leaders resolved to "prevent the creation of a Jewish state in Palestine and to conserve Palestine as a united independent state."[9] To that end they pledged to furnish the league with 10,000 rifles, 3,000 volunteers, and £1 million sterling to provide an immediate beginning for guerrilla operations against the Zionists in Palestine.

At the same time Ben-Gurion summoned his Haganah leaders to an emergency meeting in Jerusalem. "It is time," he told the men before him, "to start planning for a war against five Arab armies."[10] Ben-Gurion perceived the threat of war with the Arabs as a terrible menace that could strangle the Jewish state before it was born. On the other hand, he felt that if the Arabs insisted on going to war, the frontiers of the Jewish state would not be the boundaries assigned to it by the United Nations but those that the Jews could seize and hold by force of arms. If the Arabs rejected the United Nations decision and went to war, Ben-Gurion thought, that would give his people "the right to get what we could."[11] Thus, paradoxically, the Jewish leader turned the Arab cause into a handmaiden of Zionist aspirations.

As the two hostile armies engaged in strikes and counterstrikes that mounted in frequency and ferocity during the final months of the British mandate, events were taking place in Washington that once again placed the birth of the Jewish state in serious doubt. Shaken by the violence of Arab resistance and skeptical of Jewish military strength, President Truman was extremely reluctant to enforce the United Nations partition resolution with American troops even if such troops were part of a United Nations force. Moreover, the State Department continued to be deeply critical of partition and considered it to be legally unenforceable. In December 1947 the department prevailed upon the president to declare an arms embargo to the Middle East. Since under various agreements Britain was still free to ship arms to the Arabs, this embargo amounted to a ban on arms to the Jews. Perhaps most damaging to the Zionist cause was the fact that President Truman had become resentful of certain Zionist leaders, particularly Rabbi Abba Hillel Silver, who, in the president's opinion, had exerted improper pressure to support the Jewish cause. For all these reasons, the United States abandoned its support of the partition plan and now proposed an international trusteeship over Palestine. In desperation the Zionists appealed to the aging, almost blind Chaim Weizmann, who had enjoyed a close relationship with the American president over many years. On February 10, 1948, Weizmann wrote Truman a letter asking "for a few minutes of [his] precious time."[12] The request was refused.

Sitting at Weizmann's bedside, Frank Goldman, president of B'nai B'rith, came up with a last-ditch plan to change Truman's mind. He offered to telephone Eddie Jacobson, who had once been a partner with Harry Truman in a clothing store and who, Goldman thought, might persuade the president to receive Dr. Weizmann. Jacobson responded favorably and was granted an interview with the president on March 12. Truman at first was not receptive to the overtures of his former business partner, but Jacobson persisted. His appeal to the president made a crucial difference in Zionist fortunes:

Chaim Weizmann is a very sick man, almost broken in health, but he travelled thousands and thousands of miles just to see you and plead the cause of my people. Now you refuse to see him because you were insulted by some of our American Jewish leaders, even though you know that Weizmann had absolutely nothing to do with these insults and would be the last man to be a party to them. It doesn't sound like you, Harry.[13]

According to the same account, President Truman, after a long silence, looked Jacobson straight in the eye and said: "You win, you baldheaded son-of-a-bitch! I will see him."[14] One week later Truman met with Weizmann and promised the Jewish leader that he would work for the establishment and recognition of a Jewish state.

The battle was not yet won by the Zionists, however. On March 19 Ambassador Austin announced in the Security Council that the United States would propose the suspension of the partition plan and the establishment of a temporary trusteeship in Palestine in its place. When a shocked and angry Truman wanted to know how such a thing could have happened, he discovered that Secretary of State George Marshall, who had not been privy to the president's personal pledge to Dr. Weizmann, had directed Austin on March 16 to make the trusteeship speech at the earliest appropriate moment. The Zionists were in despair; the Arabs were jubilant; Secretary-General Trygve Lie of the United Nations briefly considered resigning; and President Truman, according to his counsel, Clark Clifford, was "boiling mad."[15] He now had to go along with the trusteeship idea, at least for the time being, since yet another reversal would have deprived the United States of all credibility.

As the British mandate drew rapidly to a close, the fighting in Palestine became increasingly desperate. In April 1948 Jewish extremists of the Irgun and Stern groups massacred the inhabitants of Deir Yassin, a small village near Jerusalem. Even though Ben-Gurion personally cabled his shock at the slaughter and the chief rabbi of Jerusalem excommunicated the Jews who had participated in it, Deir Yassin became a stain on the conscience of the Jewish state. Not only did it elicit demands for vengeance and retribution, but in the years ahead it was to become a symbol of the homelessness of hundreds of thousands of Arab refugees. The mass exodus of terrified Arabs from Jewish-controlled areas began in earnest after this event. The Arab decision to encourage the refugees to leave and to broadcast the massacre in all its horror contributed to the growing panic. Deir Yassin marked the beginning of the Palestinian problem that was to haunt the Middle East for decades to come.

Several days after the carnage of Deir Yassin, Ben-Gurion sent Golda Meir on a final peace mission. Disguised as an Arab woman, Meir traveled to Amman for a secret meeting with King Abdullah of Transjordan to discuss the possibility of preventing a collision. The king proposed that the proclamation of the Jewish state be postponed and that Palestine be kept united with the Jews autonomous in their areas. He also suggested a parliament composed equally of Arab and Jewish deputies. He desired peace, he told his visitor, but if his proposals were not accepted, war, he feared, would be inevitable. Meir replied that the postponement of the birth of a Jewish state was unacceptable and added that the Jews would fight as long as their strength lasted. Abdullah said that he realized that the Jews would have to repel any attack and that it was probably no longer in his power to act as mediator between his fellow Arabs and the Zionists. "Deir Yassin has inflamed the Arab masses," he said. "Before then I was alone. Now I am one of five and have discovered that I cannot make any decisions alone."[16] Thus this last effort to stave off the catastrophe ended in failure.

In May, with the days of the British mandate numbered, the Jews faced a crucial dilemma. Should they proclaim the Jewish state immediately, or, in light of the erosion of American support and the massing of Arab armies, should they wait? On May 12 Ben-Gurion called a secret meeting of the provisional National Council to make a decision. Opinion was sharply divided. Some council members felt that it would be wise to wait since the United States would probably not come to the aid of a self-proclaimed state but might do so if the Arabs acted first and invaded a United Nations–declared state. Others felt that the Jewish state would have to stand alone under any conditions and that therefore statehood should be proclaimed without delay. Ben-Gurion was for immediate statehood, even though he gave the Jews only a 50–50 chance for survival. When the vote was taken, six of the eleven council members voted to go ahead. By a margin of one vote the council decided to proclaim the new state on May 14, a few hours before the British mandate was to expire.

At 4 P.M. on May 14, 1948, two hours before the termination of the British mandate, Ben-Gurion announced the birth of Israel. The news triggered a frantic debate in the UN General Assembly in New York, but the world body was unable to reach a decision. A short time after Ben-Gurion's proclamation, Ambassador Austin, on the personal instruction of President Truman, announced that the United States had recognized the new state of Israel. Shortly thereafter, the Soviet delegate followed suit. "We have been duped," said Charles Malik of Lebanon in an assault of fury on the American and Soviet delegations. It was now 6:15 P.M. and the mandate had ended. Ben-Gurion broadcast a personal message of thanks from Tel Aviv to the American people. As he spoke, the building shook from the impact of an Arab bomb. "The explosions you can hear," he told his audience across the Atlantic, "are Arab planes bombing Tel Aviv."[17] The war for Palestine had broken out.

At dawn on May 15 Israel was simultaneously invaded by the Egyptian army from the south, the Transjordanian Arab Legion from the east, and the forces of Syria and Lebanon from the north. The total strength of the invading Arab armies was approximately 23,500 men, equipped with tanks, airplanes, heavy artillery, spare parts, and ammunition. The Israelis had approximately 3,000 regulars under arms plus 14,000 recruits. They also had 10,000 rifles, 3,600 submachine guns, and four ancient cannons smuggled in from Mexico; they had no tanks. The United States and the Soviet Union both disapproved of the invasion. Andrei Gromyko, speaking for the Soviet Union in the Security Council on May 29, 1948, stated: "This is not the first time that the Arab states, which organized the invasion of Palestine, have ignored a decision of the Security Council or of the General Assembly."

At the end of several months' fierce fighting, interspersed by periods of truce, Israel was left in possession of the whole of Galilee, a section of central Palestine connecting the coastal area with Jerusalem, and the whole of the Negev. Jerusalem became a divided city. The entire area controlled by Israel in 1949 was somewhat larger than the area that had been allotted to the Zionists in the partition resolution of 1947; the Arab invasion had played into the hands of the Jews. Almost 1 million Arabs were rendered homeless by the conflict and entered Syria, Transjordan, and the Egyptian-controlled Gaza Strip as refugees. From their midst would rise the fedayeen and the Palestinian resistance fighters who would hold Israel responsible for depriving them of their homeland. Thus the bloody birth of Israel set the stage for a mortal conflict between two manifestations of nationalism—one Arab, the other Jewish, both equally desperate and determined to secure what to each was holy ground.

The Sinai Campaign
and the Suez Crisis of 1956

Time did not appease antagonism even after the armistice agreements were concluded in 1949. On the Arab side, the plight of almost 1 million refugees was a constant reminder of the alien Zionist presence. No matter how defensive or conciliatory Israel's policy would be, this massive displacement would make the Jewish state into a standing provocation in the eyes of the entire Arab world. The Jews, of course, were fearful of allowing the refugees to return to their former homes. How could 700,000 Jews permit nearly 1 million Arabs to return to their land without also risking the destruction of the Jewish state? And yet how could they refuse it without inflicting on innocent people the very injustice they had themselves suffered in the diaspora? Therefore the Jews took back a few and compensated some, but most continued to linger in refugee camps in Jordan, Lebanon, Syria, and Gaza. At the same time large numbers of Jews were driven out of Iraq, Yemen, Egypt, and Morocco.

During the early 1950s Palestinian Arab fedayeen from the refugee population mounted raids on Israeli territory that steadily increased in ferocity and frequency. The Israelis in turn engaged in massive and powerful reprisals. Despite the military armistice, a state of belligerency continued to exist.

In 1952 Gamal Abdel Nasser, who had distinguished himself in the Palestine war, became president of Egypt and was soon the unrivaled champion of Arab nationalism. He instituted a blockade on Israeli shipping through the Suez Canal and in 1953 extended this blockade to include all goods being shipped to Israel. This left the Israelis with only the port of Elath, at the head of the Gulf of Aqaba in the Straits of Tiran. In late 1953 Nasser began to restrict Israeli commerce through the straits by making its ships subject to inspection by Egyptian coastguards. In 1955 he broadened the blockade and imposed a ban on overflights by Israeli aircraft. In Israel Prime Minister Ben-Gurion, who considered the port of Elath vital to Israel's survival, wanted to strike at Egypt immediately but was restrained by his colleagues. By 1956 relations between Egypt and Israel had reached the boiling point.

At this juncture the Arab-Israeli conflict blended into a broader confrontation between Arab nationalism and the remnants of the Anglo-French postcolonial presence in the Arab world. This confrontation was brought to a head by two huge engineering structures, one long in existence and the other about to be constructed: the Suez Canal and the High Dam at Aswan. President Nasser viewed the former as a leftover from colonial times and the latter as a modern pyramid to be built as a symbol of a resurgent Arab nationalism.

The United States had initially agreed to help finance the Aswan High Dam through the World Bank, but Secretary of State John Foster Dulles was irked by President Nasser's decision to purchase arms from Czechoslovakia in 1955 and his recognition a year later of Communist China. As a result, the United States reneged on its pledge to finance the dam, ostensibly because the Egyptian economy was deemed unsound, and Nasser became incensed. In his rage, he declared that the United States "should drop dead of fury, but [it would] never be able to dictate to Egypt."[18] Two days later, in an emotional "declaration of independence from imperialism," he announced the nationalization of the Suez Canal, which was partially owned by British and French financial interests. In this manner Britain and France were made to pay for Dulles's policy reversal, and fatefully the two Western European powers now perceived a common interest with Israel: the removal of Gamal Abdel Nasser from power.

The perceptions of the British and French leaders now began to play a crucial role in the gathering crisis. In Britain Prime Minister Anthony Eden's memories of Hitler at Munich were still fresh, and he now compared Nasser's actions to those of the German dictator in the 1930s. In the words of one thoughtful student of British policy at the time, the prime minister "saw Egypt through a forest of Flanders poppies and gleaming jackboots."[19] French premier Guy Mollet shared this perception. He had been an anti-Nazi resistance chief at Arras during World War II and now "saw Nasser as Hitler more plainly than anyone."[20] The two men became so obsessed with Nasser's action that "Lady Eden is believed to have complained that the Suez Canal was running through her drawing room."[21]

There was, of course, good reason for consternation in Britain and France. The International Convention of Constantinople of 1888 had provided that "the Suez Maritime Canal shall always be free and open, in time of war and in time of peace, to every vessel of commerce or of war without distinction of flag." Thus the two Western powers considered Nasser's action as a violation of their legal rights. Moreover, to Britain, control of the canal symbolized her status as an empire and as a world power. To the French, who blamed Egypt for supporting the Algerian rebellion against France, seizure of the canal served as a kind of last straw. For both, the issue at stake was not merely safeguarding the economic rights of their shareholders in the Suez Canal Company; far more important was their emotional reaction to the seemingly insolent and Hitler-like nationalism represented by the Egyptian leader.

To Nasser, on the other hand, the Suez Canal had become the symbol of a shameful colonial past. Its architect, Ferdinand de Lesseps, had become an Egyptian folk ogre. Under his brutal direction, as Nasser saw it, more than 100,000 Egyptian workers had died to build a canal that was to belong not to them or their country but to a foreign company that profited for its own enrichment and never for Egypt's benefit. "Instead of the Canal being dug for Egypt," Nasser declaimed, "Egypt became the property of the Canal and the Canal Company became a state within a state. But now the days of alien exploitation [are] over; the Canal and its revenues [will] belong entirely to Egypt. We shall build the High Dam and we shall gain our usurped rights."[22]

These sharply divergent perceptions set the stage for a violent encounter. During the weeks that followed Nasser's action, the conflict broadened. Eden and Mollet privately sounded out American reactions to the situation. They were partially reassured by the fact that Secretary of State Dulles also appeared outraged by Egypt's action. In their conversations with Dulles the British and French leaders again compared Nasser's action to Hitler's behavior at Munich and stated in the strongest terms that this type of Western appeasement must not be allowed to occur again. Dulles replied that "force was the last method to be tried, but the United States did not exclude the use of force if all other methods failed."[23] From this statement, Eden and Mollet inferred that at best the United States would present a united front with Britain and France in a show of force against Nasser and at worst would remain benevolently neutral.

Britain and France now prepared for military action. They hoped to mount a lightning attack against Egypt, occupy the canal, depose Nasser, and then negotiate with his successor from a position of strength. In the course of these preparations, highly secret meetings took place with Israeli leaders for the purpose of coordinating the attack. Prime Minister Ben-Gurion and his chief of staff, General Moshe Dayan, were intent on seizing Gaza, the main base of fedayeen activities, and Sharm el Sheik on the Tiran Straits, where the Egyptians maintained their blockade of the Gulf of Aqaba against ships bound for the port of Elath. Mollet pledged that if the Israelis would thrust into Sinai, French forces would join them, and Israel could seize Sinai and end the Egyptian blockade. Ben-Gurion hesitated; he feared that Egyptian bombers might attack Tel Aviv while Israeli forces were advancing into Sinai.[24] But when Eden pledged to use British air power to prevent Egyptian air attacks on Israel, Ben-Gurion agreed to move into Sinai.

The final plans worked out among the three prime ministers were the following: Israel was to launch the attack on October 29. As soon as Dayan's troops began their advance into Sinai, Britain and France were to issue an ultimatum to Israel and Egypt, requiring them to cease fire, to withdraw their forces 10 miles on either side of the canal, and to "accept the temporary occupation by Anglo-French forces of key positions at Port Said, Ismailia and Suez."[25] As soon as Israel had agreed to these terms and Egypt had rejected them, British bombers were to destroy the Egyptian air force and disrupt Egypt's communications and military capabilities in preparation for an Anglo-French invasion by paratroops from Cyprus and seaborne forces from Malta. Then, when these forces had occupied the canal from Port Said to Suez, a further attack was contemplated, aimed at the occupation of Cairo, if necessary, to depose Nasser. As these arrangements were being concluded, by a fateful coincidence in time, thousands of miles away Russian tanks rolled into Budapest to crush the two-day-old Hungarian revolt against Soviet domination.

On the afternoon of October 29 Israel's army launched its four-pronged advance against Egypt. Two thrusts were aimed at the canal while the third and fourth were to seal off the Gaza Strip and seize Sharm el Sheik. On the following day, while Israeli forces were advancing rapidly across the Sinai Peninsula, Britain and France issued their prearranged ultimatum, which in effect told the Egyptians to retreat and the Israelis to advance. Caught by complete surprise, Nasser rejected the ultimatum but was unable to put up much military resistance. He was convinced, however, that world opinion in the United Nations would come to his rescue.

On October 31 British and French bombers began air attacks against Egyptian targets, including Cairo. In retaliation, Nasser sank ships in order to block the canal. Within six days, Israel had overrun the greater part of the Sinai Peninsula and achieved its main military objective, the occupation of Sharm el Sheik.

The United Nations entered the picture on October 30. The American delegation called for a meeting of the Security Council and, to the consternation of Britain and France, introduced a resolution calling on Israel to leave Egypt without delay and asking all member states to "refrain from the use of force or threat of force."[26] The resolution was immediately vetoed by Britain and France. As the Security Council stood paralyzed and the Anglo-French-Israeli action continued, Soviet premier Nikolai Bulganin, in a news conference in Moscow, warned of the possibility of a third world war and declared that Soviet "volunteers" were ready to aid the Egyptian forces. He proposed that the United States and the Soviet Union restore the peace through a joint show of force. This suggestion was rejected as "unthinkable" by President Eisenhower. The United States was eager to see the Anglo-French action ended, but it was equally eager to prevent the establishment of a Soviet presence in the Middle East.

On November 2, in an emergency session of the General Assembly, the United States took a leading role in calling for a cessation of the fighting and the immediate withdrawal of the Anglo-French-Israeli forces from Egypt. The United States found support for this action from a not particularly welcome source—the Soviet Union. Thus the United States found itself in the paradoxical position of being allied in the United Nations with its great antagonist in the Cold War and at odds with its closest friends and allies, Britain and France.

By November 6 Britain had to yield. Confronted by United Nations resolutions charging her with aggression, dismayed by the action of the United States, and troubled by an increasingly hostile opposition at home, Eden terminated his abortive venture. As one critical British analyst summed it up: "The spectacle of over one hundred thousand men setting off for a war which lasted barely a day and then returning has few parallels in the long gallery of military imbecility."[27] France had no choice but to follow suit, but Israel still clutched tenaciously to what her army had conquered in the six days of the war.

The role of the American leadership, of course, was crucial in the evolution of the crisis, and personalities played an important part. Both Eisenhower and Dulles felt a sense of outrage because Eden and Mollet had not bothered to consult them on a matter as important as military action in the Middle East at a time when a national election was imminent in the United States. From a purely military standpoint, only the Israelis were attaining their objectives. The Anglo-French punitive expedition seemed to be foundering and thus could not be presented to the General Assembly as a fait accompli. The United States, by supporting the Anglo-French venture, or even by taking a neutral view of it, would have risked the ill will of a large majority of the United Nations membership and, in addition, might have had to look on helplessly while the military action failed or bogged down. Moreover, such an American response might have persuaded many neutralists that the United States, by countenancing aggression in the Middle East, differed little from the Soviet Union, which was aggressively crushing a rebellion in Hungary with military force. Most important, the United States feared the possibility of Soviet intervention in the Middle East through "volunteers" and the risk of sparking a major war through direct superpower confrontation in the contested area.

From the Soviet point of view, the Suez crisis was a windfall: The British and French appeared to be digging their own graves in the Middle East, and the United States appeared to be doing its best to help them. Thus, by appealing to the cause of Arab nationalism, the Soviet Union saw its opportunity to eject all Western influence from the Middle East and gain a foothold of its own. The fact that Israel was allied with the two colonial powers also played into Soviet hands.

Britain and France were clearly the main losers in the Suez affair. In humiliation, they had to watch Nasser snatch a political victory from a military defeat. Abandoned by their closest and oldest ally, they had to admit that they could no longer act like great powers and that, in the last analysis, their initiative in world politics depended on the decisions of the United States. The very issue that they had set out to rectify by force of arms—the internationalization of the Suez Canal—now seemed beyond redemption. For all practical purposes, the Suez crisis terminated Anglo-French authority in the Middle East. Suez had become another Dien Bien Phu.

The greatest victory in the Suez crisis was won by Arab nationalism. Nasser was now clearly master of the Suez Canal. The two great superpowers had supported him. Not only did he triumph in the showdown with Britain and France, but his other great foe, Israel, now came under increasing pressure to withdraw. Dag Hammar-skjöld, secretary-general of the United Nations, had been successful in dispatching to the Middle East a special peace force, the United Nations Emergency Force (UNEF). Under strong American pressure Israel agreed to evacuate most of the territories it had conquered from Egypt, and beginning on November 15 the UNEF soldiers replaced the Israeli troops. Only an explicit American guarantee, however, that Israel's right to free and innocent passage in the Gulf of Aqaba would not be infringed on persuaded the Israelis to evacuate the last fruits of their Sinai campaign—the Gaza Strip and the east coast of the Sinai Peninsula down to the Straits of Tiran. By March 1957 Israel had given up all the territories it had conquered, on the understanding that the UNEF would prevent fedayeen raids from Jordan and the Gaza Strip. Hence Israel emerged from the Sinai campaign with a marginal gain.

Nasser was now at the zenith of his power. Among the Egyptian people he enjoyed the title of *rais,* or captain of the ship of state. With deep satisfaction he watched Eden and Mollet resign their posts. Thus encouraged, he now planned to turn on his archenemy, the Zionist state. In March 1957 he appointed an Egyptian civil governor of Gaza, a move that was viewed with indignation and misgivings in Israel. At the same time Radio Cairo declared that "the Gulf of Aqaba will be closed to Israeli ships and our commandos will continue to sow terror in Israel."[28] Thus the seeds of the next war, which was to erupt a decade later, were sown.

The Six-Day War of 1967

Once again, time did not heal but exacerbated the tensions between the Arab states and Israel. Within the Arab world, deep rifts had appeared on the overriding question of policy vis-à-vis Israel. By early 1967 three basic positions had crystallized.

First, the Syrians, who were the most radical and whose country was a major base for border raids against Israel, had created an organization named El Fatah, or "conquest." Its commando units carried out attacks against Israel in the tradition of the earlier fedayeen raids. In addition, Syria's president Al Atassi demanded a war of liberation against Israel similar to the one being fought against the United States in Vietnam. The second position, at the other end of the spectrum, was that of King Faisal of Saudi Arabia, who was relatively friendly toward the West and who regarded the violent temper of the Syrians with considerable distrust. While the huge oil deposits of Saudi Arabia provided the king with a formidable economic weapon, they also made him dependent to some extent on the Western nations for his revenue. Nasser, therefore, found himself caught between these two rival factions. Eager to maintain his role as the embodiment of Arab nationalism, his ear was more sensitive to the gravitational pull of the Arab radicals than to the more conservative and traditional Arab leaders, such as King Faisal and King Hussein of Jordan. This made him vulnerable to Syrian efforts to involve him in a larger war with Israel.

In April 1967 a major clash took place on the Israeli-Syrian border. Six Syrian MIG fighters were shot down by Israel in the course of the battle. El Fatah raids continued to mount in ferocity, and on May 14 Israeli prime minister Levi Eshkol declared that a serious confrontation with Syria would be inevitable if the attacks continued. The Syrians responded by declaring that Israel was concentrating huge armed forces on its border in preparation for an attack against Syria. Eshkol denied this charge and invited the Soviet ambassador to visit the areas in question. The Soviet diplomat refused. The pressure on President Nasser to help the Syrians was mounting rapidly. On May 16 Nasser proclaimed a state of emergency for the Egyptian armed forces and took measures to work out a joint Syrian-Egyptian defense agreement. The Syrian leadership, however, continued to taunt the Egyptian president by accusing him of "hiding behind the sheltering skirts of the United Nations Emergency Force."[29] A wave of emotion now spread throughout the Arab world from Casablanca to Baghdad. Demonstrations against Zionism took place in virtually every Arab country. On May 16 the Palestine Service of Radio Cairo declared: "The menace and challenge of Israel have persisted far too long. The very existence of Israel in our usurped land has endured beyond all expectation. An end must be put to the challenge of Israel and to its very existence. Welcome to aggression by Israel which will send us into action to destroy it! Welcome to the battle for which we have long waited! The hour of battle is imminent. In fact, this is the hour of battle."[30]

President Nasser chose to ride the emotional tide of Arab nationalism rather than to resist it. This meant, however, that he had to take an active part in escalating the crisis, and so he decided to terminate the presence of the UNEF in Egypt and the Gaza Strip. On

May 18 Foreign Minister Mahmoud Riad asked United Nations Secretary-General U Thant to withdraw the UNEF "as soon as possible." He reminded the secretary-general that the force had been stationed on Egyptian soil at the invitation of the Egyptian government and that its continued presence depended on Egyptian approval.

The UNEF had patrolled the 100-mile-long Egypt-Israel frontier for ten years. It had been stationed on the Egyptian side of the border but not on the Israeli side. During the decade the force had been in effect, border eruptions had been kept to a minimum, and therefore the demand for its withdrawal caused considerable dismay at the United Nations. Although U Thant never questioned Egypt's legal right to demand the withdrawal of the force, he expressed "serious misgivings" about its termination. He immediately referred the matter to the UNEF Advisory Committee. The Indian and Yugoslav representatives made it clear that their contingents were likely to be withdrawn in any case. Since they made up almost half of the 3,300-man force, additional pressure for withdrawal was thus applied. Furthermore, UN forces were already being jostled out of their positions by Egyptian troops. Therefore on May 15 the secretary-general complied with the Egyptian demand, reasoning that the UNEF could no longer remain in the area if the consent of the host government was withdrawn.

Few actions have been discussed more heatedly by governments, the world press, and public opinion than U Thant's withdrawal of the UNEF. Criticism was particularly sharp in the United States, the United Kingdom, Canada, and, of course, Israel. The Israeli foreign minister, Abba Eban, noted ironically that "the umbrella was removed at the precise moment it began to rain." U Thant answered these charges by stating that he had no alternative by law but to accede to a request that was rooted in Egypt's sovereign rights. He also reasoned that if he did not comply with the request of a sovereign government, then consent for the admission of a United Nations peacekeeping force in a future crisis might be infinitely more difficult to obtain. Given all these conflicting considerations, the secretary-general made his difficult and fateful choice.

The withdrawal of the UNEF brought the crisis to a new and much graver stage. Israeli and Egyptian forces now confronted each other directly across the border. Israel ordered a limited mobilization of reserves to which Egypt, on May 21, responded in kind. Encouraged by the ease with which he had accomplished the removal of the United Nations buffer force, and spurred by the groundswell of emotions in the Arab world, President Nasser, on May 22, announced the decision that was to become the direct cause of the Six-Day War: closure of the Straits of Tiran at the entrance of the Gulf of Aqaba to Israeli shipping, thereby blockading once again the port of Elath. In an emotional speech at the Egyptian Air Force Headquarters in Sinai he declared: "The armed forces yesterday occupied Sharm el Sheik. What does this mean? It is affirmation of our rights and our sovereignty over the Gulf of Aqaba which constitutes territorial waters. Under no circumstances will we allow the Israeli flag to pass through the Gulf of Aqaba. The Jews threaten war. We tell them you are welcome, we are ready for war, but under no circumstances will we abandon any of our rights. This water is ours."[31] The imposition of the blockade catapulted the crisis into the international realm. Israel had withdrawn from the Straits of Tiran only after she had received explicit assurances that the Western powers would guarantee freedom of passage for her ships. On May 23 Prime Minister Eshkol reminded the Western powers of their obligations, and Eban was dispatched to Paris, London, and Washington to secure the necessary assurances.

The responses of the Western powers to Israel's appeal for help were sympathetic but did not amount to guarantees. President Lyndon Johnson described the blockade as "illegal and potentially dangerous to peace." It was unlikely, however, that in the light of the American experience in Vietnam, the United States would be prepared to risk military intervention in the Middle East. In fact, President Johnson emphatically urged Israel not to take unilateral action. Little support came from anyone else. The British too were sympathetic but did not offer a definite commitment to keep the waterway open, and President de Gaulle of France, observing a glacial neutrality, stated: "France is committed in no sense or on any subject to any of the states involved."[32]

These responses were not reassuring to Israel. Prime Minister Eshkol was under increasing pressure to assume a more belligerent position. On May 24 the UN Security Council convened but was unable to take any action whatsoever to lift the blockade. The sense of foreboding in Israel increased. On May 26, when Nasser asserted that the Gulf of Aqaba was only part of the subsuming problem that was caused by Israel's aggressive stance in simply existing, the response in Israel was electric. Pressure now became intense to appoint General Dayan, the hero of the 1956 Sinai campaign, to the ministry of defense. On the same day that Nasser delivered his belligerent address, his friend Mohammed Hasanein Haikal, the editor of the leading Egyptian newspaper *Al-Ahram,* wrote a remarkably frank and perceptive article:

> The closure of the Gulf of Aqaba means, first and last, that the Arab nation, represented by the UAR, has succeeded for the first time vis-à-vis Israel in changing by force a fait accompli imposed on it by force. To Israel this is the most dangerous aspect of the current situation, not who can impose the accomplished fact and who possesses the power to safeguard it. Therefore, it is not a matter of the Gulf of Aqaba but of something bigger. It is the whole philosophy of Israeli security. Hence, I say that Israel must attack.[33]

This was a fair assessment of Israel's predicament. On June 1 it was announced that Dayan had been appointed minister of defense. This move was widely interpreted as a sign that Israel had decided that she could not depend on outside help and would therefore have to resort to a preemptive attack to break the hostile encirclement. On June 2 Ahmed Shukairy, leader of the Palestine Liberation Organization (PLO), called for a holy war for the liberation of Palestine. Addressing a large congregation in the Old City of Jerusalem, he declared that the Arabs wanted "fighters, not Beatles" and called on Arab women to don battle dress, adding that "this is no time for lipstick and mini-skirts." Meanwhile, on June 3 Dayan stated at a press conference that, while Israel welcomed all the help it could get on the diplomatic front, the country wished to fight its own battles with its own troops. He added that he did "not want British or American boys to get killed" in the defense of Israel. Asked whether Israel had lost the military initiative, Dayan replied, "If you mean to say we stand no chance in battle, then I cannot agree with you."[34] The brink was reached.

At 7:45 A.M., Monday, June 5, the Six-Day War began. The Israeli air force attacked Egyptian airfields in a series of lightning strikes. By the end of the week, the armed forces of Israel occupied the Sinai

Peninsula, the Gaza Strip, the whole West Bank of the Jordan, the entire city of Jerusalem, and the Golan Heights. The armies of Egypt, Jordan, and Syria had been completely routed. Israel had destroyed or captured 430 aircraft and 800 tanks and had inflicted 15,000 fatal casualties on Arab troops. It had taken 5,500 officers and men as prisoners. Its own losses were 40 aircraft and 676 dead.

A study made by the Institute for Strategic Studies in London by Michael Howard and Robert Hunter summarizes the campaign:

> The third Arab-Israeli war is likely to be studied in Staff Colleges for many years to come. Like the campaigns of the younger Napoleon, the performance of the Israeli Defence Force provided a textbook illustration for all the classical principles of war: speed, surprise, concentration, security, information, the offensive—above all, training and morale. Airmen will note with professional approval how the Israeli air-force was employed first to gain command of the air by destruction of the enemy air-force, then to take part in the ground battle by interdiction of enemy communications, direct support of ground attacks and, finally, pursuit. The flexibility of the administrative and staff system will be examined and the attention of young officers drawn to the part played by leadership at all levels. Military radicals will observe how the Israelis attained this peak of excellence without the aid of drill sergeants and the barrack square. Tacticians will stress the importance they attached in this, as in previous campaigns, to being able to move and fight by night as effectively as they did by day. Above all, it will be seen how Israel observed a principle which appears in few military textbooks, but which armed forces neglect at their peril: the Clausewitzian principle of political context which the British ignored so disastrously in 1956. The Israeli High Command knew that it was not operating in a political vacuum. It worked on the assumption that it would have three days to complete its task before outside pressures compelled a cease-fire.[35]

On the deepest level, the secret of Israel's military success probably lay in the realization of every one of its citizens that losing would have meant the end of the nation's existence. In that light, the comparison, offered by the Soviet delegate to the UN Security Council, of Israel's offensive with Hitler's attack on the Soviet Union was hardly persuasive. In a sense, Israel's military system was the very opposite of that of nineteenth-century Prussia, which had resulted in the militarization of society. The Israeli approach led to the civilization of the army; officers maintained their authority not by

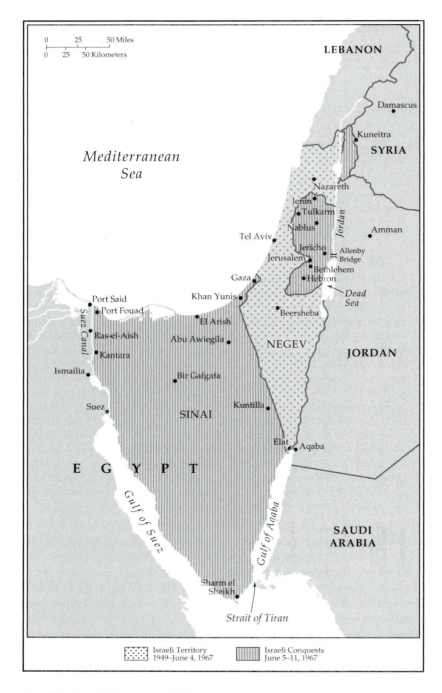

Map 10 Israeli Conquests, 1967

Inside the map:

LEBANON

Mediterranean
Sea

Damascus

Kuneitra
SYRIA

Nazareth

Jenin
Tulkarm
Nablus
Amman

Tel Aviv

Jericho
Allenby
Jerusalem
Bridge
Bethlehem
Gaza
Hebron

Khan Yunis
Dead
Sea

Port Said
Beersheba

Port Fouad
El Arish

Suez Canal
Ras-el-Aish
Abu Awiegila
NEGEV

Kantara
JORDAN

Ismailia
Bir Gafgafa

Jordan

Suez
Kuntilla

SINAI

Elat
Aqaba

E G Y P T

Gulf of Suez

Gulf of Aqaba

SAUDI
ARABIA

Sharm el
Sheikh

Strait of Tiran

Israeli Territory
1949–June 4, 1967

Israeli Conquests
June 5–11, 1967

orthodox discipline but by personal example. Therefore the Israelis got the utmost from their men and their machines.

President Nasser was so shocked by the swiftness and efficiency of Israel's offensive that he believed, or was purported to believe, that the United States and the United Kingdom had given assistance to the Zionists by maintaining an "air umbrella" over Israel. The truth was that in the Arab countries political fanaticism simply was no substitute for military expertise, and fantasies of victory could no longer mask the totality of the disaster.

Israel's leaders knew that they had to achieve their victory quickly to make it stick. They operated on the assumption that they had three days to defeat the Arabs before outside pressures compelled a cease-fire. In fact, they had four and needed five. The chorus of disapproval that arose even in the West when Israel ignored a United Nations cease-fire call and, on the fifth day of the war, opened its offensive against Syria showed how narrow was the time margin in which Israel had to work. Israel knew that there was a tacit agreement between the two superpowers not to permit the Arab-Israeli war to escalate into a larger conflict, provided that the war was quickly brought to an end. Once it had ended, the great powers were reluctant to risk a second conflict in order to undo the victory that had been achieved in the first. For this reason a premium was placed on preemption and the lightning speed of Israeli arms.

An analysis of the changes in power constellations after the Six-Day War reveals some interesting comparisons and contrasts with the crisis of 1956. First, the Soviet Union had backed a loser this time, whereas she had been on the winning side a decade earlier. Most of the military hardware that the USSR had shipped to the Arab states was destroyed or captured by the Israelis. The United States, on the other hand, was on the winning side, and superficially her policy seemed successful. But on a deeper level it was clear that the swiftness of Israel's victory had saved the United States from having to make some difficult decisions. Had the war gone badly for Israel or remained inconclusive, the United States might have been forced to intervene and risk a confrontation with the Soviet Union.

Israel, which had had to withdraw in 1956, was determined this time not to yield its military gains except in exchange for an end to belligerency. Within six days Israel had exchanged its vulnerability for a position of unprecedented military domination in the Middle

East. Within two brief decades, a fledgling Jewish state in Palestine had become a formidable power.

The October War of 1973

Israel's swift and decisive victory in 1967 had left a legacy of shame and bitterness on the Arab side. Diplomacy had not been able to dislodge the Israelis from the five territories that they had captured from three Arab countries in June 1967: Sinai and the Gaza Strip from Egypt; Old Jerusalem and the West Bank from Jordan; and the Golan Heights from Syria. The UN Security Council had been able to adopt only a single resolution on the Middle East over a period of six years. That resolution, which was passed on November 22, 1967, linked a promise of secure and recognized boundaries to Israel with a promise of withdrawal from occupied territories to the Arabs. But neither side was willing to take the first step and the entire situation remained frozen. No face-to-face negotiations between Arabs and Israelis ever took place. The Arabs gazed across the cease-fire line with increasing fury and frustration as Israel made plans to populate the territories with Jewish settlers. Israel appeared bent on de facto annexation, and the Arabs appeared equally determined to prevent it.

Anwar Sadat, who became Egypt's new president after Nasser's death in 1970, gradually and without much fanfare prepared the ground for an Arab counterattack. Unlike Nasser, the less flamboyant Sadat did not divide the Arab world but doggedly worked toward a consensus. The Soviet Union, though not prepared to give the Arabs offensive weapons for use against Israel, did replace the military hardware that had been captured or destroyed by Israel in 1967. The Soviets also trained Egyptian and Syrian commanders in Soviet military strategy and tactics in order to prevent a repetition of the debacle of the Six-Day War. By 1973 the Arabs were encouraged to believe that at least some of the lost territories could be regained by force of arms. Thus the stage was set for yet another violent encounter.

On Yom Kippur, the Jewish Day of Atonement, Syria and Egypt launched a well-coordinated surprise attack. In the north, Syria attacked the vital Golan Heights in an effort to regain the vantage point over Israeli settlements in the valley below. In the Sinai, Egypt threw a major military force across the Suez Canal, capturing Israeli positions on the eastern bank and sending Israel's defenders backward into the desert.

The Arab attack had not come as a complete surprise to the Israeli leadership. Defense Minister Dayan claimed several days later that he had had advance information that some sort of attack was imminent but had decided against a preemptive strike. The reason for this decision, according to Dayan, was to "have the political advantage of not having attacked first, even at the expense of the military advantage."[36] Israel's image abroad would thus be improved with resultant long-term political benefits.

The price that Israel paid for this apparent self-restraint was heavy. On the Suez front, the Egyptians swarmed across the canal in large numbers, laid down bridges, and landed hundreds of tanks and other war matériel. They managed to overrun the famous Israeli defense installation, the Bar-Lev line, with heavy air and artillery assaults. The lightly defended Israeli positions had to be abandoned. On the Golan Heights an enormous Syrian force equipped with 800 tanks plunged across the cease-fire line at four points. Commando units landed by helicopter on Mount Hermon and seized a major Israeli position. Overwhelmed by the force of the attack, Israeli defenders had to evacuate several outposts.

One explanation of these early Arab successes may be found in Israel's perception of its own military superiority and of the Arabs as notoriously poor, bumbling soldiers. The Israeli leadership had convinced itself of its own superiority to such an extent that it believed that any Arab attack would be suicidal. Israel, in short, was suffering from a case of military hubris.

By the end of the first week of war, Israel had stemmed the Arab onslaught, but the myth of its invincibility had nevertheless been shattered. Egypt had managed to install almost 100,000 men on the East Bank of the Suez Canal, and the fiercest tank battles since World War II were raging in the Sinai desert and the Golan Heights. Casualties were heavy on both sides, and new Soviet ground-to-air missiles presented a grave threat to the Israeli air force. Buoyed by the successes of Syria and Egypt, other Arab countries joined in the battle. Iraq and Jordan supplied troops for the Syrian front, and Saudi Arabia and other oil-rich Arab sheikdoms applied increasing pressure on the United States to abandon its support of Israel.

As casualties mounted and both sides suffered staggering losses, the superpowers entered the arena. The Soviet Union began to resupply the Arab states with ammunition and light weapons. When the United States decided to do the same for Israel, the Soviet Union escalated its supply operations to tanks and planes. This too was matched by the United States. Thus, by the end of the first week, the war had reached a new and dangerous plateau. Not only was the armor of both sides locked in a death struggle, but the fragile détente between the Soviet Union and the United States hung in the balance.

During the second week of war Israel gradually gained the upper hand on both the Syrian and Egyptian fronts. After fierce tank battles in the Golan Heights, the Israelis not only threw back the Syrians but embarked on the road to Damascus. In the words of Dayan: "We have to show them [the Syrians] that the road leads not only from Damascus to Tel Aviv, but from Tel Aviv to Damascus."[37] The Israeli advance into Syria came to a standstill at the village of Sasa, twenty miles from the Syrian capital.

On the Egyptian front, Israeli troops, in a daring tactical maneuver, entered the West Bank of the Suez Canal on Egyptian territory. Their aim was to encircle the Egyptian troops on the East Bank in Sinai and to cut off their retreat across the canal back to Egypt. After massive air and tank battles, the Israeli objectives were attained. The Egyptian troops were trapped in two large pockets in Sinai, and the Third Army was at Israel's mercy for its supply of food and water. At this juncture, with the balance shifting rapidly in Israel's favor, the superpowers once more intervened.

On October 21, acting with great urgency to protect its Egyptian ally, the Soviet leadership agreed with Secretary of State Henry Kissinger on a formula for a cease-fire resolution. This resolution, which was rushed through the UN Security Council on the following morning under joint Soviet-American sponsorship, provided for a cease-fire in place and called on all parties to start immediate negotiations toward implementing the 1967 Security Council plan for peace in the Middle East. The cease-fire began shakily, with the Egyptian forces trapped behind Israeli lines trying to break out and Israel seeking to destroy the Egyptian forces once and for all. A second cease-fire call still did not end the fighting. As a result, the Soviet Union proposed that a joint Soviet-American peace force be dispatched to the Middle East. This proposal was rejected by the United States, which feared the possibility of a military confrontation in the area. The Soviet Union then declared that it would introduce its own troops into the area unilaterally. To this Soviet threat, President Nixon responded by placing the armed forces of the United States on military alert.

During the "alert" crisis, a compromise was worked out. The UN Security Council approved a third resolution sponsored by the non-aligned countries that authorized the secretary-general to send a UN buffer force to the area. This 7,000-man emergency force would be patterned after the old UNEF that had been created by Dag Hammarskjöld in 1956. It was to exclude the permanent members of the Security Council from active participation. To save face, however, the two superpowers insisted on sending a small number of observers into the cease-fire area. The first UN troops began to arrive from Cyprus on October 27. By then, all fronts were quiet. The precarious Soviet-American détente had held after all.

As the "October war" drew to a close after seventeen days of violent fighting, Israel had won another victory, but a costly one in blood and treasure. Although it had managed to roll back the initial Arab advance and had assumed a commanding military position on both fronts, the price paid in human lives for this achievement was far higher than the toll that had been taken in the war of 1967. The heavy losses made the victory somewhat joyless. Moreover, the immediate postwar Israeli attitude on the question of the occupied territories hardened. If an Arab surprise attack had been launched along the pre-1967 armistice lines, then Tel Aviv and Jerusalem—not the Golan Heights and the Bar-Lev line—would have had to absorb the initial shock. Thus, in the Israeli view, tens of thousands of their people could be killed if such a surprise attack were only slightly more successful than the one launched in October 1973. In Eban's words: "If we had been mad enough to abandon the Golan Heights and Sharm el Sheikh and all the Sinai and the whole West Bank, would not the massive attack launched on October 6 have murdered thousands of our civilians, devastated our population centers and brought us to catastrophe? I tell you, a massacre more hideous than Auschwitz would have been a real prospect and Israel's survival would be in doubt. To suggest a restoration of the pre-1967 lines is sheer irresponsibility in the light of what has been revealed."[38]

Just as the setbacks of the first few days of war were deeply etched on Israeli minds, so the Arabs cherished and glorified their short-lived victory. Despite his ultimate defeat, President Sadat proclaimed that "Egyptian forces [had] performed a miracle by any military standard" and had thus "restored the honor of the nation." Egypt and Syria had been able to break out of the frustration and futility of unending diplomatic stalemate. They had placed Israel on notice that it could not hold on indefinitely to occupied territory unless it was prepared to accept the risk of yet another war with the odds against it. As Egypt's foreign minister, Mohamed El Zayyat, put it: "The Israeli attitude had been to assume that they were invincible and that we were meek and weak. They pictured Egyptians as people who would never fight. The argument that this occupied territory serves as a protective buffer for Israel—that was the argument of Hitler. What we are asking for is very simple: that our territorial integrity and the rights of the Palestinians be respected. These two elements are the *sine qua non* conditions for peace in the Middle East."[39]

Thus the fourth round ended with positions hardened on both sides and passions unallayed. The Israelis were embittered by the Yom Kippur surprise attack and, in their bitterness, tended to forget that the attack was launched in order to regain lost territories. The Arabs were so intent on restoring their dignity and regaining lost ground that they believed that they had won even though actually they had lost. Neither side was able any longer to understand the fears of the other. All empathy was lost. For two weeks the superpowers had made the desert a proving ground for new destructive weapons. Kings played chess while pawns bled on the battlefield. Only when the kings were fearful that the battle might engulf them as well did they stop the bloodshed. Once again the United Nations was used as a rescue operation at the edge of the abyss. Frantic cease-fire resolutions had to take the place of preventive diplomacy. And only a fragile superpower détente prevented yet another fateful escalation with dire consequences for humankind.

The October War of 1973 had one positive result. Under superpower pressure, Israelis and Arabs did agree to meet in a peace conference in Geneva in December 1973, their first face-to-face diplomatic encounter in a quarter of a century. As Eban put it, "For something to be born, the parents have to meet at least once." Chastened by four wars, Arabs and Jews alike began to feel that unless wisdom and reason ultimately prevailed, the only alternative would be mutual annihilation.

The role of the United States during and after the October War was primarily defined by Secretary of State Henry Kissinger. For the next three years, the Middle Eastern scene was dominated by the tireless peacemaking efforts of this extraordinary statesman.

Kissinger's role in the October War can be described as neither pro-Israeli nor pro-Arab but as essentially pro-equilibrium. Before the war erupted, Kissinger perceived Israel as the stronger side and thus warned the Jewish leaders "not to preempt." But when he turned out to have been mistaken and Syria and Egypt launched their coordinated surprise attack, Kissinger switched sides and provided American military aid to Israel in order to restore the military balance. And when the Israelis, with this American assistance, gained the upper hand, Kissinger switched sides again and insisted on the rescue of 100,000 trapped Egyptian soldiers. When a cease-fire was finally proclaimed by the United Nations, both sides were exhausted and roughly even—exactly what Kissinger had wanted. It had always been his firm belief that only a war without victory or defeat could contain the seeds of peace.

As Kissinger surveyed the ravages of the October War, he conceived his plan for peace in the Middle East. He decided to subdivide the problem into manageable segments instead of addressing it in its totality. He would approach it step-by-step, beginning with the least forbidding obstacle, and then, after having built a basis of trust between the rivals, he would try to negotiate the more formidable hurdles. A first tentative step had already been taken. Egypt had agreed to talk to Israel. If Kissinger could achieve a military disengagement between Israel and Egypt, a momentum toward peace might then be set in motion. It would perhaps then be possible to leap over yet another hurdle and effect a military disengagement between Syria and Israel. If such military interim agreements were possible, perhaps one might be able to move the rivals toward political accommodation. Once Egypt and Syria had entered into negotiations with Israel, Saudi Arabia might be persuaded to lift its oil embargo, and if luck held, it might even be conceivable to think about a compromise between Israel and the Palestinians and a Jerusalem settlement. Such was Kissinger's train of thought. The peacemaking process would be like a steeplechase, with each successive hurdle higher and more treacherous. But Kissinger believed that the step-by-step approach would yield at least some limited successes and should not be a total failure.

The objective that Kissinger had in mind, of course, was equilibrium. Israel would have to withdraw from some of the conquered territories, but in the context of national security. The diplomatic reemergence of the Arabs would be encouraged, but in a context of realism and responsibility. An effort would be made to woo the Arabs away from the Soviet Union. They would come to the United States because, in Kissinger's judgment, "they could get weapons from the Russians, but territory only from the United States." Therefore, by delivering some real estate to the Arabs, Soviet power in the Middle East would be diminished and American influence strengthened. To achieve this objective, however, pressure would have to be applied to Israel, which would have to be encouraged to trade territory for security. And if Kissinger's reasoning was wrong, he would have to protect Israel by always being generous with arms.

Kissinger's step-by-step approach to peace was not greeted with universal acclaim. The Soviet Union was highly critical and pushed for a general peace conference to be held in Geneva. There was also criticism in the United States. Numerous Middle East experts asserted that Kissinger's approach was that of a doctor who planned to stitch up one wound while permitting an infection to rage unattended elsewhere.

According to these critics, Kissinger, by concentrating on Egypt, intended to woo the moderate Sadat away from the Arab camp. This would not only remove the most conciliatory voice from Arab councils, but it would postpone and ultimately make more difficult the moment of truth. The heart of the matter, Kissinger's critics declared, was neither Egypt nor Syria, but the problem of the Palestinians, which Kissinger had chosen to postpone indefinitely, in addition to Jerusalem, which he had chosen to ignore completely. As George Ball, one of Kissinger's most trenchant critics, put it, "The step-by-step approach was the work of a tactician when the times called for a strategist."

Kissinger was undaunted by these attacks. He believed that the aftermath of an inconclusive war was the best time for a concentrated peace effort. Shortly after the last shot had been fired, he decided to commit his skill, energy, and reputation to a highly personal diplomatic peace offensive in the Middle East. During the next few months he would visit virtually every Arab capital and shuttle between Aswan and Jerusalem, and later between Damascus and Jerusalem. Sadat would call him "brother"; Faisal would welcome him even though he was a Jew; Hussein would pilot him in the royal helicopter; even Assad would learn to like him; and Golda Meir would have endless conversations with him in her kitchen. The end result of this extraordinary diplomatic tour de force was the successful negotiation of the first two hurdles. In January 1974 Kissinger was able to produce a military disengagement accord between Israel and Egypt, and four months later, after immense effort, he was able to achieve a similar accord between Israel and Syria.

The high point of Kissinger's "shuttle diplomacy" was the Sinai agreement between Israel and Egypt, signed in Geneva in September 1975. The Sinai agreement bore the imprimatur of a Kissinger settlement. Neither side was happy with it, but neither side could offer a better alternative that was acceptable to both. The Israelis promised to return two mountain passes and an oil field. In exchange they received pledges from President Sadat to the effect that Egypt would refrain from the threat or use of force against the Jewish state. Sadat also agreed to continue negotiations toward a final peace agreement and to extend the mandate of the UN buffer force annually for at least three years.

What finally made it possible, however, for Israel to conclude the agreement was a specific American commitment that Kissinger had not made before. Kissinger offered to station two hundred American civilian technicians in the Sinai *between* the contending parties. They would serve as a kind of early warning system in case either side planned an attack on the other, and they would report to both Israel and Egypt. In addition, Kissinger pledged to recommend an American aid commitment of $2.3 billion to Israel. Israel, which did not trust the UN buffer force, found the pledge of a small symbolic American presence reassuring. The aid package too was attractive, and furthermore, Prime Minister Yitzhak Rabin could tell the opposition that Israel still retained over 85 percent of the Sinai and the entire Gaza Strip. Sadat received his coveted mountain passes and oil fields plus an American commitment of $700 million needed for the impoverished Egyptian economy. The two hundred Americans were welcome too because their presence only underscored Sadat's growing independence from the Soviet Union. Thus Egypt gained some territorial allowances, and Israel received political concessions. What could not be bridged between the parties directly was bridged by American commitments. Some senators grumbled that the Americans in the Sinai reminded them of the beginning of Vietnam, but Kissinger was quick to point out that the Americans in the Sinai were civilians who were to aid both sides in keeping the peace, not soldiers who were to help one side to win a war.

On the whole, Kissinger was pleased with the second Sinai interim agreement. It was, after all, the first accord between Israel and an Arab nation that was not the immediate consequence of war. He knew that it was far from a genuine peace treaty, but he was convinced that his step-by-step approach was still the best way to proceed. In his judgment, most Americans were still willing to take great risks to preserve the state of Israel but were *not* willing to take such risks to preserve Israel's conquests.

During most of 1975 and 1976 a deus ex machina postponed the moment of truth for Israel. Syria and the PLO, Israel's two bitterest adversaries, turned on each other in a murderous war in Lebanon. While it lasted, Israel was in no mood to make concessions. By 1977, however, when Jimmy Carter assumed the presidency of the United States and Menachem Begin became prime minister of Israel, the Lebanese war had tapered off and a renewed Arab alliance confronted the Jewish state.

By 1977, then, it had become clear that the step-by-step approach had reached a dead end. The heart of the matter was now the fate of the Palestinians. Israel was confronted with a dreadful choice. If it agreed to negotiate with the PLO and return some territories to be used for the creation of a Palestinian state, such a state would clearly be a dagger pointed at the heart of Israel. If, on the other hand, Israel refused to negotiate, it risked another war or another oil embargo, as well as slow economic strangulation and increasing isolation. Despite the risks involved, Carter believed that ultimately Israel would have to face the Palestinians as a reality that would not go away, just as America after more than two decades had been forced to adjust to the reality of a China that was Communist. There were now 3 million Israelis and 3 million Palestinians. Both were permanent realities, and sooner or later a compromise solution would have to be discovered. The alternative was yet another war.

In November 1977 the world held its breath when, in a spectacular and unprecedented move, Sadat visited the Jewish state and addressed the Israeli Knesset. Although neither Sadat nor Begin made any substantive concessions during that first face-to-face encounter in Jerusalem, both leaders made a solemn pledge never again to go to war with one another. The Sadat mission was widely heralded as a major turning point in the thirty-year-old conflict between Arab and Jew. At last an Arab statesman had openly recognized the Jewish state. Two old enemies had suddenly become friends.

In September 1978 Carter, in an all-out effort to forge a peace settlement between Begin and Sadat, invited the two leaders to a summit meeting at Camp David. After two weeks of intense and secret deliberations, two important agreements were hammered out. First, Begin and Sadat agreed on a "Framework for Peace between Egypt and Israel" that provided for the phased withdrawal of Israeli forces from the Sinai and the signing of a full-fledged peace treaty. Second, the two leaders agreed on a broader "Framework for Peace in the Middle East" that was designed to enable the Palestinian issue and the West Bank problem to be resolved progressively over a five-year period.

But at the very moment that these agreements were being made, the Shah of Iran was deposed and driven into exile by the fundamentalist Islamic forces loyal to the Ayatollah Ruhollah Khomeini. As Iranian oil exports plummeted, the United States became increasingly dependent on Saudi Arabian oil. Recognizing their advantage, the Saudis insisted on a linkage between the separate Egyptian-Israeli peace treaty and progress toward the far more difficult issues of the West Bank, the Palestinians, and the status of Jerusalem. Motivated by American energy needs, Carter in turn exerted pressure on Israel to be more flexible. Finally, in March 1979, Begin and Sadat, after yet another Carter visit to the Middle East, signed a separate peace treaty. The president's tenacity and faith had finally borne fruit. After thirty years of war the Middle East had taken a large step toward peace.

Many vexing issues remained unresolved, of course. The fate of Jewish settlements on the West Bank continued to torment the Israelis, who also worried about the very real possibility of the ultimate creation of a Palestinian state. In 1981 Israel, using American-made planes, destroyed an Iraqi nuclear reactor that had been constructed with French and Italian help. This preemptive strike precipitated a diplomatic crisis between the United States and Israel. On the Arab side, Jordan and Saudi Arabia were dubious about the Israeli-Egyptian treaty; Syria and the PLO were bitterly opposed and regarded Sadat as a traitor. And perhaps most important, all Arabs insisted that Israel withdraw from Jerusalem and renounce the city as its capital. Israel in turn declared in 1980 that Jerusalem would remain its capital for "all eternity." In 1981, President Sadat was assassinated by Moslem fanatics. Under his successor, Hosni Mubarak, Egypt's relations with Israel cooled considerably. Worst of all, Israel launched an invasion of Lebanon which not only raised levels of violence in the region to new ferocity but upset the entire balance of power in the Middle East.

The Lebanese Tragedy

There was a time when Lebanon was a peaceful, happy land, a kind of Middle Eastern Switzerland, with its graceful seaport capital, Beirut, a major tourist attraction. This tranquillity depended on a fine balance between the Moslem and Christian populations of the country. When the balance broke down, Lebanon gradually descended into an abyss of devastation. Jealous factions fighting for turf dismembered Lebanon piece by bloody piece until it became a country without an effective government. Unable to control its own destiny, Lebanon was drawn into the vortex of the major power struggles in world politics. It became a bitterly divided country, with Beirut a divided city.

After Israel occupied the West Bank in 1967, hundreds of thousands of Palestinians moved to Lebanon over the years, gradually upsetting the fragile balance between Moslems and Christians. In 1975 the country erupted in civil war, triggered by a round of local murders, which were to become typical of the Lebanese scene. Beirut was devastated for the first time. Syria's President Assad, seeing an opportunity for expansion, sent a "peacekeeping" force into Lebanon, which signaled the beginning of the Syrian occupation of central Lebanon. Israel's Premier Begin, apprehensive about Syrian intervention, carved out for Israel a "security strip" in southern Lebanon in 1978. Four years later, in June 1982, Israeli forces invaded Lebanon in full force, going all the way to Beirut. Their goal was to drive the Palestinian guerrillas out of southern Lebanon and to counter Syria's growing influence in that war-torn country.

At this juncture, the United States, fearful that the apparent disintegration of Lebanon might play into Soviet hands, decided to become involved. The Reagan administration worked out an agreement with three of its allies—Great Britain, France, and Italy—to send about five thousand marines into Lebanon. The objective of this "multinational peacekeeping force" was to monitor the withdrawal of PLO forces from Lebanon and eventually to persuade Israel to pull out so that Syria too might withdraw. The United States hoped, in short, that it might be helpful in returning Lebanon to the Lebanese. Unfortunately this was not to be.

As the Palestinians were evacuated and the Israelis returned West Beirut to President Amin Gemayel's forces, the mission of the four-power peacekeeping force became somewhat unclear. Gradually it was redefined as providing support for the Gemayel government. But the young president acted more like the head of the Christian faction than the leader of the entire country, and the force quickly became identified as pro-Christian and anti-Moslem. A new tragedy was in the making.

In October 1983 a Moslem fanatic, kamikazelike, drove a truck loaded with explosives into the sleeping quarters of the American marines in Beirut. The vehicle exploded with such force that the structure collapsed in seconds, killing 241 American servicemen. Simultaneously another suicide mission killed 58 French soldiers, also asleep in their compounds. For the United States, this was the highest death toll since the Vietnam War; for France, it was the heaviest since the Algerian War.

When observed in the cold light of political analysis, this dreadful tragedy had all the overtones of a neocolonial conflict. The Moslem fundamentalists who committed these murders probably perceived the American, British, French, and Italian soldiers not only as partial to the Christian cause in Lebanon, but also as the vanguard of a new Western imperialism. After all, these were the very four nations that had engaged in colonial adventures not many years before: Lebanon had been a French colony; Libya had belonged to Italy; much of the Middle East had belonged to Britain; and the United States was, of course, the main instigator of this renewed colonial intrusion. Islam, especially Shi'ite Islam inspired by Iran, perceived itself as the main bulwark against Western aggression. The murderers were therefore not considered murderers. They were freedom fighters, and their reward would be immediate entry into paradise.

After the Beirut catastrophe, the days of the multinational peace-keeping force were numbered. Senator Ernest Hollings of South Carolina put it well when he called on President Ronald Reagan to withdraw the marines within sixty days: "If they've been put there to fight, then there are far too few," he said, "but if they've been put there to be killed, there are far too many." Accordingly, after some fruitless shellings by the USS *New Jersey*, the American soldiers were withdrawn from Lebanon in February 1984. Shortly thereafter, their French, British, and Italian fellow marines were removed. Lebanon by now was a carcass, and a dismembered one at that. For all practical purposes, by mid-1984 Lebanon was a divided country. Within its divisions there were further factions that made the country look like a crazy quilt. Nevertheless, these factions tended to fall, either directly or indirectly, along East-West lines. On the Western side were the Israeli forces stationed in southern Lebanon, now left to fend for themselves after the American withdrawal. The Maronite Christians and, to a lesser extent, the Sunni Moslems, were not unfriendly to Israel and the Western cause. On the other side, Druze and Shi'ite Moslems supported the Syrian presence, which in turn was backed by the Soviet Union. President Gemayel, virtually powerless after the pullout of the Western forces, had to accept the indefinite presence of the Syrians and even felt compelled to host a Soviet delegation in Beirut. When in early 1985 Israel began a phased withdrawal of its troops from Lebanon, Gemayel's hold on power became even more precarious. In historical perspective, Israel's incursion into Lebanon seemed like an ominous portent: Israel had to withdraw after three years of war, with its mission unaccomplished. And worse was yet to come.

By the late 1980s Lebanon had become a disaster area, a place of war of all against all and each for himself. Not only were Moslems pitted against Christians once again, but several outside powers continued to aggravate the conflict: Syria, which had 25,000 troops stationed on 60 percent of Lebanon's territory; Iran, which wielded influence through Shi'ite Moslems and Revolutionary Guards in the east of the country; Israel, through the continued occupation of an enclave in southern Lebanon that it called its security zone; and 400,000 Palestinians, including a guerrilla force of 10,000. Lebanon itself was virtually without a government and had a regular army of only 37,000 men. Among these men, Moslems were in the majority in the ranks, but Christians controlled the officer corps. The prime minister was a Sunni Moslem, the speaker of parliament a Shi'ite, and the president, Amin Gemayel, a Christian.

It appeared that, with all these factions, military strength would continue to dictate who controlled the country or, more accurately, who would keep it out of someone else's hands. No end appeared in sight to the destructive civil war that had erupted in 1975. Lebanon remained a tragic and dismembered land.

The Palestinian Uprising

Israel celebrated its fortieth birthday in May 1988, during a time that was marred, as Israel's birth had been, by the sound of gunfire. This time the violence did not emanate from invading armies, but erupted instead in two areas conquered by Israel in the Six-Day War of 1967: the West Bank and Gaza. Two decades of Israeli occupation had finally inflamed the passions of almost 2 million Palestinians yearning for an independent state.

By 1988 more than half of the Palestinian population of Gaza and the West Bank had lived all their lives under Israeli rule. These younger Palestinians were among the best-educated groups in the Middle East yet had only limited opportunities to apply their skills. Most made a meager livelihood in teeming villages, towns, and refugee camps. The rage and frustration of these young people finally boiled over in the West Bank. Thousands of young Palestinians began to throw rocks, iron bars, and an occasional Molotov cocktail at Israeli security forces and insisted on flying the colors— red, white, green, and black—of the banned Palestinian flag.

What began as occasional protests by groups of embittered youths quickly developed into an organized resistance movement with an underground leadership and a well-planned strategy. By the spring of 1988, the movement had gone far beyond rock throwing to an economic boycott of many Israeli products, nonpayment of taxes to Israel, mass resignations of Israeli-appointed Arab police and local government officials, and strikes that closed down trade, transport, education, and other essential public services. The movement also had a name: Intifadeh, the Palestinian Uprising. It had grown into something quite new in the context of the Arab-Israeli conflict: a massive civil-resistance movement, demanding self-determination and an end to military occupation. Israel suddenly faced an entirely new kind of challenge: war from within.

Israel's efforts to quell the uprising through thousands of arrests, imprisonments, and beatings brought no real respite. The larger the number of arrests, the wider the Intifadeh. Gradually, even though the

Palestinians were no military match for the Israelis, they gained an important political advantage: The uprising raised Palestinian national consciousness and once again focused world attention on the Palestine problem. By the summer of 1988, much of the outside world regarded Israel as an occupation power and the Palestinians as the underdog. To the dismay of the Israeli authorities, some of the Western media even began to compare Israel's occupation policies to those of South Africa. Sympathies had begun to shift. In an age of national self-determination, it had become counterproductive for a country of 3 million people to keep 2 million under permanent subjugation.

The uprising further deepened the profound rifts within Israel over the occupied territories. The Likud Party of Prime Minister Yitzhak Shamir perceived the uprising as a conspiracy to end Israel's very existence. In the Likud's view, the Palestinians were not after a Palestinian state in Gaza and the West Bank; they were out to destroy Israel altogether. Therefore a tough policy was the only appropriate response. The Labour Party under its leader, Shimon Peres, on the other hand, advocated a more flexible policy. Believing that ultimately the Jews would be outnumbered in their own country if Israel held on to the territories, the Labour Party was in favor of negotiations. The peace initiative of United States Secretary of State George Shultz, for example, was welcomed by Labour but foundered on the rock of Likud's refusal to compromise.

In a sense, the uprising redivided Israel. Many Israeli civilians became reluctant to enter the territories, and Israel's 700,000 Arab citizens became increasingly "Palestinianized." Even Jerusalem, enthusiastically described by its mayor, Teddy Kollek, as a united city of Arabs and Jews, became de facto divided once again. Very few Jews ventured into the increasingly hostile Arab sector of the city. Nor did many Palestinians cross over into the new predominantly Jewish sector. The clock had been turned back.

By late 1988, the Arab-Israeli conflict was at a complete impasse. The Palestinians demanded complete self-determination, which the Israelis were totally unprepared to grant. The Palestinians asserted that the PLO was their only legitimate representative, a premise rejected by the Israelis. Efforts by the Americans to search for mediators such as King Hussein of Jordan also came to naught when the Jordanian king, in August 1988, removed himself from the scene by relinquishing his claim to the West Bank to the PLO. A contest of wills had taken shape in which Israel remained militarily the stronger but was losing the political initiative to the Palestinians. The Arabs, after five unsuccessful wars, had at long last discovered a formula that worked.

Events now began to move more quickly. In November 1988 the PLO met in Algiers and a jubilant Yasir Arafat proclaimed national independence for a state of Palestine. He then applied for a visa to the United States to address the UN General Assembly. When the State Department denied the visa on the grounds that Arafat had been an accessory to terrorism, the United Nations decided to reconvene in Geneva, where it decided by an overwhelming vote to recognize Palestinian independence and to place the Israeli-occupied West Bank and Gaza under UN supervision. Arafat, in a shrewd political move, also declared in Geneva that he recognized "the right of all parties in the Middle East conflict to exist in peace and security," implying the recognition of Israel. Moreover, he renounced "all forms of terrorism, including individual, group, and state terrorism." Secretary of State Henry Kissinger had declared in 1975 that if the PLO ever recognized Israel and gave up terrorism, the United States would be prepared to open a dialogue with the Palestinians. According to his successor, George Shultz, these conditions had now been fulfilled, and therefore the United States decided to hold its first meeting with PLO representatives in December 1988 in Tunisia. The Israeli government, in considerable dismay, reiterated that it would not negotiate with the PLO under any conditions. Arafat had clearly succeeded in driving a large wedge between Israel and its American ally and, moreover, had won a considerable propaganda victory. He could claim that the United Nations had created Israel by majority vote in 1947 and now, more than forty years later, had passed an even more overwhelming vote on behalf of the Palestinian people; hence the time for the creation of a Palestinian state had finally arrived.

A glimmer of hope emerged in 1991. United States Secretary of State James Baker, after tireless efforts, succeeded in persuading all the parties to the conflict to participate in a peace conference in Madrid. Thus, for the first time in forty years, Israelis, Arabs, and Palestinians sat down together at a conference table. Even though each delegate used the occasion to restate familiar positions, and no concessions were made, the fact that the opposing parties had gathered in the same room and shaken hands constituted a first step toward the elusive goal of Middle Eastern peace.

The Peace Process: Between Fear and Hope

Encouraged by the events in Madrid, a small group of Israeli and Palestinian academics with good political connections met for several months in 1992 in a country mansion near Oslo, Norway, to talk peace. The site had been made available for that express purpose by the Norwegian government. The negotiators took long walks, ate hearty meals, and after dozens of collegial working sessions, emerged with a draft for a peace settlement which they submitted to their respective political leaders. The timing was excellent. On the Israeli side, Yitzhak Rabin, the hero of the war of 1967, had decided that the time had come to trade territory for peace. Shimon Peres agreed. On the Palestinian side, Yasir Arafat, eager to energize his fading image as a decisive leader and determined to become the first president of a Palestinian self-government, accepted an invitation by President Bill Clinton to meet with Rabin and Peres in Washington to sign a peace accord. Accordingly, in a historic ceremony at the White House in 1993, the old Israeli soldier and the former Palestinian terrorist shook hands and put their names to a document proclaiming peace between Israel and the Palestinians. With one stroke of the pen, Rabin and Arafat had become quasi allies against the extremists of both sides.

Because the return of Gaza and the West Bank to Arafat's newly established Palestinian Authority was an integral part of the new peace treaty, many Israeli settlers on the West Bank were bitterly opposed to it. Even before the peace accord, one fanatic had burst into a mosque near Hebron and shot several dozen Moslems at prayer. Not long afterward, bombs had gone off in Tel Aviv and Jerusalem, killing Israeli civilians. Nonetheless, Rabin and Arafat defied the fanatics and went on the offensive. To cement their new accord, Rabin severely chastised Israeli extremists and Arafat managed to place some Palestinian terrorists under arrest. Then, in a second major breakthrough in 1995, the two peacemakers succeeded in co-opting King Hussein of Jordan, who appeared on the White House lawn to make peace with Israel, once again with President Clinton presiding. Another historic handshake, this time between Prime Minister Rabin and King Hussein, sealed the accord.

Only a single holdout remained on the sidelines: President Assad of Syria.

Just as Rabin and Peres settled down to make a deal with Syria, a tragedy occurred that dealt a terrible blow to the entire peace process. In 1996 Prime Minister Rabin was shot to death by an Israeli extremist, an event without precedent in Jewish history. Emboldened by this disaster, Palestinian terrorists stepped up their attacks, which prompted Rabin's successor, Shimon Peres, to engage in retaliatory raids on terrorist strongholds in Lebanon. By mid-1996, the fanatics seemed to have checkmated the peacemakers. In their national election in May, the Israelis, by a very narrow margin, chose Likud leader Benjamin Netanyahu as their prime minister over Rabin's successor, Shimon Peres. Not surprisingly, under his leadership the peace process slowed down to a snail's pace and, in some instances, ground to a halt. In one incident, seventy-six Palestinians and Israelis were killed, and President Clinton, in a desperate effort to save the peace process, invited Netanyahu, Arafat, and King Hussein to a hastily American-arranged summit meeting in Wye, near Washington. The leaders talked but made few concessions. Netanyahu agreed to a further withdrawal of 10 percent from the West Bank but later reneged on implementation. Trapped between hope and fear, the leaders succumbed to the latter, at least temporarily.

The pendulum swung toward hope again two years later, however, when the Israeli people, frustrated by a stalled peace process, elected their most decorated soldier to lead the nation. Ehud Barak's role model was Yizhak Rabin. Like his assassinated predecessor, Barak believed in a "peace of the brave," but unlike Rabin, he built a broad comprehensive coalition under the banner of "One Israel." In a passionate inaugural address in July 1999, he described himself as one of the "gray soldiers whose hands are blackened from war and whose nostrils are filled with death." He addressed the Arab world by quoting the Jewish poet Hillel: "Our tongue is dry from the march and we cry love into the insides of your souls."[40] He gave himself a deadline of fifteen months to work out a framework for a comprehensive peace with the Palestinians, Lebanon, and Syria. Interestingly enough, this ambitious plan coincided with the time remaining to the Clinton presidency.

During the rest of 1999, the atmosphere improved considerably as Barak proceeded to mend fences with his Arab neighbors. The metaphor is apt because the Israeli leader believed that only a peace of separation rather than integration could work after so many decades of bloody conflict. He was even fond of quoting Robert Frost's famous poem "Good Fences Make Good Neighbors." First, he visited his Egyptian counterpart, Hosni Mubarak, who lent his enthusiastic support. Next, he reassured Arafat that withdrawal from the West Bank would continue if Arafat would coordinate his schedule of progress toward statehood with the Israelis. And by year's end he achieved what had eluded his predecessor: negotiations with President Assad of Syria about trading Golan for Syrian recognition of Israel. Barak knew that Arafat and Assad were both old and ill. He was eager to make peace with them rather than with unknown successors. The third Arab protagonist, King Hussein of Jordan, had already been laid to rest, but not before making a final heroic effort to contribute to the peace of his country. Time was running out for the older generation, but Barak of Israel had made hope, rather than fear, his unshakable inner compass.

By midsummer 2000 the Israeli prime minister was ready to end the step-by-step approach to peace and, in a bold and risky gamble, throw everything on the negotiating table at once. The occasion was a summit conference at Camp David between Barak and Arafat, presided over by President Bill Clinton. The foxy Arafat sensed Barak's eagerness to become the Charles de Gaulle of the Middle East and began to outmaneuver him. Every time Barak made an offer, Arafat balked and demanded more. Barak even offered what every Israeli leader before him had vowed never to do—to give up a part of East Jerusalem and permit the Palestinians to call it their capital. When Arafat rebuffed even that proposal and insisted on the right of all Palestinians to return to Israel, Barak realized that hopes for peace were waning rapidly. Both he and Clinton understood that this would be a deal breaker: The return of so many Palestinians to Israel would make the Jews a minority in their own state. In the end, even though Barak promised to return as much as 96 percent of the West Bank, Arafat still insisted on the "right of return." His stubbornness kept getting him better offers from Barak and solidified his political base at home. He was welcomed back as a hero among the Palestinians, while Barak sank into a depression and went into seclusion.

Bill Clinton made one last Herculean effort to break the deadlock in December 2000 at Taba, Egypt, but to no avail. When Arafat bid farewell to Clinton in a phone call in January 2001, three days before the president left office, he told him, "You're a great man." "The hell I am," Clinton responded. "I'm a colossal failure and you made me one."[41] High hopes had been shattered once again and fear and terror were about to take their place.

The Second Palestinian Uprising and the Road Map

In September 2000 Ariel Sharon, the leading candidate of the Likud Party for prime minister, made a visit to the Holy Al-Aqsa Mosque, whose grounds double as the Jewish Temple Mount. Surrounded by more than 1,000 soldiers and bodyguards, he visited several Palestinian holy places without asking permission. His actions sparked a second Palestinian uprising and raised the region's level of violence to heights never seen before. Before leaving office, President Clinton told Arafat that, by turning down the best peace deal he was ever going to get, he was guaranteeing the election of the hawkish Ariel Sharon. This is indeed what happened. In February 2001, Sharon was elected by a landslide, a few weeks after George W. Bush took office. Soon, a deadly duel began to take shape between Sharon and Arafat. Continuing his tradition of alternating between talks of peace when it suited his agenda and resorting to violence, Arafat now supported a new terrorist organization, the al-Aqsa Martyrs Brigade. These martyrs, taking a leaf from Osama bin Laden, introduced a new weapon—suicide attacks—into Israel. Men and women, usually working in groups of two or three, would open fire in the centers of Israeli towns, spraying everyone in sight before being shot dead themselves. Others would enter markets, nightclubs, and other crowded places with explosive belts around their waists and blow themselves up, taking dozens of innocent people with them to their deaths. On one such occasion a seventeen-year-old Palestinian girl walked into a grocery store and blew herself up, killing a seventeen-year-old Israeli girl who was doing her shopping. Sharon retaliated, using F-16 jet fighters, Apache attack helicopters, tanks, and other heavy weaponry in repeated efforts to root out the terrorists in their hideouts. In addition, Israeli tanks reduced entire neighborhoods in Gaza to rubble. When asked by a reporter whether Israel was at war, the prime minister responded in the affirmative, adding that there were funerals every day. Out of sheer frustration, Sharon placed the wily Arafat under house arrest repeatedly, but the suicide bombers, emboldened by their apparent successes, only stepped up their attacks, now reinforced by other terrorist groups such as Hamas and Hezbollah. After almost three years of steadily escalating terror, the violence had reached a dreadful inner logic of its own: It had become impossible to distinguish action from reaction and provocation from revenge.

By spring 2003 a sense of exhaustion had settled over both Israel and the Palestinians. The Bush administration had long promised a so-called road map for a solution to this most stubborn of conflicts, but it had been consumed by the war against Iraq. Now that the war was over and Saddam Hussein had been removed, British prime minister Tony Blair encouraged his American ally to turn his attention to the Arabs and the Israelis. The moment seemed ripe for another effort by a new and untested president to mediate a conflict that had dashed the hopes of so many of his predecessors.

Perhaps the most helpful event that greeted the Bush administration was the long-delayed sidelining of Arafat and the emergence of a new moderate Palestinian prime minister, Mahmoud Abbas, better known as Abu Mazen. The administration's adamant refusal to deal with Arafat had finally deprived him of his power base among his own Palestinian constituency. Accordingly, on March 18, 2003, Arafat agreed to create a new post of prime minister, and on the following day, Abu Mazen became the new leader of the Palestinian Authority at the age of sixty-eight.

The new road map was designed by the United States, with the cooperation of the European Union, Russia, and the United Nations. It was the most concerted effort to end the Palestinian-Israeli conflict since the 1993 Oslo Accords. Its basis was a dramatic statement made by Bush before the UN General Assembly on November 10, 2001, committing the United States to a two-state solution for Israel and Palestine, in which they would live peacefully together within secure and recognized borders. This commitment lay dormant during the Afghan and Iraqi wars, but was now infused with new life and came equipped with a road map and a timeline (spread out over three years) to begin immediately and to culminate in a final settlement in 2005.

First, Prime Minister Abbas was to "end all armed Palestinian activity and all acts of violence against Israelis everywhere." In return, Israel was to begin a process of dismantling settlements built since March 2001 and to freeze all settlement activity. The end of the first stage was envisaged to be new Palestinian elections, followed by a Palestinian state "with attributes of sovereignty," at first kept within provisional borders covering as yet undefined areas. Finally, this state would hold permanent agreement talks with Israel, hoping to resolve the thorny issues of Jerusalem, remaining settlements, borders, and refugees. Interestingly enough, the road map remained silent on the crucial issue of the Palestinians' right to return to Israel. Realizing that such a right would mean the destruction of Israel, all sides preferred silence to a document that would be dead on arrival.

The most hopeful aspect of the two leaders' approach to the proposed road map was their apparent willingness, for the first time, to face up to the most vexing issue: confronting the spoilers in their own midst. Thus, Ariel Sharon mustered the courage to promise in a first meeting with the new Palestinian prime minister in Aqaba, Jordan, to curb Israeli settlements. Abu Mazen, with equal courage, pledged to take on the fanatics on the fringe of the Palestinian movement and expressed his determination to use his new police force to end the violence against Israel.

To make peace in the Middle East, Israeli and Palestinian leaders realized that they might have to go to the brink of civil conflict with their own peoples. Prime Minister Sharon would have to take on the very settlers, one of whom killed Yitzhak Rabin, and Mr. Abbas would no doubt risk assassination by one of the Palestinian terror groups. The enormity of the task facing both leaders was instantly underscored when Israeli settlers and Palestinian radicals denounced the Aqaba meeting and its conclusions.

The promise was great, but the risk was clear. In the Middle East, whenever peacemakers came close to their goal, fanatics murdered them. Shockingly, the assassins usually came not from the enemy, but from their own people. It was a Jew who had killed Rabin and an Egyptian who had killed Sadat. And the greatest of the twentieth century's peacemakers, Mahatma Gandhi, has been killed by a Hindu.

True to form, the militants did not wait long. Two days after the Aqaba meeting, the three main Palestinian terror groups—Hamas, Islamic Jihad, and al-Aqsa Martyrs Brigade—staged a coordinated attack at the border crossing from Gaza into Israel. Disguised in Israeli Army uniforms, they killed four Israeli soldiers. Convinced that Abbas was too conciliatory toward Israel, they were determined to get rid of him. On the other side, Sharon faced his own hard-liners. "Go home," they jeered at him, "you surrender to terrorism."[42] The next day, Israeli helicopters rained missiles on cars carrying Hamas militants, killing five and injuring one of their leaders, Dr. Abdel Aziz Rantisi, who vowed revenge from his hospital bed. The following day, a Hamas suicide bomber, disguised as an Ortho-dox Jew, killed sixteen Israelis on a bus in Jerusalem and wounded more than one hundred people. Sharon vowed to "hound" Hamas until Palestinian security forces cracked down on them. Mahmoud Abbas found himself caught in an all-too-familiar catch-22. As one of his officials put it: "We have to get an agreement with Israel in order to get an agreement with Hamas, and we have to get an agree-ment with Hamas in order to get an agreement with Israel."[43] The vicious cycle of violence had resumed. President Bush did what many of his predecessors had done, expressing condolences to the families of the victims and exhorting both Sharon and Abbas to stop the death spiral. His "road map" seemed derailed.

One terrible example demonstrates the sheer ferocity of the con-flict. The players on the best Palestinian soccer team in Hebron began dying one by one in a wave of suicide missions against the Israelis. Their coach turned out to be the leader of Hamas's military wing in Hebron and was recruiting his players. The Israelis finally caught on to the soccer team's double life and killed the coach.

At long last, in early July, Sharon and Abbas—both near exhaus-tion after battling their own dissidents—decided to take a tentative first step on Bush's road map. Abbas managed to persuade Hamas and Islamic Jihad to accept a three-month truce and Sharon pulled back troops from parts of Gaza and the West Bank town of Bethle-hem. Standing side by side in Jerusalem on July 1—this time without an intermediary—the two leaders made yet another pledge to put the past behind them. In Mahmoud Abbas's words, "Each life that is lost is a human tragedy. No more suffering, no more death, no more pain."[44]

A few weeks later, Bush invited both Sharon and Abbas to the White House in separate meetings to encourage them to take more concrete steps along his road map. He offered Abbas an economic incentive package to initiate the development of Palestine, but warned him that terror would not be tolerated. Abbas pledged to do his best to extend the truce and to keep the militants in check.

Sharon began to dismantle several checkpoints and outposts in the West Bank and, in a major concession, released several hundred Palestinians from Israeli prisons. He insisted, however, on the completion of a "security fence" that would prevent the infiltration of suicide bombers from the West Bank into Israel, a project for which Bush showed little, if any, enthusiasm. The steps were modest on both sides, but they constituted yet another start. The main obstacle, of course, continued to loom in the background. The Palestinian militants still hoped to bomb their way to statehood and the Israelis were equally determined to retaliate, with massive force if necessary. Yet, for the first time, with a moderate Palestinian gaining ground against the wily Arafat, and an old Israeli soldier walking in the shoes of Yitzhak Rabin, a genuine coalition of moderates seemed to have emerged.

Further progress was made in August when two suicide bombings that killed two Israelis failed to destroy this new coalition of moderates. Instead, Muhammad Dahlan, the Palestinian security chief, hammered out a new agreement with his opposite number from Israel, Defense Minister Shaul Mofaz. It entailed several significant concessions by Israel: the release of seventy-three Palestinian prisoners; the handing over of two cities—Jericho and Qalqilya—to the Palestinians, with Ramallah and Tulkarm to follow at a later date; and permission for Arafat to leave his compound for a day to travel to Gaza to visit his sister's grave. Even though Hamas dismissed these concessions as "not enough," it now appeared that something new had become possible: perhaps the peace process could be freed, at long last, from being held hostage to the militants' agenda. Indeed, Israel, in a major concession, backed away from its insistence that men it regarded as wanted terrorists be held under lock and key. Instead, it accepted assurances from Dahlan to monitor these men in the cities in which they lived and to prevent them from mounting new attacks. In effect, this amounted to a grant of amnesty to militants who had agreed to abandon violence, a significant vote of faith in the Palestinian Authority to police its own extremists, yet to hold it fully responsible for any breakdown.

The very next day, however, while Abbas was meeting with leaders of Islamic Jihad and Hamas in Gaza City in an attempt to extend the truce, a suicide bomber detonated a bomb on a crowded bus in Jerusalem, killing twenty people, including six children, and wounding dozens more. Israel immediately suspended all negotiations with the Palestinians and a frustrated Abbas issued arrest warrants for the terrorists, identified as members of Hamas and Islamic Jihad. Shortly thereafter, the Israelis killed several Hamas members, including two of its senior leaders, in Gaza City. To make things even worse, Secretary of State Colin Powell appealed to the sidelined Arafat to support Abbas in his struggle against the Palestinian militants. Abbas, now wedged between a reinvigorated Arafat and his own militants, and confronted with a vote of no confidence in the Palestinian parliament, decided to offer his resignation as prime minister. The offer was accepted by Arafat who, in turn, was promptly rejected as a negotiating partner by Israel. Indeed, Israel threatened to deport or even kill Arafat, but when the UN Security Council attempted to pass a resolution calling on Israel to withdraw this threat, the United States cast a veto. Arafat, unfazed, promptly appointed a new prime minister, Ahmed Qurei, to replace Mamoud Abbas. Sharon responded by reiterating his determination to ignore Arafat and to hunt down the Palestinian militants. It appeared that the conflict had boiled down to a death struggle between two aging men, Sharon and Arafat. And, when on the eve of Yom Kippur, the holiest day in the Jewish calendar, a Palestinian suicide bomber killed nineteen people in a crowded restaurant in Haifa and wounded fifty more, Sharon retaliated with an air strike against what he called a Palestinian terror camp near Damascus, the capital of Syria. President Bush declared that Israel had the right to defend itself. This was the first overt military strike by Israel against an Arab country in thirty years, thus widening the conflict to include Syria. Not only had the road map fallen off a cliff, as Powell had warned, but the danger now loomed that the entire region might be dragged into the vortex of the deadly conflict between Israel and Palestine. To make matters even worse, in mid-October Palestinian militants killed three American security guards and wounded an American diplomat in the first fatal attack on an American target since the beginning of the second Palestinian uprising.

And yet, while Sharon and Arafat were behaving like two scorpions in a bottle, hope had risen once again, this time from unofficial sources. Ami Ayalon, a former chief of Israeli security forces, and

Sari Nusseibeh, a Palestinian university president, managed to produce a statement of principles that was signed by 100,000 Israelis and 70,000 Palestinians. In it, Israel would be recognized as the "state of the Jewish people," sovereignty in Jerusalem would be divided and shared, and the Palestinian "right to return" would not include returning to Israel.[45]

On December 1, 2003, civic leaders from across the Israeli and Palestinian political spectrum gathered in Geneva, Switzerland, to publicize a negotiated but unofficial framework known as the "Geneva Accord." The central concept was that, in exchange for peace with Israel, the Palestinians would at last gain a nonmilitarized state. The plan projected the Palestinian state occupying nearly all of the West Bank and Gaza, but with Jewish settlements along the West Bank's borders and most of Jerusalem given to Israel. In return, the Palestinians would get sovereignty over parts of East Jerusalem and the holy sites at the Temple Mount.

Even though the Sharon government rejected the Geneva Plan, U.S. Secretary of State Colin Powell decided to meet with Yossi Beilin, a former Minister of Justice in Israel and with Yasir Abed Rabbo, who led the Palestinian delegation. While Powell praised the work of the two originators of the Geneva Accord, he expressed a preference for the Bush Administration's road map emphasizing the need for the Palestinians to crack down on terrorists and for the Israelis to ease conditions for the Palestinians in the West Bank.

It appeared that the Geneva Plan dealt with final status issues while the "road map" pointed to a way of getting there.

Conclusion

When people of goodwill despair of finding a solution, they often take solace in time as the great healer of wounds. But the experience of the six wars between the Arab states and Israel has not inspired such confidence in the curative power of time. The shock inflicted on the Arab consciousness by the establishment of Israel and the resulting homelessness of a million native Palestinians grew more, rather than less, acute as Arab nationalism gathered momentum. This trauma was magnified by the fact that Israel—four times its original size—was seen by the Arab world as an ever growing menace. Many

Arabs feared that if its expansion continued at this rate, Israel would soon dominate the whole of Palestine.

On the Jewish side, time has turned Israel into a virtual garrison state. How strange it is to contemplate the fact that the Jews, who lived homeless in the diaspora for two millennia, should within the span of only four decades create a state with such fearsome military capability. Who would have guessed that the Jews, to whom things military were anathema, should now make them their first priority? Yet this is exactly what time has done.

Four times the Arabs made fatal mistakes that the Zionists used to their advantage. In 1948 five Arab armies invaded a Jewish state, whose modest boundaries had been assigned to it by the United Nations. The Jews repelled the invaders and engaged in some annexation of their own, managing to enlarge their territory. The Sinai campaign of 1956 demonstrated vividly what Israeli arms could do, even though the territorial gains had to be given up. In 1967 Nasser's blunder, the blockade of Aqaba, led directly to his humiliation and to Israel's spectacular victory. In October 1973 the Israelis turned an initial setback into yet another costly victory. Yet, in 1979, Israel signed a peace treaty with the Arab world's greatest peacemaker, Egypt's president, Anwar Sadat. But in 1982, Israel's invasion of Lebanon involved the Jewish state in a long and divisive war. And the Palestinian uprisings confronted the Jewish state with the real possibility of civil war. The question now was whether Israel and its Arab neighbors, involved in six wars in a generation, would finally settle for permanent coexistence without victory or defeat.

There was one final paradox that emerged from Israel's victories: The six wars with the Arabs created a situation in which three million Jews came to control territories that contained nearly two million Arabs. It was difficult to see how Israel could keep the fruits of victory and yet remain a Zionist state. It was this insight that transformed Yitzhak Rabin from warrior to peacemaker. Amazingly enough, he and Yasir Arafat became partners in a process that culminated in an accord between Israel and the Palestinians and, a year later, with Jordan. But the fanatics would not rest. Hopes for peace were dashed in 1996 when an Israeli extremist who regarded Rabin as a traitor shot the prime minister to death.

The legacies of Anwar Sadat and Yitzhak Rabin are clear: The strongest hope for peace in the Middle East is the building of a broad and solid coalition of moderate Arabs and Israelis standing united against the extremists of *both* sides. And indeed, as the millennium dawned over the Middle East, Ehud Barak's bold plan for a comprehensive peace once again replaced fear with hope, even for a moment.

But then, in 2003, President George W. Bush's "road map" fell off a cliff, to borrow Colin Powell's phrase, as moderates on the Palestinian side resigned and militants resorted once again to massive suicide bombings. Ariel Sharon of Israel, in turn, decided to hunt down the terrorists relentlessly. But then, out of the ashes of despair, unofficial initiatives taken by individuals from both sides produced "shadow plans" that once again raised hopes.

In this desperate struggle now going on for more than half a century, time was working against Israel. As decades passed, the shifting demographic balance increasingly entered the equation. In December 2003, Ehud Olmert, Israel's Vice Prime Minister, voiced concern that "if matters continue in the territories (West Bank and Gaza), it will lead to the loss of Israel as a Jewish state."[46] Indeed, Arab and Jewish populations were rapidly approaching parity. About 5.2 million Jews and 1.3 million Arabs were Israeli citizens, while roughly 3.5 million more Arabs were living in the West Bank and Gaza Strip with the Arab birth rate continuing to exceed the Jewish rate. Anticipating such a development, Sharon gave a major speech in December 2003 in which he warned the Palestinians that, absent a negotiated peace settlement, Israel would establish a unilateral border along a "security line" with the Palestinians. Predictably, Palestinian leaders promptly condemned the speech as an effort by Israel to force the Palestinians to live in "crowded reservations by sealing them off with a wall."[47]

The day may soon come when Palestinians may stop demanding a two-state solution to the conflict and start demanding a *single* state with a Palestinian majority. As Dan Mericor, another influential adviser to Mr. Sharon put it: One day we will get up and hear Arafat or his successor say, "I don't want a Palestinian state. I want just one thing: Annex me!"[48] Such an outcome would never be accepted by *any* Israeli government because it would mean the end of the Jewish state. Therefore, if a peaceful solution is ever to be found between these two peoples, it must be found *quickly* if a catastrophe is to be averted. Time is of the essence here.

On January 29, 2004, two events occurred that were emblematic of the entire tragic conflict. First, a Palestinian suicide bomber blew up a bus in Jerusalem killing 10 Israelis and wounding 50 more on their way to work. Second, Palestinian authorities and the Lebanese guerrilla group Hezbollah proceeded with a planned prisoner exchange with Israel. As a result, 400 Palestinian prisoners as well as 29 Lebanese members of Hezbollah were freed from Israeli jails in exchange for the return of an Israeli businessman and the remains of three Israeli soldiers who had been killed in Lebanon. Thus, the joy of reunited families coexisted uneasily with the rage of renewed terror. Both hope and despair continued to alternate in an apparently endless cycle now exceeding more than half a century.

NOTES

1. John Nary, "The Bloody Dawn of Israel," *Life* (May 1973), p. 28.
2. Dan Kurzman, *Genesis 1948* (New York: Signet, 1972), p. 26.
3. Ibid., p. 27.
4. David Horowitz, *State in the Making* (New York: Knopf, 1953), p. 140.
5. Ibid., p. 141.
6. Larry Collins and Dominique Lapierre, *O Jerusalem* (New York: Simon & Schuster, 1972), p. 27.
7. *Genesis 1948*, p. 38.
8. *O Jerusalem*, p. 30.
9. Ibid., p. 78.
10. Ibid., p. 80.
11. Ibid., p. 81.
12. *Genesis 1948*, p. 120.
13. Ibid., p. 123.
14. Ibid., p. 124.
15. Ibid., p. 126.
16. *O Jerusalem*, p. 345.
17. Ibid., p. 300.
18. Anthony Nutting, *Nasser* (New York: Dutton, 1972), p. 143.
19. Hugh Thomas, *Suez* (New York: Harper & Row, 1966), p. 163.
20. Ibid.
21. Ibid.
22. *Nasser*, p. 145.
23. Anthony Eden, *Full Circle*, quoted by Herbert Feis in *Foreign Affairs* (July 1960), p. 600.
24. *Nasser*, p. 163.
25. Ibid.
26. United Nations Document 5/3712, October 29, 1956.

27. *Suez,* p. 164.
28. Keesing's Research Report, *The Arab-Israeli Conflict* (New York: Scribners, 1968), p. 8.
29. Michael Howard and Robert Hunter, *Israel and the Arab World: The Crisis of 1967* (London: Institute for Strategic Studies, 1967), p. 17.
30. Ibid.
31. Ibid., p. 20.
32. Ibid., p. 22.
33. Cited in *Israel and the Arab World,* p. 24.
34. *Arab-Israeli Conflict,* p. 25.
35. *Israel and the Arab World,* p. 39.
36. *New York Times,* October 14, 1973.
37. *New York Times,* October 21, 1973.
38. *Time* (October 29, 1973), p. 44.
39. Ibid., p. 45.
40. *New York Times,* July 7, 1999.
41. *Newsweek,* April 1, 2002.
42. *New York Times,* June 10, 2003.
43. Ibid., June 17, 2003.
44. Ibid., July 1, 2003.
45. Ibid., October 31, 2003.
46. Ibid., December 6, 2003.
47. Ibid., December 20, 2003.
48. Ibid., December 13, 2003.

SELECTED BIBLIOGRAPHY

AJAMI, FOUAD. *The Dream Palace of the Arabs: A Generation's Odyssey.* New York: Pantheon, 1998.
ARONSON, GEOFFREY. *Creating Facts: Israel, Palestinians, and the West Bank.* Washington, D.C.: Institute for Palestine Studies, 1987.
DAWISHA, ADEED. *Arab Nationalism in the Twentieth Century: From Triumph to Despair.* Princeton, N.J.: Princeton University Press, 2003.
EBAN, ABBA. *Diplomacy for the Next Century.* New Haven, Conn.: Yale University Press, 1998.
EVRON, YAIR. *War and Intervention in Lebanon.* Baltimore: Johns Hopkins University Press, 1987.
FEINTUCH, YOSSI. *U.S. Policy on Jerusalem.* Westport, Conn.: Greenwood, 1987.
GILMOUR, DAVID. *Lebanon: The Fractured Country.* New York: St. Martin's, 1983.
GROSSMAN, DAVID. *Death as a Way of Life: Israel Ten Years after Oslo.* Trans. HAIM WATZMAN. Ed. EFRAT LEV. New York: Farrar, Straus & Giroux, 2003.
HARKABI, YEHOSHAFAT. *Israel's Fateful Hour.* New York: Harper & Row, 1988.
HOURANI, ALBERT. *A History of the Arab Peoples.* Cambridge, Mass.: Harvard University Press, 1991.

HOWARD, MICHAEL, and ROBERT HUNTER. *Israel and the Arab World: The Crisis of 1967.* London: Institute for Strategic Studies, 1967.

INDYK, MARTIN. "A Trusteeship for Palestine?" *Foreign Affairs,* May/June 2003.

ISSAWI, CHARLES. *The Arab World's Legacy.* Princeton, N.J.: Darwin, 1981.

KISSINGER, HENRY. *Crisis: The Anatomy of Two Major Foreign Policy Crises.* New York: Simon & Schuster. 2003.

KURZMAN, DAN. *Genesis 1948.* New York: Signet, 1972.

LITTLE, DOUGLAS. *American Orientalism: The United States and the Middle East since 1945.* Chapel Hill: University of North Carolina Press, 2002.

LUFT, GAL. "The Palestinian H-Bomb." *Foreign Affairs,* July/August 2002.

MORRIS, BENNY. *The Birth of the Palestinian Refugee Problem.* New York: Cambridge University Press, 1988.

MORRIS, BENNY. *Righteous Victims: A History of the Zionist-Arab Conflict, 1881–1999.* New York: Knopf, 1999.

MORRIS, BENNY. *The Road to Jerusalem: Glubb Pasha, Palestine and the Jews.* London: I. B. Tauris, 2002.

MURPHY, CARYLE. *Passion for Islam: Shaping the Modern Middle East: The Egyptian Experience.* New York: Scribner, 2002.

NUTTING, ANTHONY. *Nasser.* New York: Dutton, 1972.

OREN, MICHAEL B. *Six Days of War: June 1967 and the Making of the Modern Middle East.* New York: Oxford University Press, 2002.

POLK, WILLIAM R. *The Arab World.* Cambridge, Mass.: Harvard University Press, 1980.

POLLACK, KENNETH M. *Arabs at War: Military Effectiveness, 1948–1991.* Lincoln: University of Nebraska Press, 2002.

RABINOVICH, ITAMAR. *Waging Peace: Israel and the Arabs at the End of the Century.* New York: Farrar, Straus & Giroux, 1999.

RUBIN, BARRY. "The Real Roots of Arab Anti-Americanism." *Foreign Affairs,* November/December 2002.

RUBIN, BARRY. *The Tragedy of the Middle East.* Cambridge: Cambridge University Press, 2003.

RUBIN, BARRY, and JUDITH COLP RUBIN, Eds. *Anti-American Terrorism and the Middle East: A Documentary Reader.* New York: Oxford University Press, 2002.

RYAN, CURTIS R. *Jordan in Transition: From Hussein to Abdullah.* Boulder, Colo.: Lynne Rienner, 2002.

SAHLIYEH, EMILE. *In Search of Leadership: West Bank Politics since 1967.* Washington, D.C.: Brookings, 1988.

SATLOFF, ROBERT B., Ed. *War on Terror: The Middle East Dimension.* Washington, D.C.: Washington Institute for Near East Policy, 2002.

SAVIR, URI. *The Process.* New York: Random House, 1998.

SELA, AVRAHAM. *The Decline of the Arab-Israeli Conflict: Middle East Politics and the Quest for Regional Order.* Albany: State University of New York Press, 1998.

SHEPHERD, NAOMI. *Teddy Kollek: Mayor of Jerusalem.* New York: Harper & Row, 1988.

SHLAIM, AVI. *The Iron Wall: Israel and the Arab World since 1948.* New York: Norton, 1999.

ST. JOHN, BRUCE DONALD. *Qaddafi's World Design: Libyan Foreign Policy.* London: Sagi Books, 1987.

STEIN, KENNETH W. *Heroic Diplomacy: Sadat, Kissinger, Carter, Begin, and the Quest for Arab-Israeli Peace.* New York: Routledge, 1999.

STOESSINGER, JOHN G. *Henry Kissinger: The Anguish of Power.* New York: Norton, 1976.

STUDY GROUP. *Toward Arab-Israeli Peace.* Washington, D.C.: Brookings, 1988.

TELHAMI, SHIBLEY. *The Stakes: America and the Middle East.* Boulder, Colo.: Westview, 2002.

THOMAS, HUGH. *Suez.* New York: Harper & Row, 1966.

WALLACH, JANET, and JOHN. *Arafat: In the Eyes of the Beholder.* New York: Carol, 1990.

WICKHAM, CARRIE ROSEFSKY. *Mobilizing Islam: Religion, Activism, and Political Change in Egypt.* New York: Columbia University Press, 2002.

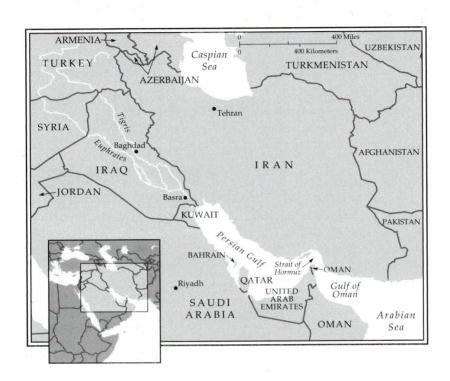

MAP 11   Iraq and the Persian Gulf Region

8

Saddam Hussein's Wars against Iran and Kuwait

Things fall apart; the centre cannot hold,
Mere anarchy is loosed upon the world,
The blood-dimmed tide is loosed, and everywhere
The ceremony of innocence is drowned;
The best lack all conviction, while the worst
Are full of passionate intensity.
. . . Somewhere in sands of the desert . . .
The darkness drops again; but now I know
That twenty centuries of stony sleep
Were vexed to nightmare by a rocking cradle,
And what rough beast, its hour come round at last,
Slouches towards Bethlehem to be born?

William Butler Yeats, *The Second Coming*

Adolf Hitler cast a long shadow over my childhood and as an adult I read dozens of biographies in an effort to understand the Nazi leader. Much was made in these books of Hitler's lonely, brutal childhood, the absence of a loving role model to guide him, and the many rejections he encountered. But something always seemed unsatisfactory about these explanations; after all, millions of youngsters all over the world have had worse childhoods than Hitler's and still managed to grow up as decent people. Now I believe that absolute evil, like great genius, may well be beyond rational explanation. Just as no biographer can really explain Shakespeare or Mozart, no historian will ever fully understand Adolf Hitler—or, for that matter, Saddam Hussein.

Perhaps our fascination with evil is that it is often more mysterious than good is, and therefore more compelling. When Shakespeare's

Hamlet warned Horatio that there were "things in Heaven and Earth that are not dreamt of in your philosophy," he was alluding to Claudius, his father's murderer. He sensed that Horatio, a man of reason, was not capable of understanding such a truly evil man. Nor can we.

Of all the people who parade through the pages of this book, I believe that only three are absolutely evil: Adolf Hitler, Saddam Hussein, and Slobodan Milosevic. Why not Stalin, one might ask? Although his crimes were horrendous, he did not love war for its own sake as did Hitler, Saddam, and Milosevic. The latter three men were classic *war lovers*. Like a vampire, the war lover feeds on the blood of the living. He thrives on the lives of the innocents, like the young Iraqi and Iranian soldiers who carried their own coffins to the front during their eight-year war. The war lover needs war without end in order to feel like a man. And only when he dies or is slain does liberation come.

Men like Generals Dwight D. Eisenhower or H. Norman Schwarzkopf hated war and abhorred casualties. Eisenhower agonized over the Normandy invasion in 1944 because he dreaded the prospect of high casualties; Schwarzkopf's entire strategy in the war against Iraq was built on keeping Allied casualties as low as possible. The Eisenhowers and Schwarzkopfs usually win their wars, whereas the war lovers invariably lose theirs. Yet only death breaks the war lover's fatal bond with his people. Therein lies his peril to humanity.[1]

This chapter will explore the two conflicts that Saddam Hussein thrust upon the world: the attack on Iran in 1980 and the invasion of Kuwait ten years later. Strangely, the Iraqi dictator conjured up echoes of all previous wars fought in this century, a unique though dubious distinction. The war with Iran, to begin with, bears an almost eerie resemblance to World War I.

The Iran-Iraq War: The Price of Martyrdom

When Saddam Hussein came to power in 1979, he ordered the construction of a statue of himself, sixty feet high, in military posture, arms outstretched in salute. Soon thereafter, thousands of portraits of the "maximum leader" made their appearance on buildings, and in lobbies, coffeehouses, and supermarkets. The Iraqi press spoke of him as "the awaited, the promised one." An orphan who had learned the craft of assassination at the knee of a murderous uncle in an obscure Iraqi village had become president-for-life of his nation.

In late 1979 Saddam launched a project to rebuild ancient Babylon. The bricks were inscribed: "The Babylon of Nebuchadnezzar was reconstructed in the era of Saddam Hussein." Nebuchadnezzar had made his name in history by destroying Jerusalem in 587 B.C.E. and driving its inhabitants into captivity.

Shortly before he decided to attack Iran, Saddam had himself photographed in a replica of the war chariot of Nebuchadnezzar. After the photograph was taken, he ordered the execution of twenty-one cabinet members, including one of his closest friends, on dubious charges of treason. "He who is closest to me is farthest from me when he does wrong," he explained.[2] Soon thereafter, he took the other cabinet ministers down to Baghdad's central prison to serve as the firing squad for a number of political prisoners. "It was to ensure loyalty through common guilt," commented a British official who witnessed the scene.[3] Saddam's secret police were everywhere and torture was commonplace. It meant death to speak against the "father-leader." And it was a crime to own a typewriter without police permission. A new gestapo was alive and well in Iraq, thirty-five years after the demise of the original model in Nazi Germany.

The war launched by Saddam against Iran in September 1980 became one of the most ferocious conflicts of the century. The dictator's personal ambition was probably the primary reason for the attack. Three role models inspired him in this adventure. The first, as we have noted, was Nebuchadnezzar, the ancient Babylonian conqueror. The second was Gamal Abdel Nasser, Egyptian president in the 1950s, whose ambition was to be leader of all the Arabs. As a young man, Saddam had been his protégé in Cairo. His third model was Nasser's successor, Anwar Sadat, who had challenged Israel successfully in the War of 1973 and whose prestige in the Arab world had soared during the 1970s. Unlike these three men, however, each of whom had a vision for his country, Saddam's purpose was brutally simple: bully, take, and kill. The above is not to say that there were no other reasons for Saddam's actions, but these were always subordinate to his main motive: conquest.

In the first place, the war between Iraq and Iran also had the earmarks of a religious conflict between two major sects of Islam. The Shi'ite Moslems, under the leadership of the Ayatollah Ruhollah Khomeini of Iran, believed that there were intermediaries between

Allah and human beings. These deputies of God were ayatollahs, an Arabic term signifying "reflection of Allah." The Sunni Moslems, who were dominant in the Iraqi leadership of Saddam Hussein, believed that there should be no such intermediaries and that each individual had a personal relationship with Allah. To some degree, the conflict was reminiscent of the religious wars in seventeenth-century Europe between Catholics, who believed in a papacy, and Protestants, who did not. It may be significant in this connection that when Christianity was torn apart by these internal struggles, it was 1,500 years old, which is the age of Islam today. So fierce was the religious nature of the struggle that the Iraqi president, in a national broadcast in November 1980, declared the conflict a jihad, a holy war to defend the ideals of the prophet Mohammed. Khomeini reciprocated by pronouncing the Iraqis enemies of God and Islam. Iraqis and Iranians alike believed that if they died in battle they would go directly to paradise. Death in a jihad assured the Moslem warrior of immortality.

Nationalism was at least as strong a force as religious fanaticism. Although more than half of Iraq's population is Shi'ite, the Iranians were unable to incite them to rebel against the Sunni leadership of Saddam. However, Iraq's appeals to Arabs in Iran's embattled Khuzistan province provoked an uprising there against Iranian rule. Territorial ambitions further fueled nationalism. The Iraqi war plan apparently hinged on seizing enough territory in an initial strike to force the Iranians into surrender. Iran, however, rebounded from the Iraq attack and, fighting with fanatical zeal, turned the war into a prolonged and bloody stalemate.

Personal hate also played a role. The Ayatollah Khomeini, the self-appointed prophet of Islam, had spent thirteen years in exile in Iraq, preparing for the uprising that eventually ousted his enemy, the shah. But in 1978, Saddam asked him to leave the country, thereby obliging him to spend the final months of his exile in France. The ayatollah never forgave nor forgot that insult. Saddam, on the other hand, eager to replace Anwar Sadat as the most powerful leader in the Arab world, was convinced that a blitzkrieg victory over Iran would enhance his status and prestige.

The course of the war itself resembled that of World War I. Predicting a two-week war, Saddam sent his infantry across 500 miles of desert front as Soviet-built MIGs bombed Iranian military targets and oil facilities. Khomeini's troops counterattacked and American-made Phantom F-11 fighter bombers streaked toward Iraqi cities and military installations. Far from achieving a quick victory, Saddam had to settle in for a long war. Once again, as so many times before, the illusion of immediate conquest was to cost the aggressor dearly. The United States and the Soviet Union had contributed to the stalemate by heavily arming both Iran and Iraq in the 1970s, when Washington had close relations with the shah of Iran and Moscow had equal influence in Baghdad. As the war progressed, the United States, fearful of Khomeini's fanatical Shi'ite fundamentalism, tilted toward Iraq, as did Kuwait, for similar reasons. The emir of Kuwait even loaned billions of dollars to Saddam, an act he was to regret bitterly a few years later.

In an era when military thinking was dominated by nuclear weapons or guerrilla warfare, the Iran-Iraq War recalled the trench battles of an earlier age. The Iranians mounted costly human-wave assaults against Iraq, whose troops were entrenched behind tanks and artillery. Iraq even resorted to the use of poison gas, banned by international conventions after World War I. And again, as in 1914, neither side could make a decisive breakthrough. After eight years of maneuvers and confrontations up and down the winding 700-mile boundary between the two countries, the battle lines returned almost exactly to their original borders. Like Britain, France, and Germany in 1918, Iran and Iraq lost a generation of their best young men.

On the Iranian side, an obsession with martyrdom helped sustain the war's popularity despite enormous casualties. In the martyrs' cemetery outside Teheran, a fountain of blood reminded visitors of the fallen heroes. Though only colored water, it was chillingly realistic. The visitors stood among row upon row, acre after acre, of graves. People came in cars, on bicycles, or on foot, the women wrapped in black *chadors*. "My country, my country is like Karbala now," they chanted. It was at Karbala, in the Persian desert, that the seventeenth-century religious leader Hussein, son of Ali, the successor to the prophet Mohammed, met his death at the hands of a rival caliph. As new victims of the war were laid to rest in the martyrs' cemetery, young men in black shirts flailed their backs with bundles of chains. *"Allah akhbar,"* they chanted. God is great.

Later in the war, when the Iranian army began to run out of men, thousands of teenage boys were recruited by the Shi'ite clergy to clear battlefields of mines and barbed wire. Their tickets to paradise were bloodred headbands reading "Warrior of God" and small metal keys signifying that the ayatollah had given them special permission to enter heaven. In some battles, the Iranian reinforcements arrived proudly carrying their own coffins. In Iraq the coffins of the dead were borne home on the roofs of taxis. These victims were also called martyrs.

In 1986 Iranian troops captured the Fao peninsula and mounted an offensive against Basra, Iraq's second-largest city. It appeared, for the moment, that Iran might be victorious. But then the fortunes of war began to tilt against the ayatollah.

In 1987 the United States decided to commit its navy to patrol the Persian Gulf. This was done for three reasons. The first was to ensure freedom of navigation for oil-carrying tankers since an interruption of such shipping would threaten the industrial democracies with a recurrence of the oil shortage of the 1970s, which had produced inflation, recession, and unemployment. The United States also wanted to prevent Soviet domination of the area. After all, Iran shared a 1,500-mile border with the Soviet Union. Finally, the United States hoped to protect the safety of friendly Arab states such as Kuwait and the oil-rich United Arab Emirates from the threat of Iranian invasion. The United States even decided to reflag Kuwaiti tankers with the American flag, thus placing them under the direct protection of its navy.

This policy suffered from an element of inconsistency, to put it mildly, since at that very time the Reagan administration was engaged in selling arms to Iran in the hope of freeing American hostages held captive in Lebanon. Not surprisingly, an accident was now merely waiting to happen. In May 1987, an Iraqi aircraft accidentally hit an American warship, the USS *Stark,* with a missile, killing 37 men. A year later, in July 1988, a second, even more tragic mistake occurred. An American warship, the *Vincennes,* shot down a civilian Iranian airliner, killing all 290 passengers. Captain Will Rogers of the *Vincennes* had had only a few seconds to decide whether the blip on his radar screen was a civilian aircraft or a hostile fighter plane. Remembering the fate of the *Stark,* he took no chances, precipitating yet another unintended disaster.

In the meantime, the Iranian offensive against Basra collapsed. The Iraqis had developed a new defense against the Iranian human-wave assaults. The attacked Iraqi units fell back just far enough to pull the Iranians into a "killing zone" of dug-in tanks, concrete bunkers, artillery, and armored units. This technique, when combined with mustard gas, wreaked havoc on the Iranians. Exhausted after eight years of war and checkmated by the United States Navy in the Gulf, Khomeini finally had had enough. In July 1988 he personally endorsed a cease-fire, declaring that his decision was more painful than taking poison. Saddam, equally exhausted, was quick to accept the offer and, by way of celebration, turned savagely on the rebellious Kurdish minority in northern Iraq, killing at least 5,000 Kurds with poison gas.

What can be said of this conflict in historical perspective? First, it took over 1 million lives and therefore may claim the dubious distinction of being one of the most vicious wars of the twentieth century. Second, like most religious conflicts, it ended inconclusively, very near the borders where it had erupted in the first place. And finally, it devastated the resources of both combatants, leaving their economies destroyed and deeply in debt. Ultimately, the war accomplished nothing. The ambitions of two ruthless men had created a wasteland. In larger historical perspective, perhaps the Thirty Years' War within Christendom in the seventeenth century may serve as the best analogy. Neither Catholics nor Protestants came out as winners after thirty years and several million casualties. Both had to settle for compromise and coexistence.

From a war twice the length of World War I, Saddam Hussein gained a few barren borderlands from Iran. Three years later, after having provoked another war, this time with the United States and its allies, he was to return these meager spoils in a grand gesture. It was for nothing, then, that 400,000 Iraqis had died and the country rendered bankrupt. Yet its dictator wasted no time in plotting the next assault. To the war lover, even three years of peace were far too long.

Saddam's Aggression against Kuwait

On March 12, 1938, as a boy of ten, I watched Hitler's motorcade enter Vienna, my hometown. Three days later, I heard his shrill, rasping voice on Austrian radio: "As the Führer and Chancellor of the German Nation and the Reich, I now declare before history the incorporation of my native land into the German Reich." The *Anschluss* was complete. Henceforth my homeland was to be known as *Ostmark,* a province of the German Reich.

Exactly one year later, on March 15, 1939, I saw Hitler's tanks enter Prague, where we had gone after having fled Vienna. "Czechoslovakia has ceased to exist," Hitler proclaimed from Hradčany

Castle. "It is now the Protectorate of Bohemia and Moravia, part of German *Lebensraum.*"

Neither Britain nor France nor the United States made the slightest effort to save either Austria or Czechoslovakia. Consequently, on September 1, 1939, an emboldened Hitler attacked Poland. The German Führer called his invasion a "counterattack." "The Poles fired first," he insisted, and the German move was a "defensive action." World War II had begun.

More than half a century later, on August 2, 1990, quite by coincidence, I found myself on a tour bus in Turkey, near the Iraqi border. Suddenly, the tour guide interrupted her routine travelogue and announced in a strained voice, "Iraq has just invaded Kuwait; please do not be agitated, you have nothing to fear." My neighbor, a Turkish businessman, turned to me and asked, "Saddam is like Hitler. Will you Americans stop him?" "I hope so," I replied, "I remember Hitler. It's déjà vu."

The parallels between Hitler's assault on his neighbors and Saddam's invasion of Kuwait appear to be so glaring that comparison becomes inevitable. The Iraqi attack on Kuwait was a replica of Nazi blitzkrieg tactics. At dawn on August 2, 1990, approximately 100,000 Iraqi troops and three hundred tanks crossed the border and rolled unimpeded down an empty superhighway that Kuwait had built several years earlier as a token of friendship with Iraq. Appealing to an "all-merciful compassionate God" for support, Saddam announced that he had entered the country at the invitation of a "free interim government" which had supposedly seized control of Kuwait from the emir. Hitler had used that type of pretext for his invasions of Austria and Czechoslovakia.

The Iraqi tanks covered the 80 miles to Kuwait City in less than four hours. Resistance was impossible since Kuwait's entire population was smaller than the active Iraqi armed forces. The troops went straight to the emir's palace hoping to capture him, but the monarch had escaped just in time, by helicopter to neighboring Saudi Arabia. The Iraqis seized the central bank where Kuwait's gold reserves were stored as well as the Ministry of Information building, which housed all radio and television studios and the country's telephone exchanges. Within a few hours, the deed was done. Saddam announced that Kuwait had ceased to exist. Henceforth, it was to be the nineteenth province of Iraq. A sole hidden transmitter broadcast a desperate plea for help to other Arab states: "O Arabs, Kuwait's blood and honor are being violated. Rush to its rescue; the children, the women, the old men of Kuwait are calling on you."[4] Saddam named a new puppet regime made up of nine Kuwaiti collaborators who were to report to him directly. On August 8 he defended his actions in Kuwait as "necessary to redress flawed regional borders drawn up by colonial powers that had installed a corrupt minority in the Arab world's richest territory." He also ordered all foreign embassies to close down because Kuwait was now an integral part of Iraq.

Few were fooled by Saddam's explanations. President George Bush called the Iraqi dictator's act "naked aggression," and the real reasons for it were widely held to be obvious. The move was a power grab, pure and simple. Kuwait was a timely acquisition for Iraq whose war with Iran had left it $70 billion in debt and with tremendous reconstruction costs. And even though the long war had weakened Saddam's military muscle, the little monarchy would be no match for him. Not only could he now loot Kuwait's treasury, but by acquiring its enormous oil fields he would control 20 percent of the world's oil supply and thus exercise a stranglehold over the Western countries he hated. Even more important than the financial spoils would be his new economic power. He would make himself the new Gamal Abdel Nasser and become the hero of the Arab world. And if he could march into Saudi Arabia as well before anyone thought of stopping him, his domain would resemble that of his idol, Nebuchadnezzar.

Saddam followed Hitler's example not only in his blitzkrieg attack on Kuwait but also in the tactics of deception leading up to the attack. First he complained that Kuwait had not only been producing oil in excess of the quota established by the Organization of Petroleum Exporting Countries (OPEC), but had also drilled horizontally in order to tap into Iraq's Rumalia oil field. OPEC met in July, and in order to underline his policy of intimidation, Saddam sent 30,000 elite troops of his Republican Guard to the Kuwaiti border. He promised, however, that he would not attack his neighbor if Kuwait would abide by its production quota. The emir complied meekly and OPEC raised its production price for the first time in four years. Egypt's president Hosni Mubarak called the quarrel between Iraq and Kuwait "a cloud that will pass with the wind," a comment he was to regret bitterly a few days later. Saddam, instead of withdrawing his 30,000 troops now that his demands had been met, sent 70,000 more to the Kuwaiti border.

Saddam's second demand was that Kuwait forgive the $40 billion in loans it had extended to Iraq to help Saddam finance his eight-year war with Iran. His logic was that he had fought off Khomeini's fundamentalist threat on behalf of all Arabs and therefore was entitled to cancel his debt. He forgot, conveniently, that it was he who had begun the war against Iran. This demand was accompanied by impassioned threats such as, "If they don't give it to me, I will know how to take it," and "If anyone tries to stop me, I will chop off his arm at the shoulder."

The terrified Kuwaitis agreed to a meeting in Jidda, Saudi Arabia, prepared not only to accede to Saddam's financial demands but also to cede Bubiyan Island, which blocked Iraq's unimpeded access to the sea. During the two-hour meeting, the Kuwaitis capitulated completely. Yet the Iraqi delegation walked out of the meeting. Six hours later, Saddam marched into Kuwait.

The echoes of the 1930s were unmistakable: fiery speeches full of grievances, the exploitation of border disputes, negotiations that were intended all along to be fruitless, and phony requests for intervention by fictitious locals in the target country.

Saddam's father-figure, his uncle Khairallah, a Nazi sympathizer, had written a leaflet in the 1940s entitled "Three Things That God Should Not Have Created: Persians, Jews, and Flies." When Saddam came to power, he had his uncle's leaflet reprinted and widely distributed.[5] Another book that he admired and had read repeatedly was *Mein Kampf* by Adolf Hitler.

Saddam's policy in Kuwait, once he had annexed the country, had all the earmarks of Hitler's treatment of Russian "subhumans" after his invasion of the Soviet Union in June 1941. Torture, murder, and mass arrests began on the day of the invasion. There were thousands of interrogations. Wrong responses brought mutilation and death. The rape of Kuwaiti women was commonplace. Twenty-one university professors who refused to take down a picture of the emir and replace it with one of Saddam were summarily executed.[6]

Amnesty International published a seventy-nine-page report on human rights violations carried out by the Iraqis in Kuwait. President Bush happened to read it just before a television interview with David Frost about Saddam's aggression. All he could talk about was the barbarism of Saddam's troops:

> It was so terrible, it's hard to describe. Barbara read two pages and could not read any more. The torturing of a handicapped child; the shooting of

young boys in front of their parents; the rape of women dragged out of their homes and repeatedly raped and then brought into the hospital as basket cases; the tying of those that were being tortured to ceiling fans so they turn and turn; the killing of a Kuwaiti and leaving him hanging so that others will see him; electric shocks to the private parts of men and women. Broken glass jabbed into people. I'm afraid I'd get very emotional if I described more of it.[7]

The Iraqis stole everything of value. They looted the museums and the jewelry stores. They drove stolen cars full of loot back to Iraq. They even attacked Kuwait's national zoo and used the caged animals for target practice. Later, when food became scarce, they ate the zoo's sheep, deer, and gazelles.

All this was done in the name of an "all merciful, all-compassionate God." But then Hitler's soldiers, too, while committing the most heinous crimes in history, wore belt buckles with the motto *Gott Mit Uns*—God Be with Us.

Before the invasion, most American officials responded to Saddam's warnings with an equanimity bordering on indifference. In late July Saddam had once again delivered one of his many threats: "The oil quota violators have stabbed Iraq with a poison dagger. Iraq will not forget the saying that cutting necks is better than cutting means of living. Oh God Almighty, be witness that we have warned them!"

The next day, July 23, even though 30,000 Iraqi troops had massed on the Kuwaiti border, U.S. State Department spokesperson Margaret D. Tutweiler declared that the United States had "no defense treaties with Kuwait, no special defense or security commitments to Kuwait."[8]

Two days later, U.S. Ambassador April Glaspie, an Arabist scholar, met with Saddam and, according to the Iraqi transcript of the meeting, told him that the United States had "no opinion on Arab-Arab conflicts, like your border disagreement with Kuwait."[9] The State Department never challenged the accuracy of the transcript even though Glaspie later told the Senate Foreign Relations Committee that the Iraqis had deleted her warning to Saddam that the United States would insist that settlements be made "in a nonviolent manner."[10]

Could it be that Saddam was emboldened or even misled by this apparent American passivity the way Kim Il Sung of North Korea might have been emboldened forty years earlier to invade South

Korea? After all, the United States had neglected to include South Korea in its defense perimeter in 1950. Or, to extend our earlier analogy, did the United States make the same mistake with Saddam that Britain and France had made with Hitler before his attacks on Austria and Czechoslovakia?

America's top military men, who would play such a pivotal role in the coming war, did not see it coming. Even with 100,000 Iraqi troops on the Kuwaiti border, General Schwarzkopf, the hero-to-be of Operation Desert Storm, submitted a brief to his boss, Colin Powell, chairman of the Joint Chiefs of Staff, stating that it looked "at most as if Iraq was poised to launch a punitive but limited strike at Kuwait."[11] Neither Powell, nor his boss, Defense Secretary Richard Cheney, disagreed. Powell could not say for certain what Saddam was going to do; therefore, there was no immediate response for the military to take. As late as August 1, General Thomas Kelly, Powell's chief of operations, believed an invasion to be unlikely. Cheney agreed that there was no way to distinguish between a bluff and the real thing. The bluff was only credible if Saddam did all the things he had done: uncoiled his tanks, moved them to the line, and massed troops on the border.[12] The Central Intelligence Agency too was ambivalent. Deputy Director Richard Kerr allowed for the possibility of an invasion but emphasized that Iraq's real enemy was Israel and that a military attack by one Arab state on another would be unprecedented.

To explain this American misperception as a cultural misunderstanding would be too simple. After all, Mubarak had also dismissed Saddam's threats as a "passing cloud." The only political leader who was convinced that Saddam was not bluffing and would indeed invade Kuwait was Israel's defense minister, Moshe Arens. Arens remembered Hitler. His warnings to the United States, however, were not given much weight until the invasion was virtually under way.

Perhaps we must conclude from the preceding discussion that rational analysis may not reveal the war lover's intent. Even Stalin, that most cunning and ruthless of individuals, did not believe that Hitler would actually invade the Soviet Union. And when he did, Stalin suffered a nervous breakdown. The Americans were not guilty here of cultural myopia. They simply failed to see that the war lover *will* go to war, no matter what.

Bush's reaction to the invasion was that of a man who had known combat in World War II. "It's naked aggression," he exclaimed on

August 2. "It's good versus evil; we have a clear moral case here; nothing like this since World War II; nothing of this moral importance since World War II." Later that day, the president met with British Prime Minister Margaret Thatcher, who affirmed that her country was "standing shoulder to shoulder with the United States." Thatcher had her childhood memories of Britain under the Nazi blitz, not to mention her successful campaign to expel the Argentinean invaders from the Falkland Islands in 1982. Her support would become the cornerstone of a thirty-nation coalition against Saddam Hussein under the United Nations flag. On the evening of that eventful day, the UN Security Council, by a vote of 14 to 0, passed a resolution calling for Iraq's immediate and unconditional withdrawal from Kuwait. There was only a single abstention, by the government of Yemen. Even the Soviet Union voted with the majority.

The Security Council vote of August 2 was a historic occasion. Not since the North Korean aggression of June 25, 1950, had the Security Council cast a vote on such a matter without being paralyzed by a Soviet veto. And the 1950 vote, as we noted in Chapter 3, was an aberration because of the absence of the Soviet delegate from the council that day. The vote of August 2, 1990, on the other hand, was to be not a fluke but a harbinger of things to come.

On the day after the invasion, Secretary of State James Baker and Soviet Foreign Minister Eduard Shevardnadze issued a joint communiqué denouncing Saddam's aggression. This document also set a precedent. Soviet President Mikhail Gorbachev, eager for America's goodwill and economic assistance in his own domestic travails, decided to make common cause with the United States. He did this even though the Soviet Union had been Iraq's chief arms supplier and still had several hundred advisers there at the time of the invasion. The next day, the United States and the European Community imposed broad economic sanctions against Iraq and froze Iraqi and Kuwaiti assets in their countries.

The Americans, of course, were fearful that Saddam would develop an appetite for Saudi Arabia and continue his march from Kuwait into the desert kingdom. Saudi Arabia would not be a pushover like Kuwait, but it would still be no match for Saddam's army. On August 6, therefore, the top American military leaders flew to Riyadh to confer with King Fahd about the Iraqi threat to his country. They did not do this for purely altruistic reasons, of course, even though there was no reason to doubt the president's principled position that "this aggression must not stand." There was also the matter of oil to consider. If Saddam were to conquer the oil fields of Saudi Arabia, he would be in control of almost half of the world's proven oil reserves. This would strike at the lifeline of the United States and the entire Western world. The defense of Saudi Arabia was clearly a strategic imperative. The president had instructed his commanders to ask the king to request the United States to provide military assistance to his kingdom. According to Schwarzkopf's recollections, the king's immediate response was, "We want you to come."[13] This was the invitation the president had been hoping for. Now his diplomacy could be backed up by military force.

Bush welcomed this challenge. Domestic problems had always bored him, and he considered foreign policy to be the true measure of presidential achievement. In 1980, as he was losing the presidential nomination to Ronald Reagan, he had made some revealing comments about the job he coveted: "Domestic problems drag you down and nag all the time. But sooner or later something major happens, something abroad that only we [the United States] can do something about. Then you show if you can cut it. If you can't everything can be going beautifully and you are probably out of there next time. If you pull it off, a lot else can go wrong and you'll be all right. I know I can handle the foreign policy side."[14]

On August 4, 1988, exactly two years before he ordered troops to the Persian Gulf, Bush had delivered a foreign policy speech in which he praised John F. Kennedy's inaugural address: "We shall bear any burden, meet any hardship, support any friend, oppose any foe to assure the survival and success of liberty." That formulation, he declared, reflected the principles and policies he would follow as president. In his view, the single most important concern of the president was the national security. On August 6, 1990, after receiving King Fahd's invitation to protect Saudi Arabia, Bush said to a reporter, "Watch and learn; maybe I'll turn out to be a Teddy Roosevelt."[15] In an emotional conversation with the emir of Kuwait, Bush promised the exiled leader that the United States would help win back his country and restore him to his throne. On the next day, August 7, Bush ordered United States troops, military aircraft, and warships to Saudi Arabia. Operation Desert Shield had been born.

As commander in chief, Bush was determined that Desert Shield should not become another Vietnam War. As 200,000 American troops poured into Saudi Arabia in August, the president repeated this pledge again and again. And indeed, he kept his word by avoiding three fatal mistakes that Lyndon Johnson had made during the Vietnam years: first, Bush worked through the United Nations, whereas Johnson had made Vietnam essentially an American war; second, Bush labored to obtain congressional endorsement of the use of force, something Johnson never bothered to do; and finally, Bush left the actual fighting to the generals, whereas Johnson had become obsessed with every tactical detail of the war.

Building on Thatcher's support as well as on the new Soviet-American détente, Bush managed to stitch together a formidable military coalition against Iraq in a matter of days. By mid-August, a total of thirty nations had made troop commitments to the new multinational force. Nations like Japan and Germany, whose constitutions precluded them from combat, pledged substantial financial contributions. Saudi Arabia and Kuwait contributed both troops and money. While Bush and Cheney worked on the NATO allies, Mubarak of Egypt appealed to the members of the Arab League. When the league met in Cairo on August 10, thirteen of its twenty-one members including Syria agreed to send military forces. Within two weeks, Saddam's window of opportunity to invade Saudi Arabia was closed. The question now was whether the coalition forces arrayed against him could dislodge him from Kuwait.

On August 12 Saddam tried a new ploy to divide the coalition. He offered to resolve the crisis if Israel would agree to withdraw from the occupied West Bank, Golan Heights, and Gaza. This attempt to link the invasion of Kuwait to the Palestinian issue was so transparently opportunistic that not even Syria was induced to leave the coalition. Yet the move drew Yasir Arafat, the leader of the PLO, to Saddam's side and forced neutral King Hussein of Jordan, who was fearful of the Palestinian majority within his kingdom, to tilt toward Iraq. On November 8 Bush, now more determined than ever to reverse Saddam's aggression, ordered another 250,000 American troops to the gulf. In response Saddam, convinced that Bush was bluffing, announced on November 19 that he was sending another 250,000 troops into Kuwait. By late November half a million troops on each side were facing each other. On November 29 the UN Security Council established a six-week deadline for Saddam to withdraw from Kuwait. It authorized the coalition to "use all necessary means" to achieve its objectives. The deadline was midnight, January 15, 1991.

Saddam tried a few other diversionary maneuvers. He took hundreds of Western nationals as hostages, describing them as "guests."

When this device did not work, he released the hostages and announced that he would return the borderlands he had captured in the war against Iran. By doing so, he hoped to convert his mortal enemy into an ally. Iran accepted Saddam's gift but did not change its neutral stance. On December 22, still convinced that the coalition would not fight him, Saddam announced that he would never relinquish Kuwait and, if attacked, would attack Israel and use chemical weapons. Through all of this provocation, the coalition stood fast and did not lose a single member. Bush, ever mindful of Johnson's mistakes in Vietnam, reminded everyone repeatedly that Kuwait was not a matter between Iraq and the United States, but one between Iraq and the world community.

By early January, with the moment of truth approaching, Bush turned his attention to the Congress. Determined not to repeat Johnson's second mistake, the president tried his utmost to get the Congress to back him. Concerned that the best way to avoid a war was to be prepared to fight one and to prove this to Saddam, he now used his persuasive powers on the Senate and the House.

The members of the 102nd Congress were confronted with a fateful choice: whether to authorize the president to use force to back up the UN mandate or to delay action and give the economic sanctions more time. Those who supported the president argued that Saddam should not be allowed to defy the United Nations. Congressman Stephen J. Solarz, for example, declared that appeasing Saddam, like appeasing Hitler, would bring disaster.[16] Those opposed, like Senator Edward M. Kennedy, warned against a long land war with at least seven hundred Americans killed every week.[17]

On January 12, 1991, the "use of force" resolution was passed in the Senate by a vote of 52 to 47 and in the House by 250 to 183. For the first time since World War II, the Congress had formally authorized a president to go to war should he deem it necessary.

The nation now closed ranks behind the president. A last-ditch diplomatic effort by UN Secretary-General Javier Pérez de Cuéllar came and went. On January 15, the day of the deadline, Bush announced that every minute after midnight would be borrowed time. At 6 P.M. Washington time the next evening, the first allied bombs fell out of the skies on Baghdad from 30,000 feet. Desert Shield had become Desert Storm.

As we survey the events between August 2, 1990, and January 15, 1991, one truth emerges with striking clarity: None of the military men around the president believed that Saddam would go to war over Kuwait. Cheney, Powell, and Schwarzkopf were convinced that Saddam was no martyr and would withdraw to save himself. The president concurred, but on December 21, 1990, just to make sure, he asked Prince Bandar, the Saudi ambassador to the United States, for his opinion. Bandar agreed emphatically that "if Saddam had to choose between his own neck and leaving Kuwait, he would act to save his neck."[18] All these men were wrong.

On countless occasions between August 2 and January 15, Saddam declared that the Americans were too cowardly to fight. And if they would dare to take him on, they would drown in a sea of their own blood. Like a modern-day Nebuchadnezzar, he would conduct a victorious campaign against the infidel in the "mother of all battles." In other words, he would be victorious with or without a war. He too was wrong.

Once again, as so many times before, misperception played a crucial role. Each side misread profoundly the character, intent, and resolve of its adversary. The Americans and their allies believed that Saddam would respond rationally and withdraw in the face of overwhelming odds. Saddam, blinded by a war lover's hubris, believed himself to be invincible and underestimated his enemy's resolve. These profound misperceptions on both sides precipitated the outbreak of the war.

The air campaign that began on January 16 was an unqualified success. It subjected the Iraqi forces to the most severe pounding endured by any land army in history. And it achieved this with incredibly low casualties for the UN forces. It was probably the only case in military history of a victory achieved almost by air power alone. The ground war that followed in late February lasted only one hundred hours. Iraqi resistance to the air attacks turned out to be so weak that Air Force Captain Gunther Drummond, who took part in the opening assault, remarked, "It was as if we had no adversary."[19]

On January 15 the White House gave members of Congress and the press disinformation to the effect that Saddam might have a few days' grace if he began a pullout. According to Arab intermediaries, Saddam believed this and relaxed a bit. He would have done better to consult the Washington branch of Domino's Pizza (a national restaurant chain), which put out a warning at 5 A.M. on January 16 that war was likely that day. Domino's was receiving record delivery orders from the White House and the Pentagon, presumably to fuel officials through imminent crisis meetings.[20] In fact, at 11 A.M. that morning the president ordered the attack and that afternoon Cheney signed an order putting the directive into effect.

The air war was fought in three phases. Phase One concentrated on gaining air superiority. This goal was achieved very quickly. Few Iraqi aircraft challenged the coalition planes, and during the week of January 22–29 over one hundred Iraqi planes flew to Iran, presumably a safe haven, where they were impounded by the Iranians. Phase Two was to try to shatter the nervous system of Saddam's army and to destroy his nuclear, chemical, and biological weapons capability. During Phase Three, coalition air forces would pound the Iraqi field army relentlessly over a period of three to four weeks in order to soften it up for the ground campaign to follow.

On January 17 Saddam committed his third blunder since the invasion of Kuwait. Hoping to pull Israel into the war and thus to break up the coalition, Saddam launched Soviet-made Scud missiles—named Al Hussein—into Tel Aviv, the largest city of this noncombatant country. Reportedly, he made this decision after executing two of his air commanders who had dared to remind him of his earlier misjudgments: that he could invade Kuwait with impunity and that the coalition would not resort to force.[21]

Saddam's hope was that Egypt and Syria, not wanting to appear to be fighting in defense of Israel, would pull out of the coalition or switch sides. Even Saudi Arabia, he hoped, would come under heavy pressure to abandon the Americans. The dictator was wrong again.

Bush quickly implored Israeli Prime Minister Yitzhak Shamir to exercise restraint and promised not only to make the destruction of the mobile Scud-launchers a top priority but also to equip the Israelis with Patriot missiles capable of shooting down the Scuds in midair. Shamir agreed, even though Saddam launched forty Scuds into Israel and another forty-six at Saudi Arabia. The Scuds, like the German V-2s that fell on London during World War II, were of no real military value. They were intended to induce panic in the cities and to incite the frightened population against the government.

Fortunately, none of the Scuds carried chemical or biological warheads, probably because the air attacks had severely damaged Saddam's facilities. Nor, apparently, did the Scuds have the capability to deliver these unconventional weapons. At any rate, the Scuds did little to disrupt the air attacks. Most of them were shot down by Patriots. And the coalition, to the fury of Saddam, held together.

The moral issue of sending missiles into the cities of a noncombatant country was another matter. As General Schwarzkopf succinctly put it, "The difference between Saddam Hussein and myself is that I have a conscience and he doesn't."[22]

On February 22, after a Soviet-brokered attempt to mediate had failed, the president gave Saddam a final ultimatum: get out of Kuwait by Saturday noon, February 23, or face the consequences.

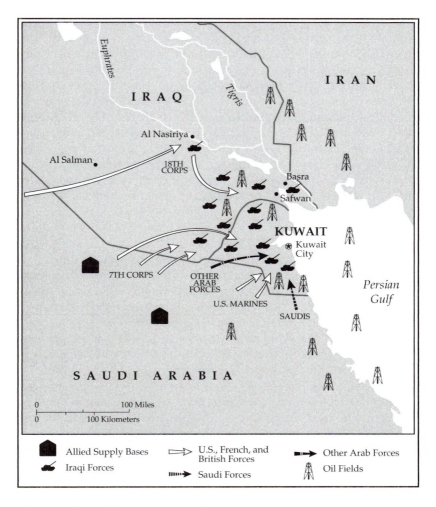

MAP 12 **The Gulf War, February 1991**

Saddam responded once again by inviting the coalition to drown in its own blood in the "mother of all battles." This was yet another costly error. By stalling and haggling, the Iraqi dictator doomed his army to a terrible defeat.

When Bush authorized the ground campaign, he was determined not to repeat Lyndon Johnson's third mistake in Vietnam by second-guessing his generals. This was a wise decision. As it turned out, Schwarzkopf achieved a victory that made military history.

After observing Saddam's movements during the air war, Schwarzkopf had reached the conclusion that Saddam, like so many commanders before him in history, would fight the last war over again. Saddam had lured the Iranian troops into frontal assaults on heavily defended fortifications. Trapped in the "killing zones," the Iranians were annihilated. And indeed, aerial reconnaissance revealed the same defensive strategy and the same "killing zones" in southern Kuwait. Taking a lesson from Erwin Rommel, the "Desert Fox" of World War II, Schwarzkopf decided on a daring flanking maneuver he would later compare to the Hail Mary play—a football maneuver in which a quarterback hoping for a last-minute touchdown sends his receivers far off to one side and then deep into the opponent's end zone. Leaving enough troops and equipment on Kuwait's southern border to convince Saddam that he was going to attack him in a frontal assault, Schwarzkopf decided to move 250,000 troops with their armor, artillery, and supplies 200 miles westward in a matter of a few days. As he put it later: "I can't recall any time in the annals of military history when this number of forces have moved over this distance to put themselves in a position to attack."[23] Indeed, he out-did not only Rommel but also Patton and Montgomery, Rommel's American and British adversaries.

Saddam, completely taken by surprise, broadcast a message to his troops: "Oh, Iraqis, fight them with all the power you have, men of the Mother of Battles, fight them for your faith in God! Show no mercy! Fight them!"[24]

It was useless. Iraqi soldiers, exhausted and demoralized, emerged from their foxholes by the tens of thousands to surrender. On the third day of the ground war, Schwarzkopf knew he had won a spectacular victory. As he recounted later: "It was literally about to become the battle of Cannae, a battle of annihilation."[25] Schwarzkopf, a student of history, was referring to Hannibal's slaughter of 50,000 Romans in 216 B.C.E., which was accomplished by trapping them in a classic encirclement. As the coalition forces entered Kuwait

City to the cheers of its jubilant inhabitants, thousands of vehicles, commandeered by Iraqi troops fleeing to their homeland, crowded the road north to Basra. The road became a highway of doom as ferocious allied air attacks turned the escape route into a graveyard. Corpses and smoking vehicles littered the highway for miles.

At this moment, in sight of victory, Schwarzkopf told the press how things stood: "We were 150 miles from Baghdad and there was nobody between us and Baghdad. If it had been our intention to take Iraq, if it had been our intention to destroy the country, if it had been our intention to overrun the country we could have done it unopposed, for all intents and purposes, from this position at that time."[26] President Bush, however, ordered a cease-fire on February 27, proclaiming that the objectives of the coalition had been achieved. One month later, this produced a small tiff between the president and his field commander. The spat started when, during an interview with David Frost, Schwarzkopf said that he had recommended that the United States keep fighting because "we could have completely closed the door and made it, in fact, a battle of annihilation." The implication was that he could have finished off Saddam's regime altogether. Bush, eager to avoid the impression that he had "wimped out," instructed Cheney to state to the press that the general had "raised no objections to the termination of hostilities."[27] The matter was settled at week's end when Schwarzkopf closed the debate with a graceful apology. Nonetheless, the question continued to linger. Did the president stop the war too soon?

In answering this question, we must remember the enormous effort that the president had expended to put the coalition together. Had he attempted to take Baghdad, the Soviet Union and the Arab partners might have defected from the alliance and Operation Desert Storm might have ended up as an American war, not a United Nations collective security action. After all, the UN mandate did not include the destruction of Saddam's regime. It confined itself to Iraq's expulsion from Kuwait. It is not impossible, moreover, that the president, a student of history, might have recalled the Korean War of 1950. On that occasion, as we saw earlier, another American general, Douglas MacArthur, had decided to strain the limits of his UN mandate and to invade the invader, North Korea. By doing so, MacArthur provoked a Chinese intervention, prolonging the war by more than two years. That cost the United States large additional casualties. Bush did not want to be sucked into such a trap. He wanted the war to end and the troops to come home.

In any case, Schwarzkopf was right when, in his celebrated final briefing, he termed the coalition's success "almost miraculous." Not only were the pessimists wrong, but the optimists were too. American casualties were less than 5 percent of the lowest prewar Pentagon estimates. Iraqi casualties were estimated at 100,000 at the very least. When Schwarzkopf was asked to evaluate Saddam's military leadership, the general gave a memorable answer: "As far as Saddam Hussein being a great military strategist, he is neither a strategist nor is he schooled in the operational arts nor is he a tactician, nor is he a general, nor is he a soldier. Other than that, he is a great military man."[28]

But perception of the human quality of General Schwarzkopf emerged less from that famous statement and more from an afterthought following his description of the low allied casualty rate as "miraculous." "It will never be miraculous to the families of these people," he added sadly. For one moment he bore the burden of every life that had been lost. At that moment, he was not a warrior but a grieving father to every allied soldier.

"By God, we've kicked the Vietnam syndrome once and for all," President Bush exclaimed after announcing the cease-fire. He and most Americans were savoring the country's first major military victory since 1945. When the soldiers of Desert Storm raced across Kuwait, they not only defeated Saddam's army; they also exorcised the lingering demons of self-doubt from the Vietnam era. One marine who helped liberate Kuwait City brought with him an old American flag that had been given to him twenty-three years earlier by a dying comrade in Vietnam. A circle had been completed, a chapter closed. Or had it?

A jarring note disturbed the victory celebrations: Saddam Hussein was still alive. Not only was he alive; he still ruled. April 28, his birthday, was still a national holiday in Iraq. It was not often that a national leader of a defeated country survived not only one catastrophic war but two. Somehow, despite endless rumors of assassination attempts and palace coups, Saddam was able to hold on to power. As one Iraqi put it, "Since we could not cut his hand off, we now have to kiss it." And true to form, the war lover soon found himself other victims: his own people and the Kurdish and Shi'ite minorities.

After his defeat, Saddam fought with relentless tenacity for his own survival. One of his methods was to sacrifice millions of Iraqis to starvation and disease in order to shock the United Nations into easing economic sanctions. His health minister decided to cut off international food relief on numerous occasions because providing the relief was easing the conscience of the Americans and Europeans. In short, he wanted more pain, not less, to demonstrate Saddam's determination.

The ink was not yet dry on the cease-fire agreement when Saddam began a brutal assault on the Kurdish minority in northern Iraq. Encouraged by President Bush, who had publicly urged the overthrow of Saddam, the Kurds had attempted to oust the ruler. Saddam had used poison gas against them in 1988. On February 24 clandestine Arab radio stations urged the Kurds to "hit the headquarters of the tyrant," and on March 10 the Voice of Free Iraq predicted that "a bullet will be coming for the tyrant very soon."

Saddam's army was still strong enough to crush a rebellion in Basra and then vent its full fury on the rebellious Kurds in the north and an unruly Shi'ite minority in the south. The result was a floodtide of refugees desperately seeking sanctuary in the craggy mountains on the borders of Turkey and Iran. Saddam's troops pursued both Kurds and Shi'ites ruthlessly; death tolls were immense and are still unknown. In northern Iraq advancing Iraqi tanks were seen with Kurdish children strapped to their flanks as shields, and in the south large signs were painted on the tanks proclaiming: "No Shi'ites after today."

For several weeks Bush hesitated. But as the slaughter grew and refugees were dying by the thousands every day of cold and hunger, he had no choice but to act. The result was Operation Haven. In late April, 10,000 American, 5,000 British, 1,500 French, and 1,000 Dutch soldiers worked around the clock to build tent cities for the desperate refugees and provide them with at least one meal a day. The wily Saddam promised the Kurds autonomy, but his victims, not surprisingly, refused to trust his word. By July, only 4,000 coalition soldiers remained, but thousands of Kurds and Shi'ites continued to die daily. Plainly, Saddam was calculating that he would outlast the humanitarian remnants of Desert Storm and then resume his vengeance.

The plight of the refugees was not the only tragic and problematic element in the dénouement of the war. The UN cease-fire resolution of April 3 enjoined Saddam to turn over for destruction all of his large ballistic missiles and chemical, biological, and nuclear bomb-making equipment. The goal, of course, was to defang the Iraqi dictator permanently. Saddam complied with all but one of these conditions. He refused steadfastly to submit to UN inspection several secret bomb-making installations that somehow had survived Desert Storm. These installations probably contained enough enriched uranium for two Nagasaki bombs.[29] Such a capability could be the vehicle for Saddam's political resurrection in the Arab world, and symbolically "it would be the ultimate thumb in the eye of George Bush."[30] Little wonder that, in May, Saddam emerged from his presidential residence in Baghdad firing a pistol in the air in defiance of the Americans. Thousands of Iraqis watched and cheered him on. One year after his defeat, Saddam still continued to defy the United Nations.

Perhaps the grimmest legacy that Saddam Hussein left to posterity was his decision to torch more than six hundred oil wells in Kuwait. As the coalition forces entered Kuwait City, the country's oil fields were like a scene from Dante's *Inferno.* Across the darkened landscape hundreds of orange fireballs roared like dragons, spewing poisonous vapors high into the air. From overcast skies dripped a greasy black rain polluting everything it touched. Black, choking smoke blotted out the sun. Oil-soaked workers turned in twelve-hour shifts, struggling with hand tools to control the burning flow. Some 5 million gallons of oil a day, worth about $100 million, were going up in flames. Oil covered thousands of acres, killing plants and animals and threatening subsurface water. Hospitals reported a dramatic increase in respiratory cases. Antipollution masks were selling briskly for thirty dollars apiece in supermarkets. Breathing, said one Kuwaiti, was "like taking the exhaust pipe of a diesel truck in your mouth and breathing that."[31]

It is impossible to tell what the long-range ecological consequences of this insanely vindictive act will be. The immediate fear was that the dense smoke would block the sun's rays and trap dirty air close to the ground. As a Western diplomat in Riyadh observed, "When the winds stop, a lot of people are going to die."[32] Some scientists were predicting that the smoke from the oil fields could disrupt the monsoon on the Indian subcontinent and pelt rich croplands with acid rain. At worst, the thick black clouds could reach the upper atmosphere, snuffing out an entire growing season and threatening millions with starvation in a Saddam-induced nuclear winter.

The last of the oil field fires was not extinguished until November 1991. In historical perspective, one conclusion is already certain: Saddam Hussein committed an act of ecological terrorism unprecedented in history. Like Hitler, when he lost the war he scorched the earth. The war lover turned nature into hell, his favorite habitat.

The 1990s bore witness to a Saddam Hussein who was down but not out. Not only did the war lover cling to power by the most brutal means imaginable, but he was busy assembling arsenals of weapons of mass destruction. In 1991 the UN Security Council created a Special Commission (UNSCOM) and charged it with the responsibility to search out and destroy as many of the hidden weapons caches as possible. Saddam pursued a tenacious "cheat and retreat" policy, leading UNSCOM inspectors around by the ear year after year. It almost worked, but then in 1995, Saddam's son-in-law, Hussein Kamel, defected from Baghdad and handed over to UNSCOM thousands of incriminating documents that had been hidden—of all places—on his chicken farm. This discovery spurred the UN agency to pursue its search in earnest and it did, indeed, destroy more Iraqi weapons during the next three years than had been destroyed during the entire Persian Gulf War. Not surprisingly, UNSCOM inspectors were barred from Iraq completely and, as a result, the United States and Britain launched four days of air attacks in retaliation. This was followed by a year of tedious negotiations that led to a new arms inspection agency called the UN Monitoring, Verification, and Inspection Commission (UNMOVIC), which replaced UNSCOM. As an incentive for Iraq, the UN lifted the cap on how much oil it was allowed to sell under the UN's "oil for food" program. A suspension of economic sanctions was also held out as an additional carrot if Iraq would cooperate fully with the new inspection agency. As the year 2000 dawned, one fact was beyond dispute: Saddam still ruled Iraq.

George Herbert Walker Bush's decision to confine the war to the expulsion of Saddam from Kuwait echoed down the years to become George W. Bush's conviction that his father had made a serious mistake. And when Saddam tried to assassinate the older Bush during a visit to Kuwait, the son's conviction congealed into a fixation to conclude unfinished business. "After all," he said, "this is the guy who tried to kill my dad."[33] This fixation led to Saddam's third and final conflict, in which he became the target of the first preemptive war in American history. An analysis of this dramatic event constitutes the bulk of the following chapter.

NOTES

1. For a more extended discussion of Stalin's possible addition to the trio of war lovers, please see my concluding chapter.

2. *Time,* August 13, 1990, p. 23.

3. Ibid.
4. Ibid.
5. CNN publication: Thomas B. Allen, F. Clifton Berry, and Norman Polmar, *War in the Gulf* (Atlanta: Turner, 1991), p. 54.
6. Ibid., p. 70.
7. Bob Woodward, *The Commanders* (New York: Simon & Schuster, 1991), p. 343.
8. *War in the Gulf,* p. 62.
9. Ibid.
10. Ibid.
11. *The Commanders,* p. 209.
12. Ibid., p. 220.
13. *War in the Gulf,* p. 74.
14. *Time,* August 20, 1990, p. 20.
15. Ibid.
16. Ibid., p. 82.
17. Ibid.
18. *The Commanders,* p. 350.
19. *Time,* January 28, 1991.
20. Ibid.
21. *War in the Gulf,* p. 149.
22. Ibid., p. 178.
23. Ibid., p. 198.
24. Ibid., p. 203.
25. Ibid., p. 214.
26. Ibid., p. 212.
27. *Time,* April 18, 1991, p. 22.
28. Quoted in *War in the Gulf,* p. 213.
29. *New York Times,* July 7, 1991.
30. Ibid.
31. *War in the Gulf,* p. 221.
32. *Time,* March 18, 1991.
33. Quoted in *Time,* October 7, 2002, p. 28.

SELECTED BIBLIOGRAPHY

ABDO, GENEIVE, and JONATHAN LYONS. *Answering Only to God: Faith and Freedom in Twenty-first-Century Iran.* New York: Henry Holt, 2003.

AJAMI, FOUAD. "Iraq and the Arabs' Future." *Foreign Affairs,* January/February 2003.

AMUZEGAR, JAHANGIR. "Iran's Crumbling Revolution." *Foreign Affairs,* January/February 2003.

BILL, JAMES A. *The Eagle and the Lion: The Tragedy of American-Iranian Relations.* New Haven, Conn.: Yale University Press, 1988.

BLACKWELL, JAMES. *Thunder in the Desert: The Strategy and Tactics of the Persian Gulf War.* New York: Bantam, 1991.

BULLOCH, JOHN, and HARVEY MORNS. *The Gulf War: Its Origins, History, and Consequences.* London: Methuen, 1989.

CALABRESE, JOHN, Ed. *The Future of Iraq.* Washington, D.C.: Middle East Institute, 1997.

CNN: THOMAS B. ALLEN, F. CLIFTON BERRY, and NORMAN POLMAR. *War in the Gulf.* Atlanta: Turner, 1991.

COCKBURN, ANDREW, and PATRICK COCKBURN. *Out of the Ashes: The Resurrection of Saddam Hussein.* New York: HarperCollins, 1999.

COTTAM, RICHARD W. *Iran and the United States: A Cold War Case Study.* Pittsburgh, Pa.: University of Pittsburgh Press, 1988.

DAVIES, CHARLES, Ed. *After the War: Iraq and the Arab Gulf.* Chichester: Carden, 1990.

GRIMSLEY, MARK, and CLIFFORD ROGERS, Eds. *Civilians in the Path of War.* Lincoln: University of Nebraska Press, 2002.

HENDERSON, SIMON. *Instant Empire: Saddam Hussein's Ambition for Iraq.* San Francisco: Mercury House, 1991.

JANSEN, G. H. *Militant Islam.* New York: Harper & Row, 1980.

KARSH, EFRAIM. *Saddam Hussein: A Political Biography.* New York: Free Press, 1991.

KHADDURI, MAJID. *The Gulf War: The Origins and Implications of the Iraq-Iran Conflict.* New York: Oxford University Press, 1988.

LEEDEEN, MICHAEL, and WILLIAM LEWIS. *Debacle: The American Failure in Iran.* New York: Knopf, 1981.

LEWIS, BERNARD. *The Political Language of Islam.* Chicago: University of Chicago Press, 1988.

MAUGERI, LEONARDO. "Not in Oil's Name." *Foreign Affairs,* July/August 2003.

OBALLANCE, EDGAR. *The Gulf War.* London: Brassey's, 1988.

PENROSE, EDITH, and E. F. PENROSE. *Iraq: International Relations and National Development.* Boulder, Colo.: Westview, 1978.

POLLACK, KENNETH M. "Next Stop Baghdad?" *Foreign Affairs,* March/April 2002.

POTTER, LAWRENCE G., and GARY G. SICK, Eds. *Security in the Persian Gulf: Origins, Obstacles, and the Search for Consensus.* New York: Palgrave, 2002.

RAMAZANI, R. K. *The Persian Gulf and the Strait of Hormuz.* Alphen aan der Rijn, Netherlands: Sijthoff, 1979.

RITTER, SCOTT. *Endgame: Solving the Iraq Problem Once and for All.* New York: Simon & Schuster, 1999.

RUBIN, BARRY. *Paved with Good Intentions: The American Experience in Iran.* New York: Oxford University Press, 1980.

SCIOLINO, ELAINE. *The Outlaw State: Saddam Hussein's Quest for Power and the Gulf Crisis.* New York: Wiley, 1991.

SEGAL, DAVID. "The Iran-Iraq War: A Military Analysis." *Foreign Affairs,* Summer 1988.

SIFRY, MICAH L., and CHRISTOPHER CERF, Eds. *The Iraq War Reader: History, Documents, Opinions.* New York: Simon & Schuster, 2003.

SMITH, PERRY M. *How CNN Fought the War: A View from the Inside.* New York: Birch Lane Press, 1991.

WOODWARD, BOB. *The Commanders.* New York: Simon & Schuster, 1991.

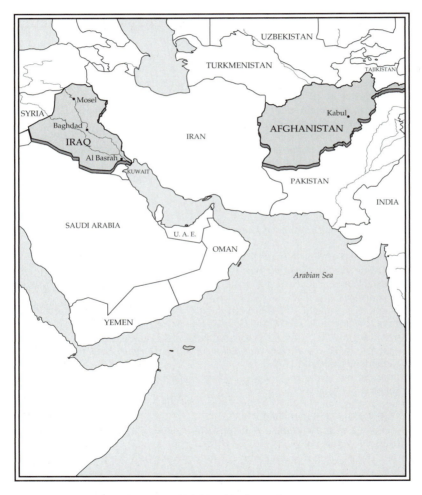

MAP 13   Iraq, Afghanistan, and Neighboring Countries

9

New Wars for a New Century: America and the World of Islam

The Americans worship life, while we worship death.
Osama bin Laden

The ink of a scholar's pen is more sacred than the blood of a martyr.
The Prophet Muhammad, the *Koran*

On Tuesday morning, September 11, 2001, I was sitting on an American Airlines flight on the runway of San Diego Airport waiting to take off for Chicago. Departure time came and went and the captain made a cryptic announcement about a delay ordered by the tower. After an hour had passed the passengers grew restless. A bearded pilot emerged from the cockpit and disappeared into the lavatory. He returned to the cockpit a few minutes later. Shortly thereafter there was another announcement of a further, indefinite delay. At long last, the plane slowly taxied back to the gate. I noticed that the bearded captain in a white uniform quickly got off first. A few moments later, the passengers were allowed to disembark. The airport was strangely silent, with people crowded around TV sets. That is when I first learned of the horrible events of what is now known as 9/11. I shall never know whether my aircraft was still one more that might have been destined to be a part of that barbarous plot.

None of us alive today will ever forget that terrible day when nineteen religious fanatics, armed with box cutters, hijacked four commercial airliners carrying innocent civilians. The terrorists crashed two planes into the Twin Towers of New York City's World Trade

Center, bringing both down in a holocaust of fiery debris. A third plane was flown into the Pentagon, but the passengers on the fourth plane, made aware of their impending doom during cell phone conversations with loved ones, put up a desperate struggle and managed to divert the aircraft from its intended target in Washington D.C., instead crashing in a field in rural Pennsylvania. When it was all over, 3,000 men, women, and children were lost in a sneak attack more barbarous than Pearl Harbor in 1941. Then, the Japanese had chosen a military target and killed 2,300 sailors; the terrorists, on the other hand, had taken 3,000 civilian lives in the very heart of America—its capital and its largest metropolis. No one in America would ever be quite the same again. Something truly unimaginable had occurred: All of us that day had looked into the face of absolute evil.

Absolute evil is a mystery. Nonetheless, I shall attempt an explanation, with the caveat that no argument, no matter how persuasive, should ever be confused with a condonement of an act as barbarous as 9/11. In this effort, I am indebted to an excellent book, *What Went Wrong* by Bernard Lewis, a British historian with vast knowledge of the Moslem world. The book, published before 9/11, describes the Ottoman Empire as a lazy and corrupt bureaucracy that for almost half a millennium had walled itself in against any kind of change from the outside world. When, in the eighteenth century, the empire found itself confronted by four revolutions going on simultaneously in Western Europe, it rejected them as dangerous threats to its survival. First, the Ottoman Turks regarded the scientific inventions of the English Industrial Revolution as potentially destabilizing. Second, the French Revolution, with its slogan of "liberty, equality, and fraternity," was unacceptable to the rigid class system of the Ottoman Empire. When some of the French ideals were adopted by the Founding Fathers of the United States, the danger seemed only to grow more acute. Third, the American principle of the separation of church and state flew right in the face of one of the most cherished beliefs of the Ottoman rulers: that the mosque and the state were forever joined under the Prophet Muhammad. Finally, and perhaps most dangerous of all, was the Western concept of the emancipation of women. In the Ottoman Empire's culture women were seen as chattel or playthings, never as equal partners in love or in work. Scheherazade was allowed to live only as long as she could entertain the Sultan by telling him 1,001 stories.

When the Ottoman Turks discovered that they had been left behind, they blamed the Western countries for their decline. It was a classic example of projecting their own failure onto someone else; after all, they had walled themselves in. The Ottoman Empire had become the "sick man of Europe" by choice, not by conquest.[1]

The Ottoman Turks were replaced by British and French rulers, who turned most of the Middle East into colonies for another century and a half. After they were humbled by Gamal Abdel Nasser of Egypt during the Suez Crisis of 1956, the Europeans were replaced by the Americans. Gradually, American Coca-Cola plants and other commercial enterprises went up in Mecca and Medina, two holy Islamic cities in Saudi Arabia. Even worse, there was now the threat of Israel, protected by the United States. European Jews not indigenous to the region had settled Arab countries, had declared a sovereign state with a new flag, and had forced half a million Palestinians to leave their homes: The homeless Arab refugees of today had become the Jews of yesterday. Moslem rage was boiling over. As if all this were not enough, the Soviet Union invaded Afghanistan in 1979. Afghan freedom fighters turned on the "godless Bolsheviks" with a vehement ferocity. One of them was Osama bin Laden, who had been expelled by his family in Saudi Arabia and was now building a network of supporters in Afghanistan. In 1989, the freedom fighters drove the Soviet Army out of Afghanistan in a humiliating defeat that signaled the death knell of the Soviet Union.

1989 was the year of democratic revolutions in Europe. One by one, like dominoes, Soviet satellites threw off the Communist yoke and declared democracies. Hungary, Poland, Romania, Czechoslovakia, Bulgaria, and the Baltic states joined the parade. The Berlin Wall came down and the two Germanys celebrated their reunification. The United States, eager to facilitate this process and sensing the impending implosion of the Soviet Union itself, decided to join the party, so to speak, and abandoned Afghanistan. Osama bin Laden and many like him felt outraged and betrayed. After all, they, too, had fought the "godless Bolsheviks." Bin Laden's anger flamed into a bottomless hatred and a relentless determination to kill as many Americans and Jews as possible in the name of Islam.

It should be emphasized at this point that religious fanatics like Osama bin Laden should not be confused with Islam as a whole. The Al Qaeda, as bin Laden's followers came to be known, were promised immediate entry into paradise, as well as seventy-two virgins each, as rewards for their martyrdom. Most Moslems, on the other hand, are ordinary people who simply wish to pursue their daily lives. In two instances—Kuwait and Kosovo—the United States had decided to come to their rescue.

Once again, there should be no misunderstanding about the above analysis: An explanation of an unspeakable act is not the same as its condonement.

George W. Bush:
From Pragmatist to Crusader

In my studies of American presidents I have identified two basic personality types that have characterized their leadership styles. First, there has been the *crusader,* whose hallmark is a missionary zeal to make the world better. The crusader tends to make decisions on the basis of a preconceived idea rather than on the basis of experience. Even though there are alternatives, he usually does not see them. If the facts do not square with his philosophy, it is too bad for the facts. Thus, the crusader tends toward rigidity and finds it difficult, if not impossible, to extricate himself from a losing posture. He does not welcome dissent, and advisers tend to tell him what he wants to hear. He sets out to improve the world but all too often manages to leave it in worse shape than before.

The second basic type is the *pragmatist.* The pragmatist is guided by the facts and his experience in a given situation, not by wishes or unexamined preconceptions. He is generally aware of the alternatives to his chosen course of action and explores the pros and cons of each as objectively as possible. He encourages advisers to tell him what he ought to know, not what they think he wants to hear. Always flexible, he does not get locked into a losing policy. He can change direction and try again, without damaging his self-esteem. Neither hope nor fear, but evidence alone, governs his decision making. And when there is no evidence as yet, there is always common sense to guide him.

Naturally, these two basic types are not mutually exclusive: A pure crusader would be a saint or a fanatic, and a pure pragmatist would be an efficient machine. Both types usually are present to some degree in each personality, but one typically predominates. Over the years, crusading and pragmatic leaders have tended to alternate in cycles. The crusading spirit dominates American foreign policy in times of crisis or national trauma, whereas the pragmatic mode is more in evidence during periods of relative calm and consolidation. Like a pendulum, America has swung between two moods: Sunday evangelism and week-day realism.[2]

The purest crusader I have encountered in my research was Woodrow Wilson, locked in his battle with the Senate over ratification of the League of Nations. On his arrival in Paris in 1919, Wilson astounded the European diplomats with his sense of messianic mission:

> Why has Jesus Christ so far not succeeded in inducing the world to follow his teachings in these matters? It is because he taught the ideal without devising any practical means for attaining it. That is why I am proposing a practical scheme to carry out His aims.[3]

David Lloyd George of Great Britain and Georges Clemenceau of France decided to go along with Wilson in Versailles reluctantly but the American president met his nemesis in Henry Cabot Lodge of the U.S. Senate. The senator and some of his allies insisted on amendments to the League of Nations Covenant, but Wilson would brook no compromise: "The facts are marching and God is marching with them. You cannot resist them. You must either welcome them or subsequently, with humiliation, surrender to them. It is welcome or surrender."[4] To Woodrow Wilson, it was all or nothing and he got nothing. The League of Nations, born in an American cradle, died in an American grave.

The purest pragmatist I ever came across was John F. Kennedy during the Cuban Missile Crisis of 1962. The evidence alone governed his conduct. Under enormous pressure from most of the military members of his War Council to bomb the Soviet bases in Cuba, he nonetheless refused to give the order to go ahead. Even when John McCone, director of the Central Intelligence Agency, and Vice President Lyndon Johnson implored him to act after an American U2 aircraft had been shot down over Cuba, he still held out for more evidence that the Soviets truly wanted nuclear war. And after one last effort, he succeeded in making a deal with Nikita Khruschev, the Soviet leader. By so doing, he contained a nuclear superpower bristling with thousands of missiles stationed ninety miles from Florida, and pulled back from the nuclear abyss. New evidence made public by Mikhail Gorbachev during his tenure as Soviet president revealed that the Soviets would have fired their nuclear missiles if the United States had bombed their sites. Humanity had escaped oblivion by a whisker.

There are times when a crusader is able to alter his particular course and become a pragmatist. Ronald Reagan is one example. Reagan, who habitually referred to the Soviet Union as "the evil empire," changed his mind about his adversary when British Prime Minister Margaret Thatcher informed him that she believed Gorbachev was an honest man with whom one could do business. Reagan and Gorbachev signed their first disarmament treaty shortly thereafter, and Reagan never mentioned the "evil empire" again. He had been able to assimilate new facts and to abandon a dangerous fixation.

It is the thesis of this chapter that George W. Bush began his term as President of the United States as a pragmatist and then gradually, over a period of several months, moved ever closer to the crusading end of the spectrum until his pursuit of terrorists—and Saddam Hussein—hardened into an obsession.

I remember well that defining moment when President Bush, his arm around a fireman, sounded his stern warning to the perpetrators of the barbarous crime committed on September 11, 2001. "I can hear you," he shouted to the crowd around him. "The rest of the world hears you and the people who knocked these buildings down will hear from all of us soon." The slogan "United We Stand" had become a reality that day. The entire country, indeed the entire world, was behind the president in his determination to seek out and punish the 9/11 criminals. When he declared, in the manner of the Old American West, that Osama bin Laden was wanted "Dead or Alive," there were few if any objections by anyone. The president was calm and measured in his statements. "I'm a patient man," he said. He was prepared to give the Taliban government of Afghanistan time to extradite bin Laden to the United States. If the Taliban would not cooperate it would be destroyed. Bush seemed almost too generous to many Americans, but when September gave way to October his patience ran out. With the support of the American people he invaded Afghanistan on October 7. The Taliban regime collapsed by November 9 with the fall of Mazar-e Sharif, a strategic town in the north of the country. Shortly thereafter, the cities of Herat, Kabul (the capital), and Jalalabad were captured, as the remnants of the Taliban surrendered. The arrest of bin Laden, however, proved elusive. Somehow, the crafty Al Qaeda leader outfoxed the Americans by slipping away into the vast and almost ungovernable region of the Afghan-Pakistani border. Thus, bin Laden, who had himself videotaped boasting about the "huge success against the infidel Americans," went unpunished. It seemed that nineteen fanatics armed with nothing but box cutters had outsmarted the country with the most advanced technology in the world.

The slow shift in President Bush's makeup from pragmatist to crusader cannot be explained in terms of any one single factor. The terrible frustration of having to admit that bin Laden had gotten away no doubt gnawed at him. It seemed that evil had triumphed over good. To the president, who as a younger man had undergone a religious epiphany that made him perceive the world in clear-cut terms such as "good versus evil" or "you are with us or against us," this was clearly an unacceptable outcome. He became increasingly attracted to a small but highly intelligent group of neoconservative intellectuals who believed that containment was no longer the answer in a post-9/11 world. The most prominent of these was a trio of men who were said to be indebted to the late Professor Leo Strauss of the Department of Political Science at the University of Chicago. Strauss's best-known work, *On Tyranny,* dealt with classical Greece and had nothing to do with modern international events. His daughter, Jenny Strauss Clay, wrote in an article in June 2003 that her father "was a teacher, not a right-wing guru" and that she did not recognize him from the articles written by his alleged disciples.[5] The first of these was Deputy Under Secretary of Defense Paul D. Wolfowitz, who developed several strategic analyses for the president, contending that a new doctrine of preemptive war should be applied to dictatorships that presented a direct threat to the United States. Wolfowitz in fact advocated a policy that would overturn more than two hundred years of American foreign policy: Dictatorships dangerous to America should be turned into democracies, by force of arms if necessary. Richard Perle of the American Enterprise Institute and an influential adviser to the Pentagon declared that "we could deliver a short message, a two-word message: you're next." Michael Ledeen, a former U.S. National Security official and key strategist, proclaimed that "it may turn out to be war to remake the world."[6] In short, the three men advocated a policy of making the world safe for democracy through full use of America's status as the world's sole remaining superpower.

Reporter Bob Woodward of Watergate fame, whose book *Bush at War* is based on numerous lengthy interviews with the president, suggested that the ease with which Bush had defeated the Taliban was a further source of encouragement to change direction now that a new regime—under a pro-American leader, Hamid Karzai—had been installed in Afghanistan. There was, finally, the element of a personal grudge match. Saddam Hussein had, after all, attempted to assassinate the president's father on a visit to Kuwait and the son was eager to bring his father's unfinished business to a successful conclusion.

These, then, are the links in the fateful chain of events that took George W. Bush to the crusading end of the personality spectrum. The opportunity for unveiling this grand design occurred when David Frum, the president's speechwriter, came up with a new phrase that the president used in his State of the Union Address on January 29, 2002. States like Iraq, Iran, and North Korea, the president declared, constituted an "axis of evil." By seeking weapons of mass destruction, "the regimes posed a grave and growing danger. I will not stand by as peril draws closer and closer. The United States of America will not permit the world's most dangerous regimes to threaten us with the world's most destructive weapons."

The implication of the president's speech was unmistakable. The dictators of Iraq, Iran, and North Korea would not be permitted to develop nuclear, chemical, or biological weapons, with Iraq first on the list. I must confess that at this juncture I began to develop a malaise with this new policy. Like most Americans, I believed that preemption made perfect sense against terrorists like bin Laden's Al Qaeda cells, for the simple reason that these fanatics were quite prepared to die for their cause—in fact, they welcomed death. Such people could not be contained, and one had to bring the battle to them *before* they decided to strike or it was too late, as 9/11 had so grimly demonstrated. But this was not the case, I believe, with the dictator of a sovereign state, like Saddam Hussein, whose highest priority was to survive as ruler. He knew that if he so much as twitched in the direction of the United States he would be doomed. Hence, he could be deterred as Khruschev had been during the Cuban Missile Crisis.

Not surprisingly, the "evil axis" speech triggered immediate responses by the three targeted dictators. They were evil, but not stupid. In April 2002, Saddam Hussein announced an increase in the amount offered to the families of martyred Palestinian suicide bombers from $10,000 to $25,000. He was careful not to offer such bounties to Al Qaeda terrorists so as to not provoke the United States into a preventive attack. Almost simultaneously, the Iranians sent huge shipments of arms to the Palestinians. One such vessel was intercepted by the Israelis. Thus, Iran and Iraq raised the ferocity of the Israeli-Palestinian conflict to new levels without directly confronting the United States. They placed a roadblock in front of the American president in order to deflect attention from themselves. "Here, deal with this problem first," they seemed to say. Kim Jong Il, North Korea's dictator, condemned the "axis of evil" speech as a declaration of war by the United States. In January 2003 he threatened North Korea's withdrawal from the Nuclear Non-Proliferation Treaty (NPT) and began to step up his nuclear weapons program. Soon thereafter, in February, he went so far as to threaten to nullify the truce of Panmunjon, which had ended the Korean War half a century earlier. North Korea's withdrawal from the NPT actually became effective on April 10, 2003.

The Bush administration's response to these events was to create a curious double standard. The road to war with Iraq continued unimpeded while, on the other side of the world, the United States entered into negotiations with North Korea, which was building a growing nuclear arsenal. Saddam Hussein may have wished that he was North Korean.

By the summer of 2002, the preemption doctrine was fully in place. "Containment is not possible," Bush declared in a commencement speech at West Point on June 1. "In the world we have entered, the only path to safety is the path to action. And this nation will act." Clearly, Saddam Hussein was now the target; Osama bin Laden had virtually disappeared from the president's radar screen.

War Drums

During the fall of 2002, the run-up to war against Iraq began in earnest. On September 12, Bush appeared before the UN General Assembly. He listed the numerous UN Security Council resolutions that had been ignored by Saddam Hussein since 1991. He also asserted that Saddam had deceived UN inspectors for years and that he still possessed large stockpiles of chemical and biological weapons. He declared that, if the Iraq regime desired peace, "it would have to immediately forswear, disclose, or remove or destroy all weapons of mass destruction." One month later, on October 11, an increasingly frustrated Bush went before Congress and received a 77 to 23 vote of support for a resolution authorizing war against Iraq in the Senate; a similar resolution passed in the House by 296 to 133. On November 8, after intensive lobbying, the United States succeeded in securing a unanimous UN Security Council resolution threatening Saddam with "grave consequences" if he was not prepared to rid himself of all weapons of mass destruction. On November 27, UN inspection teams were admitted back into Iraq after a four-year absence. Dr. Hans Blix of Sweden was placed in charge of chemical and biological weapons and Dr. Mohammad el-Baradei of the International Atomic Energy Agency had the same responsibilities for nuclear weapons. In their first report to the UN Security Council the inspectors noted that progress was being made on the process, but not on the substance of the inspections. However, the report concluded on a note of cautious optimism. On February 5, 2003, Secretary of State Colin Powell appeared before the Security Council and delivered a scathing speech, based largely on U.S. intelligence sources, accusing Saddam Hussein of continuing his policy of deception and declaring that time was rapidly running out. Shortly thereafter, British prime minister Tony Blair, America's staunchest ally in the United Nations, delivered a similar address before the British House of Commons. On February 15, over 10 million protesters gathered in numerous world capitals to express their opposition to a war against Iraq. Perhaps the most prominent of these was Nelson Mandela, the former president of South Africa, who declared that the American president was a man "who [had] no foresight and who [could] not think properly."[7]

On February 24, the United States and Britain introduced a draft resolution declaring that Iraq had missed its last chance to disarm and demanding that the Security Council pass a resolution specifically authorizing war. This initiative ran into stiff resistance. France, Russia, and China, all veto-bearing permanent members of the Council, demanded that the UN inspectors be given more time. Progress was being made, they declared, and Saddam had begun to destroy some of his Al-Samoud II missiles, which exceeded the range permitted under UN criteria. Germany and Syria, two nonpermanent members of the Council, objected for similar reasons. Only two member states, aside from Britain, supported the American position: Spain and Bulgaria. In the center were six uncommitted nations collectively referred to as the "swingers": Chile, Mexico,

Pakistan, Angola, Cameroon, and Guinea. The Americans were particularly concerned about France and Russia, which threatened to veto the resolution. Russia, after intensive lobbying, softened its stance somewhat, but France remained adamant. A comment made by Secretary of Defense Donald Rumsfeld describing France as "Old Europe" did not help matters. Bush's continued assertions that there was no room for neutrality in this debate annoyed the three African countries, which responded that, in their case, a neutral stance was completely justified because Iraq was no threat to them and they had different priorities. Dismissive comments by Rumsfeld about the increasing irrelevance of the United Nations further angered the "swinger" states. Finally, Bush realized that even if France and Russia were to abstain from a vote, the United States would not be able to muster the necessary nine votes for the passage of a war resolution. The situation seemed hopelessly deadlocked.

It is interesting to note that, in the midst of this debate and shortly after the UN inspectors had reported further progress in Iraq, notably on the destruction of a large number of Al-Samoud II missiles, Bush decided to raise the bar for Saddam Hussein: This new standard was not just Saddam's disarmament, but his complete removal from Iraq through regime change. Since the UN inspectors were responsible only for disarmament and were unable to affect a decision by Saddam to go into exile, the administration clearly set the bar beyond the reach of the United Nations. In other words, President Bush had decided to go to war no matter what.

While these debates were going on, American and British troop deployments increased dramatically. Two hundred fifty thousand American and 50,000 British troops had massed on the Iraqi border, mostly in Kuwait in the south. Turkey had demanded $26 billion in exchange for permitting American bases there, but a few days later the Turkish parliament rescinded that vote by a narrow margin. After several days of haggling, the Turks permitted overflights, but no bases. Hence, the United States was in effect deprived of a northern front against Iraq, forcing it to station most of its troops in other areas, such as Kuwait. Nonetheless, preparations for war continued at an ever accelerating pace.

On March 7, in a last effort to help avert a war, I published an article in the *San Diego Union Tribune* proposing that the Security Council designate Saddam Hussein as a War Criminal using the precedent of Slobodan Milosevic. Then, I decided to approach the

UN delegation of Pakistan, one of the swing votes in the Council and yet a nation friendly to the United States that had helped in the capture of leading Al Qaeda criminals. The Pakistanis responded favorably to the war criminal concept and offered to propose a compromise resolution on March 17 that also would have quadrupled the number of UN inspectors in Iraq in an effort to speed up the inspection process. That afternoon, however, the president announced that the time for diplomacy had run out and that he had decided to meet with Tony Blair and the president of Spain, Jose Maria Aznar, in the Azores to prepare for war. He did this even though UN Secretary-General Kofi Annan had declared that such a war outside the United Nations would violate its Charter. In an address to the nation from the White House, Bush declared that waiting to act after America's foes "have struck first is not self-defense, it is suicide."[8] It was the clearest statement yet in defense of the preemption doctrine. That day he also gave Saddam Hussein an ultimatum to leave Iraq within forty-eight hours or else face the consequences. When Saddam, not surprisingly, ignored this ultimatum, the president decided to act without the United Nations. On March 19, Bush went to war with a "coalition of the willing," which included Britain, Australia, Spain, Poland, and a group of small states from Eastern Europe, Asia, and Africa. The die was cast.

To begin our analysis of the course of the war, let us make some general observations. First, it went much better than many, including myself, had feared. The worst did not happen: No weapons of mass destruction, chemical, biological, or nuclear, were ever used against the United States or against Israel. No Scuds were launched against the Jewish state as had been the case in the first Gulf War. Only one Silkworm missile landed near a Kuwait City marketplace, inflicting little damage, while others fell harmlessly into the ocean. Second, my own worst fear of a Stalingrad in Baghdad never materialized. The Iraqi army turned out to be so degraded by its losses in the first Gulf War and so completely outclassed by the coalition forces' new technology that it never had a chance to put up a strong defense of Baghdad. Not a single Iraqi aircraft took to the sky. Third, coalition casualties were kept generally in the same range as those in the first Gulf War, although a relatively large percentage of them turned out to be self-inflicted through accidents or friendly fire. On the other hand, there were some negative surprises, in particular, Iraqi Republican Guard troops disguised as civilians pretending to surrender and then opening fire, devastating unsuspecting coalition troops. As in the first Gulf War, the number of Iraqi casualties, both military and civilian, was huge, with an exact figure almost impossible to determine.

The main objective of the war was obtained within three weeks; the regime of Saddam Hussein fell on April 9 when American marines entered Baghdad and toppled a huge statue of the dictator from its pedestal in the capital's central square. In Washington, Rumsfeld proclaimed that Saddam had gone the way of other dictators in history, comparing his fate to other, even deadlier tyrants, such as Hitler and Stalin. However, he noted, the war was "most assuredly not yet over."[9] Saddam himself, who had apparently survived a "decapitation" attempt on his life with dozens of cruise missiles on the first day of the war, had disappeared from view and was believed to be in hiding somewhere near his hometown, Tikrit, with his two sons.

Unlike the first Gulf War, which began with four weeks of fierce air attacks and ended with the destruction of much of Saddam's army in a three-day ground war executed brilliantly by General Norman Schwarzkopf, the second Gulf War began with "shock and awe" aerial bombardments delivering seven times the punch of those twelve years earlier, in conjunction with a massive tank invasion that entered Iraq from the south, then raced north across the desert straight for Baghdad. American tank commanders speeding through the Iraqi desert encountered more resistance from fierce sand storms than from Iraqi troops. The Iraqis tried to make a stand in Nasiriya, south of Baghdad, which resulted in the most challenging battle of the war for the Americans, with considerable casualties. The Iraqi losses, however, were huge—and demoralizing—as the "shock and awe" attacks gradually devastated most military targets in Baghdad. As American troops approached the Iraqi capital, they were instructed to wear suits shielding them against chemical attacks as well as gas masks. As the troops entered the outskirts of Baghdad, Central Command Chief General Tommy Franks instructed them to kill as many soldiers as possible, to destroy Iraqi tanks and communication systems, and to attack the regime's remaining pillars of power in the city. Arab media now portrayed the war as a killing field. Surrenders by Iraqi troops began to multiply, but so did Republican Guard suicide attacks. To the Americans' astonishment, few if any organized Republican Guard units were in evidence as

American troops entered Baghdad while the British thrust into Basra, Iraq's second-largest city. On April 8, General Franks made his first visit to the troops in the battle zone and on April 9, coalition forces entered the heart of the Iraqi capital. Saddam's statue was pulled down by Iraqis helped by American marines, who supplied a crane to do the job. Saddam himself was photographed that day when he made an appearance somewhere in Baghdad surrounded by cheering admirers. No one knew when the picture had been taken and whether it was really Saddam, or one of his numerous doubles. After that day, Saddam's whereabouts became a mystery.

Saddam Hussein's final act before leaving power is worth noting. At 3 A.M. on April 9, Saddam's older son Qusay appeared at the Iraqi Central Bank and delivered a note from the dictator demanding $1 billion in $100 notes and €1 million in euro notes. The hapless teller, awakened from his sleep, complied out of fear when he saw Saddam's signature. Two trucks loaded with banknotes disappeared into the night after the largest bank robbery in world history. Perhaps Saddam considered it his severance pay for three decades in power.

The "War after the War": Dilemmas of Occupation

It became clear very quickly in post-Saddam Iraq that the Americans had prepared very well for waging war, but hardly at all for waging peace. The jubilant welcome that many Iraqis extended to the American troops when they entered Baghdad did not last long. The population of Baghdad quickly discovered that Saddam had been replaced by a power vacuum.

The pent-up rage against thirty years of tyranny exploded in scenes of frenzied looting, with mobs setting fire to remaining government ministries and private homes, and backing trucks up to offices and department stores to fill them with stolen merchandise. Gun battles broke out between packs of looters and defenders of their property; Baghdad's hospitals received more casualties from rioting and looting than from the war.[10] Most of the city remained without electricity and potable water, and almost every shop remained shuttered. In fact, most of the country operated essentially without a government and without police protection. Rumsfeld, apparently caught unprepared, commented that "freedom is untidy and free people are free to make mistakes and commit crimes."[11]

The administration quickly dispatched retired Lieutenant General Jay Garner as Overseer. He arrived in Baghdad without fanfare and quickly toured a heavily looted hospital, promising to get its services back as fast as possible. The next day, pillagers stripped Baghdad's National Museum of priceless artifacts dating back thousands of years. A leading repository of ancient civilizations fell victim to looters and chaos. On April 14, at last there was some good news. Seven American military personnel were discovered alive in a town north of Baghdad, three weeks after they vanished during the fighting with the Iraqis. The group included a thirty-year-old African American cook, Shoshana Johnson, who had been shot in both her ankles by her captors. All seven were quickly reunited with their families.

By July 2003, however, barely three months after the end of the war, more than 100 American soldiers had been killed in assaults and firefights, mostly in and around Baghdad. On one occasion it took 4,000 G.I.s to pacify a thirty-square-mile area north of Baghdad infested with die-hard Saddam loyalists. "We won the war, so

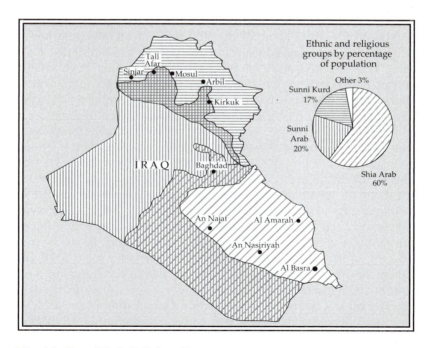

MAP 14   Iraq: Ethnic-Religious Groups

why are people dying?" a distraught relative moaned in despair. It
was becoming increasingly apparent that, out of the chaos that was
Iraq, organized resistance against the American occupation had
begun to form.[12] It was, in fact, guerrilla war. The new commander
of the American occupation forces, General John B. Abizaid, forced
to admit the obvious, declared that American troops in Iraq were
under attack from a "classical guerrilla-type campaign," whose
forces were largely drawn from Saddam's supporters and foreign terrorist elements. New troop replacements would be needed, the general added. When the United States appealed for help, Poland and
Spain offered to deploy a modest number of troops, but Germany,
France, and Canada refused unless their forces were placed under a
United Nations mandate. An embarrassed Rumsfeld now considered a call-up of 10,000 National Guard soldiers for duty in Iraq. "If
they are needed, they will be there," he said.[13] By this time, U.S. casualties in the "war after the war" had risen to an unacceptable rate of
two fatalities a day. In the meantime, the elusive Saddam Hussein
not only remained at large, but appeared on a new audiotape exhorting his followers to kill as many "infidels" as possible.

Around this time, some of the first signs of an emerging power
structure in Iraq revealed itself in one of Islam's holiest cities, Karbala. Tens of thousands of Iraqi Shi'ites, who had been cruelly
oppressed by Saddam's regime for over twenty years, organized a
pilgrimage for the first time in a generation. The Shi'ites, who com-
prised 60 percent of Iraq's population, had managed to maintain a
network of underground organizations through their clerics. Saddam had been too busy devastating any potential opposition among
his secular Sunni population to pay close attention to the Shi'ites.
The Kurds in the north, meanwhile, who had enjoyed considerable
autonomy despite Saddam because of the no-fly zones enforced by
the Americans in the first Gulf War, now insisted on their continued
independent status in the new Iraq. When Lieutenant General Garner arranged a meeting with potential Iraqi leaders, he discovered
that the most vocal group were the Shi'ites, who mistrusted the
Americans because they had been encouraged to revolt against Saddam in 1991 and then had been abandoned and subsequently were
savagely oppressed by the Iraqi dictator. Garner did not prove equal
to the task of stopping the chaos and was soon replaced by Paul Bremer III, a retired diplomat and counterterrorism expert. Around the
same time, Ahmed Chalabi, an Iraqi opposition leader favored by

the Pentagon, raised an interesting question: Should former Baath party members who had worked for the Saddam regime be admitted to administrative jobs, such as running the water supply and electrical grids, because of their competence and experience in these areas? The question reminded many of the post-World War II German government that retained low-level Nazis in administrative positions for similar reasons. The American response was to dissolve the Baath party as a political institution, but to consider the appointment of individuals on a case-by-case basis.

As Iraqi demands for a larger role in running their country became more and more strident, Bremer convened a new Governing Council consisting of twenty-five members: thirteen Shi'ites, five Sunnis, five Kurds, one Christian, and one Turkoman. Though the Council's first decision was to abolish all of Saddam's national holidays, there was a consensus that priority should be given to the restoration of security and of essential services, such as water and electricity. Only one day after the new Council convened, a militant Shi'ite cleric whipped up an anti-American frenzy among thousands of fellow Shi'ites, who began chanting slogans like "No Americans after today!" and "No to America, no to colonialism!" It was a precarious beginning, at best.

In late August, a leading moderate Shi'ite cleric, Ayatollah Muhammad Bakr al-Hakim, was killed by an explosion so powerful that only shreds of the man's turban and his watch could be found. Baathist terrorists were blamed for the assassination. The cleric's funeral procession became a massive outpouring of grief mixed with cries for revenge against the perpetrators and of anger against the Americans for not providing sufficient protection. In response, the Iraqi Governing Council appointed a twenty-five-member cabinet to begin taking over day-to-day control of the government including internal security, oil, and finance. However, most of the new cabinet's members feared for their safety and did not trust the Americans to ensure it. "The Governing Council could become a morgue," one of the newly appointed cabinet ministers exclaimed in despair.

All things considered, perhaps Pentagon planners had been focused too much on technological innovation and not enough on past experience. As the NATO operation in Kosovo should have made clear, two armies would be needed for a massive operation like Iraq, requiring occupation and reconstruction. The first would be the fighting force that would remove Saddam's regime and the second, following the military, would be composed of military police, civilian affairs officers, and humanitarian aid groups. The Pentagon prepared the first force brilliantly, but neglected the second.[14]

As chaos in Iraq continued into the summer of 2003 it became increasingly clear to the occupying powers that their jobs might last not months but years. The UN Security Council, in an effort to mend fences, decided to relinquish its control over the Iraqi Food for Oil Program, and, in the same resolution, endorsed the occupation of Iraq by the United States and Great Britain. An additional request by the United Nations to permit the return of its inspectors was turned down. UN Secretary-General Kofi Annan, in a rather subdued speech, recommended that the United Nations be permitted to share in the reconstruction of Iraq in a significant manner.

As we survey Iraq after the storm of war, it must be concluded that the damage done was considerable. Both the United Nations and NATO emerged from the war as fractured organizations badly in need of repair. In the United Nations, the president had alienated almost all the members of the Security Council except for Great Britain and Spain. In NATO, he had managed to offend its largest member, neighboring Canada, which had requested another thirty days' extension for UN inspectors and had been rebuffed by the president. When the U.S. ambassador to Canada, Paul Celluci, expressed his disappointment at Canada's refusal to participate in the war against Iraq, he was reminded that Canadians had fought side by side with Americans not only in two world wars but also in Korea and in Kuwait.

Finally, the economic costs of preemption would be enormous for the United States: $160 billion had been spent for the war and subsequent occupation of Iraq. On September 7, 2003, the president announced that he would request $87 billion for occupation and reconstruction costs in Iraq and Afghanistan for 2004. In the first Gulf War, America's UN allies paid almost 90 percent of the costs, but this time it would be the other way around. Moreover, the American idea of having Iraqi oil revenues pay for the country's reconstruction did not materialize as planned. Even though the war itself inflicted relatively little damage, looters and saboteurs after the war virtually destroyed the oil industry's infrastructure. However, by late summer 2003, American oil-field experts, together with Iraqi engineers, had managed to increase the output of oil to 1 million barrels a day, roughly half that of prewar levels. Improved security provided by several hundred militiamen from a Moslem sect made a signifi-cant contribution to this encouraging trend.

The Bush administration declared repeatedly that its plan to rebuild Iraq was modeled on the Marshall Plan, which had helped rebuild Europe after World War II. On closer scrutiny, the analogy seems flawed. European countries were required by the Truman administration to match every dollar of American aid. In the words of then–Secretary of State George C. Marshall in a speech on June 5, 1947: "It would be neither fitting nor efficacious for this government to undertake to draw up unilaterally a program designed to place Europe on its feet economically. This is the business of the Europeans. The initiative, I think, must come from Europe."[15] This seemed a far cry from Bush's "coalition of the willing," in which the United States and Britain shouldered 90 percent of the cost in lives and materiel.

The great positive consequence of the war, of course, was the fall of a tyrant. It was difficult not to rejoice at the spectacle of Sad-dam's statues coming down, especially after hundreds of mass graves of murdered Iraqis had been discovered all over the country. Yet the victory was marred by the fact that American casualties con-tinued at the rate of at least two a day after the president's proclama-tion on May 1 that the war had ended. On July 22, at long last, Saddam's two sons Uday and Qusay—the two henchmen of the regime—were killed by U.S. troops in a firefight in the city of Mosul. This action was undertaken on a tip supplied by an Iraqi informant. Saddam himself, however, remained at large.

We will now turn to an overall analysis of these pivotal events in history.

The core reason for Bush's decision to apply his preemption doc-trine to Iraq was Saddam's reluctance to cooperate with UN inspec-tors in giving up his weapons of mass destruction. When Saddam, who felt his doom was near, began to comply and bulldozed dozens of Al-Sammoud missiles, the president raised the bar from disarma-ment to regime change. Defense Secretary Rumsfeld commented dryly after the invasion that Saddam probably had destroyed his weapons before the war began. This seemed like an argument for containment, not preemption, because, if Rumsfeld was correct, Saddam wanted to survive as ruler of Iraq at any cost, even of his weapons of mass destruction. He *was,* in fact, contained. At any rate, the fact remains that no such weapons were found and none were used. Saddam's mandated compliance was raised to an impossible height: Bush simply wanted him gone.

These facts are consistent with accumulating evidence that the Bush administration took a very selective approach to intelligence reports about the mysterious disappearance of any weapons of mass destruction. Because most intelligence reports—in the absence of a "smoking gun"—were inherently ambiguous, administration officials tended to accept the worst-case scenarios as fact. In short, they glossed over ambiguities and instead looked for things that confirmed their world view. Sometimes there were even outright mistakes, such as the claim made in the president's State of the Union speech in January 2003 that Saddam had sought to buy uranium from an African nation, later identified as Niger. This claim was based on a British intelligence report that turned out to be a forgery. CIA Director George Tenet accepted the blame for the mistake when he stated, "I am responsible for the approval process in my Agency."[16] A few days later, Stephen J. Hadley, Bush's deputy national security adviser, was even more specific: "I should have asked that the sixteen words be taken out of the State of the Union address," he said. "I failed in that responsibility."[17]

In this connection, it should be noted that the alleged terror links between bin Laden and Saddam were never definitively proved. Indeed, there is strong circumstantial evidence that there was no love lost between these two men. Bin Laden was a religious fanatic while Saddam was a secular, womanizing despot living in opulent imperial palaces reminiscent of Emperor Caligula in ancient Rome. Moreover, numerous interrogations of Al Qaeda detainees in Guantanamo, Cuba, have revealed that bin Laden categorically refused even to consider any collaboration with Saddam. Nor was there ever any proven initiative on Saddam's part to work together with bin Laden. Indeed, the former Iraqi intelligence officer, Ahmad Khalil Samir al-Ani, who was alleged to have met with Muhammad Atta in Prague in April 2001, denied categorically under U.S. interrogation that such a meeting took place.[18] The irony is that Iraq became a magnet for Al Qaeda fighters *after* the war, when they swelled the ranks of the anti-American resistance in ever increasing numbers during the occupation.

During the late summer of 2003, Al Qaeda–related attacks escalated to new heights of ferocity. In addition to killing Americans, the terrorists attacked oil pipelines, water supplies, and the Jordanian Embassy. In a climax of random horror, a suicide bomber drove a truck into the wall of the unguarded UN headquarters in Baghdad, killing twenty UN humanitarian workers and injuring dozens more—in the most devastating attack on the United Nations in its history. Among the dead was the UN's High Commissioner for Human Rights, Sergio Vieira de Mello, a dedicated UN diplomat and peacemaker. It appeared that Al Qaeda had begun to use chaos as a deliberate strategy. Why else would they attack men and women who were there to help the Iraqi people? The terrorists sensed, probably not altogether incorrectly, that they enjoyed a measure of support among the broader population, which chafed under an occupation that was unable to provide basic services, let alone public safety. Thus, in a tragic way, the United States had taken a country that was not an imminent terrorist threat and turned it into one.[19]

The United States appealed to the world to contribute more troops to the American-led occupation of Iraq. Not surprisingly, the Bush administration continued to insist that additional troops be subject to coalition control. Germany, France, Canada, and numerous other UN members were equally insistent on the blessing of the Security Council before they would send troops to Iraq. A melancholy Kofi Annan, still grieving over his slain colleagues in the UN Secretariat, tried hard to bridge these differences by pointing out the common need to stabilize Iraq, but the rifts that had opened before the war persisted in its aftermath.

All this leads to some important philosophical questions. First, what if, from the chaos that has ruled after the war, there emerges a confederation of three entities—Kurdish, Sunni, and Shi'ite—presided over by a Shi'ite cleric? Rumsfeld went on record that such a development would not be permitted by the United States. Would it not be an ultimate irony of history if Saddam were replaced by a Shi'ite cleric who would seek to guide the Iraqis away from Western secularism and toward a theocratic form of government? How do we define democracy? As something that grows from the ground up or is imposed from the top down?

It is interesting, from this perspective, to look at the destiny of Afghanistan, which had been living in the shadow of Iraq since the invasion of Iraq. The United States installed a pro-American leader, Hamid Karzai, as president in 2002, but less than two years later, Karzai was little more than the de facto mayor of Kabul; the real power in Afghanistan has passed back to traditional tribal chief-tains. What was worse, remnants of the ousted Taliban, apparently taking a leaf from the postwar Iraqi insurgency, killed several senior members of the Clerics' Council who supported the American-installed Karzai regime, and issued a call for a jihad against all pro-American forces. As a result, American soldiers began to die in Afghanistan. In response to this new threat, in August 2003, NATO, for the first time in its history, decided to extend its reach beyond Europe and place the multinational peacekeeping force operating in Afghanistan under its direct control.

Speaking of Afghanistan, Al Qaeda seemed to have made a remarkable resurgence *after* the fall of Saddam Hussein. Vicious attacks that killed numerous Americans took place in May 2003 in Riyadh, Saudi Arabia, and in Casablanca, Morocco. In August, Al Qaeda was involved in a murderous bombing of a Marriott Hotel in Jakarta, Indonesia. Bin Laden was believed to be very much alive and plotting more calamities for the United States. Two years after 9/11, two *Newsweek* reporters encountered an old man named Khan Kaka who made his home in a mud hut in the foothills of the huge peaks along the Afghan-Pakistani border. Kaka's son-in-law had been a special bodyguard of the man Kaka called "big chief," Osama bin Laden. Asked where bin Laden was now, "Kaka grinned and waved without a word toward the peaks surrounding the valley: Up there."[20] Maureen Dowd of the *New York Times* put it more elo-quently: "If all those yuppies can climb Mount Everest at 29,000 feet," she wrote, "can't we pay somebody to nab Osama at 14,000 feet?"[21] No one had the answer.

To add insult to injury, Saddam Hussein was organizing his own insurgency from his hiding place, believed to be somewhere in Iraq. He knew that his crack troops had avoided contact with the Ameri-cans during the war and had now melted into the population. Thus, both bin Laden and Saddam, each in his unique fashion, managed to deny the Americans the taste of victory. Was Henry Kissinger right when he wrote that "the guerrilla wins by not losing, but an army loses by not winning?"

Finally, there was an even more far-reaching question. Was Amer-ica's preemptive strike against Iraq a precedent for similar endeavors? "Where is the list?" Canada's Prime Minister Jean Chretien wanted to know. Who may be next? The other two members of the "axis of evil," Iran or North Korea? Or could it be Syria or an as-yet unnamed dictator who provokes America's anger? If the United

States went that route, it would embark on the road to empire. Empires, sooner or later, enter the dustbin of history because they spend too much of their national wealth on imperial "overstretch," until they end up in economic ruin. That way went ancient Rome, Britain, and the Soviet Union.

In this context, Iran presented a new challenge during the summer of 2003. The third member of Bush's "evil axis" was warned that the United States would "not tolerate the construction of a nuclear weapon."[22] American officials had been focusing for several years on nuclear plants in Iran that were producing enriched uranium in a laboratory process. When the International Atomic Energy Agency (IAEA) expressed similar concerns about Iran's program and demanded that Iran allow IAEA inspectors to visit all of its nuclear plants, the president decided to issue his tough warning. He did so even though Iran's weapons program was not as advanced as that of North Korea. Iran, unlike North Korea, which had brazenly decided to withdraw from the Nuclear Proliferation Treaty (NPT), remained within its official guidelines and emphasized that its nuclear program was designed for purely peaceful purposes. Critics continued to maintain, however, that Iran, while observing the NPT's letter of the law, nonetheless had every intention of going nuclear. The IAEA, increasingly suspicious of Iran's real plans, refused to extend its deadline for admission of its inspectors. In October 2003, Iran finally decided to accept the IAEA's demands, thus defusing a major crisis, at least temporarily.

Suppose Iran were to follow North Korea's example and decide to withdraw from the NPT? It is interesting to note that Iran's nuclear programs rapidly accelerated after Bush's "evil axis" speech in January 2002 and that the country's conservative clerics agreed with more reformist elements on the need for such a program. Fortunately for the United States, a wave of democratic protesters demanding freedom of expression has also been in evidence in Tehran and other cities of Iran. Should these elements succeed in transforming the governing theocracy into a more democratic form of government, the United States might be spared the agonizing decision of taking yet another fateful step.

Fortunately, it seems that Americans make poor empire builders. Perhaps Americans' reluctance is in their collective memory because the nation was born in the crucible of an anticolonial revolution— they even had a tea party in Boston to prove it. To the British, empires came naturally. Parents in the nineteenth century sent their children to the best schools in England to prepare them for her Majesty's colonial service. Generations of men and women built the British empire, but even it went down in the end.

One of those British men was T. E. Lawrence, better known as Lawrence of Arabia, whose life provides some fascinating lessons for would-be empire builders. (For classic-movie lovers, David Lean's brilliant biopic with Peter O'Toole in the leading role is a good introduction to Lawrence's career.)

During World War I, Lawrence forged many disparate Arab tribes into a unified guerrilla force that drove the Turks out of what was then Mesopotamia. But when British troops replaced the Ottoman Empire, Arab nationalists turned on the British. An increasingly disenchanted Lawrence, writing in the *Sunday Times* of London on August 22, 1920, said:

> The Baghdad communiqués are belated, insincere, incomplete. Things have been far worse than we have been told, our administration more bloody and inefficient than the public knows. We are today not far from disaster.[23]

By then, the country was in full rebellion, with a loss of more than 400 British and 10,000 Iraqi lives. The British-sponsored monarchy fell in 1958 when the royal family was murdered, their bodies dragged through the streets. This event was followed by a succession of violent coups, culminating in the dictatorship of Saddam Hussein in 1979.

Lawrence's memoir, *The Seven Pillars of Wisdom,* is relevant to the guerrilla warfare being waged against the Americans after Saddam's removal from power. Lawrence advised that direct confrontations with a superior conventional force should be avoided. Instead, he recommended stealthy hit-and-run attacks to keep the enemy always nervous, never knowing where and when the next attack would occur.

The occupation of Iraq was constituted as a mostly Anglo-Saxon operation. The United States and Britain provided 95 percent of the troops and regarded this near monopoly as a prize to be coveted. In Kosovo and Afghanistan, on the other hand, occupation became a responsibility broadly shared among NATO, the United Nations, and indigenous personnel. I suspect it was the Anglo-Saxon nature of the Iraqi occupation that fired up the fierce guerrilla resistance. The purpose of a guerrilla insurgency is not to defeat an enemy militarily, but to defeat him politically by appealing to the local population. While in Kosovo and Afghanistan postwar occupation casualties remained minimal; in Iraq, by August 2003, they exceeded the war casualties.

When it was announced that American postwar casualties were exceeding war casualties, the Bush administration, in a major strategic reversal, agreed to negotiations in the UN Security Council authorizing a multinational force in Iraq, with the proviso that such a force be placed under American command. The proposed resolution also invited the Iraqi Governing Council to develop a timetable for drafting a constitution and holding elections that would lead to the restoration of Iraqi sovereignty and the withdrawal of all foreign troops. The United States's reversal was not only influenced by the rising death toll of American troops but by a new congressional study that indicated that the United States did not have enough active-duty troops to keep the current occupation force in Iraq past March 2004 without significant help from other countries. In light of the dismissive manner in which the president had treated the United Nations before the war, a tough round of negotiations with countries that felt particularly offended, such as France and Germany, was all but certain. At issue, of course, was the degree of political control that the United States would be prepared to cede to the United Nations as a price for a substantial number of troops. In the end, the model might be the UN police action in Korea in 1950, which was authorized by the UN Security Council but placed under the command of an American general, Douglas MacArthur.

When, on September 23, 2003, President Bush addressed the UN General Assembly and not only refused to offer an apology for earlier bypassing it, but also declared that "the United States had rescued the credibility of the United Nations," his audience remained unmoved.[24] And when, a few weeks later, he invited the members of the Security Council to contribute troops for the occupation and reconstruction of Iraq, the response was negative. Kofi Annan, the UN's Secretary-General, sided with those opposing the United States and strongly urged that political authority be transferred as speedily as possible from the Americans to the Iraqis themselves. Only Turkey offered troops but the Iraqi Governing Council, with an eye on the Kurds, pressed the United States to turn the offer down. The next day the Turkish Embassy in Baghdad was bombed, apparently as a warning. After a few more days of intensive negotiations, the Security Council managed to pass a unanimous resolution authorizing an

American-led multinational force in Iraq. Resolution 1511 also set a December 15, 2003, deadline for the Iraqi Governing Council to lay out a timetable for creating a constitution and democratic government. No time limit was set on the Governing Council's plans, however, giving the United States additional room to maneuver.

On the positive side, this compromise ended the Bush administration's isolation in the Security Council, at least on the surface. Underneath, however, the fissures remained. As soon as the resolution had passed, France, Germany, Russia, and Pakistan emphasized that it was still too flawed to spur contributions of troops or money beyond current levels of assistance. Their comments made it clear that they would have preferred a quick, time-limited transfer of responsibility from the United States to the Iraqi people. They had decided to vote in favor of the resolution not because they trusted the United States but because they did not want to be blamed for its failure.

All things considered, the pressure was now on the Americans to deliver. Not surprisingly, rifts had appeared within the Bush administration, to such a degree that the president found it necessary to assert that he alone was in charge of Iraq policy. The first challenge was a "donors conference" held in Madrid one week after the passage of Resolution 1511. In anticipation of that conference, the United States decided to make a further concession to the United Nations. It set up a new agency, to be run by the United Nations and the World Bank independent of the U.S.-led occupation, to administer some of the reconstruction assistance earmarked for Iraq. The hope was, of course, to attract more generous contributions from a larger number of donors.

In Madrid, seventy donors contributed a total of $13 billion. Roughly half of this sum, however, was pledged in loans rather than as outright grants. The total fell far short of the $55 billion that the United States and the World Bank had assessed as Iraq's needs through the year 2007. Even with the $20 billion pledged by the United States for reconstruction included in the total, $33 billion was still a disappointment. "Security is a problem, we don't deny it," Secretary of State Powell said at a news conference closing the donors' meeting. As if to bear out his words, guerrillas attacked Baghdad's biggest hotel and its International Red Cross headquarters two days later.

When moreover, in early November, insurgents shot down five helicopters killing 40 GIs and crashed a car bomb into the Italian headquarters in Nasiriya killing 19 Italian soldiers, the Bush Administration decided on a dramatic change in its policy. It would turn over sovereignty to an Iraqi provisional government by mid-2004 and postpone the controversial issues of drafting a constitution and the holding of national elections. The United States would maintain a military presence, not as an occupation force, but by "invitation from the Iraqi people."

Thus, a determined guerrilla force consisting of several thousand militants from both inside and outside Iraq had apparently taken its toll on the U.S.-led occupation. For the first time, the coalition began to prepare for an exit strategy after a "decent interval."

Predictably, this American "exit strategy" encountered major opposition, especially from Shi'ite leaders who demanded that nothing less than an election would be acceptable. Given the fact that Shi'ites constitute 60 percent of the Iraqi population, a national election would, in all probability, confer control over the country to a Shi'ite leader. "We're boxed in," said an administration official. "We have a highly difficult set of issues to deal with here. We can't just settle for anything that gets us out of Iraq."[25]

Al Qaeda, not to be outdone, managed to kill 55 Turkish civilians in two synagogues and two British sites in Istanbul, Turkey. Al Qaeda's objective, apparently, was to sever ties between the West and Turkey's Islamic society.

In early December, in a public acknowledgment of the urgent problems in Iraq, President Bush decided to appoint James A. Baker III as his personal envoy to explain the administration's exit strategy to skeptical nations in Europe and in the Arab world. In addition, the former secretary of state under George H. W. Bush was assigned the role of restructuring Iraq's huge debt of $120 billion, $40 billion of which was owed to France, Germany, Russia, and Japan and the bulk of the remaining $80 billion to Arab nations. Baker, who had assembled an impressive coalition under the UN's aegis to help the U.S. fight Saddam Hussein in the first Gulf War, was seen as the man best qualified to persuade UN members to "forgive or forget" large amounts of Iraq's indebtedness to them, and to facilitate an orderly exit for the United States by mid-2004.

Mr. Baker's assignment was rendered a great deal more difficult when Deputy Defense Secretary Paul Wolfowitz announced a decision approved by the President, that barred countries that had not supported the invasion, notably France, Germany, Russia, and Canada, from competing for $18.6 billion in prime reconstruction contracts in Iraq. The move was justified in terms of "essential security interests." Since the Wolfowitz memorandum appeared only a few hours before the President asked world leaders to receive Mr. Baker, the timing seemed particularly awkward.

Predictably enough, responses from the excluded nations were angry, to say the least. Russia declared that it would not agree to any debt write-off whatsoever for Iraq. France and Germany rejected the American decision as unacceptable and the European Union announced that it would demand an investigation into whether the American decision was compatible with the rules of the World Trade Organization. Canada expressed shock, given that it, alongside with France and Germany, had troops in Afghanistan and had already contributed substantially to the reconstruction of Iraq. The list of barred countries also included China at the very moment when that country's new prime minister had just concluded a visit to the White House. In a subsequent meeting with reporters, the President justified his decision with the argument that only those nations that had contributed militarily to the American effort in Iraq should reap the benefits of the $18.6 billion the Congress had approved for reconstruction. The fact that the excluded countries would have the right to bid on subcontracts did little to assuage their anger. In those capitals, the Americans were seen at best as clumsy, but at worst, as regarding Iraq as a spoil of war.

To state matters as objectively as possible, the Bush Administration's poor timing had reopened old wounds with countries at a time when it desperately needed their support in fashioning an exit strategy from Iraq.

While all this was going on, Iraqis were watching Afghanistan next door where, after tortuous discussions, a commission of lawyers and experts had drawn up a draft constitution to be placed before the Afghan people by the end of 2003. With the help of the United Nations, hundreds of thousands of questionnaires, written opinions, and cassettes recorded by illiterate people formed the basis of this draft which tried to achieve a balance between the Afghan peoples' yearning for an Islamic republic and their recognition of the need for democratic institutions. A *loya jorga,* or grand assembly of Afghanistan's many tribes, convened in late 2003 to engage in a national debate for the purpose of approving a final Afghan constitution. After difficult and often heated discussions, the grand assembly achieved a compromise by year's end. The new constitution would be based on a strong presidency, but would also provide checks and balances to protect the rights of the country's numerous ethnicities. Women were given equal rights with men. It was a hopeful beginning.

There was a terrible setback to these efforts, however, in two separate incidents. American air strikes killed 15 children by mistake in an area suspected of harboring Taliban fighters. As hundreds of delegates were arriving in Kabul for the constitutional grand assembly, President Karzai voiced his profound concern and promptly opened an investigation. The timing of this tragedy could not have been more unfortunate.

But then—after months and months of bad news in Iraq and steadily rising casualties inflicted on the Americans by the guerrillas—there was, at last, rejoicing. On December 13, Saddam Hussein was captured by American soldiers—alive.

The Capture of Saddam and Beyond

"Don't shoot," the bearded man said to the soldiers as he emerged from a hole in the ground next to a farmhouse near Tikrit. It was Saddam Hussein giving himself up without a shot even though he was armed with a pistol. In stark contrast to his two sons who had perished in a hail of bullets a few months earlier, their father had chosen to survive, even at the price of total humiliation at the hands of his American captors.

The first image the world had of the captured tyrant was that of a shaggy, haggard derelict undergoing a health check. An army doctor wearing rubber gloves was seen searching the hair of an apparent homeless man for lice and prodding open his mouth with a tongue depressor. Then viewers saw the pink flesh of the man's throat as the doctor scraped off a few cells for DNA identification.

In the world of Islam where pride and dignity were all-important, shame had taken a terrible toll. The man who had called himself the "Glorious Leader" and the "Direct Descendant of the Prophet" had become a prisoner. And yet, Saddam Hussein clearly preferred a life of shame to the death of martyrdom. This, I believe, and have always believed, has been the tyrant's core, his very essence: Survival.

Lt. Colonel Todd Megill, intelligence officer for the Fourth Infantry Division at Tikrit, pieced together a fascinating mosaic of Saddam Hussein as a fugitive during one of the most intensive manhunts in modern history. Saddam apparently depended on a kind of Iraqi "underground railroad" consisting of 25 to 30 people tied to him by a bond of blood and trust, all tribal men with secure positions on his extended family tree. They would shuttle him from one safe house to another among about 30 such hiding places. Saddam would rest at one of them for a few hours and then flee to the next, often dodging his pursuers by only a few hours. He was lavish in bestowing money he had stolen from the Bank of Iraq upon his numerous hosts as a reward for a short respite.

During his nine months as a fugitive, Saddam gave general guidance to his subordinates, according to Colonel Megill. "He would say, focus on this, focus on that; in this area, recruit, in that area, make trouble; or, I would like to see more attacks."[26] According to the Colonel, the 66-year-old Saddam had little difficulty reverting to a fugitive's life, something he knew well from his experience. As a 22-year-old youth, he had been part of a failed assassination attempt against Iraq's military ruler, Abdul Karim Kassem, and he claimed that he had to flee from his pursuers by swimming across the Tigris River. In an ironic twist, 44 years later, the aging fugitive was caught a few hundred yards from the riverbank where he came each year to mark the anniversary of his political legend with a choreographed swim.

But when his pursuers caught up with him, this time, there were no heroics. Saddam left a pistol and a Kalashnikov rifle lying in the bunker. He decided not to emulate his idol, Adolf Hitler, by committing suicide. Instead, he emerged from his hiding place, hands raised high, into the night.

Saddam Hussein was a monstrous dictator who caused the deaths of hundreds of thousands of his own people, fought a needless war with Iran, and invaded neighboring Kuwait inflicting untold misery on millions more. And even when he lost the first Gulf War, he survived as a ruler who lived to murder thousands of Kurds and Shi'ites. Through all of this, his grip on Iraq never weakened. Surviving his enemies *was* winning.

During the run-up to the war with the United States, Saddam gradually came to understand that "young Bush," unlike his father, was really out to get him. As this realization sank in, Saddam made more and more concessions to the UN inspectors, but to no avail. Bush simply wanted him gone. So far as weapons of mass destruction were concerned, he either had none or had destroyed them in a last effort to avert a war which, he now knew, he was bound to lose. And then, with time rapidly running out, he used an intermediary to make one last desperate offer which was rejected out of hand by the Americans.

When war did finally come, Saddam did not lead the charge against the enemy. He stole a billion dollars and went underground. The hole in the ground from which he was pulled on December 13 was within sight of one of his palaces that resembled vulgar hotels in Las Vegas. Instead of enjoying the luxuries of a Nero or a Caligula, he had suffered the company of rats and lice for many months. But he had come through it all alive and that was yet another victory. This was no martyr who worshipped death. This was a man who worshipped life—his own.

Saddam's capture conferred both tangible and intangible benefits on the U.S.-led coalition. First, of course, December 13, 2003 was the greatest morale booster since the outbreak of the war. Moreover, Saddam would have to stand trial as a war criminal, probably before Iraqi judges with UN assistance, to answer for his countless atrocities before the peoples of the world to bear witness.

Second, France, Germany and Russia not only congratulated the United States on its success but made commitments to President Bush's envoy, James A. Baker III, to help Iraq restructure its debt. Deep wounds that had fractured alliances in both NATO and in the United Nations had begun to heal.

Then, on December 19, President Bush and Britain's Prime Minister Tony Blair announced that Libya's leader, Colonel Muammar el-Qaddafi, had agreed to give up all of his nuclear, chemical, and biological weapons and to open his country to inspection. The President was quick to link this decision to the war in Iraq, suggesting that Qaddafi had decided to give up his weapons rather than face off against the United States and its allies.[27] Moreover, in a clear reference to Iran and North Korea, the President declared, "I hope other leaders find an example in Libya's action."

It is interesting to note, in this connection, that in February 2004, Dr. Abdul Qadeer Khan, the "father of Pakistan's nuclear bomb," confessed to President Musharraf that he had been selling nuclear weapons secrets to Libya, Iran, and North Korea for over three decades. This outrageous example of clandestine nuclear proliferation underlined the temptations that were available to leaders of rogue states who were determined to go nuclear. Early in his tenure as ruler of Libya, Qaddafi had apparently been among Dr. Khan's customers. It appears that the three members of Bush's "evil axis" had been offered illicit weapons by a person working under the very nose of his country's head of state, a man who had been helpful to the Americans in their war against Al Qaeda. Proliferation was indeed a tangled web. And, most important, while the past cannot be undone, what about the future? Libya might prove to be the exception. Unless the NPT is taken seriously at long last, Al Qaeda or other terrorist groups might still find men like Dr. Khan of Pakistan in other countries to sell them the means of mass destruction.

In January 2004, British and American weapons experts were given extensive access to dozens of Libya's military laboratories. CIA teams were permitted to visit several sites involved in nuclear programs. The experts were also allowed to view tens of tons of mustard gas that had been produced about a decade earlier. One of the most senior analysts said that this was the most extraordinary disclosure in his 30 years of doing this.[28]

While there is no doubt some truth to the President's linkage between the Libyan leader's decision, particularly its timing, to the war in Iraq, the facts suggest a far more complex pattern.

The tragedy of Pan Am Flight 103, which had been brought down by a Libyan bomb in 1988 over Lockerbie, Scotland, with a loss of 270 lives, was one of the most heinous acts in modern history and had made Qaddafi the terrorist most feared and despised by the United States. However, after narrowly escaping an American "decapitation" attempt, the Libyan leader began to turn away from state-sponsored terrorism and embarked on a gradual process of negotiating his reentry into the community of nations. In 1999, Qaddafi decided to turn over the two men accused of the crime to a Scottish court. This was followed by protracted negotiations over compensation for the families of the victims. In August 2003, Qaddafi's regime decided to pay the sum of $2.7 billion for distribution of $10 million to each of the aggrieved families. In addition, Libya admitted culpability for the Pan Am 103 disaster. In return, the UN Security Council decided to lift the sanctions it had imposed on Libya in 1988.

The above facts suggest that the Libyan leader's change of heart occurred years before the Iraqi war as a result of a deft combination of American and British diplomacy backed up by force, but well short of war and invasion.

This story raises some disturbing questions. If Libya could be contained after its overt act of aggression against an American airliner, why not Saddam Hussein who had never attacked the United States? If Qaddafi showed a capacity for change, possibly even for contrition, over a period of 15 years, why not an aging Saddam? We shall never know. What we do know is that a preemptive war imposed heavy burdens on the United States. Americans continued to die in Iraq even after Saddam's capture. Yet containment did work in the long run with the Soviet Union and, apparently, with the leader of Libya—a rogue state—who ultimately decided to abandon state terrorism for diplomacy.

Saddam will no doubt go down in history as an absolutely evil figure, especially after the "Mother of All War Crimes Trials" is done with him. Yet he did not pose an imminent threat to the United States when the President decided to go to war with him. Indeed, after his capture, the Americans discovered a directive by Saddam, issued to his supporters after his fall from power, in which he warned them not to join forces with other Arab insurgents. All along, his agenda had not been that of Al Qaeda's holy war against the West, but his own survival.

It was Osama bin Laden who had killed innocent civilians in New York and in Washington. Where was he now? No one seemed to know. It almost appeared that the effort that was expended on the war in Iraq and on dealing with the post-war guerrilla insurgency and hunting down Saddam had absorbed most of the energies of the Bush administration, the media, and the public. America's rage had shifted from bin Laden to Saddam, in an example of massively displaced aggression unparalleled in recent times. Only time and distance will unravel the remaining mysteries of this, one of the strangest chapters in American history.

On May 1, 2003, I joined the throng of people on the docks of San Diego to welcome home the USS *Abraham Lincoln* from its deployment to Iraq. The President, after landing on the warship by navy jet, declared that the war was over. The applause was loud and sustained. But then he added that he would bring the troops back home as soon as possible. This statement triggered deafening applause which would not stop. I believe that even the Bush administration, given the multitude of post-war problems, may shrink from taking the fateful step into another preventive war. I continue to believe that President Bush did not use war truly as a last resort. It was a war of choice and not of necessity. I also believe that it was a good thing that Saddam Hussein was gone. But the way it was done should stand as a warning, not as an inspiration.

Perhaps preemptive war is a "quick-fix" that provides the illusion of an easy victory. Containment demands patience and fortitude, and yet more patience. But it does *not* demand a "rendezvous with death" for young men and women on some distant battlefield.

NOTES

1. Bernard Lewis, *What Went Wrong?* (Oxford: Oxford University Press, 2002) *passim*.

2. John G. Stoessinger, *Crusaders and Pragmatists*, 2nd ed. (New York: W. W. Norton, 1985).

3. Alexander L. George, and Juliette L. George. *Woodrow Wilson and Colonel House: A Personality Study* (New York: John Day, 1956), p. 230.

4. Ibid., p. 295.

5. *New York Times*, June 7, 2003.

6. Dreyfuss, Robert, "Just the Beginning," *The American Prospect,* April 2003.

7. *New York Times,* February 1, 2003.

8. Ibid., March 18, 2003.

9. Ibid., April 10, 2003.

10. Ibid., April 12, 2003.

11. Ibid.

12. *New York Times,* June 2, 2003.

13. *New York Times,* July 13, 2003.

14. Thomas L. Friedman, "Bad Planning," *New York Times,* June 25, 2003.

15. *New York Times,* September 27, 2003.

16. *New York Times,* July 12, 2003.

17. *New York Times,* July 23, 2003.

18. *New York Times,* December 13, 2003.

19. Jessica Stern, "How America Created a Terrorist Haven," *New York Times,* August 20, 2003.

20. Sami Yousafzai and Ron Moreau, "Rumors of Bin Laden's Lair," *Newsweek,* September 8, 2003.

21. *Newsweek,* September 3, 2003.

22. *New York Times,* June 19, 2003.

23. Quoted by John Kifner, *New York Times,* July 20, 2003.

24. *New York Times,* September 24, 2003.

25. Ibid., November 29, 2003.

26. Ibid., December 21, 2003.
27. Ibid., December 20, 2003.
28. Ibid., December 21, 2003.

SELECTED BIBLIOGRAPHY

ACKERMAN, SPENCER, and JOHN B. JUDIS. "The First Casualty." *New Republic,* June 30, 2003.

ALMOND, GABRIEL A., R. SCOTT APPELBY, and EMMANUEL SIVAN. *Strong Religion: The Rise of Fundamentalisms Around the World.* Chicago and London: University of Chicago Press, 2003.

BENJAMIN, DANIEL, and STEVEN SIMON. *The Age of Sacred Terror.* New York: Random House, 2002.

BIDDLE, STEPHEN. "Afghanistan and the Future of Warfare." *Foreign Affairs,* March/April 2003.

BOOT, MAX. "The New American Way of War." *Foreign Affairs,* July/August 2003.

BYFORD, GRENVILLE. "The Wrong War." *Foreign Affairs,* July/August 2002.

CHUA, AMY. *World On Fire.* New York: Doubleday, 2003.

CORDESMAN, ANTHONY H. *Saudi Arabia Enters the Twenty-First Century: The Political, Foreign Policy, Economic, and Energy Dimensions.* London: Praeger, 2003.

EPOSITO, JOHN L. *Unholy War: Terror in the Name of Islam.* New York: Oxford University Press, 2002.

FELDMAN, NOAH. *After Jihad: America and the Struggle for Islamic Democracy.* New York: Farrar, Straus & Giroux, 2003.

FRUM, DAVID. *The Right Man.* New York: Random House, 2003.

GUNARATNA, ROHAN. *Inside Al Qaeda: Global Network of Terror.* New York: Columbia University Press, 2002.

HARRIS, NIGEL. *Thinking the Unthinkable: The Immigration Myth Exposed.* London: I. B. Tauris, 2002.

HIRSH, MICHAEL. *At War with Ourselves: Why America Is Squandering Its Chance to Build a Better World.* New York: Oxford University Press, 2003.

HIRSH, MICHAEL. "Bush and the World." *Foreign Affairs,* September/October 2002.

IKENBERRY, JOHN G. "America's Imperial Ambition." *Foreign Affairs,* September/October 2002.

KINZER, STEPHEN. *All the Shah's Men: An American Coup and the Roots of Middle East Terror.* Hoboken, N.J.: John Wiley & Sons, 2003.

LAQUEUR, WALTER. *First Century.* New York: Continuum, 2003.

LEWIS, BERNARD. *What Went Wrong?* New York: Oxford University Press, 2002.

MACKEY, SANDRA. *The Reckoning: Iraq and the Legacy of Saddam Hussein.* New York: W. W. Norton, 2002.

MURRAY, WILLIAMSON, and ROBERT H. SCALES JR. *The Iraq War.* Cambridge, Mass.: The Belknap Press / Harvard University Press, 2003.

NAKASH, YITZHAK. "The Shi'ites and the Future of Iraq." *Foreign Affairs,* July/August 2003.

NYE, JOSEPH S., JR. "U.S. Power and Strategy After Iraq." *Foreign Affairs,* July/August 2003.

PERKOVICH, GEORGE. "Bush's Nuclear Revolution." *Foreign Affairs,* March/April 2003.

PETERSON, PETER G. "Public Diplomacy and the War on Terrorism." *Foreign Affairs,* September/October 2002.

PICKERING, THOMAS R., and JAMES R. SCHLESINGER. *Iraq: The Day After.* New York: Council on Foreign Relations Press, 2003.

POLLACK, KENNETH M. "Securing the Gulf." *Foreign Affairs,* July/August 2003.

POLLACK, KENNETH M. *The Threatening Storm: The Case for Invading Iraq.* New York: Random House, 2002.

PRESTOWITZ, CLYDE. *Rogue Nation: American Unilateralism and the Failure of Good Intentions.* New York: Basic Books, 2003.

RIEFF, DAVID. "Blueprint for a Mess." *New York Times Magazine,* November 2, 2003.

ROTBERG, ROBERT I. "Failed States in a World of Terror." *Foreign Affairs,* July/August 2002.

ROULEAU, ERIC. "Trouble in the Kingdom." *Foreign Affairs,* July/August 2002.

ST. JOHN, ROBERT BRUCE. *Libya and the United States: Two Centuries of Strife.* Philadelphia: University of Pennsylvania Press, 2002.

STERBA, JAMES P., Ed. *Terrorism and International Justice.* New York: Oxford University Press, 2003.

STERN, JESSICA. *Terror in the Name of God: Why Religious Militants Kill.* New York: Ecco/HarperCollins, 2003.

STERN, JESSICA. "The Protean Enemy." *Foreign Affairs,* July/August 2003.

VIDAL, GORE. *Perpetual War for Perpetual Peace: How We Got to Be So Hated.* New York: Thunder's Mouth, 2002.

WOODWARD, BOB. *Bush at War.* New York: Simon & Schuster, 2003.

WRIGHT, SUSAN, Ed. *Biological Warfare and Disarmament: New Problems/New Perspectives.* Lanham, Md.: Rowman & Littlefield, 2002.

10

Why Nations Go to War

Even in our sleep
Pain that we cannot forget
Falls drop by drop upon the heart
Until in our own despair
Against our will
Comes Wisdom
Through the awful grace of God.

Aeschylus

"If you look too deeply into the abyss," said Nietzsche, "the abyss will look into you." The nature of war in our time is so terrible that the first temptation is to recoil. Who of us has not concluded that the entire spectacle of war has been the manifestation of organized insanity? Who has not been tempted to dismiss the efforts of those working for peace as futile Sisyphean labor? The face of war, Medusa-like with its relentless horror, threatens to destroy anyone who confronts it.

Yet we must find the courage to brave the abyss. I believe deeply that war is a sickness, though it may be humanity's "sickness unto death." No murderous epidemic has ever been conquered by avoiding exposure, pain, and danger, or by ignoring the bacilli. Human reason and courage have frequently prevailed, and even the plague was overcome; the Black Death that ravaged our planet centuries ago is today but a distant memory.

I know that the analogy between sickness and war is open to criticism. It has been fashionable to assert that war is not an illness but, like aggression, an ineradicable part of human nature. I challenge this assumption. Whereas aggression may be inherent, war is learned behavior and as such can be unlearned and ultimately selected out entirely. Humans have overcome other habits that previously had seemed unconquerable. For example, during the Ice Age, when people lived among small, isolated populations, incest was perfectly acceptable, whereas today incest is almost universally taboo. Cannibalism provides an even more dramatic case. Thousands of years ago, human beings ate one another and drank one another's blood. That, too, was part of "human nature." Little more than a century ago, millions of Americans believed that God had ordained white people to be free and black people to be slaves. Why else would He have created them in different colors? Yet slavery, once considered part of human nature, was abolished because human beings showed capacity for growth. Growth came slowly, after immense suffering, but it did come. Human nature had been changed. Like slavery and cannibalism, war too can be eliminated from humanity's arsenal of horrors.

It does appear, however, that people abandon their bad habits only when catastrophe is close at hand. Intellect alone is not enough. We must be shaken, almost shattered, before we change, just as a grave illness must pass its crisis before it is known whether the patient will live or die. Most appropriately, the ancient Chinese had two characters for crisis, one connoting danger and the other, opportunity. The danger of extinction is upon us, but so is the opportunity for a better life for all people on the planet. We must therefore find a way to confront Medusa and to diagnose the sickness. Diagnosis is no cure, but it is a necessary first step.

To begin with, the dawn of the twenty-first century coincided with two sea changes in the nature of war. First, September 11, 2001, demonstrated that nineteen fanatical terrorists armed with hijacked passenger planes could inflict serious damage on the world's only remaining superpower. In the wake of that horrible event, Al Qaeda cells, lurking in the shadows, have continued to target victims in countries all over the world, including Morocco, Indonesia, Kenya, Saudi Arabia, and Turkey. Twentieth-century wars, on the whole, had fairly clear-cut beginnings and endings. The war against terrorism, by contrast, has ignored national boundaries and will only end on some distant day when ordinary people, going about their daily business, lose their fear of another September 11.

The second sea change occurred when President George W. Bush decided to go to war with Saddam Hussein's Iraq by invoking the doctrine of preemption, or first strike. This decision flowed from the president's conviction that "to wait for America's foes to strike first

[was] not self-defense, it [was] suicide." In Osama bin Laden's case, the new doctrine made eminent sense, as it would be fatal to wait for a suicide bomber to complete his murderous mission. But in the case of Saddam Hussein, the doctrine was widely criticized because the Iraqi leader, despite his brutality toward his own people, did not pose a direct and imminent threat to the United States. Thus, Bush chose to overturn more than 200 years of American foreign policy on a dubious assumption. Be that as it may, the new century ushered in two new kinds of armed conflict: an apparently endless war against men and women who hated so passionately that they would welcome death to achieve their ends; and a preemptive war against an evil tyrant who murdered his own people and was perceived as a threat by a superpower intent on replacing him with a democratic government.

Let us now proceed to the major findings of my research for this book.

The Determinants of War

The first general theme that compels attention is that no nation that began a major war in the twentieth century emerged a winner. Austria-Hungary and Germany, which precipitated World War I, went down to ignominious defeat. Hitler's Germany was crushed into unconditional surrender. The North Korean attack was thwarted by collective action and ended in a draw. Although the Vietnam War ended in a Communist victory, it would be far too simple to blame the Communists exclusively for its beginning. The Arabs, who invaded the new Jewish state in 1948, lost territory to the Israelis in four successive wars. Pakistan, which sought to punish India through preemptive war, was dismembered in the process. Iraq, which invaded Iran in 1980 confident of a quick victory, had to settle for a costly stalemate eight years and half a million casualties later. And when Saddam provoked most of the world by invading Kuwait in 1990, he was expelled by UN forces. Slobodan Milosevic, whose henchmen "cleansed" much of Bosnia of Croats and Moslems in the pursuit of a Greater Serbia, was forced to give back most of his conquests. And his "final solution" for the Albanians in Kosovo was nullified by an aroused NATO, which was repelled by barbarisms similar to those of the Nazi era.

In all cases, those who began a war took a beating. Neither the nature nor the ideology of the government that began hostilities made any difference. Aggressors were defeated whether they were capitalists or Communists, white or nonwhite, Western or non-Western, rich or poor. In the nineteenth century, by contrast, most wars were won by the governments that started them: War was still a rational pursuit, fought for limited objectives. Only those who, like Napoleon, aspired to the big prize suffered ultimate defeat. Twentieth-century aggressors, on the other hand, tended to be more demanding and more ruthless: They fought for total stakes and hence made war a question of survival for their intended conquests. Those who were attacked had to fight for life itself, and courage born of desperation proved a formidable weapon. In the end, those who started the war were stemmed, turned back, and, in some cases, crushed completely. In no case did any nation that began a war achieve its ends.

It would be premature to draw any definitive conclusions about the two wars that have made the dawn of the new century a watershed. We do not have enough distance from the events in question. But some things can be said with certainty. First, none of us will ever be the same again after September 11, 2001. We now know that everything is possible, even the unthinkable. Even though there has not been another 9/11, there can be no real closure to that barbarous event as long as its perpetrator, Osama bin Laden, is alive or evades justice. In the meantime, the shadowy struggle against unseen enemies in every part of the globe must continue unabated.

It would also be too facile to assert that George W. Bush won his war against Saddam. To be sure, there was a swift military victory after three weeks. However, Saddam was missing, and marauding guerrilla bands still loyal to him had killed more American soldiers after the war than during the war itself. The oft-repeated statements made by the Bush administration that the war's outcome was not in doubt certainly did not reflect conditions three months after its official end, which Bush had declared on May 1, 2003, aboard the USS *Abraham Lincoln*. On July 3, a day when ten more American soldiers were wounded in three separate guerrilla attacks, the commander of allied forces in Iraq declared that "we're still at war" and the United States announced a reward of $25 million for the capture of Saddam Hussein or confirmation of his death, plus $15 million for each of his two sons. "Until we know for sure, their names will continue to cast a shadow of fear over this country," Paul Bremer, the American civil administrator of Iraq, declared.[1] When Saddam's two sons were killed in a fierce firefight by U.S. troops, their funerals were attended by Iraqis shouting anti-American slogans. And, at Fort Stewart, Georgia, a colonel had to be escorted out of a meeting with 800 angry wives who wanted their husbands to come home. In August, there was the disastrous attack on the headquarters of the United Nations in Baghdad claiming 21 lives including that of a top UN official. Moreover, November ushered in a quantum leap in violence when five U.S. helicopters were shot down, killing 55 GIs. Nineteen Italian soldiers, seven Spanish intelligence agents, and several Japanese and South Koreans were killed as well. The November total of coalition casualties approached the one-hundred mark.

As a result, the Bush administration adopted a somewhat hasty exit strategy: It decided to turn over sovereignty to an Iraqi provisional government by mid-2004 and postpone the drafting of a constitution and the holding of national elections to a later date. Moreover, the Americans embarked on tough new tactics including aerial bombardments, the erection of barriers, detentions, and razings that echoed Israel's antiguerrilla methods. As a result, some of the violence diminished in the targeted areas, but the apparent calm masked a seething fury. "I see no difference between us and the Palestinians," an Iraqi man complained while waiting to pass through an American checkpoint. "We didn't expect anything like this after Saddam fell."[2]

The steady escalation of insurgency attacks during the months of the "war after the war" clearly denied the Americans the victory they had announced with such confidence when Saddam's statue was toppled from its pedestal in Baghdad.

The capture of Saddam on December 13 by American soldiers was no doubt the best day for the United States since the outbreak of the war. The President who regarded Iraq as the central front against terrorism lauded the event as a major victory.

The facts suggest that Saddam's capture was a significant success, but by no means a decisive victory. In the first place, Americans continued to die in Iraq. Second, Iraq was *not* in fact at the center of the war on terrorism. Al Qaeda certainly had a presence there, but its most devastating attacks had occurred elsewhere: suicide bombings in Morocco in May, Indonesia in August, Saudi Arabia and Turkey in November. And bin Laden continued to threaten the United States itself with another major calamity, even more catastrophic than the one of September 11, 2001.

The lesson of all this was that, for America, the fundamental challenge continued to be the willingness and ability to fight terrorism on several fronts and not to be lulled into a false sense of security by a single success, impressive though it was, on the Iraqi front. In short, victory was likely to elude the Americans if they chose to concentrate on one battleground to the exclusion of others, equally dangerous.

Finally, and perhaps most important, it was impossible to determine what Iraq would look like in mid-2004 when the United States was planning to turn over sovereignty to the embattled country without first holding elections or drafting a constitution. Could democracy sink roots in such an uncertain political climate? If so, the Americans could justly claim victory. But such a prospect, by the close of 2003, seemed far-fetched, at best.

With regard to the problem of the outbreak of war, the case studies indicate the crucial importance of the personalities of leaders. I am less impressed by the role of abstract forces, such as nationalism, militarism, or alliance systems, which traditionally have been regarded as the causes of war. Nor does a single one of the ten cases examined here indicate that economic factors played a vital part in precipitating war. The personalities of leaders, on the other hand, have often been decisive. Conventional wisdom has blamed the alliance system for the outbreak of World War I and the spread of the war. Specifically, the argument runs, Kaiser Wilhelm's alliance with Austria dragged Germany into the war against the Allied powers. This analysis, however, totally ignores the part the Kaiser's personality played during the gathering crisis. Suppose Wilhelm had had the fortitude to continue in his role as mediator and restrain Austria-Hungary instead of engaging in paranoid delusions and accusing England of conspiring against Germany? The disaster might have been averted; conventional wisdom would then have praised the alliance system for saving the peace instead of blaming it for causing the war. In truth, the emotional balance or lack of balance of the German Kaiser turned out to be crucial. Similarly, the relentless mediocrity of the leading personalities on all sides no doubt contributed to the disaster.

If one looks at the outbreak of World War II, there is no doubt that the financial burden of the victors' peace terms at Versailles after World War I and the galloping inflation of the 1920s brought about the rise of Nazi Germany. But once again, it was the personality of Hitler that was decisive. A more rational leader would have consolidated his gains and certainly would not have attacked the Soviet Union. And if it had to be attacked, then a rational man would have made contingency plans to meet the Russian winter instead of anticipating a swift victory.

In the Korean War the hubris of General MacArthur probably prolonged the conflict by two years, and in Vietnam at least two American presidents, whose fragile egos would not allow them to face facts, first escalated the war quite disproportionately and then postponed its ending quite unreasonably. In the Middle East the volatile personality of Gamal Abdel Nasser was primarily responsible for the closing of the Gulf of Aqaba, the event that precipitated the Six Day War of 1967. In 1971 Yahya Khan, the leader of West Pakistan, took his country to war with India because he would not be cowed by a woman, Indira Gandhi. In 1980, and again in 1990, Saddam Hussein made a personal decision to begin a war. Around the same time, Slobodan Milosevic, driven by personal ambition to become the leader of a Greater Serbia, launched his expansionary moves into neighboring Croatia and Bosnia, and finally, disastrously for him, into Kosovo.

There is no doubt that Osama bin Laden's personality and his fanatical hatred of America inspired the nineteen terrorists who perpetrated the heinous deeds of September 11, 2001. If ever there was a quintessential fanatic, it certainly was the man who organized Al Qaeda in the wastelands of Afghanistan.

George W. Bush's road from Afghanistan to Iraq was paved by gradual steps toward the crusading end of the personality spectrum: First, his evangelical conversion predisposed him toward a Manichean, good-versus-evil world view; second, the influence of neoconservative intellectuals reinforced that world view; third, bin Laden's slipping from his grasp frustrated him; and lastly, Saddam Hussein's attempt to assassinate his father triggered a personal grudge. All of these factors culminated in a fixation on Saddam, until Bush was convinced his tyrannical and dangerous presence had to be removed, peacefully if possible but by force of arms if necessary.

In all these cases, a leader's personality was of critical importance and may, in fact, have spelled the difference between the outbreak of war and the maintenance of peace.

The case material reveals that perhaps the most important single precipitating factor in the outbreak of war is misperception. Such distortion may manifest itself in four different ways: in a leader's image of himself; in a leader's view of his adversary's character; in a leader's view of his adversary's intentions toward himself; and finally, in a leader's view of his adversary's capabilities and power. Each of these is important enough to merit separate and careful treatment.

1. There is remarkable consistency in the self-images of most national leaders on the brink of war. Each confidently expects victory after a brief and triumphant campaign. Doubt about the outcome is the voice of the enemy and therefore insupportable. This recurring optimism is not to be dismissed lightly by the historian as an ironic example of human folly. It assumes a powerful emotional momentum of its own and thus itself becomes one of the causes of war. Anything that fuels such optimism about a quick and decisive victory makes war more likely, and anything that dampens it facilitates peace.

This common belief in a short, decisive war is usually the overflow from a reservoir of self-delusions held by a leader about both himself and his nation. The Kaiser's appearance in shining armor in August 1914 and his promise to the German nation that its sons would be back home "before the leaves had fallen from the trees" was matched by similar expressions of military splendor and overconfidence in Austria-Hungary, Russia, and the other nations on the brink of war. Hitler's confidence in an early German victory over the Soviet Union was so unshakable that no winter uniforms were issued to the Wehrmacht's soldiers and no preparations whatsoever were made for the onset of the Russian winter. In November 1941, when the mud of autumn turned to ice and snow, the cold became the German soldier's bitterest enemy. Tormented by arctic temperatures, men died, machines broke down, and the quest for warmth all but eclipsed the quest for victory. Hitler's hopes and delusions about the German "master race" were shattered in the frozen wastes of the Soviet Union. The fact that Hitler had fought in World War I and had seen Germany's optimism crumble in defeat did not prevent its reappearance.

When North Korea invaded South Korea, its leadership expected victory within two months. The Anglo-French campaign at Suez in 1956 was spurred by the expectation of a swift victory. In Pakistan Yahya Khan hoped to teach Indira Gandhi a lesson modeled on the Six-Day War in Israel. In Vietnam every American escalation in the air or on the ground was an expression of the hope that a few more bombs, a few more troops, would bring decisive victory. Saddam Hussein expected a quick victory over Iran but got instead a bloody stalemate. Ten years later, he once again expected an easy triumph, this time over Kuwait, but instead provoked the world's wrath and took a severe beating. In Serbia, Slobodan Milosevic's belief that destiny had chosen him to be the leader of a Greater Serbia nourished his conviction that he was invincible. He did gain much ground early in the war, but later was forced to give it back even more quickly. Finally, the Americans were so confident of victory in Iraq that they failed to prepare adequately for postwar reconstruction. The resulting power vacuum invited a serious guerrilla war, which placed the Americans' early military victory very much in question. Saddam's capture after nine months on the run, encouraging though it was, did not, by itself, guarantee an early victory. Indeed, coalition casualties rose to even greater heights.

Leaders on all sides typically harbor self-delusions on the eve of war. Only war itself provides the stinging ice of reality and ultimately helps to restore a measure of perspective in the leadership, and the price for recapturing reality is high indeed. It is unlikely that there ever was a war that fulfilled the initial hopes and expectations of both sides.

2. Distorted views of the adversary's character also help to precipitate a conflict. As the pressure mounted in July 1914, the German Kaiser explosively admitted that he "hated the Slavs, even though one should not hate anyone." This hatred no doubt influenced his decision to vacate his role as mediator and to prepare for war. Similarly, his naïve trust in the honesty of the Austrian leaders prompted him to extend to them the blank-check guarantee that dragged him into war. In reality the Austrians were more deceitful than he thought and the Russians were more honest. Worst of all, the British leadership, which worked so desperately to avert a general war, was seen by Wilhelm as the center of a monstrous plot to encircle and destroy the German nation. Hitler, too, had no conception of what the Soviet Union really was like. He knew nothing of its history and believed that it was populated by subhuman barbarians who could be crushed with one decisive stroke and then made to serve as German supermen's slaves. This relentless hatred and ignorant contempt for the Soviet Union became a crucial factor in Hitler's ill-fated assault of 1941.

Perhaps the most important reason for the American military intervention in Vietnam was the American leadership's misreading of the nature of Communism in Asia. President Lyndon Johnson committed more than half a million combat troops to an Asian land war because he believed that Communism was still a monolithic octopus, with North Vietnam its tentacle. He did this more than a decade after the death of Stalin, at a time when Communism had splintered into numerous ideological and political fragments. His total ignorance of Asia in general, and of Vietnam in particular, made him perceive the Vietnam War in purely Western terms: a colossal shoot-out between the forces of Communism and those of anti-Communism. The fact that Ho Chi Minh saw Americans as successors of French imperialism—whom he was determined to drive out—was completely lost on Johnson. Virtue, righteousness, and justice, so Johnson thought, were fully on his side. America, the child of light, had to defeat the child of darkness in a twentieth-century crusade.

Mutual contempt and hatred also hastened the outbreak of the wars between the Arab states and Israel and between India and Pakistan. In the former case, the Arab view of Israel as an alien and hostile presence was a precipitating cause of conflict. In the latter, the two religions of Hinduism and Islam led directly to the creation of two hostile states that clashed in bloody conflict four times in half a century. Saddam Hussein's contempt for the Americans and his boast that he would annihilate them in the "mother of all battles" led straight to his defeat. Milosevic's distorted perception of the Turkish victory over the Serbs at Kosovo in 1389 prompted him to turn his fury against the Moslem Albanians in Kosovo six hundred years later. In January 2002, President Bush designated Iraq, Iran, and North Korea as members of an "evil axis." Iran and Iraq responded by fanning the fires of the Israeli-Palestinian conflict, and North Korea regarded Bush's statement as a declaration of war. Bush's primary target clearly was Saddam Hussein. Yet, while the Bush administration liked to compare him to Hitler and Stalin, the Iraqi dictator's reach was never global, unlike that of his two predecessors. Besides, the man who had precipitated 9/11 and murdered 3,000 civilians continued to remain at large. And, perhaps, Bush unwisely diverted resources from the real criminal, bin Laden, to Saddam.

3. When a leader on the brink of war believes that his adversary will attack him, the chances of war are fairly high. When both leaders share this perception about each other's intent, war

becomes a virtual certainty. The mechanism of the self-fulfilling prophecy is then set in motion. When leaders attribute evil designs to their adversaries, and they nurture these beliefs for long enough, they will eventually be proved right. The mobilization measures that preceded the outbreak of World War I were essentially defensive measures triggered by the fear of the other side's intent. The Russian czar mobilized because he feared an Austrian attack; the German Kaiser mobilized because he feared the Russian "steamroller." The nightmare of each then became a terrible reality. Stalin was so constrained by the Marxist tenet that capitalists would always lie that he disbelieved Churchill's accurate warnings about Hitler's murderous intent, and the Soviet Union almost lost the war. Eisenhower and Dulles were so thoroughly convinced that the Chinese would move against the French in Indochina, as they had against MacArthur's UN forces, that they committed the first American military advisers to Vietnam. The Chinese never intervened, but the Americans had begun their march along the road into the Vietnam quagmire. Arabs and Israelis generally expected nothing but the worst from one another, and these expectations often led to war. The Palestinians' conviction that Israel intended to hold on to the occupied territories forever precipitated two intifadas and countless suicide bombings that in turn prompted Israeli retaliatory attacks—a cycle of ferocity unprecedented even in that tortured region. And Milosevic's belief at Kosovo that the Albanians were out to oust the Serbs launched his subjugation of other ethnic groups in Yugoslavia, especially the Albanians.

It was in this area—a leader's view of his adversary's intention—that the Americans found the fundamental basis for going to war with Iraq. For the Bush administration, the invasion's core rationale was the suspected existence of hidden arsenals of weapons of mass destruction in Iraq, including chemical and biological agents and possibly even nuclear weapons that, if real, posed a direct and imminent danger to the United States. "I will disarm Saddam," the president declared repeatedly.

This perception persisted despite several reports from UN inspectors that struck a far more cautionary note. Finally, when Saddam began to destroy some of his conventional missiles, Bush changed his goal from disarmament to regime change. His fixation had solidified into a determination to rid the world of Saddam, no matter what.

After the war, when no weapons of mass destruction were found anywhere in Iraq, the Bush administration, despite accumulating evidence that it had selected only those intelligence reports that supported its view of Saddam and rejected all that cast doubt on Saddam's weapons caches, clung to its assumptions that "we will find them." Even when, in October 2003, six months after the end of the war, David Kay, the U.S.'s chief weapons inspector, informed Congress that no illicit weapons had been found, but suggested that the search be continued, the Bush administration requested $600 million to carry on the hunt for conclusive evidence. Yet, in January 2004, Mr. Kay, who had decided to retire, announced that he had concluded that Iraq did not possess any large stockpiles of illicit weapons at the start of the war in 2003. The UN inspectors, whose reports on weapons of mass destruction turned out, after the war, to be quite accurate, were belittled and denied access to postwar Iraq by the Americans.

Regarding the alleged ties between Saddam and bin Laden, when no definitive proof of any such link was ever found—when in fact it was emphatically denied by captured Al Qaeda operatives—the administration remained adamant that such a conspiracy had existed. It did finally admit that there was no evidence that Saddam had been involved in the attacks of 9/11. So far as the presence of Al Qaeda in Iraq was concerned, it became a self-fulfilling prophecy when that nation, during the U.S.-led occupation, became a magnet for terrorists.

There may be fine lines of distinction between a misperception, an exaggeration, and an outright lie. But it must be asserted that the decision to go to war is the most solemn one a president can make and therefore must be made on the basis of *all* the available evidence, not those parts only that fit the doctrine of a crusader. Yet, to persuade the American people to go to war on the basis of Saddam's evil character alone might not have been enough. The direct threat of lethal weapons had to be added to make the case convincing. It was here that truth might have become a casualty.

When it came to describing Saddam's weapons program, Bush never hedged before the war. "If we know Saddam has dangerous weapons today—and we do—does it make any sense for the world to wait to confront him as he grows even stronger and develops even more dangerous weapons?" Bush asked during a speech in Cincinnati in October 2002.[3] After the war, however, when no such weapons were actually found, the president shifted his emphasis from the immediacy of the threat to the assertion that, no matter what, the world was better off without Saddam Hussein in power. When pressed on the topic by Diane Sawyer of ABC News on December 16, with Saddam already in American custody, the President responded sharply: "So, what's the difference?" he asked rhetorically.[4]

The answer, I believe, is as follows: "With respect, Mr. President, more than 600 American casualties and more than 4,000 American wounded, numerous other coalition casualties, tens of thousands of Iraqi civilian casualties, and enormous sums of money that the United States can ill afford. That's the difference."

This point was underlined by Barton Gellman of the *Washington Post* on January 7, 2004. Based on numerous interviews with leading Iraqi scientists, he concluded: that Iraq's unconventional weapons arsenal existed "only on paper."

> Investigators have found no support for the two main fears expressed in London and Washington before the war that Iraq had a hidden arsenal of old weapons and built advanced programs for new ones. In public statements and unauthorized interviews, investigators said they have discovered no work on former germ-warfare agents such as anthrax bacteria, and no work on a new designer pathogen—combining pox virus and snake venom—that led U.S. scientists on a highly classified hunt for several months. The investigators assess that Iraq did not, as charged in London and Washington, resume production of its most lethal nerve agent, VX, or learn to make it last longer in storage. And they have found the former nuclear weapons program, described as a "grave and gathering danger" by President Bush and a "mortal threat" by Vice President Cheney, in much the same shattered state left by U.N. inspectors in the 1990s.[5]

4. A leader's misperception of his adversary's power is perhaps the quintessential cause of war. It is vital to remember, however, that it is not the actual distribution of power that precipitates a war; it is the way in which a leader thinks that power is distributed. A war will start when nations disagree over their perceived strength. The war itself then becomes a dispute over measurement. Reality is gradually restored as war itself cures war; the fighting will end when nations form a more realistic perception of each other's strength.

Germany and Austria-Hungary in 1914 had nothing but contempt for Russia's power. This disrespect was to cost them dearly.
Hitler repeated this mistake a generation later, and his misperception led straight to his destruction. One of the clearest examples of
this phenomenon took place in the Korean War. MacArthur, during
his advance through North Korea toward the Chinese border, stubbornly believed that the Chinese Communists did not have the capability to intervene. When the Chinese crossed the Yalu River into
North Korea, MacArthur clung to the belief that he was facing
40,000 men; the true figure was closer to 200,000. When the Chinese
forces temporarily withdrew after an initial engagement to assess
their impact on MacArthur's army, the American general assumed
that the Chinese were badly in need of rest after their encounter with
superior Western military might. When the Chinese attacked again
and drove MacArthur all the way back to South Korea, the leader of
the UN forces perceived this action as a "piece of treachery worse
even than Pearl Harbor." Most amazing about MacArthur's decisions is that the real facts were entirely available from his own intelligence sources, if only the general had cared to look at them. But he
thought he knew better and thus prolonged the war by two more
years. Only at war's end did the Americans gain respect for China's
power and take care not to provoke the Chinese again beyond the
point of no return.

Despite the lessons of Korea, in the Vietnam War the American
leadership committed precisely the same error vis-à-vis North Vietnam. Five successive presidents believed that Ho Chi Minh would
collapse if only a little more military pressure was brought to bear
on him, either from the air or on the ground. The North Vietnamese
leader proved them all mistaken, and only when America admitted
that North Vietnam could not be beaten did the war come to an end.
In both Korea and Vietnam the price of reality was high indeed. As
these wars resolved less and less, they tended to cost more and more
in blood and money. The number of dead on all sides bore mute testimony to the fact that America had to fight two of the most terrible
and divisive wars in her entire history before she gained respect for
the realities of power on the other side. In Pakistan, Yahya Khan
had to find out to his detriment that a woman for whom he had
nothing but disdain was better schooled in the art of war than he,
did not permit her wishes to dominate her thoughts, and was able
finally to dismember Pakistan. Only a quarter century later, when

both India and Pakistan went nuclear, did these two nations regard each other with respect and gradually develop their own regional balance of power. In 1948 the Arabs believed that an invasion by five Arab armies would quickly put an end to Israel. They were mistaken. But in 1973 Israel, encouraged to the point of hubris after three successful wars, viewed Arab power only with contempt and its own power as unassailable. That too was wrong, as Israel had to learn when, a decade later, Palestinian suicide bombers drove the Israelis to despair with a campaign of terror. In the Persian Gulf, the invading Iraqis were amazed at the "fanatical zeal" of the Iranians, whom they had underestimated. And in 1991 Saddam Hussein's belief that the Americans were too weak and cowardly to expel him from Kuwait led straight to his defeat. The Bosnian Serbs' contemptuous prediction that they would drown the Moslems and the Croats in the ocean came back to haunt them when they were put to flight by their intended victims. And, like Saddam before him, Milosevic's conviction that NATO was too passive and divided to intervene in the former Yugoslavia led directly to his own surrender in Kosovo.

Finally, the Americans underestimated Iraqi resistance in 2003, not during the war itself, but afterwards when, to their dismay, a tenacious guerrilla movement loyal to Saddam claimed a growing number of American lives. "Bring 'em on," Bush exclaimed in growing frustration, but the casualties kept rising nonetheless. This realization forced the allied military commander to admit that the war was not yet over, three months after the president had proclaimed victory from the flight deck of a warship. Indeed, the Americans admitted that they now had a classic guerrilla war on their hands, and that war included Al Qaeda.

In the case of North Korea, by contrast, Bush, despite his "loathing" for Kim Jong Il, had an accurate perception of North Korea's military capabilities.[6] Kim's nuclear weapons and his 1-million-man standing army no doubt helped deter the American president from a preemptive strike on North Korea à la Iraq. Thus, misperception hastens war, while recognition of reality tends to avert it.

Hence, on the eve of each war, at least one nation misperceives another's power. In that sense, the beginning of each war is an accident. The war itself then slowly, and in agony, reveals the true strength of each opponent. Peace is made when reality has won. The outbreak of war and the coming of peace are separated by a road that leads from misperception to reality. The most tragic aspect of this truth is that war itself has remained the best teacher of reality and thus has been the most effective cure for war.

Heart of Darkness

Ours is still a far from peaceful world. September 11, 2001, is embedded in the collective memory of our generation, and George W. Bush's war with Iraq will echo through history for decades. But there are other wars on a horrendous scale that threaten humanity's future and must not be ignored. As the year 2003 began, approximately fifty tribal, ethnic, or religious wars were underway around the world. Some of these, like the genocide of the Tutsi tribe in Rwanda, involved horrible massacres on an almost unimaginable scale. Others, like the Irish "Troubles," seemed to move toward resolution after decades of bloodshed. Still others, like the Chechnya rebellion and the uprising in East Timor, were suppressed with considerable brutality. Although none of these conflicts threatened the survival of humanity, the level of lawlessness involved in each situation seemed to be particularly high.

Of these several dozen conflicts, the genocide that took place in Rwanda in 1994 particularly warranted a chapter. Clearly, the violent death of almost 1 million people should not be ignored. Yet, during my research, I was confronted by a frustrating information gap. With the exception of a shattering report by American journalist Philip Gourevitch, *We Wish to Inform You That Tomorrow We Will Be Killed with Our Families,* and Alan J. Kuperman's article, "Rwanda in Retrospect," in *Foreign Affairs*'s January/February 2000 issue, there were few objective sources on which I could rely. Yet, the following truth had become clear: This was not a war between two hostile African tribes; it was the massacre of close to a million Tutsi in the spring of 1994 by Hutu extremists. In Kuperman's words, it was "the fastest genocide in recorded history," and it was genocide by stealth.[7]

Gourevitch's preface is worth quoting at length:

Decimation means the killing of every tenth person in a population, and in the spring and early summer of 1994, a program of massacres decimated the Republic of Rwanda. Although the killing was lowtech—

performed largely by machete—it was carried out at a dazzling speed: of an original population of about seven and a half million, at least eight hundred thousand people were killed in just a hundred days. Rwandans often speak of a million deaths, and they may be right. The dead of Rwanda accumulated at nearly three times the rate of Jewish dead during the Holocaust. It was the most efficient mass killing since the atomic bombings of Hiroshima and Nagasaki.[8]

The reason? More than a hundred years ago, German and then Belgian colonizers had elevated the Tutsi tribe to leadership positions in their colony, apparently because the Tutsi were taller and of lighter color than the Hutu. The genocide of 1994 was the Hutus' ultimate revenge after decades of Tutsi oppression. Tens of thousands of Tutsi were found with their hands and feet chopped off by machetes, the Hutus' way to "cut the tall people down to size."

By the time the Western world learned of the Rwandan disaster, most of the intended victims were dead. Neither President Clinton nor UN Secretary-General Boutros Boutros-Ghali was aware of the true dimensions of the slaughter. Both Kofi Annan, Boutros-Ghali's successor, and Clinton apologized in 1998 for their ignorance, if not their indifference.

It appears that by the millennium a consensus had been reached that international intervention was justified in cases of aggression by one country against another—as with Iraq in Kuwait—and in cases of genocide by dictators against their own peoples—like Milosevic in Kosovo. But this understanding is not all-encompassing. It does not as yet include the continent of Africa, which still seems to evoke Joseph Conrad's *Heart of Darkness* in Western minds. Perhaps it was this indifference that the Hutu counted on in the pursuit of their genocidal goals. Kuperman concludes that more UN forces deployed prior to the genocide could have deterred the killing.[9] But such a deployment would have presupposed a collective will, and it was precisely that will that was absent.

In December 2003, almost a decade after the massacre, a United Nations Tribunal in Arusha, Tanzania, convicted three Rwandans of genocide and crimes against humanity for using radio stations and newspapers to mobilize the Hutus against the Tutsis and to lure the victims to killing grounds where they were exterminated. The panel of three African judges, drawing a legal boundary between free speech and criminal incitement, meted out two life sentences and one twenty-seven-year prison sentence. "There is a wide range for free expression," the court declared, "but when you pour gasoline on the flames, that's when you cross the lines into unprotected expression." Prosecutors called the verdict an historic victory.[10]

In August 2003, however, there was another false start, this time by the United States. After several weeks of hesitation, President Bush intervened in a bloody civil war in Liberia, an African nation that had been founded by freed American slaves in 1847. He demanded that the president of the country, Charles Taylor, step down immediately. Taylor, who earlier had precipitated incendiary civil wars in neighboring Ivory Coast, Guinea, and Sierra Leone, had been indicted as a war criminal by an international court in Sierra Leone. The British had managed to restore a fragile peace in Sierra Leone and the French had done the same in Guinea and Ivory Coast. They now urged the United States to join a UN peacekeeping force that would try to restore order in America's former colony, as the British and French had done in theirs. The wars in West Africa had cost millions of lives, and worst of all, the warring tribes, especially in Sierra Leone, had used child soldiers to do their bidding, in yet another example of barbarism.

On August 1, 2003, the UN Security Council, meeting in emergency session, approved an American resolution for a UN peacekeeping force to quell the violence in Liberia. Despite this initiative, the Bush administration insisted that its troops be granted immunity from prosecution by any country other than their own while on duty in Liberia. In addition, the American peacekeepers were ordered to wait on warships off the African coast until Nigerian troops had arrived in the Liberian capital. These reservations prompted the president of Nigeria to compare the United States to a fire engine that had arrived but could not be put to use until the fire was out. Once again, American willingness to put even modest amounts of military might behind its principles seemed to evaporate where Africa was concerned, even though the local populations had begged for American intervention.

The lesson here is clear enough: As playwright Arthur Miller put it in *Death of a Salesman:* "Attention must be paid!" To be truly humanitarian, however, intervention against barbarism should be color-blind and should be organized by the United Nations as in the Arusha Trial, not undertaken by any one power unilaterally. Unless the international community, at long last, truly embraces Africa, hope itself may become genocide's ultimate victim.

As far as the nature of warfare is concerned, a fundamental change seems to be in the making. War *between* states seems to be giving way to war *within* states. This is clearly true of Chechnya, Kosovo, and Rwanda. As states have weakened and some, like the Soviet Union and Yugoslavia, have disappeared completely, this trend may well continue. But most unfortunately, intrastate war seems no less ferocious than interstate war, and is perhaps even more so. Wars between blood brothers, like the American Civil War, have always been savage. And, of course, there is the matter of international terrorism, where there is no end in sight.

Why does the human species learn so slowly and at such terrible cost? I keep wondering. What I do know is that, in the last analysis, the answer to war must be sought in humanity's capacity to learn from its self-inflicted catastrophes. Why did the Germans and the French make war between them well-nigh impossible after a century that had witnessed three horrendous wars and the Holocaust? Perhaps because Germany and France produced visionary postwar leaders like Konrad Adenauer and Jean Monnet, who said *No* to war once and for all. Why was Nelson Mandela able to prevent a bloody civil war in South Africa? Perhaps it is total exhaustion and despair that produces visionaries. And perhaps it is the same as with ordinary people, some of whom learn and grow from shattering experiences, while others just get older—and more stupid.

Learning from History

My concluding reflections concern the United States, the country that granted me refuge from Nazi, Soviet, Japanese, and Chinese dictatorships and that is now the world's only remaining superpower. It is also the leading democracy in a world where democracy has become the prevailing form of government. In my boyhood, it was tyranny. And yet, the United States, for the first time in its history, fought a war of choice, not of necessity. By going to war with Iraq in March 2003, it put into action a doctrine of preemption in order to remove a dictator and to attempt to turn his country into a democracy. By doing so, the American republic took a first step toward becoming an imperial power.

Top officials in the Bush administration actually convened a seminar on June 16, 2003, on the subject of "Rules and Tools for Running an Empire."[11] It is my hope that their readings for another such event would include Aeschylus's play *The Persians* and Paul Kennedy's *The Rise and Fall of the Great Powers*.

The Persians is the earliest surviving play in Western literature, written by Aeschylus in 479 B.C. The playwright had fought against Persia in the Battle of Marathon eleven years before. His play is an elegy for a fallen civilization and a warning to Greece lest it, too, be overtaken by imperial hubris. "Defeat is impossible, defeat is unthinkable," proclaims the hero, before disaster overtakes him. The message is clear: Through our own pride, we invite fate and nature to do their worst. The gods are not to blame.[12]

Paul Kennedy, in his exhaustive work, demonstrates how the great imperial powers in history declined and fell through "imperial overstretch," while nations that concentrated on their domestic economies grew and prospered. Rome, Britain, and the Soviet Union found themselves in the former category, with postwar Germany and Japan, as well as China, in the latter.

I believe that the United States presently stands at a fateful crossroads in its history. Empires in the past survived only so long as they understood that diplomacy backed by force was to be preferred to force alone. Once they succumbed to force alone, decline would swiftly follow. The Greeks taught the Romans to call this failure hubris. Perhaps it is not possible for a nation to be *both* a republic and an empire. I believe that democracy is best transmitted to other nations by example, not by war.

A word should be said here about the Americans' attitude toward the United Nations after the Iraq war. Only after the realization that the war's aftermath was costing more casualties than the war itself, did Bush decide to go back to the United Nations. Even then, there were no apologies for his earlier dismissive behavior—only requests for troops and funds, without a real quid pro quo of shared authority. The unanimous resolution authorizing a multinational force passed by the Security Council in October 2003 was largely symbolic and designed to end the perception of America's isolation. The reality was quite different. Some of the members who voted in favor of the resolution did so not out of sympathy for the United States, but out of fear that they would be blamed for America's ultimate failure if they were to oppose it or abstain. Despite its UN veneer, the predominantly Anglo-Saxon nature of the Iraqi occupation continued unabated. Indeed, American casualties continued in Iraq and Osama bin Laden released yet another audiotape urging Al Qaeda to carry on the struggle worldwide.

In retrospect, it probably would have been better had the president gone to war only with a clear UN mandate from the start, as Harry Truman had in Korea in 1950. At the very least, he could have been generous and swift in sharing power with the United Nations after the war, while there was still time. But crusaders, when they make mistakes, are usually unable to say three simple words: "I am sorry." What then often follows was described eloquently a very long time ago: "Pride goeth before a fall." One may hope that, with the Bush administration, a more forgiving cliché might apply: "Better late than never."

As the year 2003 drew to a close, there seemed little hope that the U.S.-led occupation of Iraq would be bolstered by large infusions of troops or money from other countries. Instead, the President ordered the Pentagon to supplement the 130,000 American troops in Iraq with tens of thousands of Iraqis who—after a few weeks of training—would be put on the front lines in areas where guerrilla attacks had been the fiercest. There was considerable debate about the wisdom of putting armed young Iraqis—around 18 or 19 years old—on the streets with only a few weeks of formal training, but the President decided that the risk was worth taking because troops drawn from the local population would be more likely to see an attack coming than the American troops.[13]

The American plan to turn over sovereignty to the Iraqis before they had completed work on a constitution and decided on the nature of elections seemed like a huge gamble that put at risk Bush's grander vision of Iraq as a "free and democratic society." What about Iraq, then, as a model for the rest of the Middle East? Besides, America's new "exit strategy" was instantly challenged by leading Shi'ite clerics, who demanded early national elections, for the reason, understandably enough, that Shi'ites made up the majority of the Iraqi population. A trap was threatening to close.

The Americans faced a turning point in Iraq not unlike the British who, after World War I, had tried to fuse together three disparate provinces of the defeated Ottoman Empire under a Sunni Arab monarchy. They failed in that attempt. One can only hope that their modern-day successors fare better in their own efforts to invent a new Iraq.

Shakespeare described the challenge well in *Julius Caesar:*

There is a tide in the affairs of men
Which, taken at the flood, leads on to fortune.
Omitted, all the voyage of our life
Is bound in shallows and in miseries.
On such a full tide are we now afloat
And we must take the current when it serves
Or lose our ventures.

I love my country and wish it well. But I also know that history does not take reservations. It does, however, reward respect.

Iraq, like Yugoslavia, became a united country only through overwhelming force imposed by a dictator, such as Tito or Saddam Hussein. Unity did not come any more naturally to the Croats, Serbs, and Moslems of Yugoslavia then it did for the Kurds, Sunnis, and Shi'ites of Iraq. Unity has never been a natural state for these countries. The Habsburgs of Austria knew this, as did the Ottoman Turks who ruled all three peoples of Iraq successfully for centuries— by ruling them *separately.*

History *does* provide us with clues for a successful exit strategy: First, encourage an autonomous Kurdistan in the north, an autonomous Shi'ite entity in the south, and an autonomous Sunni entity in the middle. Second, reassure the Sunnis by financing their access to oil in both the north and south. Supporting the Sunnis in this fashion would be far less painful and probably a lot cheaper than suffering even greater casualties at the hands of militant Sunni elements. Third, encourage democratic elections *within* each region, supervised by the United Nations. Perhaps, after the passage of some time, the three entities might be willing to agree on a loose confederation in which the parts would have greater power than the whole, a variant of the Indian constitution. If not, then the only remaining solution would be complete autonomy.

Even this formula might not work in the end, but it stands a far better chance for success than the present strategy. It respects the different ethnicities involved, and it respects their histories.

In January 2004, the American exit strategy was undermined when the leading Shi'ite cleric in Iraq, Grand Ayatollah Ali al-Sistani, reiterated his insistence on direct national elections instead of a complex caucus system advocated by the Americans. Adnan Pachachi, the president of Iraq's Governing Council, recommended the enlargement of that body into a legislative assembly as a possible compromise. Most important, however, since it appeared that the Ayatollah seemed receptive to the views of UN Secretary-General Kofi Annan, the Americans quickly decided that the time had come to ask the UN for help. This time they were more diplomatic than they had been before the war. After Saddam's capture, James Baker III had been busy cutting deals with France, Germany, Russia, and Canada to forgive the Iraqis large chunks of their debts in exchange for the right to bid on lucrative reconstruction contracts. The UN Secretary-General, realizing that there was no substitute for the UN's vast experience in nation-building, overcame serious misgivings and decided to deploy a team of specialists to Iraq in order to forge a consensus among the quarreling factions despite the continuing violence in that country.

Thus, the UN and the U.S. had changed roles. The U.S., at long last, realized its need for the UN, but the latter, while willing to be helpful, had become wary of the Americans. Most important, however, a national election would not resolve the problem, but merely change its complexion. It would be welcomed by the Shi'ites, but might inflame both Kurds and Sunnis who made up the remaining 40 percent of Iraq's population. Hence, the confederation formula outlined earlier might still remain the course of last resort.

A related fallacy of the Bush administration's policy has been its assumption that the road to a Middle Eastern peace would lead through Baghdad. The facts seem to point in a different direction. After all, the United States did unseat one Moslem leader but, thus far, has failed to secure a state for the Palestinians. Indeed, as the Arab population of Israel and its occupied territories approaches parity with its Jewish population, demography has turned that 50-year conflict into a ticking time bomb. Unless the United States, at long last, invests its full power and prestige in pressing for a resolution to that desperate struggle, it may well be that the insurgents in Iraq might gather momentum and join with the Palestinians in a kind of "struggle for national liberation" against a "neo-colonial" America and its ally, Israel. This, in turn, could bear the seeds of a "clash of civilizations" between the Western and the Moslem worlds with the potential of an apocalyptic confrontation. Once again, a policy-maker who ignores history does so at his peril.

If we are to seek understanding from history's vast tapestry, we must also pay attention to its "might-have-beens." These "might-have-beens" are not just ghostly echoes; in some instances, they are *objective possibilities* that were missed—most of the time, for want of a *free intelligence* prepared to explore alternatives. Hence, it is our responsibility not to ignore these "ifs" and "might-have-beens" for they *could* have been.

If George W. Bush had gone to the UN Security Council shortly after the 9/11 attacks when most of the world supported the United States, he could easily have gained approval for a UN police action to seek out and arrest Osama bin Laden as a war criminal. After all, bin Laden had proudly claimed responsibility on videotape for his deed. It is difficult to believe that a sharply focused UN police action, under an American commander and with the support of President Musharraf of Pakistan, would not have been successful in ferreting out bin Laden, even in the formidable terrain of the Pakistan-Afghanistan border. The UN could have brought to justice a criminal who had killed 3,000 innocent civilians from more than 80 of its member states. This would have done much to end the interminable debates on terrorism in the United Nations. Like with pornography, you know it when you see it. Bin Laden could have joined Milosevic in The Hague on charges of mass murder and, if he had been killed, few would have grieved for him at that early date. International law would have been greatly strengthened, there would have been no wide rifts in the UN and in NATO and, in all probability, there would have been no war with Iraq. Most likely, American, and quite possibly, world history, would have taken a more benign turn. *It seems that the most tragic "ifs" and "might-have-beens" of history tend to apply more to crusaders than to pragmatists.*

Yet another tragic "might-have-been" has echoed down the corridors of time. It concerns an earlier crusader, John Foster Dulles, U.S. Secretary of State under President Dwight D. Eisenhower. Dulles, a stern Puritan, had scoffed at the containment policy and had advocated a new policy of "rollback" and "liberation" of Eastern Europe from the Soviet Union.

During the Geneva Conference of 1954, which marked the exit of France from Indochina, Chou En-lai, Communist China's Foreign Minister, quite by accident, ran into Dulles in one of the corridors of Geneva's Palais des Nations. The Chinese statesman stretched out his hand to Dulles in a gesture of reconciliation, but the American put his hands behind his back and walked away. A good Puritan would have no commerce with the Devil. It is tempting to speculate about the repercussions of this episode. What if Dulles had responded? Might the Vietnam War have been avoided? We shall never know. But one is forced to wonder, especially when one contemplates the 58,000 American deaths and the one million Vietnamese deaths that were to follow.

One final warning: How often have we heard that a particular war was "inevitable?" In my research, I have come across this phrase dozens of times since the "iron dice" of World War I. Crusaders are particularly fond of making such assertions. In truth, *no* event in the affairs of states has *ever* been inevitable. History does not make history. Men and women make foreign policy decisions. They make them in wisdom and in folly, but they make them nonetheless. Often, after a war, historians look back and speak of fate or inevitability. But such historical determinism becomes merely a metaphor for evasion of responsibility. There is, after all, in our lives, a measure of free will and self-determination.

One such case in point is deeply troubling. In November 2003, it was revealed that Imad Hage, a Lebanese-American businessman, had been sent by the chief of Saddam's intelligence services to contact the Bush Administration, during the final days of its rush to war, with three major concessions:[14] First, Baghdad was prepared to invite 2,000 FBI agents in addition to American weapons experts to Iraq in order to prove that there were no hidden weapons of mass destruction; second, the regime would pledge to hold elections under UN supervision; and third, Iraq would extradite to the Americans a leading suspect in the 1993 bombing of the World Trade Center.

At the time this offer was made, the Bush Administration's preparations for war were complete. There was no turning back; war was seen as inevitable. The point here is not that a deal might have been reached; it is that the United States rejected the offer out of hand and thereby *made* the war inevitable. Now we shall never know and *that,* given the lives that are being lost, is a tragedy.

In his testimony before Congress on January 28, 2004, David Kay, who had served as chief U.S. weapons inspector in Iraq over a nine-month period since the end of the war, declared simply, "We were all wrong, probably in my judgment, and that is most disturbing."[15] He did add, however, that there had been no political pressure exerted by the Bush administration on intelligence analysts to exaggerate the threat from Saddam's Iraq. In short, the books were wrong, he believed, but they weren't "cooked."

What is clear in the end, is the *absolute certainty* with which all members of the Bush administration justified the war on the basis of the alleged existence of large stockpiles of illicit weapons in Iraq, when, in fact, there was plenty of room for doubt. Moreover, the administration refused to grant a little more time to the UN inspectors who, as it turned out, had done a creditable job in disposing of Iraq's illegal weapons.

Finally, Dr. Kay declared in his testimony that it was "important to acknowledge failure." I believe that people learn more from failure than from success—if one keeps an open mind. But it is precisely *that* which a crusader finds almost impossible to do.

Responding to mounting pressures from the Congress, including members of his own party, to set up an independent commission to investigate the intelligence controversy precipitated by Dr. Kay, President Bush agreed. He did so, however, with the proviso that the commission's findings would not be announced until March 2005, that is, after the presidential election of November 2004. He also reasserted that America had done "the right thing in Iraq" to remove Saddam Hussein from power by force of arms.

In their efforts to find out what really happened, the commission *and* the President might bear in mind a simple human truth: We are more likely to "know" what we *want* to know than what we don't want to know.

Let there be no misunderstanding about this: Saddam was, and remains to this day, a murderous thug who demonstrated once again, when he meekly surrendered to American soldiers, that his highest priority was his own survival. But, as I have attempted to show in this and in the preceding chapter, he posed *no* imminent threat to the United States when President George W. Bush decided to go to war with him. *I believe that Saddam Hussein was not worth the loss of a single allied soldier's life nor that of a single innocent Iraqi civilian. I believe that he could have been brought down without a war.*

As the reader may recall, during the final days of diplomacy in March 2003 I had approached the UN delegation of Pakistan with a proposal for the UN Security Council to designate Saddam Hussein as a War Criminal while also quadrupling the number of UN inspectors in an effort to speed up the inspection process. The Pakistanis were prepared to sponsor this resolution on March 17, but that very afternoon the President announced that the time for diplomacy had expired. Two days later the United States was at war.

From my experience with the United Nations for which I worked for seven years, I believe that this resolution would have been passed by the Security Council as an acceptable alternative to an invasion of Iraq which had deadlocked the Council. Moreover, the United States could have avoided the breach which it confronted with its NATO allies and with the United Nations.

The precedent of Slobodan Milosevic is instructive here. He was indicted by the then Chief Prosecutor of the International War Crimes Tribunal, Louise Arbour, for war crimes and crimes against humanity in May 1999 when he was still in power as president of Yugoslavia. Two years later he had gone from power to prison as a defendant in The Hague. In short, he had become a pariah before the world. The massing of a quarter million of American and British troops around Iraq, combined with more vigorous UN inspections might well have led Saddam to propose much earlier the desperate measures which he *did in fact* propose several days before the war broke out. And his new role as an international pariah would probably have motivated the survivor in him to act while there was still time. At the very least, he could have been defanged, and, at best, deposed without a war.

The cliché is wrong: History does *not* repeat itself, at least not exactly. But it *does* teach us through analogy. I believe that, when this alternative was overlooked, yet another precious opportunity to save lives was lost.

I should like to conclude on a note of hope. Since the last edition of this book appeared, there has been a slow dawning of compassion and of global consciousness over humanity's bleak horizons. This is true despite, or perhaps even because of, the catastrophe of 9/11. Increasingly, war criminals are being held individually accountable for their actions before international tribunals. Slobodan Milosevic, a former head of state, is facing trial on charges of genocide before a newly formed International Criminal Court in the Hague. And in December 2003, in a landmark decision half a world away, in Arusha, Tanzania, a UN War Crimes Tribunal convicted three Rwandans for genocide against the Tutsi tribe and handed down stiff prison sentences. These are hopeful signs.

There *is* progress though it is maddeningly slow. Yet, I must remain an optimist. If I were not, I probably would not be alive today, as the epilogue to this book makes clear. Humanity has built *both* cathedrals and concentration camps. Though we have descended to unprecedented depths in our time, we have also tried to scale new heights. We are not burdened with original sin alone; we also have the gift of original innocence.

Finally, I ask my readers' indulgence to permit me to close with my favorite poem. It was written by William Ernest Henley a century and a half ago in England and expresses the need to transcend despair and tragedy with courage and with hope—qualities which this generation too must live by if we are to live meaningful and caring lives in a world still beset by war.

Invictus

Out of the night that covers me,
Black as the Pit from pole to pole,
I thank whatever gods may be
For my unconquerable soul.

In the fell clutch of circumstance
I have not winced nor cried aloud.
Under the bludgeonings of chance
My head is bloody, but unbowed.

Beyond this place of wrath and tears
Looms but the Horror of the shade,
And yet the menace of the years
Finds, and shall find, me unafraid.

It matters not how strait the gait,
How charged with punishments the scroll,
I am the master of my fate:
I am the captain of my soul.

NOTES

1. *New York Times,* July 4, 2003.
2. Ibid., December 7, 2003.
3. Ibid., December 18, 2003.
4. Ibid.
5. *Washington Post,* January 7, 2004.
6. Bob Woodward, *Bush at War* (New York: Simon & Schuster, 2002), p. 340.

7. Alan J. Kuperman, "Rwanda in Retrospect," *Foreign Affairs* (January/February 2000), p. 98.

8. Philip Gourevitch, *We Wish to Inform You That Tomorrow We Will Be Killed with Our Families* (New York: Farrar, Straus & Giroux, 1998).

9. Kuperman, "Rwanda in Retrospect," p. 115.

10. *New York Times,* December 4, 2003.

11. "Philosophers and Kings," *The Economist,* June 21, 2003.

12. Margaret Jefferson, "Empire and the Pride before a Fall." Review of *The Persians, New York Times,* June 11, 2003.

13. *New York Times,* October 30, 2003.

14. Ibid., November 6, 2003.

15. Ibid., January 29, 2004.

SELECTED BIBLIOGRAPHY

BACEVICH, ANDREW J. *American Empire: The Realities and Consequences of U.S. Diplomacy.* Cambridge: Harvard University Press, 2002.

BEIGBEDER, YVES. *Judging War Criminals: The Politics of International Justice.* New York: St. Martin's, 1999.

BERKOWITZ, BRUCE. *The New Face of War: How War Will Be Fought in the 21st Century.* New York: Free Press, 2003.

BIALER, SEWERYN. "The Death of Soviet Communism." *Foreign Affairs,* Winter 1991/1992.

BLAINEY, GEOFFREY. *The Causes of War.* New York: Free Press, 1973.

BOOT, MAX. *The Savage Wars of Peace: Small Wars and the Rise of American Power.* New York: Basic Books, 2002.

BROKAW, TOM. *The Greatest Generation.* New York: Random House, 1998.

BROOKS, STEPHEN G., and WILLIAM C. WOHLFORTH. "American Primacy in Perspective." *Foreign Affairs,* July/August 2002.

BRZEZINSKI, ZBIGNIEW. "Post-Communist Nationalism." *Foreign Affairs,* Winter 1989/1990.

CLAUSEWITZ, KARL VON. *On War.* New York: Modern Library, 1943.

COHEN, ELIOT A. *Supreme Command: Soldiers, Statesmen, and Leadership in Wartime.* New York: Free Press, 2002.

COLLEY, LINDA. *Captives: Britain, Empire, and the World, 1600–1800.* New York: Pantheon, 2003.

DAWISHA, ADEED, and KAREN DAWISHA. "How to Build a Democratic Iraq." *Foreign Affairs,* May/June 2003.

DYSON, FREEMAN. *Weapons and Hope.* New York: Harper & Row, 1984.

EBERSTADT, NICHOLAS. "The Future of AIDS." *Foreign Affairs,* November/December 2002.

FERGUSON, NIALL. *Empire: The Rise and Demise of the British World Order and Its Lessons for Global Power.* New York: Basic Books, 2003.

FUKUYAMA, FRANCIS. *Our Posthuman Future.* New York: Farrar, Straus & Giroux, 2002.

GLENNON, MICHAEL J. "Why the Security Council Failed." *Foreign Affairs,* May/June 2003.

GORBACHEV, MIKHAIL. *The August Coup.* New York: Harper & Row, 1991.

GORBACHEV, MIKHAIL, and ZDENEK MLYNAR. *Conversations with Gorbachev: On Perestroika, the Prague Spring, and the Crossroads of Socialism.* New York: Columbia University Press, 2002.

GOUREVITCH, PHILIP. *We Wish to Inform You That Tomorrow We Will Be Killed with Our Families.* New York: Farrar, Straus & Giroux, 1998.

GRAHAM JR., THOMAS. *Disarmament Sketches: Three Decades of Arms Control and International Law.* Seattle: University of Washington Press, 2002.

HAMBURG, DAVID A. *No More Killing Fields: Preventing Deadly Conflict.* Lanham: Rowman & Littlefield, 2002.

HANNIGAN, ROBERT E. *The New World Power: American Foreign Policy, 1898–1917.* Philadelphia: University of Pennsylvania Press, 2002.

HEDGES, CHRIS. *War Is a Force That Gives Us Meaning.* New York: PublicAffairs, 2002.

HEDGES, CHRIS. *What Every Person Should Know About War.* New York: Free Press, 2003.

HOUGH, JERRY. *Russia and the West.* New York: Simon and Schuster, 1988.

Human Development Report 2002. United Nations Development Program. New York: Oxford University Press, 2002.

IGNATIEFF, MICHAEL. *The Warrior's Honor: Ethnic War and the Modern Conscience.* New York: Holt, 1998.

IRIYE, AKIRA. *Global Community: The Role of International Organizations in the Making of the Contemporary World.* Berkeley: University of California Press, 2002.

KAGAN, DONALD. *On the Origins of War and the Preservation of Peace.* New York: Doubleday, 1995.

KAGAN, DONALD. *The Peloponnesian War.* New York: Viking, 2003.

KAGAN, ROBERT. *Of Paradise and Power: America and Europe in the New World Order.* New York: Alfred A. Knopf, 2003.

KAHN, HERMAN. *On Thermonuclear War.* Princeton: Princeton University Press, 1960.

KENNAN, GEORGE F. "Communism in Russian History." *Foreign Affairs,* Winter 1990/91.

KENNEDY, PAUL. *The Rise and Fall of the Great Powers.* New York: Random House, 1987.

KISSINGER, HENRY. *White House Years.* Boston: Little, Brown, 1979.

KUPCHAN, CHARLES. *The End of the American Era: U.S. Foreign Policy After the Cold War.* New York: Alfred Knopf, 2002.

KUPERMAN, ALAN J. "Rwanda in Retrospect." *Foreign Affairs,* January/February 2000.

LIEVEN, ANATOLE. *Chechnya: Tombstone of Russian Power.* New Haven: Yale University Press, 1998.

MALONE, DAVID M., and YUEN FOONG KHONG, Eds. *Unilateralism and U.S. Foreign Policy: International Perspectives.* Boulder: Lynne Rienner, 2003.

MANDELBAUM, MICHAEL. *The Ideas That Conquered the World: Peace, Democracy, and Free Markets in the Twenty-First Century.* New York: PublicAffairs, 2002.

MILWARD, ALAN, Ed. *The Rise and Fall of a National Strategy, 1945–63.* Portland: Frank Cass, 2002.

MOLAVI, AFSHIN. *Persian Pilgrimages: Journeys Across Iran.* New York: W. W. Norton, 2002.

ODOM, WILLIAM E. *Fixing Intelligence: For a More Secure America.* New Haven: Yale University Press, 2003.

SCHELL, JONATHAN. *The Fate of the Earth.* New York: Knopf, 1982.

SCHELLING, THOMAS C. *Arms and Influence.* New Haven: Yale University Press, 1966.

SCHRAM, MARTIN. *Avoiding Armageddon.* New York: Basic Books, 2003.

SHEVTSOVA, LILIA. *Putin's Russia.* Washington: Carnegie Endowment for International Peace, 2003.

STIGLITZ, JOSEPH. *Globalization and Its Discontents.* New York: W. W. Norton, 1992.

TALBOTT, STROBE. "From Prague to Baghdad." *Foreign Affairs,* November/December 2002.

TAUBMAN, WILLIAM. *Khrushchev: The Man and His Era.* New York: W. W. Norton, 2003.

WALZER, MICHAEL. *Just and Unjust Wars.* New York: Basic Books, 1977.

VAN EVERA, STEPHEN. *Causes of War: Power and the Roots of International Conflict.* Ithaca, N.Y.: Cornell University Press, 1999.

WRIGHT, QUINCEY. *A Study of War.* Chicago: University of Chicago Press, 1942.

Epilogue

A few weeks before an earthquake devastated Kobe, I was in the Japanese port city as the keynote speaker to the World Congress of Junior Chamber International. The Jaycees were celebrating their fiftieth anniversary year. It was a festive event with a huge gathering of delegates from every continent.

I was seated on the stage about to be introduced by the JCI's world president, a charming man from the island nation of Mauritius. As I looked over my audience, I noticed a large group of Japanese VIPs in the gallery. They stood out from the glittering assemblage by their dark, solemn-looking suits. A sudden flash of memory came back to me. I had been in Kobe before, under very different circumstances. It was in April 1941 and I was then a boy of thirteen, en route from Prague, Czechoslovakia, to Shanghai, China, fleeing for my life from the Nazi Holocaust.

The story of my family was not unusual for those unusual times. I was growing up in Vienna, Austria, in a middle-class Jewish family when Hitler annexed Austria in 1938.

My parents divorced when my father emigrated to Palestine, where my mother refused to follow him. She did not want to leave her parents behind in Prague. She and my grandparents were convinced that matters would not get worse for the Jews; hence my mother and I moved to Prague to join them.

Shortly after Hitler entered Prague in 1939, my mother learned that my father had died in Palestine, and a year later, lonely and frightened, she remarried. By late 1940, terrible fights erupted between my stepfather and my grandparents, with my mother caught in the middle. My stepfather, who seemed to understand Hitler, insisted upon leaving Europe immediately.

"You are an adventurer," my grandparents shouted. "This is, after all, the twentieth century. It can't get any worse."

However, the evidence to the contrary was mounting steadily. Hitler had conquered most of Western Europe and the war against the Jews was beginning in earnest. By January 1941, my stepfather dragged my mother and me to dozens of consulates in Prague, begging for visas.

Finally, an official at the Chinese Embassy, in a gesture of compassion, granted us a visa to Shanghai in exchange for "landing money," which cost us most of our belongings. This visa, however, was useless unless we could procure a transit visa across the Soviet Union, and that, in turn, was unavailable unless we could prove that we could leave the Soviet Union and somehow get to Shanghai. This meant yet another transit visa, this time via Japan.

But it was well known in the Prague Jewish community that the Japanese were sympathetic to the Germans and therefore reluctant to help the Jews. Thus without this indispensable Japanese link in the chain of flight, the Shanghai visa was worthless. In February 1941, however, long lines suddenly formed in front of the Japanese Consulate in Prague. The news had spread like wildfire that a new consul was issuing Japanese transit visas via Kobe to hundreds of desperate Jews.

After several days in line, we were ushered into the office of an elegant, kindly looking man who, after patting me on the head, issued us three visas without the slightest difficulty. "Good luck," he said to us in German as the next applicants were already being ushered in. Three days later, my stepfather procured the transit visa across the Soviet Union, the final link in the chain. Departure date was set for March 4, 1941, my mother's birthday.

Pain has etched the memory of that night into my mind forever. My grandparents had come to the station to say goodbye. We were taking the train to Moscow, where we were to connect to the Trans-Siberian "Express" to Vladivostok on the Soviet Pacific coast. My mother was frantic with grief, my stepfather icy and determined. The train was to leave at 8 P.M.

"I don't want to go, I want to stay with you," I screamed, leaping from the train into my grandparents' arms.

"No," my grandfather admonished. "You must go."

He gently lifted me back onto the train, and a few minutes later the train left the station. My grandparents waved a flashlight, the light flickering up and down in the darkness. Up and down. A few weeks later, they were deported to Theresienstadt, the way station to Auschwitz, where they perished in 1944.

The journey through Siberia seemed endless. Most of the time, I stared out at the vast expanses of the Russian landscape, infinitely patient in its snow-covered silence. We shared a compartment with a Japanese diplomat who introduced himself as Dr. Ryoichi Manabe. He was being transferred from Berlin to Shanghai to a new diplomatic post, he explained to us in fluent German. He seemed quite young, perhaps in his early thirties, and had a courtly, gentle manner about him.

We shared our meals with him and I played chess with him occasionally. After the first week of the long journey, my mother mentioned to him that we too were headed for Shanghai, as refugees. After all, the Japanese consul in Prague had helped us, and she saw no reason to fear this nice young man, so well versed in German literature. Before we parted, he handed us his card and invited my mother, quite matter-of-factly, to call him in Shanghai if we should ever need his help.

We then crossed on a small fishing vessel from Vladivostok to Kobe, Japan, where we were allowed to await passage to Shanghai. The three weeks of waiting were tinged with trepidation since we knew absolutely no one in Shanghai. Finally, we were able to book passage and arrived in the Chinese port city in April 1941.

My stepfather, a resourceful man, was able to land a job as a teller in a small bank in the international settlement. My mother developed a talent for millinery, and I was enrolled in a British public school with excellent teachers who thrived on Shakespeare. We lived in two little rooms in the French concession of the city, and my mother prepared modest Chinese culinary miracles. Things were looking up. But this brief interlude came to an abrupt end.

In June 1941 Hitler invaded the Soviet Union, and in December the Japanese, in another surprise assault, attacked Pearl Harbor. Germany and Japan were now military allies in a war for world domination. Not surprisingly, the Germans now instructed the Japanese what to do with the Jews under their control.

There were approximately 15,000 European Jews living in Shanghai at the time of Pearl Harbor. In early 1943 all Jews were ordered to move into a ghetto in Hongkew, an impoverished and neglected section of the city. Within a few weeks, most of Shanghai's Jews were herded into large, overcrowded communal centers, or tiny, equally overcrowded dwelling places. Food was scarce, sanitation terrible, and education for the ghetto children sporadic and disorganized at best. The ghetto was placed under the direct control of the Japanese military, complete with barbed wire and police dogs. Then, with eviction from our little apartment in the French concession only a week or so away, my mother remembered Dr. Manabe.

I recall my mother agonizing over whether she should take up Dr. Manabe's invitation to call him. After all, the political situation had deteriorated drastically since that long trek across Siberia. We knew nothing about Dr. Manabe except that he was assigned to Shanghai as part of the Japanese Diplomatic Corps.

Finally, with the move to the ghetto only three days away, my mother decided to take the chance and see him. My stepfather had developed a heart ailment and was afraid to accompany her. He and I spent the day anxiously awaiting her return. She came back at 6 P.M., her eyes shining—Dr. Manabe had been as kind as ever.

Not only had he remembered us, but when my mother asked him to allow us to remain outside the ghetto, he immediately issued a one-year extension of stay so that my stepfather could be near a good hospital and I could continue my education in the British public school where the teachers protested against the Japanese occupation of the city by continuing to teach us Shakespeare.

Thus it came about that, in the midst of war and devastation, I received a first-class education. My mother went back in 1944 and again in 1945 to ask Dr. Manabe for another extension, and both times he complied. We eked out a living from my mother's millinery work; my stepfather had become too ill to hold a job.

I learned excellent English, good French, and passable Chinese and Japanese at a school that, despite the noise of war all around, somehow maintained superior standards. When I graduated in the spring of 1945, I knew the part of Hamlet by heart. Then, after V-J Day, I became a shoeshine boy because that was the best way to meet one of the American demigods who had liberated us and might help me build a future.

Luck smiled on me. In September 1946 a young lieutenant from Iowa, Peter Delamater, wrote a letter on my behalf to his alma mater, Grinnell College, and that fine Midwestern school admitted me with a scholarship in 1947.

My mother and stepfather followed me to America in 1949. In 1950, incredibly enough, I was admitted to Harvard, where I earned a Ph.D. in International Relations in 1954. Thus I became one of the lucky few who had survived the Holocaust and was able to fashion a life in the New World.

After the war, my mother tried to track down Dr. Manabe, to thank him for what he had done for us. She finally received a letter from him in 1952 from an address in Tokyo, thanking her for thanking him for the "small favor" he had extended us. He was living in obscurity now, he wrote. He added that he was happy, though, that in our case, "Humanity had triumphed over evil." Then he simply disappeared.

Despite repeated efforts to contact him again we failed, and, finally, we assumed that he had died. Yet two questions never ceased to haunt me: Who was the mysterious consul in Prague who gave us that transit visa via Kobe, and why did Dr. Manabe put himself at risk to help us?

I was nearing the end of my speech in Kobe. Then, I briefly told the story of my stay in Kobe over half a century ago and asked the press corps if they could help me find any information they could about the two Japanese diplomats who had saved my life during the Holocaust years. Since I had to return to the United States the following evening, I begged the reporters to give the search priority.

That night the phone rang in my hotel room. It was Mr. Toshinori Masuno of the *Kobe Shimbun,* a leading Japanese newspaper.

"We found out how you got your visas," the reporter said. "It was Consul Chiune Sugihara who issued thousands of visas to Jewish refugees against the express orders of his superiors in Tokyo."

I began to tremble. *Was this a Japanese Oskar Schindler or Raoul Wallenberg?* I wondered. "Sugihara issued most of these visas in Lithuania until they posted him to Prague in early 1941," Masuno continued. "And the three of you were on the list. You were among the last before they shut down his consulate."

"How did he do it?" I inquired.

"He saw this as a conflict between his government and his conscience," the reporter replied, "and he followed his conscience."

"When did he die?" I asked.

"In 1986, in disgrace for not having followed orders," Masuno said sadly. "But he was a moral hero in Israel. They planted a tree in his honor in Jerusalem."

"And what about Dr. Manabe?" I queried.

"We are still searching," the reporter replied. "But he's probably deceased."

That night I returned to the United States to teach my classes at Trinity University in San Antonio, Texas. My emotions were in turmoil. *Too late,* I thought. *I cannot thank either one of them; it's too late.*

The next morning, the phone woke me from a troubled sleep. It was Mr. Masuno.

"We've found Dr. Manabe," he exclaimed. "He is eighty-seven years old and quite frail, but he remembers everything. He lives alone and has an unlisted phone number. We managed to get it for you, though. Here it is."

I thought of little else that day, November 16, 1994. And then, in the middle of the night—the middle of his day—I dialed the number.

He did indeed remember everything. We were not the only ones he had helped more than fifty years ago. Other desperate Jews had benefited from his selfless generosity. A music lover, he had come to the rescue of the Shanghai Philharmonic Orchestra by saving its Jewish members from the ghetto. We both tried not to weep as we recalled those far-gone events that seemed to have taken place on another planet. I sent him one of my books that would never have been written without him, and a picture of my mother taken in 1991, a year before her death.

Yet letters and phone calls were not enough. Thinking of his age, I flew to Tokyo and went to see him in the small apartment where he lived, surrounded by his books. I found a man with a beautiful, deeply spiritual face, and a natural grace and dignity. Bridging half a century proved surprisingly easy. He, like myself, had chosen an academic life after the war and had served as a professor of German literature at Tokai University in Tokyo.

We saw each other every day for a week and I quickly grew to love him. On my last day in Tokyo I finally asked the question that had always haunted me: "Weren't you ever afraid to help us?" I asked. "After all, you could have lost your job, or worse, they could have killed you."

He looked at me in amazement. "That thought never occurred to me," he answered. "Besides, people should not be forced to live in ghettos."

I hugged him goodbye, and by so doing, embraced my long-dead father and my murdered grandparents who had been wrenched out of my childhood during the Hitler years. An old wound, open for more than fifty years, had begun to heal.

Dr. Manabe died in April 1996.

I had the privilege to express my gratitude to one of the true moral heroes of our time and to do so while he was still alive. Most of us who carry such unredeemable debts must somehow try to honor them after our benefactor's death. I was given the chance to do so in the here and now.

As a teacher of young college students, I see now that I must teach a most important truth: that there is no such thing as collective guilt, and that, in dark times, there are always men and women who will confront evil, even in its most absolute form, and reaffirm our humanity. In the depths of the abyss, moral courage still survives, and at times even prevails.

My life was saved that way not once, but twice.

348   *Acknowledgments (continued from the copyright page)*

Page 245: Twelve lines from "The Second Coming" by William Butler Yeats, from *The Collected Works of W.B. Yeats,* Revised Second Edition, edited by Richard J. Finneran. Reprinted with the permission of Scribner, a Division of Simon & Schuster. Copyright © 1924 by Macmillan Publishing Company, renewed 1952 by Bertha Georgie Yeats and A.P. Watt Ltd.

MAP 3: Operation Barbarossa and the Eastern Front, 1941–1942. From *The Experience of World War II,* edited by John Campbell, p. 56. Copyright © 1989 Equinox (Oxford) Limited. Used by permission of Oxford University Press, Inc., and by kind permission of Andromeda Oxford Limited.

MAP 7: Crisis in Kosovo. Adapted from the *Boston Globe,* Tuesday, April 6, 1999. Used by permission.

MAP 10: Israeli Conquests, 1967. From p. 70 in *Atlas of the Arab-Israeli Conflict,* Sixth Edition, by Martin Gilbert. Copyright © 1993. Used by permission of Oxford University Press, Inc., and G. Weidenfield & Nicolson Ltd., The Orion Publishing Group Ltd. (UK).

MAP 14: Iraq: Ethnic-Religious Divisions. Adapted from CIA; Perry-Castaneda Map Collection, University of Texas, http://www.lib.utexas.edu/maps/index.html.

Index

Abbas, Mahmoud, 232–236
Abdullah, King of Transjordan,
    189, 190, 196
Abizaid, John B., 288
Absolute evil, 274
Abu Mazen. *See* Abbas, Mahmoud
Acheson, Dean, 57, 59–60, 61, 62,
    63–64, 66, 68, 70, 71
Adenauer, Konrad, 327
Advani, L. K., 180
Adversary's character,
    misperception of, as cause of
    war, 317–318
Adversary's power, misperceptions
    of, as cause of war, 321–324
Aechylus, 328
Afghanistan, 275–276, 278–279,
    280, 293–294, 296–297,
    300–301
Africa, 284, 324–327
Aggressors, defeat of, 311–314
Al-Aqsa Martyrs Brigade, 231,
    233–234
Albania, 139, 147

Albanian Kosovars, 138–149, 153,
    311
Albright, Madeleine, 144–145, 179
Alexander, Czar of Russia, 43
Alexander, King, 119
Alliance systems, as cause of
    World War I, 2
Al Qaeda, 275–276, 280, 281, 284,
    292–293, 294, 299, 313, 320,
    323
Altschiller (Austrian espionage
    agent), 10
Amnesty international, 254
Angola, 283
Ani, Ahmad Khalil Samir al-, 292
Annan, Kofi, 284, 290, 293, 297,
    325, 331
Anti-Comintern Pact, 29
Aqaba, Gulf of, 201, 204, 207–208,
    238
Arab-Israeli conflict, 187–240, 275,
    281, 311, 323
    Lebanese tragedy in, 220,
    222–225

Arab-Israeli conflict, (*continued*)
  misperceptions in, 199–200, 238
  and October War of 1973,
    212–222
  and Palestine uprising in 2000,
    231–237
  and Palestine War of 1948,
    188–198
  and Palestinian uprising of 1988,
    225–228
  peace process in, 228–231
  and prospects for peace,
    237–240
  reason for, 187–188
  and Sinai campaign and the Suez
    crisis of 1956, 198–204
  and Six-Day War of 1967,
    204–212
  See also Israel; Palestine
Arab League, 193, 259
Arafat, Yasir, 227–232, 235, 236,
    238–239, 259
Arbour, Louise, 145, 335
Arens, Moshe, 256
Assad, Hafex al-, 218, 222, 229, 230
Atassi, Al, 204
Atta, Muhammad, 292
Aufbau Ost, 32, 33
Aurora, Jagjit Singh, 175
Austin, Warren R., 66–67, 68, 195,
    197
Australia, 69
Austria-Hungary
  and Serbia, ultimatum to, 5–8
  in World War I, 1–8, 14, 20–22
  See also Austro-Serbian conflict

Austro-Serbian conflict, 1–12,
    14–15
Awami League, 171–172
"Axis of evil" speech, 280–281, 295
Ayalon, Ami, 236–237
Aznar, Jose Maria, 284
Azzam Pasha, 189–191, 193

Baker, James, 227, 299–300, 303,
    331
Balfour, Lord Arthur James, 188
Balfour Declaration, 188–189
Ball, George, 99, 103–104,
    105, 218
Bandar, Prince, 261
Bangladesh, 169–178
Banja Luka, 133
Bao Dai, 95
Baradei, Mohammad el-, 282
Barak, Ehud, 229–230, 239
Bar-Lev line, 215
Barrett, Edward W., 63
Basra, 250, 267
Bay of Pigs, 96
Begin, Menachem, 220–221, 222
Beilin, Yossi, 237
Beirut, 222–223
Belgium, 2, 16, 18, 325
Bengal, 170–175
Ben-Gurion, David, 189, 192,
    193–194, 195–197, 198, 201
Berchtold, Leopold von, 5, 6–8,
    8–9, 10–11, 15, 20–21, 22
Beria, Lavrenti, 41
Bethlehem, 234

Bethmann-Hollweg, Theobald von,
  1, 11–12, 13, 17, 22
Bhutto, Zulfikar Ali, 171–172, 176
Bin Laden, Osama, 275–276,
  278–281, 292, 294, 305,
  311–313, 318, 320, 329, 332
Blair, Tony, 232, 282, 284, 303
Blix, Hans, 282
Bombing policy, in Vietnam war,
  102–104, 105, 110–112,
  113
Bose, Subhas Chandra, 163
Bosnia, 120, 149, 152
  conflict in, 125–131, 133–134,
    311, 323
  and Dayton Peace Accords,
    132, 133–134
  post-war, 136–138
  See also Yugoslavia
Boutros-Ghali, Boutros, 128,
  130, 325
Boyd, Charles G., 136
Bradley, Omar, 64, 66
Bremer, Paul, 288, 312
Brezhnev, Leonid, 120
Broz, Josip, 120. See also Tito
Budapest, 201
Buddhists, beliefs of, 158–159
Bulganin, Nikolai, 202
Bulgaria, 4, 33, 282
Bundy, McGeorge, 102,
  104, 105
Bush, George H. W., 125, 127,
  133, 232–237, 258–269
  and Hussein, Saddam, 253,
    254–255, 256–257, 269

Bush, George W., 80–83, 180, 231,
  239, 291–292, 299, 310–311,
  313, 318, 323, 326, 332,
  333–334
  and "axis of evil" speech,
    280–281, 295
  and Hussein, Saddam, 269,
    280–281, 302–303, 305,
    312–313, 319–321, 333
  leadership style of,
    276–281
  personality of, 315
  Bush at War (Woodward), 280

C. *Turner Joy*, 103
Cadogan, Sir Alexander, 46
Cairo, 201
Calcutta, 175
Cambodia, 93, 94, 110–111,
  112–113, 114
Cameroon, 283
Camp David talks, 230
Canada, 69, 94, 206, 288, 290,
  293, 294
Cannibalism, 310
Carter, Jimmy, 220–221
Caste system, 158, 160
Casualties
  in Gulf War of 1990, 266,
    284–285
  in Gulf War of 2003, 284–285,
    297, 313, 321, 328
  in Iran-Iraq War, 251
  in Korean War, 79–80
  in Vietnam war, 114

Cavendish-Bentinck, Victor, 46
Celluci, Paul, 290
CENTO. *See* Central Treaty
  Organization
Central Africa, 33
Central Treaty Organization
  (CENTO), 166
Chalabi, Ahmed, 288–289
Chamberlain, Neville, 44
Charles XII of Sweden, 38
Chelius, General von, 12
Cheney, Richard, 256, 259, 261,
  262, 265, 321
Chernomyrdin, Viktor,
  145, 146
Chiang Kai-shek, 68
Chile, 282
China, 89, 199, 265, 282
  and India-Pakistan conflict, 166,
    167, 168, 169, 174, 175
  in Korean War, 57–58, 64, 65, 67,
    68, 70–78, 79–80
  and North Korea, 81, 82
  in Vietnam war, 91–96, 95,
    102, 115
Chou En-lai, 332
Chretien, Jean, 294–295
Christmas Truce of 1914, 23
Churchill, Winston, 20, 32, 39,
  45–46, 51–52
Civil disobedience, 161
Clark, Wesley, 152
Clausewitz, Karl von, 16
Clay, Jenny Strauss, 279
Clemenceau, Georges, 277
Clifford, Clark, 105, 195

Clinton, Bill, 80–81, 133, 136, 138,
  142, 144, 147, 151, 179,
  228–231, 325
Cold War, 89, 91, 202
Colonialism, 75, 88–95, 99, 107,
  157, 159–163, 164, 223, 275,
  295–296, 325
Commissar Order, 36
Communism, 28, 89–90, 97–98,
  106, 112–113, 114
Comprehensive Test Ban Treaty,
  179
Conrad, Joseph, 325
Contact Group, 131–132, 139–140
Containment, 291, 304–305, 332
Cooper, John Sherman, 103
Crankshaw, Edward, 169
Cripps, Stafford, 45–46
Croatia, 120, 123–125, 131–132,
  133, 134, 146, 149, 152
Croat-Moslem Federation, 134
Crusader, as leadership style, 276
Cuba, 67
Cuban Missile Crisis of 1962, 182,
  277–278
Cuéllar, Javier Pérez de, 260
Cuny, Fred, 130–131
Cyprus, 138, 149, 201
Czechoslovakia, 29–30, 44, 199

Dahlan, Muhammad, 235
Dayan, Moshe, 201, 208, 213, 214
Dayton Accords, 132, 133–134,
  136, 137, 140
Death of a Salesman (Miller), 326

Deir Yassin massacre, 195–196
Delamater, Peter, 344
Democracy, vs. dictatorship, 279
Denmark, 31
Dictatorship, vs. democracy, 279
Diem, Ngo Dinh, 95–96, 98, 100
Dien Bien Phu, battle for, 92, 107
Divide and conquer, British
    strategy of, 159
Djindjic, Zoran, 151, 152
Dobrorolski, Gen., 14–15
Dowd, Maureen, 294
Drummond, Gunther, 261
Dubrovnik, 124
Dudakovic, Atif, 133
Dulles, John Foster, 91, 92, 94, 199,
    200, 202–203, 319, 332

Eastern Europe, 284
East India Company, 159, 160
Eban, Abba, 190, 206, 215, 216
Ecological terrorism, 268
Ecuador, 67
Eden, Anthony, 46, 199, 200, 201,
    202–203, 204
Egypt, 67, 197, 198–204, 238, 259,
    262
  in October War of 1973, 212–222
  in Six-Day War, 204–212
Egyptian-Israel peace treaty, 221
Eichmann, Adolf, 140
Eisenhower, Dwight D., 91–96,
    202–203, 246, 319, 332
El Fatah, 204
Ely, Paul, 92

Emancipation, of women, 274
Empires, fate of, 295–296
Erikson, Erik, 49–50
Eshkol, Levi, 205, 207
Estonia, 31, 43
Ethnic cleansing, 124–125,
    127–132, 134–136, 139–140,
    142, 144, 151–152
Ethnic wars, 324
European Community, 124, 125,
    257
European Union, 133, 232
Evan, Abba, 207
Evil, 245–246, 274

Fahd, King, 257–258
Faisal, King of Saudi Arabia,
    204–205, 218
Fall, Bernard, 93
Fay, Sidney B., 6
Fear, as cause of war, 2
Fedayeen, 197, 198, 201
Ferdinand I (of Bulgaria), 4
Fernandez, George, 180
Finland, 31, 32
*The First Strike—The Story of a
    Future War* (Shpanov), 39
Ford, Gerald R., 113
France, 43, 44, 67, 75, 88–95, 99,
    107, 129, 133, 275, 332
  and Arab-Israeli conflict,
    199–204, 207, 222–224
  and Gulf War of 2003, 282–283,
    293, 297, 298
  and post-Saddam Iraq, 288

France, (*continued*)
  in World War I, 13, 14, 16–17,
    19, 21, 31
Franks, Tommy, 285–286
Franz Ferdinand, assassination
  of, 2, 3–7
Franz-Joseph, Emperor of
  Austria-Hungary, 1–8,
    15, 22
Freedom fighters, 223, 275
French Communist Party, 107
French Revolution, 274
Freud, Sigmund, 27
Friedheim, Jerry, 111
Frost, David, 254, 265
Frum, David, 280
Fulbright, William, 103

Galilee, 197
Gandhi, Indira, 173–178
Gandhi, Mahatma, 157, 161–163,
  233
Gandhi, Rajiv, 178
Garner, Jay, 287, 288
Gaulle, Charles de, 207
Gaza Strip, 197, 201, 204, 209, 212,
  219, 225, 227–228, 231,
  234–237, 239
Gellman, Barton, 321
Gemayel, Amin, 223, 224
Geneva Accords, 93–95, 112
Geneva Conference, 93–94, 332
Genocide, 324–327
George, David Lloyd, 277
George, King of England, 18

Germany, 133, 259, 282, 288, 293,
  297, 298, 325
  and Stalin, 27–28, 38–48, 51–52
  in World War I, 1–8, 14, 33
  See also Russo-German War
Giesl, Baron W., 7–8
Glaspie, April, 255
Glubb Pasha, 189, 190
Goering, Hermann, 35, 37, 50
Golan Heights, 209, 212–213, 215,
  230
Goldman, Frank, 194
Goodwin, Richard N., 109
Gorazde, 128, 129, 130
Gorbachev, Mikhail, 123, 257, 278
Gourevitch, Philip, 324–325
Great Britain, 32, 43, 44–46, 48,
  130, 133, 275
  and Arab-Israeli conflict,
    188–189, 191–197, 199–204,
    207, 208, 222–224
  and Gulf War of 1990, 257, 259,
    269
  and Gulf War of 2003, 282–284,
    286, 333
  and India, 157, 159–163, 164
  and Kosovo, 144
  and post-Saddam Iraq, 290
  in World War I, 11–13, 17,
    19–20, 21, 23, 31
Greater Serbia, 121, 146
Great Purge of the 1930s, 39–42,
  43, 51
Greece, 35
Grey, Sir Edward, 11, 13, 19
Griffin mission, 90

Gromyko, Andrei, 197
Gross, Ernest A., 60–61, 61–62,
    63, 64–65, 66
Guillain, Robert, 93
Guinea, 283, 326
Gulf War of 1990, 255–269
    casualties of, 266, 284–285
    as compared to Gulf War of
    2003, 284–286
    misperceptions in, 256,
    261–262, 264, 323
    See also Kuwait, Iraq attack on
Gulf War of 2003, 269, 281–286,
    293, 297–298, 304–305,
    310–314, 319–321, 327,
    332–334
    casualties of, 284–285, 288, 291,
    297, 313, 321, 328
    as compared to Gulf War of
    1990, 284–286
    and debt restructuring, 299–300,
    303
    and exit strategy, 299,
    313, 330
    misperceptions in, 323
    occupation cost of, 296–297
    and post-war reconstruction
    costs, 290–291
    and post-war U.S. occupation,
    286–293, 294, 296–300,
    328–329
    and reconstruction contracts,
    299–300
The Guns of August (Tuchman),
    18
Gurtov, Melvin, 93

Hácha, Emil, 29–30
Hadley, Stephen J., 292
Haganah, 193–194
Hage, Imad, 333
Hague Conference, 36
Haikal, Mohammed Hasanein, 208
Hakim, Ayatollah Muhammad
    Bakr al-, 289
Halberstam, David, 97, 99, 107
Halder, Franz, 31, 34, 35–36
Hamas, 232, 233–234, 235, 236
Hammarskjöld, 204, 215
Harkins, Paul D., 99–100
Heart of Darkness (Conrad), 325
Herzegovina, 120. *See also* Bosnia;
    Yugoslavia
Herzl, Theodore, 188
Hezbollah, 232
Hickerson, John D., 60–61
High Dam at Aswan, 199
Hillel, 229
Hindu Nationalist Party, 179
Hindus
    beliefs of, 158–159
    vs. Moslems, 157–183
Hitler, Adolf, 39, 136, 138, 139,
    144, 199, 200, 216, 245–246,
    251–252, 254, 256, 311, 316,
    317, 318, 319, 322
    charismatic appeal of, 49–51
    as compared to Hussein,
    Saddam, 252–255, 268, 285,
    302
    and Jews, persecution of, 187,
    189
    personality of, 315

Hitler, (*continued*)
and Russia, 27–38, 49, 51
and Stalin, 29, 30–31, 32–33, 34,
37, 42–43, 43–45, 46, 47–48, 52
Hitler-Stalin pact, 31, 42–45
Hitler Youth, 50
Ho Chi Minh, 88, 89, 90, 91–96,
102, 104, 105, 106–108, 318,
322
Ho Chi Minh City, 113, 115
Holbrooke, Richard, 133,
136, 140
Hollings, Ernest, 223–224
Hollingworth, Larry, 128–129
Hope, as basis of misperceptions in
Vietnam war, 87, 133
Hötzendorff, Conrad von, 5–6, 15,
20–21
Howard, Michael, 209
Hughes, Emmett John, 104
Huk rebellion, 97
Hull, Cordell, 46–47
Humphrey, Hubert, 104
Hunter, Robert, 209Hitler,
Adolf209
Hussein, King of Jordan, 205, 218,
226, 228–229, 230, 259
Hussein, Qusay, 286, 291, 312–313
Hussein, Saddam, 133, 138, 145,
232, 245–246, 278, 291–292,
311, 315–318
and Bush, George H. W., 253,
254, 255, 256–257, 269
and Bush, George W., 269,
280–281, 302–303, 305,
312–313, 319–321, 333

capture of, 301–305, 317
as compared to Hitler, 252–255,
268, 285, 302
fall of, 285, 291, 313, 333
insurgency plans of, 294
and Iran-Iraq War, 246–251
and Kurds, 251, 267
and oil wells, torching of, 268
personality of, 247
rise of, 296
role models of, 247
Hussein, Uday, 291, 312–313
Husseini, Haj Amin el-, 189
Husseini, Jamal, 191
Hyderabad, 164

IAEA. *See* International Atomic
Energy Agency
Ianushkevich, Gen., 14–15
ICC. *See* International Criminal
Court
Imperial power, U.S. as, 327–328
Imperial powers, fall of, 328
Incest, 310
India, 13, 67, 94, 149
and Great Britain, 157, 159–163,
164
nuclear weapons in, 178–182
and partition, 163
religions of, 158–159
India-Pakistan conflicts, 157–183,
311, 322–323
in 1947, 157–165
in 1965, 166–169
in 1971, 169–178

in 1998 to present, 178–182
misperceptions in, 172–173
reasons for, 182–183
Indochina, 149, 332
Inevitability, as theme in World
War I, 1–2
Institute for Defense Studies and
Analysis in New Delhi, 174
Instrument of Accession to India,
165
International Atomic Energy
Agency (IAEA), 295
International Control Commission,
94
International Convention of
Constantinople of 1888,
199–200
International Criminal Court
(ICC), 152–153
International law, 153, 331
International terrorism, 327
International War Crimes Tribunal,
127, 335
Intifadeh. *See* Palestinian uprising
Iran, 132, 223, 224, 260, 280, 281,
294–295, 295, 303
nuclear plants in, 295
Iran, shah of, 221, 249
Iran-Iraq War, 246–251, 311
casualties of, 251
in historical perspective, 251
and World War I, as compared
to, 246, 248–249
Iraq, 133, 180, 280, 296–297
and Kuwait, attack on, 251–269,
311, 323

nuclear weapons in, 80–81
"oil for food" program in, 269,
290
post-war U.S. occupation of,
286–293, 294, 296–300,
328–329
religious groups in, 288–289, 293
See also Gulf War of 1990;
Gulf War of 2003;
Iran-Iraq War
Iraqi Governing Council, 297–298
Isaacs, Robert, 107–108
Islam, 149, 223. *See also* Moslems
Islamic Jihad, 233–234, 235, 236
Ismailia, 201
Israel, 259, 260, 262. *See also* Arab-
Israeli conflict; Israel;
Palestine
Israelis, 149
Italy, 33, 222–224
Ivory Coast, 326
Izetbegovic, Alija, 125, 130, 132,
137

Jackson, Andrew, 59
Jacobson, Eddie, 194–195
Jagow, Gottlieb von, 8
Jammu, 180
Japan, 9, 29, 33, 59, 75, 81, 82, 259
Jefferson, Thomas, 59
Jericho, 235
Jerusalem, 197, 209, 226, 234
Jessup, Philip C., 66
Jewish Agency, 189
The Jewish State (Herzl), 188

Jews
  immigration of, to Palestine,
    187–188
  persecution of, and Hitler,
    187,189
  treatment of, in Shanghai,
    343–344
  in World War II, 341–342
Jihad, 248
Jinnah, Mohammed Ali, 157, 162,
    170
Jodl, Alfred, 32
Joffre, Joseph, 19
Johnson, Herschel, 191
Johnson, Louis A., 64, 65
Johnson, Lyndon B., 98, 100,
    101–109, 207, 259, 260, 264,
    277, 318
Johnson, Robert, 102
Johnson, Shoshana, 287
Jorda, Claude, 135
Jordan, 204, 205, 209, 228–229, 259
Junagadh, 164

Kaka, Khan, 294
Kamel, Hussein, 269
Karadzic, Radovan, 125–128, 130,
    131–132, 134, 135, 136–137,
    137, 152
Kargil, 179
Karzai, Hamid, 280, 293–294, 301
Kashmir, 177, 178, 179, 180,
    181–182
  1947 battle over, 163–165
  and War of 1965, 166–169

Kassem, Abdul Karim, 302
Kay, David, 320, 333, 334
Kelly, Thomas, 256
Kennedy, Edward M., 260
Kennedy, John F., 96–101, 182,
    258, 277–278
Kennedy, Paul, 328
Kerr, Richard, 256
KFOR, 148
Khan, Dr. Abdul Qaadeer,
    303–304
Khan, Ayub, 166, 168
Khan, Liaquat Ali, 164, 170
Khan, Yahya, 171–173, 175–177,
    315, 316, 322
Khmer Rouge government,
    112–113, 114
Khomeini, Ayatollah Ruhollah,
    221, 247–251
Khrushchev, Nikita, 42, 48, 52, 96,
    120, 182, 277–278
Khuzistan, 248
Kiev, 38
Kijevo, 124
Kim Il Sung, 58, 80, 255–256
Kim Jong Il, 80–81, 281, 323
Kirov, Sergei, 39
Kissinger, Henry, 109–110, 112,
    138, 214, 216–220, 227, 294
KLA. *See* Kosovo Liberation
    Army
Knin, 123–124, 132
Kobe, 341–342
Kollek, Teddy, 226
Korbel, Josef, 144
Korea, 149, 297

Korean War, 58–80, 90, 91, 92,
    93, 322
  casualties of, 79–80
  misperceptions in, 73–78
  reasons for outbreak of,
    57–58
Kosovo
  conflict in, 120–122, 138–151,
    296–297
  misperceptions in, 142
  See also Yugoslavia
Kosovo battle of 1389, 139, 150
Kosovo Covenant, 150
Kosovo Liberation Army, 139–140,
    142, 147–149
Kosovo Protection Corps, 149
Kostunica, Vojislav, 151
Kosygin, Aleksei, 169
Krajina, 123–124, 132
Krajisnik, Momcilo, 136–137, 138
Krebs, Colonel, 47
Krogh, Peter, 144–145
Kucan, Milan, 123
Kuperman, Alan J., 324, 325
Kurds, 250, 267, 297
Kuwait, 249, 250, 283
  Iraq attack on, 251–269,
    311, 323
  See also Gulf War of 1990
Kuwait, emir of, 249, 258
Kuznetsov, N. G., 48

Lansdale, Edward, 97
Laos, 93, 94, 110
Latvia, 31, 43

Lawrence, D. H., 1
Lawrence, T. E., 296
Lawrence of Arabia, 296
Lazar, Tsar, 150
Leaders
  and fear of attack, as cause of
    war, 318–321
  personalities of, as cause of war,
    2, 314–315
  self-image of, as cause of war,
    315–317
Leadership styles, 276–277
League of Nations, 188, 277
Learned behavior, war as,
    309–310
Lebanon, 193, 197, 220, 222–225,
    229, 238, 250
Lebensraum, 28, 33
Ledeen, Michael, 279
Leningrad, 38
Lesseps, Ferdinand de, 200
Levin, Carl, 179
Lewis, Bernard, 274
Liberia, 326
Libya, 223
  nuclear weapons in, 303–305
Lichnowski, Karl Max, 17, 18
Lie, Trygve, 61, 63, 66, 69, 195
Lincoln, Abraham, 59
Lithuania, 31, 43
The Living and the Dead
    (Simonov), 52
Ljubljana, 122
Loas, 112
Lodge, Henry Cabot, 100, 277
Luxembourg, 2, 19

MacArthur, Douglas, 62, 64,
    66–79, 265, 297, 315, 319, 322
Macedonia, 120, 139, 147. *See also*
    Yugoslavia
Maddox, 103
Madrid "donors conference,"
    298
Magsaysay, Ramon, 97
Maisky, Ivan, 46
Malcolm, Noel, 150
Malik, Charles, 197
Malik, Yakov, A., 66, 69
Malta, 201
Manabe, Ryoichi, 343, 344,
    345–347
Mandela, Nelson, 282, 327
Mao Zedong, 57–58, 77, 107
Markovic, Ante, 122
Marshall, George, 195, 291
Marshall Plan, 291
Masuno, Toshinori, 345–346
McCarthy, Joseph, 61, 98
McCone, John, 277
McNamara, Robert, 100,
    102, 103, 104, 105, 106
McNaughton, John, 102
Megill, Todd, 301–302
Mein Kampf (Hitler), 28, 254
Meir, Golda, 190, 196, 218–219
Mello, Sergio Vieira de, 293
Memoirs (Tirpitz), 3
Memoirs (Truman), 62, 64, 65, 66,
    74
Mericor, Dan, 239
Mexico, 282
Middle East

oil in, 217, 221, 250, 253,
    258, 268
and Ottoman Empire, 274–275
peace in, and United States,
    330–331
See also individual countries
Militarism, as cause of war, 2
Miller, Arthur, 326
Milosevic, Mira, 121
Milosevic, Slobodan, 121–125,
    135, 138–147, 150–153, 246,
    311, 315, 317–319, 323,
    325, 335
as compared to Hitler, 136, 138,
    139, 144
as compared to Hussein,
    Saddam, 138, 145
fall of, 131–132
and rise of power, 121–122
surrender of, 145–147
Misperceptions
    in Arab-Israeli conflict, 199–200,
    238
    as cause of war, 2, 315–324
    in Gulf War of 1990, 256,
    261–262, 264, 323
    in Gulf War of 2003, 323
    in India-Pakistan conflicts,
    172–173
    in Korean War, 73–78
    in Kosovo, 142
    in Vietnam war, 87, 88–113, 133
    in World War I, 20–22
    in World War II, 27–28, 37–38,
    43–48, 52
    in Yugoslavia, 131–132

Mladic, Ratko, 124, 127–128, 129, 130, 131–132, 134, 135, 136, 152

Mofaz, Shaul, 235

Mollet, Guy, 199, 200, 201, 203, 204

Molotov, Vyacheslav, 32–34, 45, 47

Moltke, Helmuth von, 1, 17–18, 19

Monnet, Jean, 327

Montenegro, 120, 122, 139, 147. *See also* Yugoslavia

Morillon, Phillipe, 128

Moscow Trials, 42

Moslem-Croat Federation, 131

Moslem League, 162, 170

Moslems
  beliefs of, 159
  vs. Christians, 222–224
  vs. Hindus, 157–183
  vs. Moslems, 169–178, 247–248
  in Yugoslavia, 120–121
  See also Albanian Kosovars; Islam

Mountbatten, Lord, 164, 165

Moyers, William, 109

Mubarak, Hosni, 222, 230, 253, 256, 259

Muccio, John J., 64

Mujibur. *See* Rahaman, Sheik Mujibar

Mukti Bahini, 173, 174

Musharraf, Perves, 179, 180

Mussolini, Benito, 35, 38

Mutual Defense Assistance Program, 90

Myths and legends, 150–151

Nagra, Gandharv, 178

Napoleon Bonaparte, 38, 43, 51, 312

Nasser, Gamal Abdel, 198–207, 211, 212, 238, 247, 275, 315

National Assembly, 171–172

Nationalism, 119–153, 120–121, 158, 161–163, 179, 198, 203, 248
  as cause of war, 2

National socialism, 50

NATO. *See* North Atlantic Treaty Organization

NATO implementation force (IFOR), 133–134, 138

Nazi Holocaust, 142, 144

Nebuchadnezzar, 247, 253, 261

Negev, 197

Nehru, Jawaharlal, 164, 166, 167

Netanyahu, Benjamin, 229

Netherlands, 69

New Zealand, 69

Niazi, Lt. Gen., 176–177, 178

Nibelungentreue, 4, 6–7

Nicholas II, 7, 9–13

Nietzsche, 309

Niger, 292

Nigeria, 326

9/11, 273–274, 278–279, 280, 294, 310, 312, 320, 332. *See also* Terrorism

Nixon, Richard M., 92, 109–113, 214
"Nixon Doctrine," 110
Nol, Marshal Lon, 112
Nolting, Frederick E., Jr., 97–98
North Atlantic Treaty, 88
North Atlantic Treaty Organization (NATO), 57, 97, 129–130, 152, 311, 323, 332
   and Afghanistan, 294
   and Bosnia, 138
   and Gulf War of 1990, 259
   and Gulf War of 2003, 335
   and international law, 153
   and Kosovo, 139–150
   and occupation, costs of, in post-war Iraq, 296–297
   and post-Saddam Iraq, 290
   and Yugoslavia, 131
North Korea, 255–256, 257, 265, 280, 281, 294, 303, 311
   and attack on South Korea, 57–58, 58–59, 60–62, 63, 67–68, 79
   nuclear weapons in, 80–81, 82–83, 295, 323
   and United States, 80–83
Norway, 31, 32, 67
NPT. *See* Nuclear Non-Proliferation Treaty
Nuclear Command Authority, 181
Nuclear Non-Proliferation Treaty (NPT), 81, 281, 295
Nuclear plants, in Iran, 295
Nuclear weapons
   in India, 178–182
      in Iraq, 80–81
      in Libya, 303–305
      in North Korea, 80–81, 82–83, 295, 323
      in Pakistan, 178–182
      See also Weapons of mass destruction
Nuremberg war crimes trials, 36
Nusseibeh, Sari, 237

Occupation, cost of, in post-war Iraq, 296–297
October War of 1973, 212–222, 214–215
Oil, in Middle East, 217, 221, 250, 253, 258, 268
"Oil for food" program, in Iraq, 269, 290
Old Jerusalem, 212
Olmert, Ehud, 239
On Tyranny (Strauss), 279
OPEC. *See* Organization of Petroleum Exporting Countries
Operation Barbarossa, 33–38, 45, 47
Operation Desert Shield, 258, 260
Operation Desert Storm, 256, 260
Operation Green, 29–30
Operation Horseshoe, 140, 141, 146
Operation Rolling Thunder, 104
Operation Sea Lion, 32
Organization of Petroleum Exporting Countries (OPEC), 253

Ottoman Empire, 274–275, 296
Ottoman Turks, 121, 150, 274–275
Owen, Lord Peter, 128

Pace, Frank, Jr., 68
Pachachi, Adnan, 331
Pakistan, 149, 283, 284, 298, 332
  nuclear weapons in, 178–182
  See also India-Pakistan conflict
Paléologue, Maurice, 9–10
Palestine, 187–188. *See also* Arab-
  Israeli conflict; Israel
Palestine Liberation Organization
  (PLO), 208, 220, 223, 226–227
Palestine War of 1948, 188–198
Palestinian Authority, 228, 235
Palestinian resistance fighters, 197
Palestinian uprising of 1988,
  225–228
Palestinian uprising of 2000,
  231–237
Palistine Liberation Organization
  (PLO), 259
Pam Am Flight 103, terrorist
  bombing of, 304
Panikkar, K. M., 71, 74, 78
Panmunjon Truce Agreement of
  1953, 81, 281
Paris Accords, 110, 111, 112
Pashich, Nikola, 7–8
Passive resistance, 161
Paul, King of Yugoslavia, 35
Paulus, Friedrich von, 41
Pentagon Papers, 104, 105
Peres, Shimon, 226, 228–229

Perle, Richard, 279
The Persians (Aechylus), 328
Peter, Serbian prince regent, 7, 35
Philippines, 65
Plavsic, Biljana, 136–137
PLO. *See* Palestine Liberation
  Organization
Poland, 30–31, 43–44, 94, 284, 288
Pol Pot, 114
Ponte, Carla del, 151
Port of Elath, 198, 201
Port Said, 201
Pourtalés, Friedrich von, 10, 19
Powell, Colin, 82, 180–181, 236,
  237, 239, 256, 261, 282, 298
Power, perceptions of, in World
  War I, 21–22
Pragmatist, as leadership style, 276
Preemption doctrine, 279, 281, 284,
  290, 291, 294–295, 304–305,
  310–311

Qaddafi, Muammar el-, 303–305
Qalqilya, 235
Qurei, Ahmed, 236

Rabbo, Yasir Abed, 237
Rabin, Yitzhak, 219, 228–229, 232,
  233, 235, 238–239
Radford, Arthur W., 92
Rahaman, Sheik Mujibar, 171–173,
  174, 176
Ramallah, 235
Rambouillet peace accord, 140

Rann of Kutch, 167–168
Rantisi, Abdel Aziz, 234
Rasputin, 9
Rayburn, Sam, 98
Reagan, Ronald, 222, 223, 250,
    258, 278
Refugees, 128, 141–142, 145,
    146–148, 173–174, 183, 198,
    267, 275
Religion, as cause of war, 182–183.
    See also Religious war
Religious war, 275–276, 324
    in India and Pakistan, 157–183
    in Iran and Iraq, 246–251
    in Yugoslavia, 120
Remembering America (Goodwin),
    109
Rhee, Syngman, 64
Riad, Mahmoud, 206
Ribbentrop, Joachim von, 30,
    32–34, 44
*The Rise and Fall of the Great
    Powers* (P. Kennedy), 328
Rogers, Will, 250
Romania, 31, 32, 33
Rommel, Erwin, 264
Roosevelt, Eleanor, 153
Roosevelt, Franklin D., 32,
    59, 88
Roosevelt, Theodore, 59
Rose, Sir Michael, 130
Rostow, Walt, 97, 98–99, 100–101,
    102
Rostow-Taylor Report, 98–99,
    100–101
Rothschild, Baron de, 188

Rumsfeld, Donald, 81, 283, 285,
    286, 288, 291, 293
Rusk, Dean, 77–78, 102,
    104, 113
Russia, 82, 133, 201
    and Bosnia, 130
    and Gulf War of 2003,
        282–283, 298
    and Hitler, 27–38, 49, 51
    and Kosovo, 148
    in World War I, 2, 3, 5, 8–13,
        14–19, 20–22
Russo-German War, 27–38, 38–48,
    49–52
Rwanda, genocide in, 324–326

Sadat, Anwar, 212, 215, 218, 219,
    220–222, 232, 233, 238, 239,
    247, 248
Saigon, 109, 113
Sarajevo, 125, 126–128, 129,
    130, 134
Saudi Arabia, 204–205, 217, 221,
    257–259, 262
Sazonov, Sergei, 9, 10, 11, 12,
    14–15, 19, 21
Schlesinger, Arthur, Jr., 99, 105
Schlieffen, Alfred von, 16, 17
Schlieffen Plan, 16
Schmidt, Paul, 29, 33–34, 35
Schopenhauer, Arthur, 30
Schultz, George, 227
Schwarzkopf, H. Norman, 133,
    246, 256, 258, 261, 263,
    264–266, 285

SEATO. *See* Southeast Asia Treaty
Organization
Selective Service Act, 67
Separation of church and state, 274
Sepoy Rebellion of 1857, 160
Serbia, 120–122, 131–132, 133, 134,
137, 140–141, 146, 149,
151–153, 153, 311
Austria-Hungary ultimatum to,
5–8
in World War I, 2, 3, 8–12,
20–21, 22
See also Austro-Serbian conflict;
Yugoslavia
Serbo-Croatian language, 124
The Seven Pillars of Wisdom
(Lawrence), 296
Shamir, Yitzhak, 226, 262
Shanghai, treatment of Jews in,
343–344
Sharett, Moshe, 191
Sharif, Prime Minister, 179
Sharm el Sheik, 201, 207
Sharon, Ariel, 231, 235, 236, 239
Shastri, Lal Bahadur, 167–168
Shevardnadze, Eduard, 257
Shi'ite Moslems, vs. Sunni
Moslems, 247–248
Shirer, William L., 35
Shmushkevich, Gen., 39
Shpanov, N., 39
Shukairy, Ahmed, 208
Shultz, George, 226
Sickness, and war, analogy
between, 309–310
Sierra Leone, 326

Sikhs, 178
Silver, Abba Hillel, 194
Simonov, Konstantin, 52
Sinai agreement, 219–220
Sinai campaign, and the Suez crisis
of 1956, 198–204
Sinai Peninsula, 201–202, 204,
208–209, 212
Singh, Hari, 164–165
Sistani, Grand Ayatollah Ali al-,
330–331
Six-Day War of 1967, 204–212
Slavery, 310
Slovenia, 120, 122–123, 125. *See
also* Yugoslavia
Solarz, Stephen J., 260
Sophie, Crown Princess of Austria-
Hungary, 3
Sorge, Richard, 47
Southeast Asia Treaty
Organization (SEATO), 93,
94–95, 166
South Korea, 81–82
and North Korea attack on,
57–58, 58–59, 60–62, 63,
67–68, 79
and United States, 81–82
South Vietnam, 94
Soviet Union
and Afghanistan, 275
and Arab-Israeli conflict, 191,
197, 202–203, 205, 211–215,
218–219, 222, 224
collapse of, 275
and Cuban Missile Crisis,
277–278

Soviet Union, (*continued*)
   and Gulf War of 1990, 257, 263,
      265
   and India-Pakistan conflict, 167,
      169, 174, 175
   in Iran-Iraq War, 249, 250
   in Korean War, 61, 62–63, 65, 66,
      67, 69
   in Vietnam war, 93, 94, 95, 107,
      111–112, 115
   in World War I, 33
Spain, 282, 283, 284, 288, 290
Special Forces, creation of, 97
Special International War Crimes
      Tribunal, 133
Srebrenica, 128, 129, 130, 135, 152
Staab, Gen. von, 18
Stalin, Joseph, 88, 107, 120, 141,
      144, 246, 256, 285, 318, 319
   and Germany, 27–28, 38–48,
      51–52
   and Great Purge of the 1930s,
      39–42, 43, 51
   and Hitler, 29, 30–31, 32–33, 34,
      37, 42–43, 43–45, 46, 47–48, 52
   in Korean War, 57–58
   and United States, 45, 46–47, 48
Stambolic, Ivan, 120–121
Straits of Tiran, 201, 204, 207
Strasser, Gregor, 50
Strauss, Leo, 279
Straw, Jack, 180
Suez Canal crisis, and the Sinai
      campaign, 198–204
Sukhomlinov, Vladimir, 9–10,
      10–11, 14–15

Sunni Moslems, vs. Shi'ite
      Moslems, 247–248
Syria, 193, 197, 222–224, 224, 229,
      230, 236, 259, 262, 282, 294
   in October War of 1973,
      212–222
   in Six-Day War, 204–205, 209,
      211
Syrian-Egyptian defense
      agreement, 205
Szápary, S., 10

Taiwan, 75
Taliban, 278, 294
Tashkent, 169
Taylor, Charles, 326
Taylor, Maxwell, 98–99, 100–101,
      102
Tel Aviv, 197
Tenet, George, 292
Terrorism, 227, 231–232, 237, 268,
      280–281, 304, 313. *See also*
      9/11
Thatcher, Margaret, 257, 259, 278
Thirty Years' War, 251
Thuggee, Hindu custom of, 160
Tikrit, 301
Tirpitz, Alfred von, 3, 19
Tito, 58, 120–121, 122, 123
Tonkin Gulf Resolution, 103, 111
Transfordanian Arab Legion, 197
Transjordan, 189, 190, 196, 197
Trepper, Leopold, 47
Tribal wars, 324
Trueheart, William, 97–98

Truman, Harry S, 191, 194–195,
    197, 291
  and atomic bombing of Japan,
    59
  in Korean War, 58–70, 70–74,
    76, 79
  and United Nations,
    commitment to, 59, 60
  and Vietnam war, 88–91
Truman Doctrine, 88
Tuchman, Barbara, 9, 16–17, 18
Tudjman, Franjo, 123, 124,
    131, 137
Tukhachevsky, Gen., 41
Tulkarm, 235
Turkey, 283, 297, 299
Tutweiler, Margaret D., 255
Tuzla, 129

Umansky, Konstantin, 46–47
UN Commission for India and
    Pakistan, 165
UN Committee on Palestine
    (UNSCOP), 190
UNEF. *See* UN Emergency Force
UN Emergency Force (UNEF),
    204, 205–206, 215
UNHCR. *See* UN High
    Commissioner for Refugees
UN High Commissioner for
    Human Rights, 293
UN High Commissioner for
    Refugees (UNHCR), 128,
    147, 149
United Arab Emirates, 250

United Kingdom, 67, 69, 206, 211
United Nations, 152–153
  and Afghanistan, 300
  and Arab-Israeli conflict,
    191–192, 194–197, 202,
    205–207, 212, 214–215, 216,
    219, 227, 232, 236, 238
  and Bosnia, 128–131
  and Gulf War of 1990, 257, 259,
    260, 261, 265, 266–269
  and Gulf War of 2003, 281–284,
    293, 297–298, 333
  and India-Pakistan conflict,
    165
  in Korean War, 60–70, 70–80
  and occupation, costs of,
    296–297
  and October War of 1973, 212,
    214–215
  and post-Saddam Iraq, 288,
    290, 331
  Truman commitment to,
    59, 60
  U.S. attitude toward, 328–329
  and Yugoslavia, 124
United States
  and Afghanistan, 275–276,
    278–279, 280, 293–294
  and Arab-Israeli conflict,
    191, 193–197, 199–204,
    206–208, 211–224,
    226–237
  attitude of, toward United
    Nations, 328–329
  and Bosnia, 125, 129, 130, 131,
    133–134

United States, (*continued*)
  and Cuban Missile Crisis,
    277–278
  and empire building, 295
  and Gulf War of 1990, 255–269
  and Gulf War of 2003, 269,
    281–286, 304–305, 333–335
  and ICC, 152
  as imperial power, 327–328
  and India-Pakistan conflict, 167,
    170, 175, 179–181
  in Iran-Iraq War, 249, 250–251
  in Korean War, 58–80
  and Kosovo, 144–145
  in Middle East, 275
  and Middle Eastern peace,
    330–332
  and North Korea, 80–83
  and post-war occupation of
    Iraq, 286–293, 294, 296–300,
    328–329
  and South Korea, 81–82
  and Stalin, 45, 46–47, 48
  in Vietnam war, 87–115
  and World War II, 45
  and Yugoslavia, 125, 136
Universal Declaration of Human
  Rights, 153
UN Monitoring, Verification,
  and Inspection Commission
  (UNMOVIC), 269
UNMOVIC. *See* UN Monitoring,
  Verification, and Inspection
  Commission
UNPROFOR. *See* UN Protection
  Force

UN Protection Force
  (UNPROFOR), 124–125, 128,
    130–131
UNSCOM, 269
UNSCOP. *See* UN Committee on
  Palestine
UN War Crimes Tribunal,
    135–138, 151–152
U Thant, 206

Vajpayee, Atal Behari, 178–179,
    180, 181
Vietnam, 75, 88, 89–91, 92–94, 95,
    99, 107
Vietnamization, 109–110
Vietnam war, 87–115, 259, 264,
    311, 322, 332–333
  bombing policy in, 102–104, 105,
    110–112, 113
  casualties of, 114
  and Eisenhower, 91–96
  and Ford, 113
  in historical perspective, 114
  and Johnson, 98, 101–109
  and Kennedy, 96–101
  misperceptions in, 87,
    88–113, 133
  and Nixon, 92, 109–113
  and Truman, 88–91
  withdrawal of American troops
    in, 109–113
Viviani, René, 19
Vojvodina, 120, 121–122. *See also*
  Yugoslavia
Vukovar, 124

Walters, Barbara, 136
War
  and aggressors, defeat of,
    311–314
  determinants of, 311–324
  inevitability of, 333
  interstate and intrastate, 327
  as learned behavior, 309–310
  nature of, 310–311, 327
  reasons for, 310–324
  and sickness, analogy between,
    309–310
War, cause of
  alliance systems as, 2
  fear as, 2
  and leaders, and fear of attack,
    318–321
  and leaders, personalities of, 2,
    314–315
  and leaders, self-image of,
    315–317
  militarism as, 2
  misperception as, 2, 315–324
  nationalism as, 2
  religion as, 182–183
War lovers, 138, 151, 246, 251, 256,
  261, 266
Watergate hearings, 110
Weapons of mass destruction,
  268–269, 280–284, 290–291,
  302–303, 319–321, 333.
  See also Nuclear weapons
Weizmann, Chaim, 188, 194–195
Welles, Sumner, 46
West Bank, 209, 212, 221, 225, 227,
  228, 229, 234–235, 237, 239

West Bengal, 173
Westmoreland, William, 104–105
What Went Wrong (Lewis), 274
Whitney, Courtney, 76–77
Wicker, Tom, 110–111
Wiesel, Elie, 127
Wilhelm II, 1–22, 51, 314, 316,
  317, 319
Willoughby, Charles A., 75
"Willy-Nicky" telegrams,
  12–13, 21
Wilson, Harold, 167
Wilson, Woodrow, 277
Wolfowitz, Paul, 279, 299–300
Women, emancipation of, 274
Woodward, Bob, 280
The World as Will and Idea
  (Schopenhauer), 30
World Trade Center, 1993
  bombing of, 333
World War I, 1–23, 33, 296, 311,
  321–322
  causes of, 1–2
  inevitability of, as theme
    in, 1–2
  and Iran-Iraq War, as compared
    to, 246, 248–249
  misperceptions in, 20–22
  perceptions of power in, 21–22
World War II, 49–52, 162–163,
  341–342, 252, 256, 291
  misperceptions in, 27–28, 37–38,
    43–48, 52
  See also Hitler, Adolf, and
    Russia; Stalin, Joseph, and
    Germany

Yeltsin, Boris, 130
Yemen, 257
Yezhov, N. I., 41
"Yogurt Revolution," 122
Yugoslavia, 35–36, 63, 67,
    323, 335
  conflict in, 119–153
  dismemberment of, 122–125
  misperceptions in, 131–132
  See also Croatia; Bosnia;
    Kosovo; Macedonia;
    Montenegro; Serbia; Slovenia;

*under individual republics and
autonomous regions;*
Vojvodina; Yugoslavia

Zayyat, Mohamed El, 216
Zepa, 129
Zhou En-lai, 72–73
Zhukov, Georgi, 46
Zionism, 188–198, 205, 211
Zivkovic, Zoran, 152
Zubak, Kresimir, 137